Don't Roll Your Eyes at ME, Young Man!

Also by Jerry Scott and Jim Borgman

Zits: Sketchbook 1
Growth Spurt: Zits Sketchbook 2

Humongous Zits: A Zits Treasury

Don't Roll Your Eyes at ME, Young Man!

WELL...?
SCOTT and BORGMAN
WOW! THAT MUST HAVE BEEN A REALLY STUPID QUESTION!
DON'T YOU ROLL YOUR EYES AT ME, YOUNG MAN!

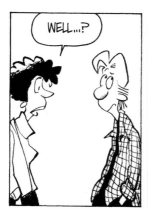

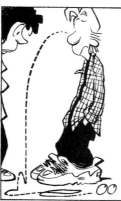

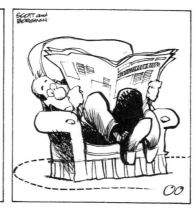

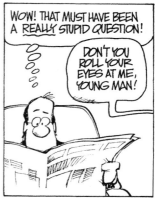

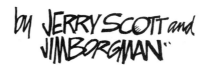

A ZITS® Collection
Sketchbook 3

by JERRY SCOTT and JIM BORGMAN

Andrews McMeel Publishing, LLC
Kansas City • Sydney • London

Zits® is syndicated internationally by King Features Syndicate, Inc. For information, write King Features Syndicate, Inc., 300 West 57th Street, New York, New York 10019.

Andrews McMeel Publishing, LLC
an Andrews McMeel Universal company
1130 Walnut Street, Kansas City, Missouri 64106

www.andrewsmcmeel.com

11 12 13 14 15 BAH 11 10

ISBN: 978-0-7407-1166-4

Library of Congress Control Number: 00-103482

Zits® may be viewed online at:
www.kingfeatures.com

To The New School community, with thanks.
—J.B.

To Peter, Hedley, Alf, Illka, and Mika
with many thanks for helping to broaden our horizons.
—J.S.

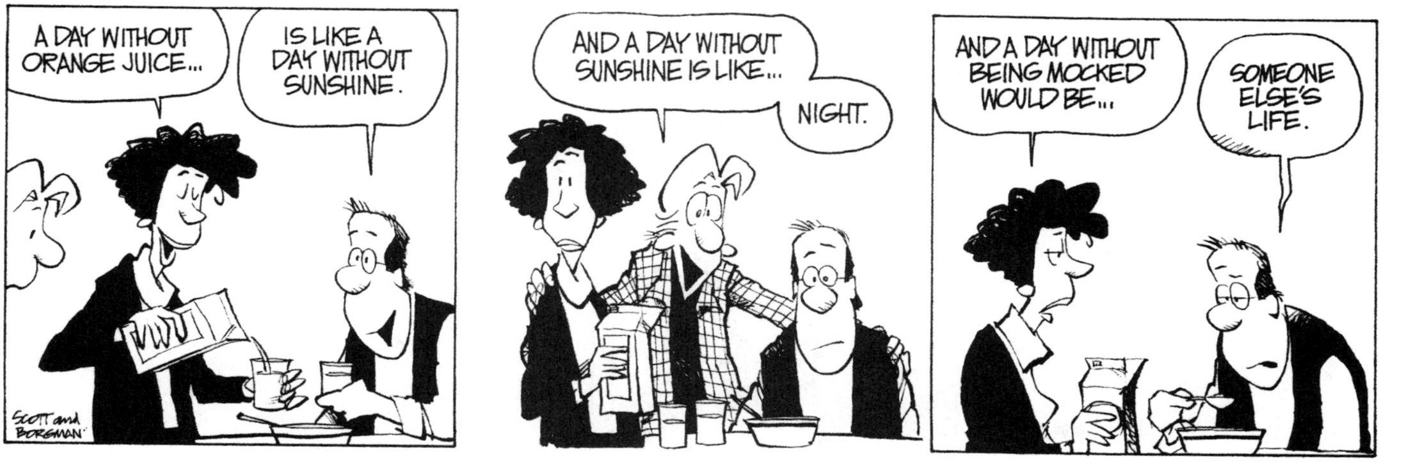
A DAY WITHOUT ORANGE JUICE...
IS LIKE A DAY WITHOUT SUNSHINE.
SCOTT and BORGMAN
AND A DAY WITHOUT SUNSHINE IS LIKE...
NIGHT.
AND A DAY WITHOUT BEING MOCKED WOULD BE...
SOMEONE ELSE'S LIFE.

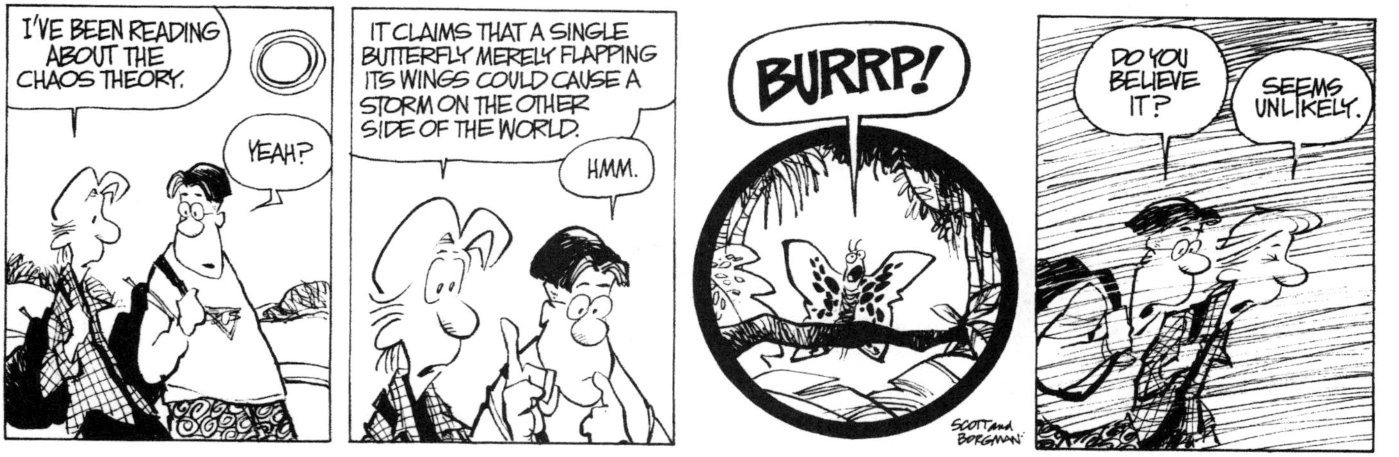
I'VE BEEN READING ABOUT THE CHAOS THEORY.
YEAH?
IT CLAIMS THAT A SINGLE BUTTERFLY MERELY FLAPPING ITS WINGS COULD CAUSE A STORM ON THE OTHER SIDE OF THE WORLD.
HMM.
BURRP!
SCOTT and BORGMAN
DO YOU BELIEVE IT?
SEEMS UNLIKELY.

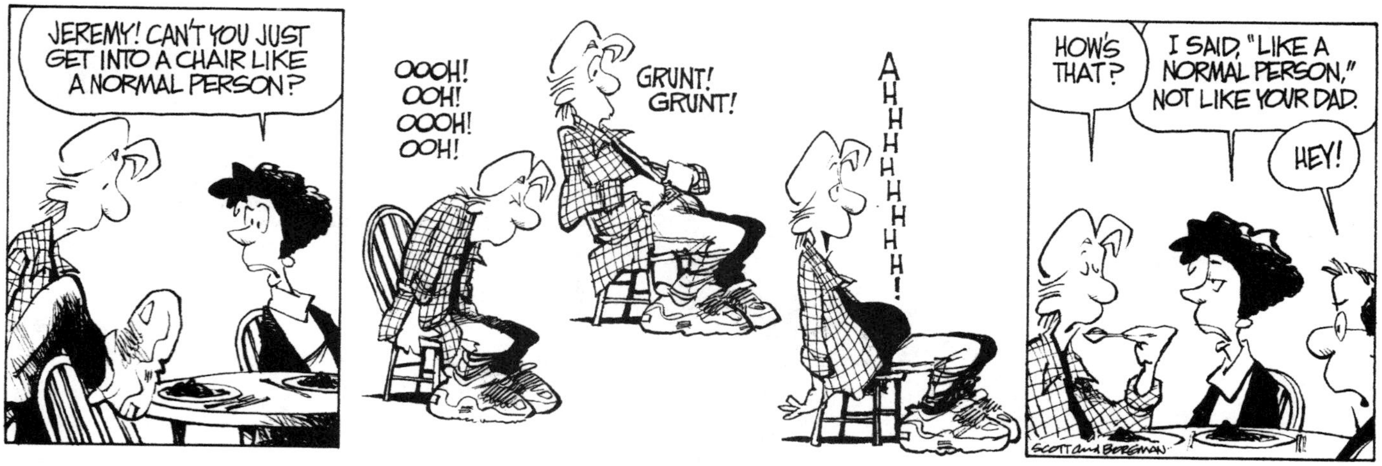
JEREMY! CAN'T YOU JUST GET INTO A CHAIR LIKE A NORMAL PERSON?
OOOH! OOH! OOOH! OOH!
GRUNT! GRUNT!
AHHHHHHH!
HOW'S THAT?
I SAID, "LIKE A NORMAL PERSON," NOT LIKE YOUR DAD.
HEY!
SCOTT and BORGMAN

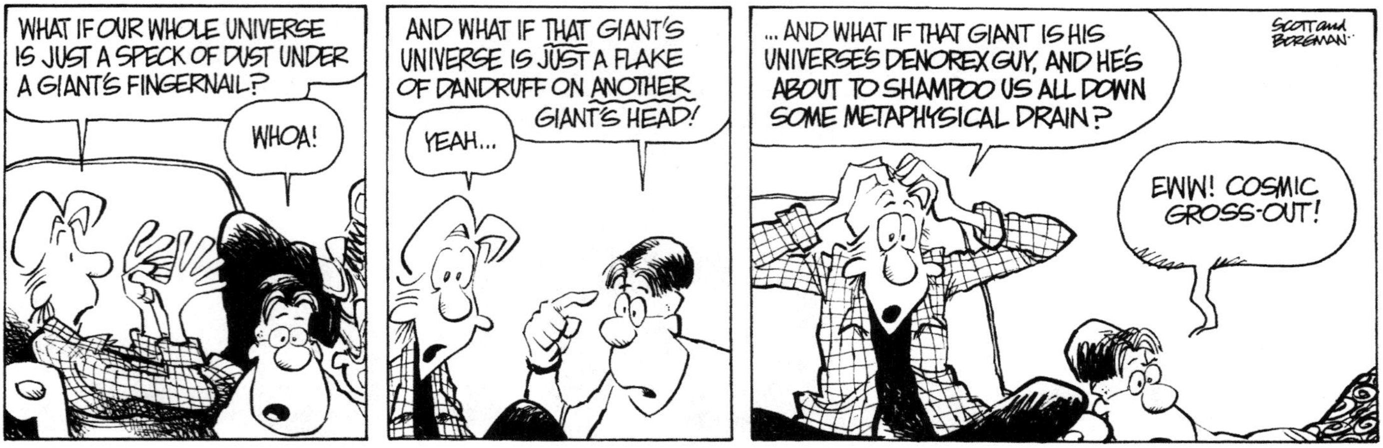
WHAT IF OUR WHOLE UNIVERSE IS JUST A SPECK OF DUST UNDER A GIANT'S FINGERNAIL?
WHOA!
AND WHAT IF THAT GIANT'S UNIVERSE IS JUST A FLAKE OF DANDRUFF ON ANOTHER GIANT'S HEAD!
YEAH...
...AND WHAT IF THAT GIANT IS HIS UNIVERSE'S DENOREX GUY, AND HE'S ABOUT TO SHAMPOO US ALL DOWN SOME METAPHYSICAL DRAIN?
SCOTT and BORGMAN
EWW! COSMIC GROSS-OUT!

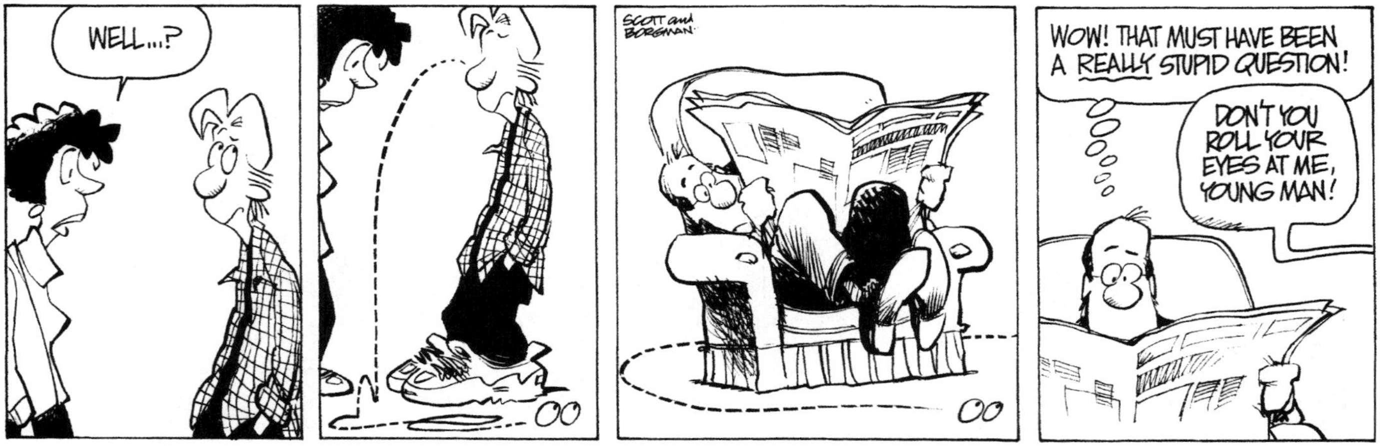
WELL...?
SCOTT and BORGMAN
WOW! THAT MUST HAVE BEEN A REALLY STUPID QUESTION!
DON'T YOU ROLL YOUR EYES AT ME, YOUNG MAN!

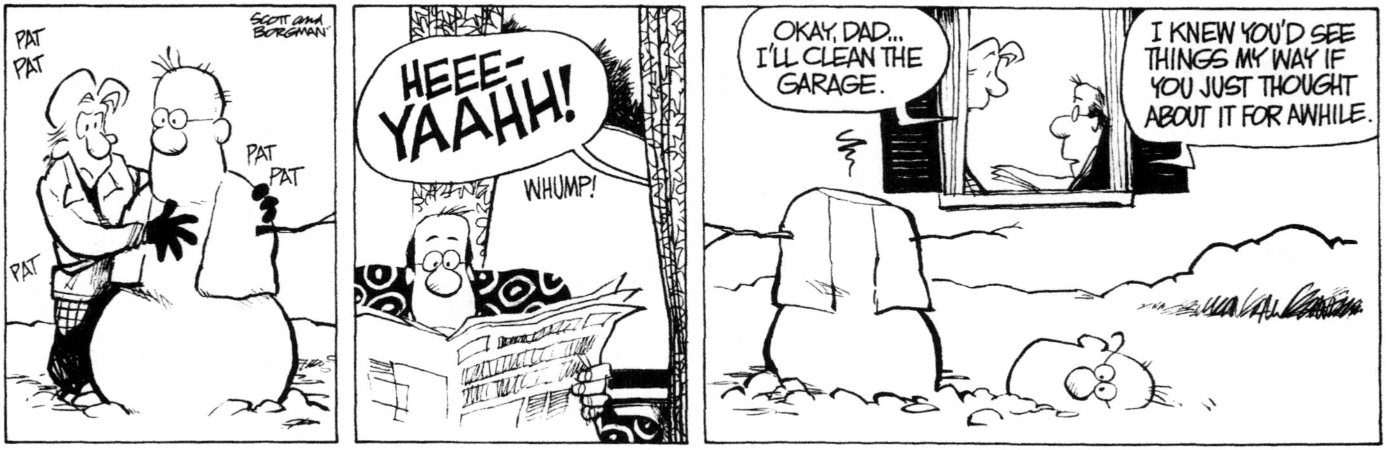
PAT PAT
SCOTT and BORGMAN
PAT PAT
PAT
HEEE-YAAHH!
WHUMP!
OKAY, DAD... I'LL CLEAN THE GARAGE.
I KNEW YOU'D SEE THINGS MY WAY IF YOU JUST THOUGHT ABOUT IT FOR AWHILE.

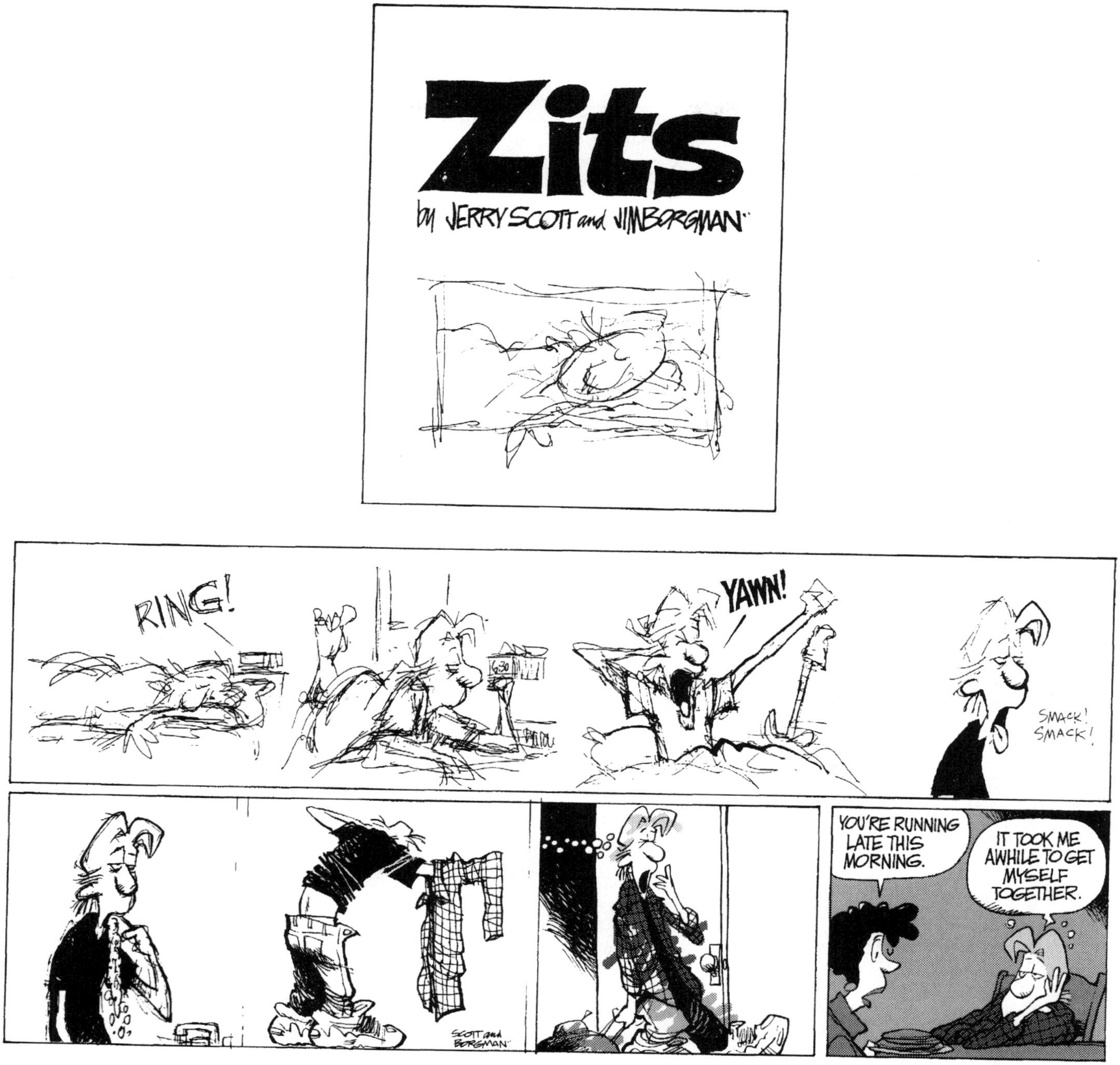
Zits
by JERRY SCOTT and JIM BORGMAN
RING!
YAWN!
SMACK! SMACK!
SCOTT and BORGMAN
YOU'RE RUNNING LATE THIS MORNING.
IT TOOK ME AWHILE TO GET MYSELF TOGETHER.

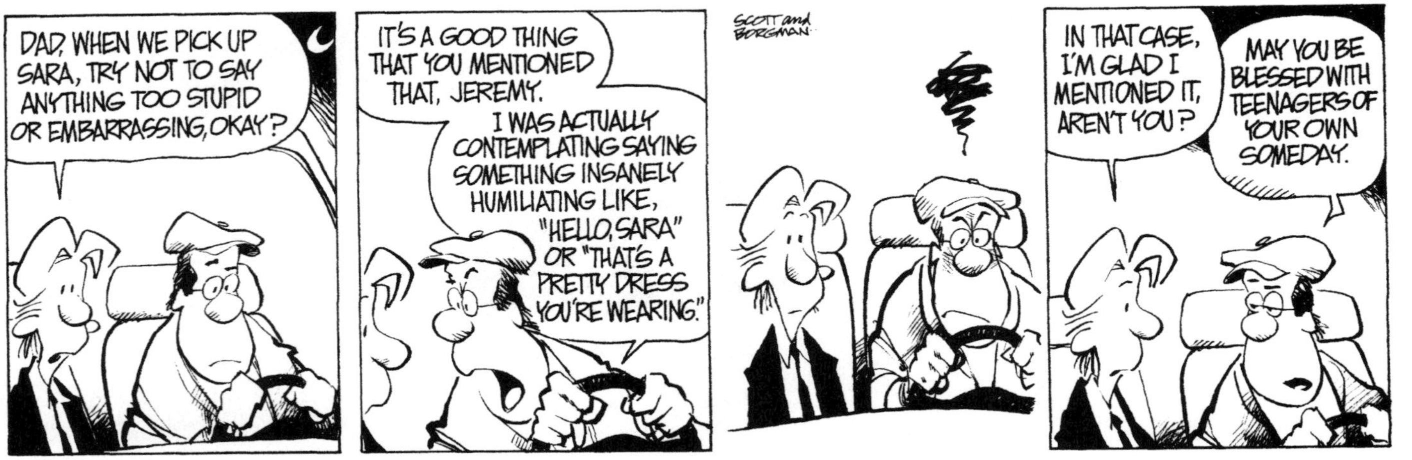
DAD, WHEN WE PICK UP SARA, TRY NOT TO SAY ANYTHING TOO STUPID OR EMBARRASSING, OKAY?
IT'S A GOOD THING THAT YOU MENTIONED THAT, JEREMY.
I WAS ACTUALLY CONTEMPLATING SAYING SOMETHING INSANELY HUMILIATING LIKE, "HELLO, SARA" OR "THAT'S A PRETTY DRESS YOU'RE WEARING."
SCOTT and BORGMAN
IN THAT CASE, I'M GLAD I MENTIONED IT, AREN'T YOU?
MAY YOU BE BLESSED WITH TEENAGERS OF YOUR OWN SOMEDAY.

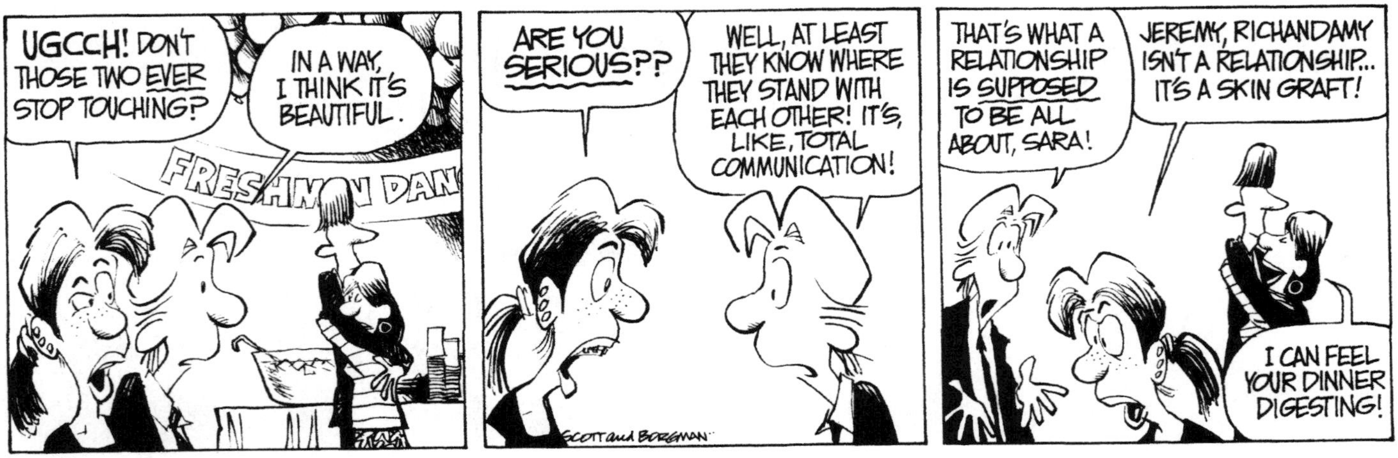
UGCCH! DON'T THOSE TWO EVER STOP TOUCHING?
IN A WAY, I THINK IT'S BEAUTIFUL.
FRESHMAN DAN
ARE YOU SERIOUS??
WELL, AT LEAST THEY KNOW WHERE THEY STAND WITH EACH OTHER! IT'S, LIKE, TOTAL COMMUNICATION!
SCOTT and BORGMAN
THAT'S WHAT A RELATIONSHIP IS SUPPOSED TO BE ALL ABOUT, SARA!
JEREMY, RICHANDAMY ISN'T A RELATIONSHIP... IT'S A SKIN GRAFT!
I CAN FEEL YOUR DINNER DIGESTING!

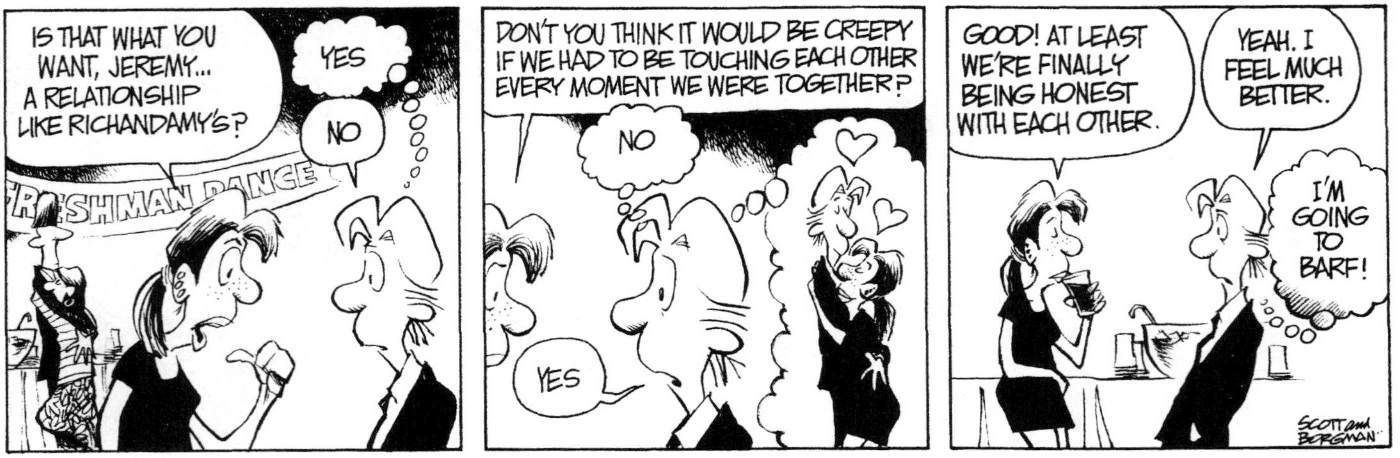
IS THAT WHAT YOU WANT, JEREMY... A RELATIONSHIP LIKE RICHANDAMY'S?
YES
NO
FRESHMAN DANCE
DON'T YOU THINK IT WOULD BE CREEPY IF WE HAD TO BE TOUCHING EACH OTHER EVERY MOMENT WE WERE TOGETHER?
NO
YES
GOOD! AT LEAST WE'RE FINALLY BEING HONEST WITH EACH OTHER.
YEAH. I FEEL MUCH BETTER.
I'M GOING TO BARF!
SCOTT and BORGMAN

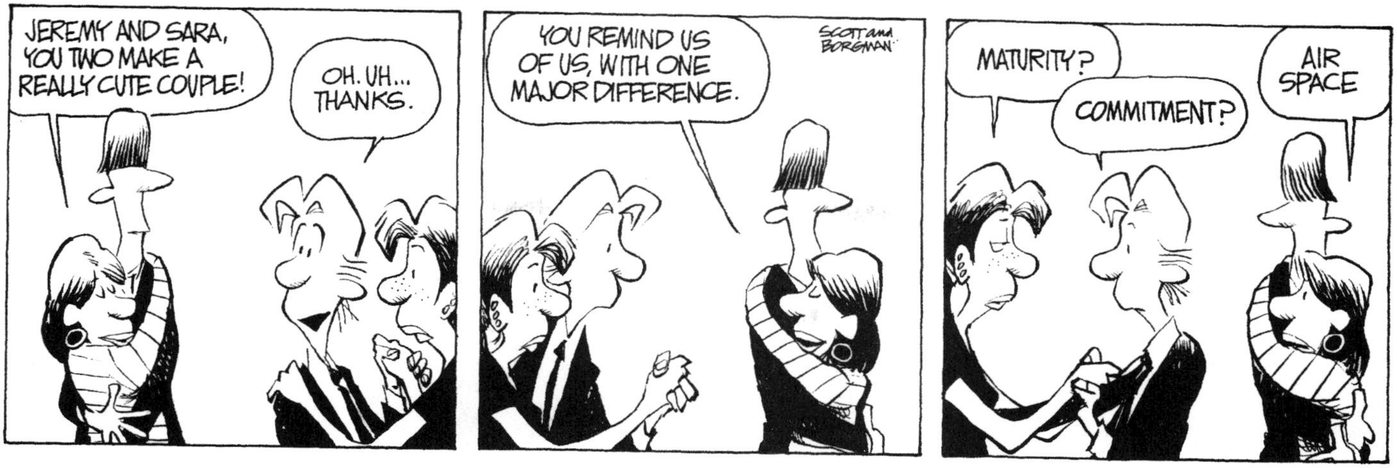
JEREMY AND SARA, YOU TWO MAKE A REALLY CUTE COUPLE!
OH. UH... THANKS.
YOU REMIND US OF US, WITH ONE MAJOR DIFFERENCE.
SCOTT and BORGMAN
MATURITY?
COMMITMENT?
AIR SPACE

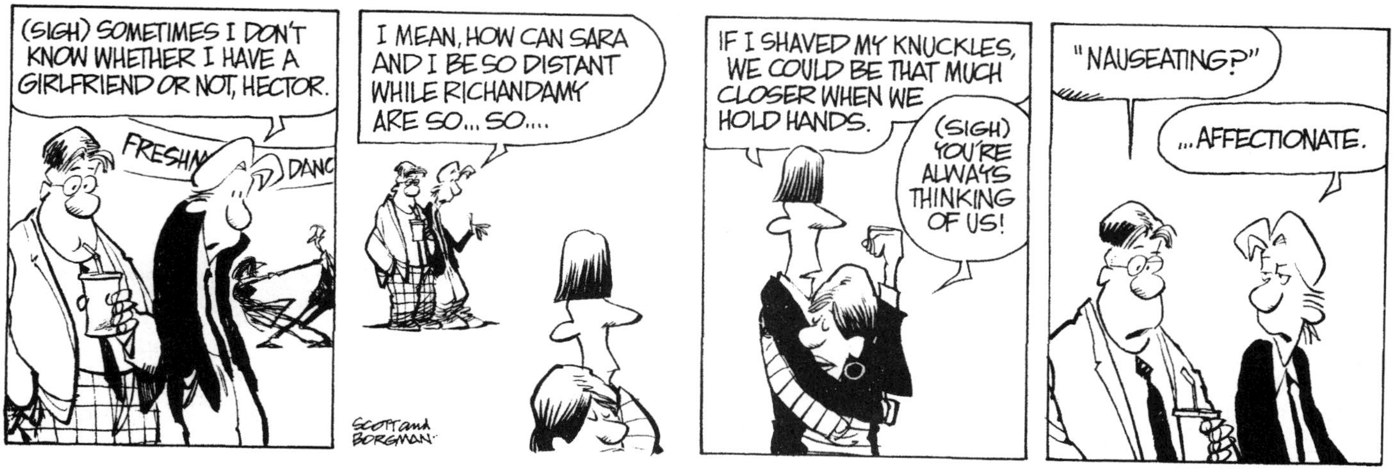
(SIGH) SOMETIMES I DON'T KNOW WHETHER I HAVE A GIRLFRIEND OR NOT, HECTOR.
I MEAN, HOW CAN SARA AND I BE SO DISTANT WHILE RICHANDAMY ARE SO... SO....
SCOTT and BORGMAN
IF I SHAVED MY KNUCKLES, WE COULD BE THAT MUCH CLOSER WHEN WE HOLD HANDS.
(SIGH) YOU'RE ALWAYS THINKING OF US!
"NAUSEATING?"
...AFFECTIONATE.

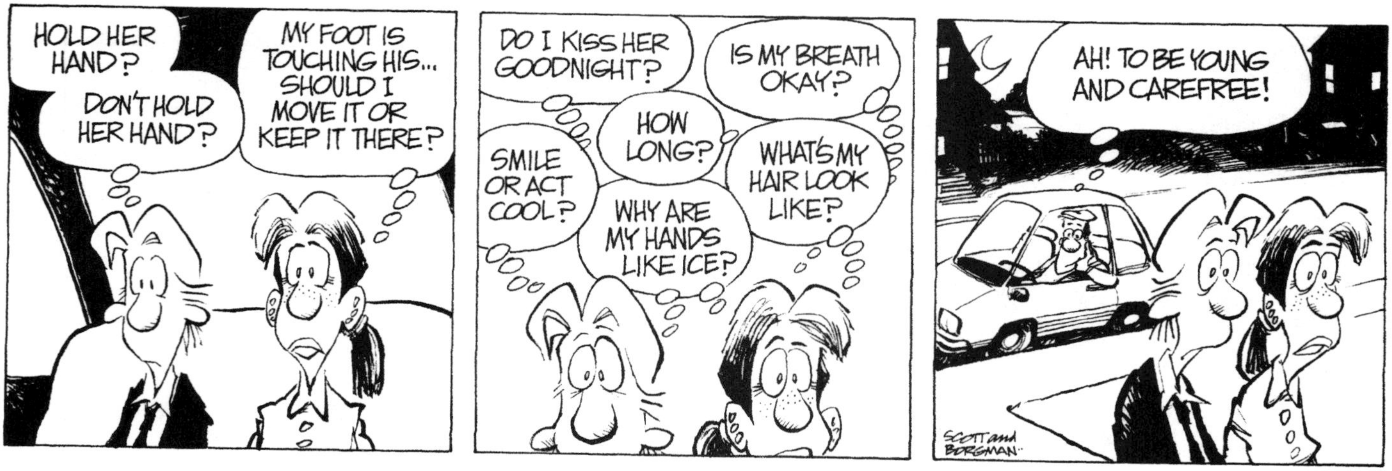
HOLD HER HAND?
DON'T HOLD HER HAND?
MY FOOT IS TOUCHING HIS... SHOULD I MOVE IT OR KEEP IT THERE?
DO I KISS HER GOODNIGHT?
IS MY BREATH OKAY?
HOW LONG?
SMILE OR ACT COOL?
WHAT'S MY HAIR LOOK LIKE?
WHY ARE MY HANDS LIKE ICE?
AH! TO BE YOUNG AND CAREFREE!
SCOTT and BORGMAN

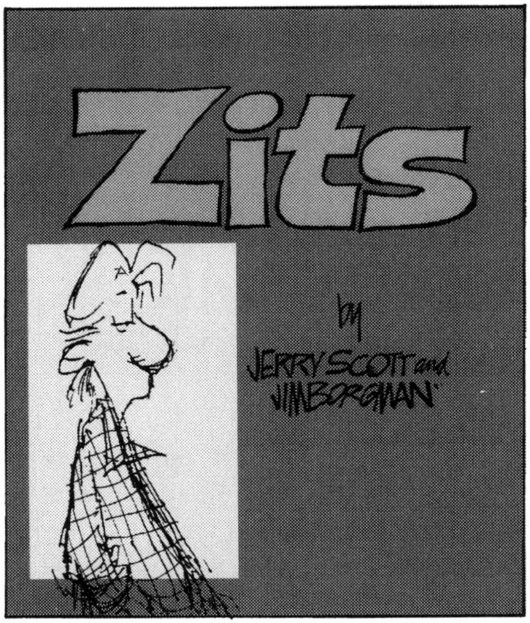
Zits
by
JERRY SCOTT and
JIM BORGMAN

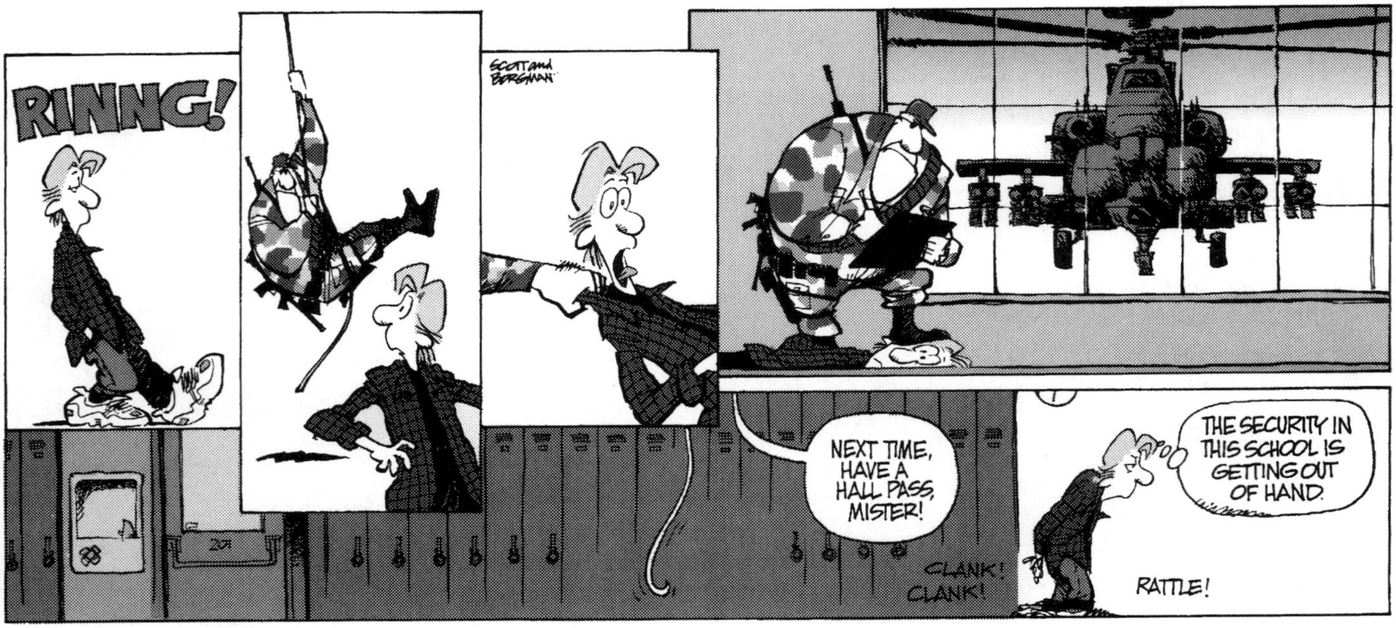
RINNG!
SCOTT and BORGMAN
NEXT TIME, HAVE A HALL PASS, MISTER!
CLANK! CLANK!
THE SECURITY IN THIS SCHOOL IS GETTING OUT OF HAND.
RATTLE!

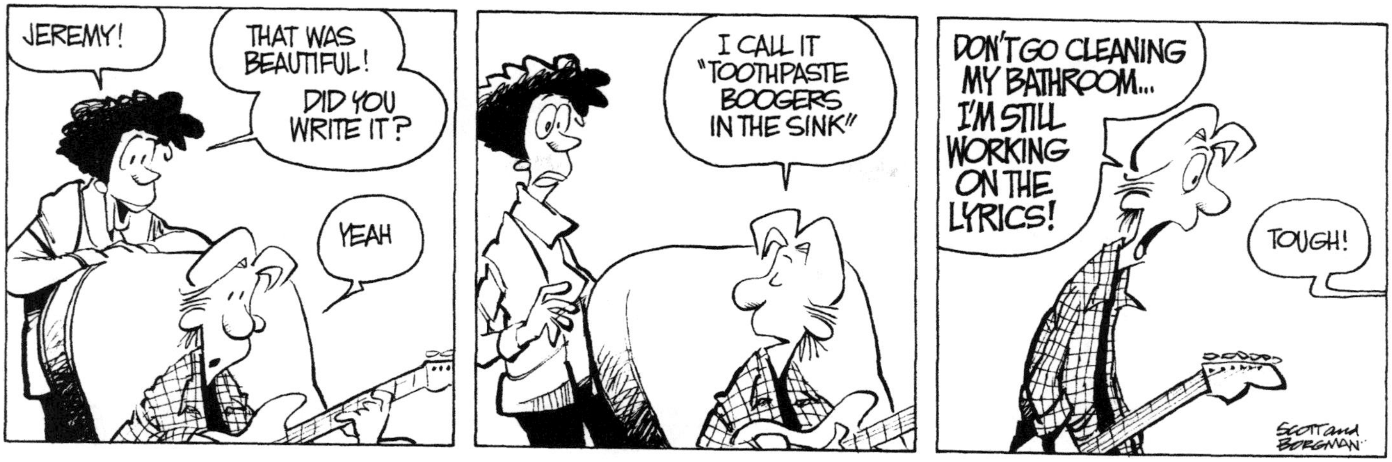
JEREMY!
THAT WAS BEAUTIFUL!
DID YOU WRITE IT?
YEAH
I CALL IT "TOOTHPASTE BOOGERS IN THE SINK"
DON'T GO CLEANING MY BATHROOM... I'M STILL WORKING ON THE LYRICS!
TOUGH!
SCOTT and BORGMAN

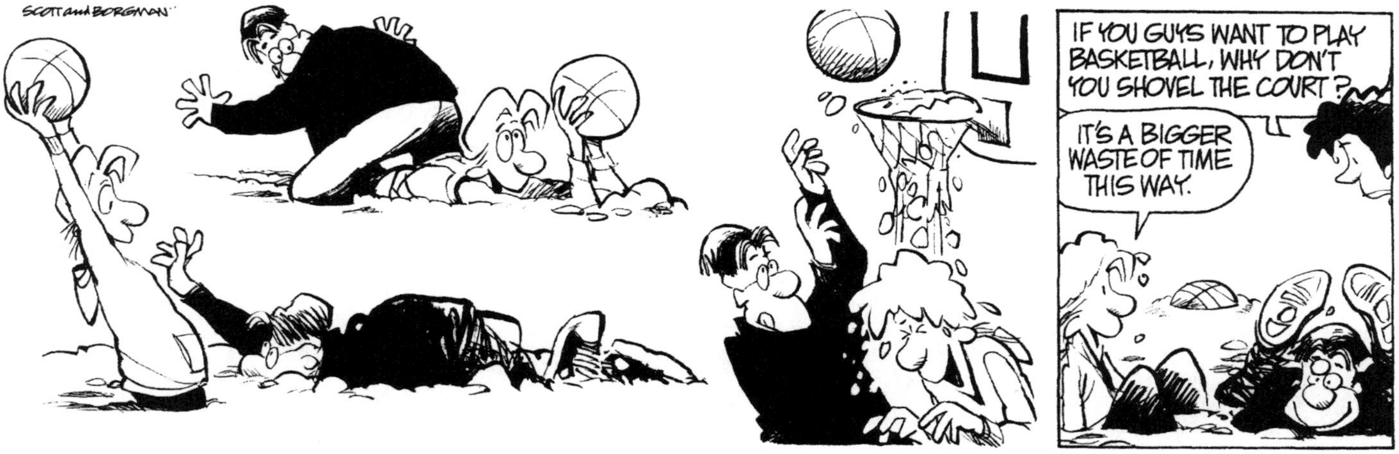
SCOTT and BORGMAN
IF YOU GUYS WANT TO PLAY BASKETBALL, WHY DON'T YOU SHOVEL THE COURT?
IT'S A BIGGER WASTE OF TIME THIS WAY.

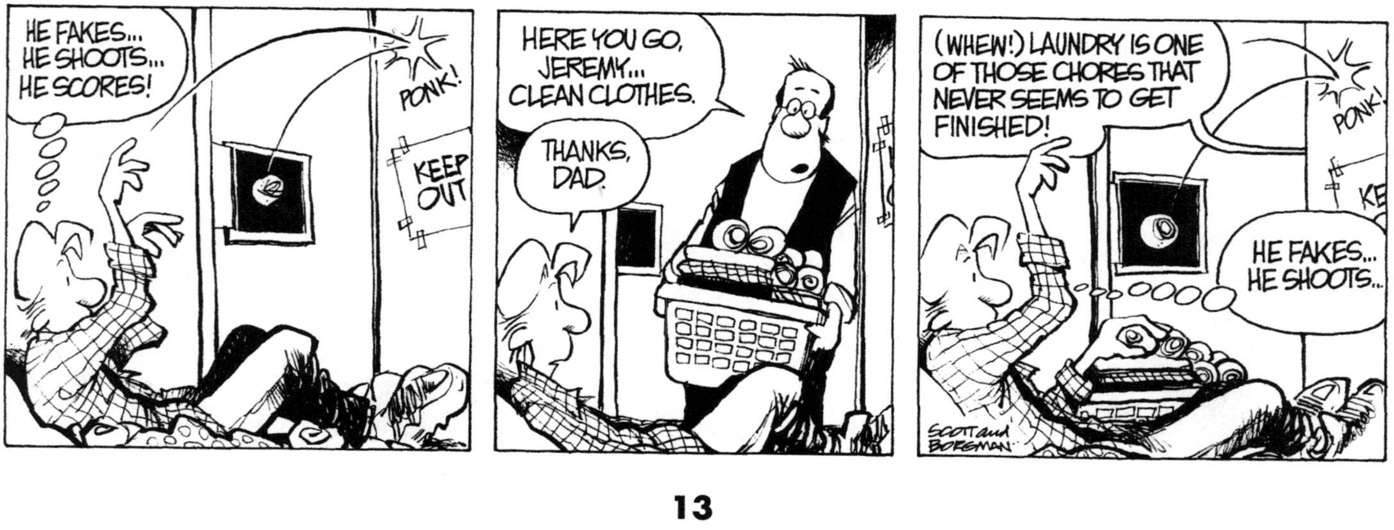
HE FAKES... HE SHOOTS... HE SCORES!
PONK!
KEEP OUT
HERE YOU GO, JEREMY... CLEAN CLOTHES.
THANKS, DAD.
(WHEW!) LAUNDRY IS ONE OF THOSE CHORES THAT NEVER SEEMS TO GET FINISHED!
PONK!
HE FAKES... HE SHOOTS...
SCOTT and BORGMAN

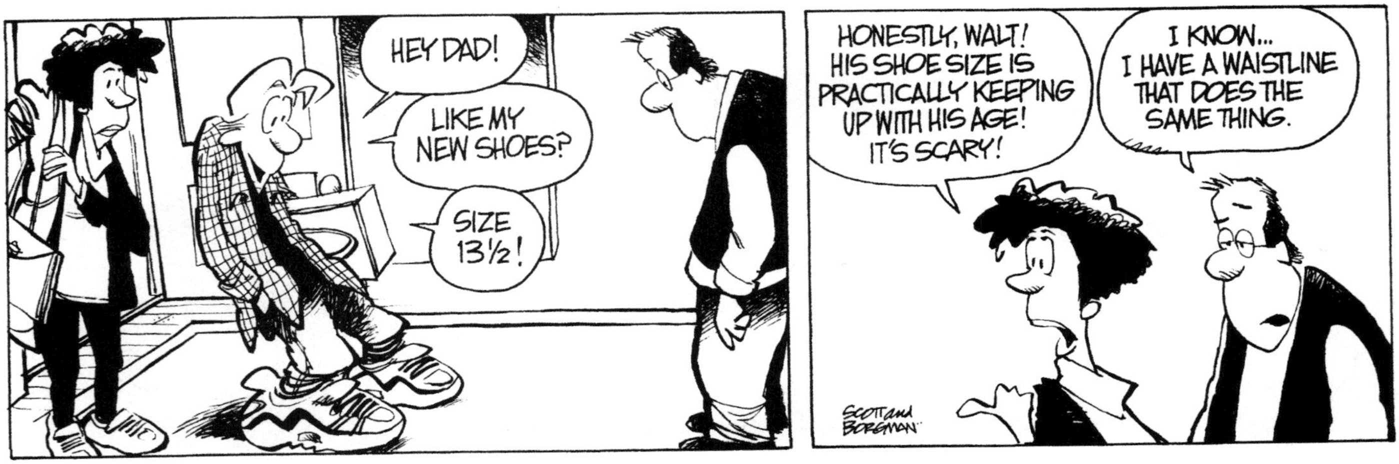
HEY DAD!
LIKE MY NEW SHOES?
SIZE 13½!
HONESTLY, WALT! HIS SHOE SIZE IS PRACTICALLY KEEPING UP WITH HIS AGE! IT'S SCARY!
I KNOW... I HAVE A WAISTLINE THAT DOES THE SAME THING.
SCOTT AND BORGMAN

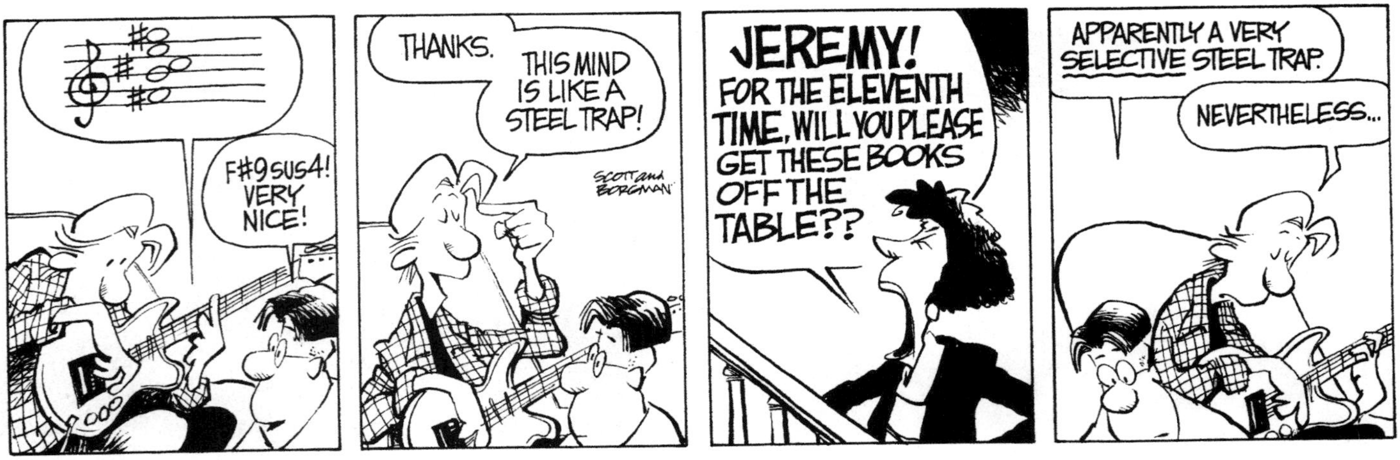
F#9SUS4! VERY NICE!
THANKS.
THIS MIND IS LIKE A STEEL TRAP!
SCOTT AND BORGMAN
JEREMY! FOR THE ELEVENTH TIME, WILL YOU PLEASE GET THESE BOOKS OFF THE TABLE??
APPARENTLY A VERY SELECTIVE STEEL TRAP.
NEVERTHELESS...

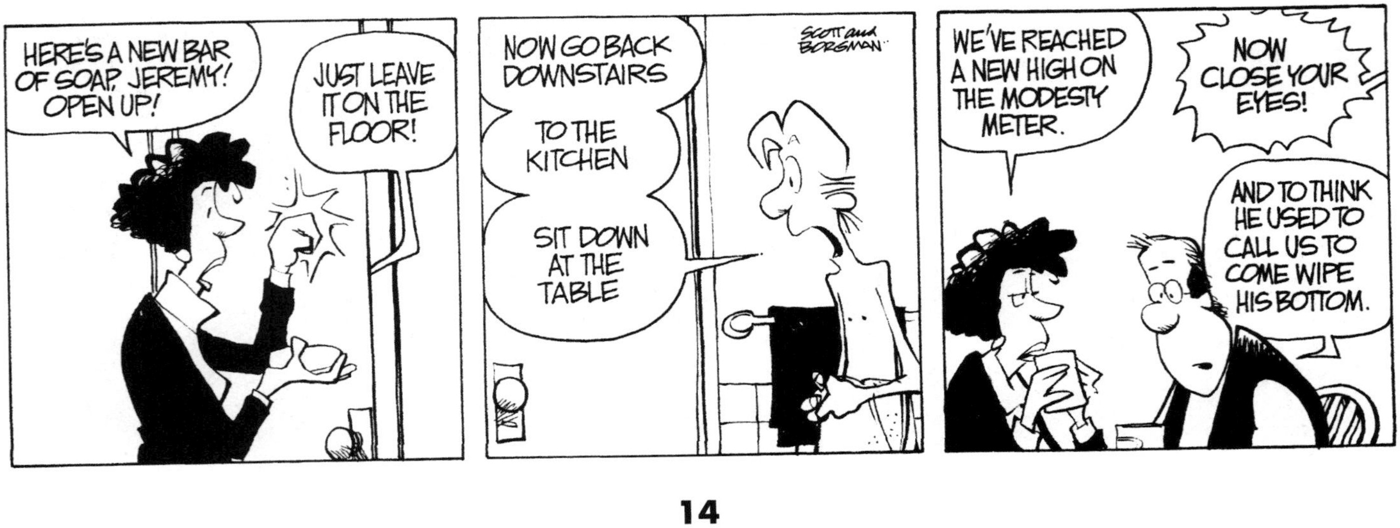
HERE'S A NEW BAR OF SOAP, JEREMY! OPEN UP!
JUST LEAVE IT ON THE FLOOR!
NOW GO BACK DOWNSTAIRS
TO THE KITCHEN
SIT DOWN AT THE TABLE
SCOTT AND BORGMAN
WE'VE REACHED A NEW HIGH ON THE MODESTY METER.
NOW CLOSE YOUR EYES!
AND TO THINK HE USED TO CALL US TO COME WIPE HIS BOTTOM.

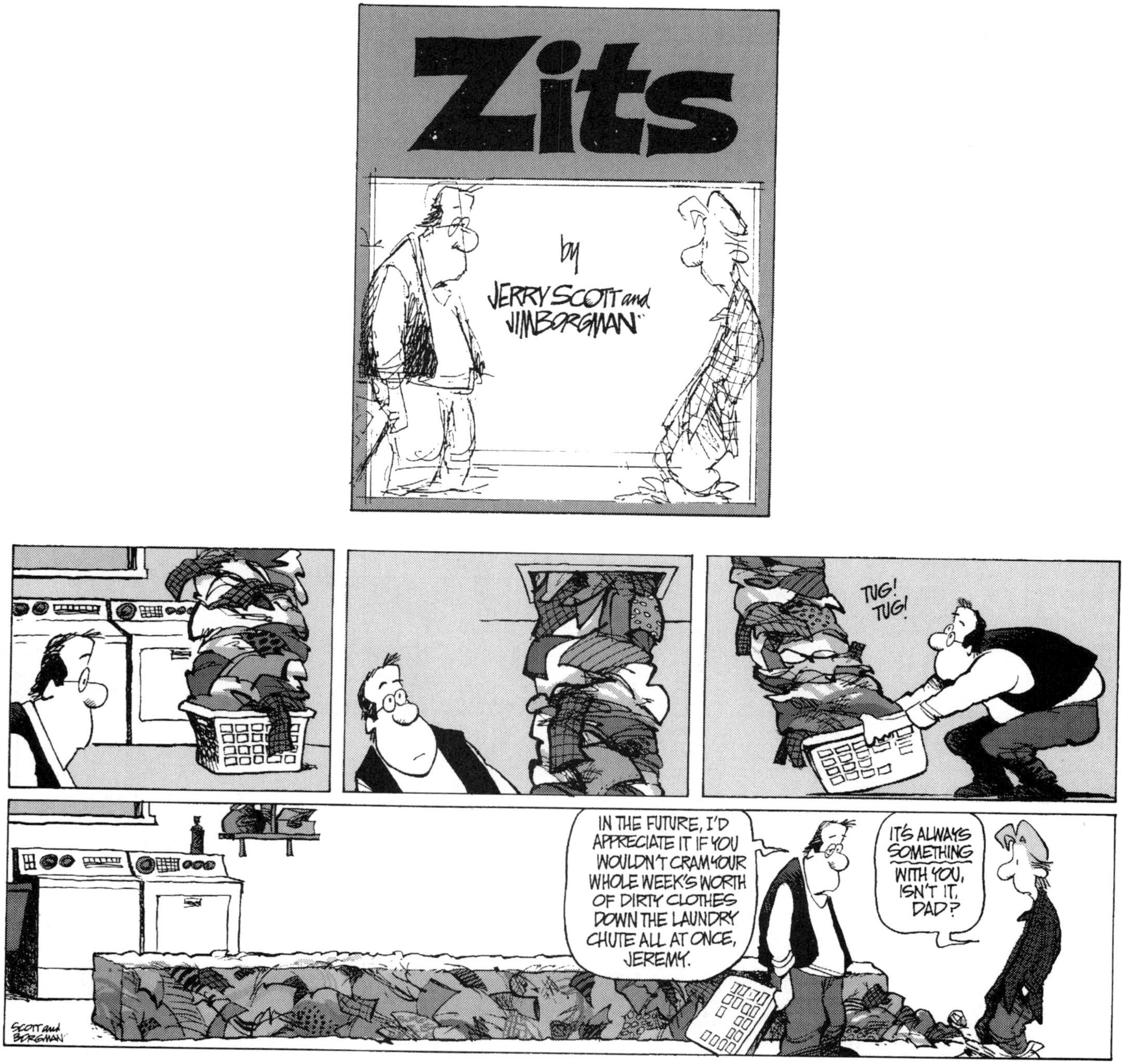
Zits
by
JERRY SCOTT and JIM BORGMAN
TUG! TUG!
IN THE FUTURE, I'D APPRECIATE IT IF YOU WOULDN'T CRAM YOUR WHOLE WEEK'S WORTH OF DIRTY CLOTHES DOWN THE LAUNDRY CHUTE ALL AT ONCE, JEREMY.
IT'S ALWAYS SOMETHING WITH YOU, ISN'T IT, DAD?
SCOTT and BORGMAN

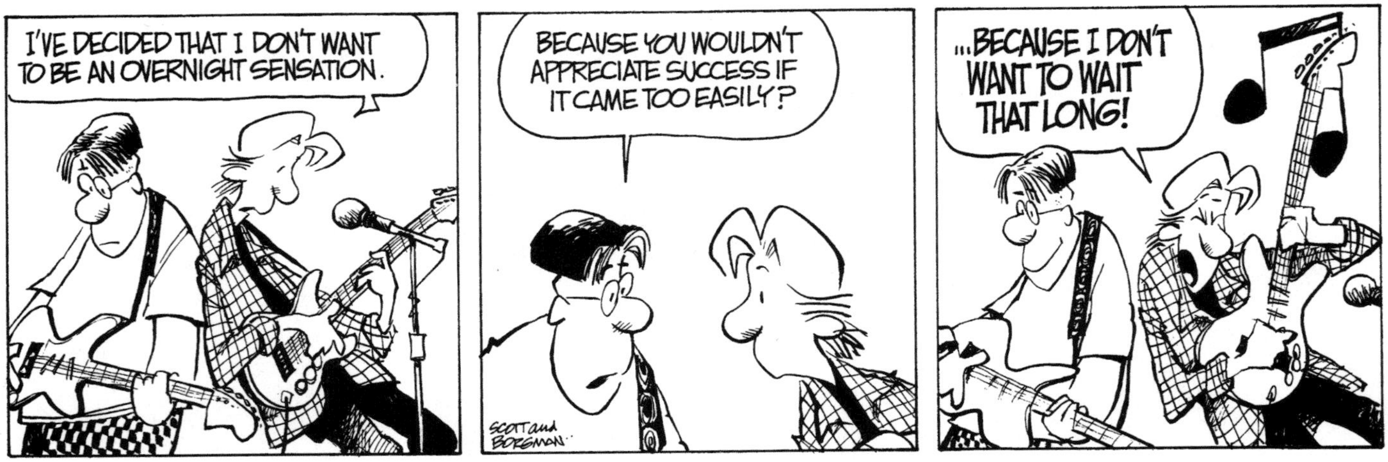
I'VE DECIDED THAT I DON'T WANT TO BE AN OVERNIGHT SENSATION.
BECAUSE YOU WOULDN'T APPRECIATE SUCCESS IF IT CAME TOO EASILY?
SCOTT and BORGMAN
...BECAUSE I DON'T WANT TO WAIT THAT LONG!

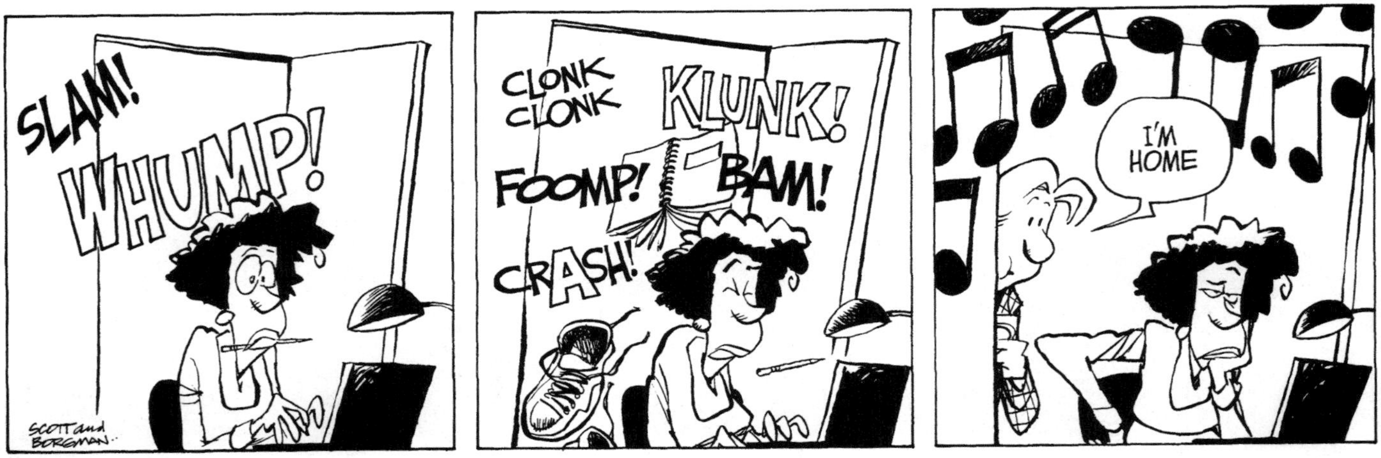
SLAM!
WHUMP!
SCOTT and BORGMAN
CLONK CLONK
KLUNK!
FOOMP!
BAM!
CRASH!
I'M HOME

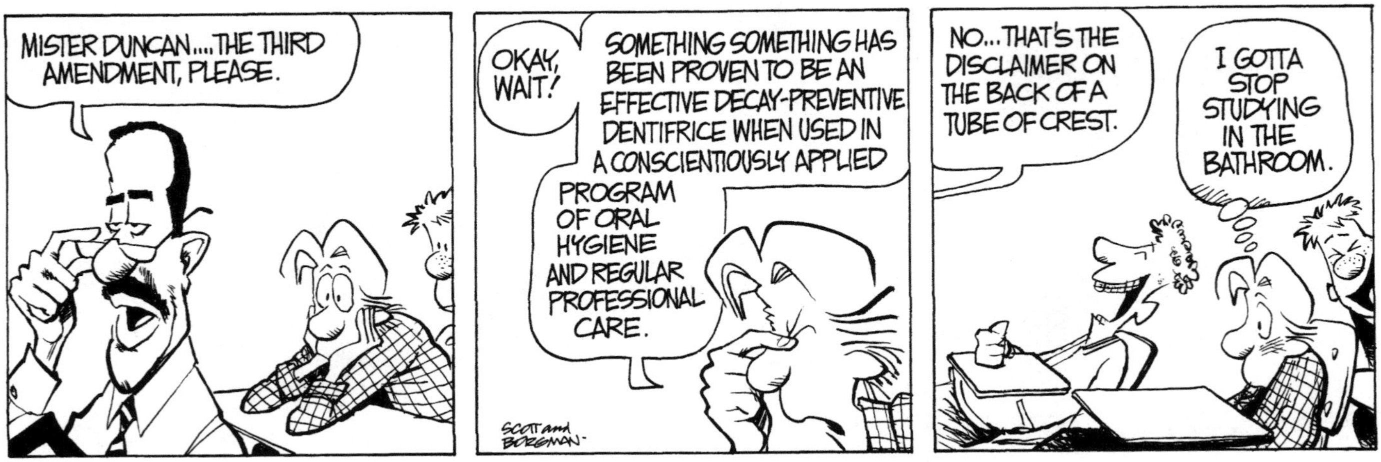
MISTER DUNCAN....THE THIRD AMENDMENT, PLEASE.
OKAY, WAIT!
SOMETHING SOMETHING HAS BEEN PROVEN TO BE AN EFFECTIVE DECAY-PREVENTIVE DENTIFRICE WHEN USED IN A CONSCIENTIOUSLY APPLIED PROGRAM OF ORAL HYGIENE AND REGULAR PROFESSIONAL CARE.
SCOTT and BORGMAN
NO...THAT'S THE DISCLAIMER ON THE BACK OF A TUBE OF CREST.
I GOTTA STOP STUDYING IN THE BATHROOM.

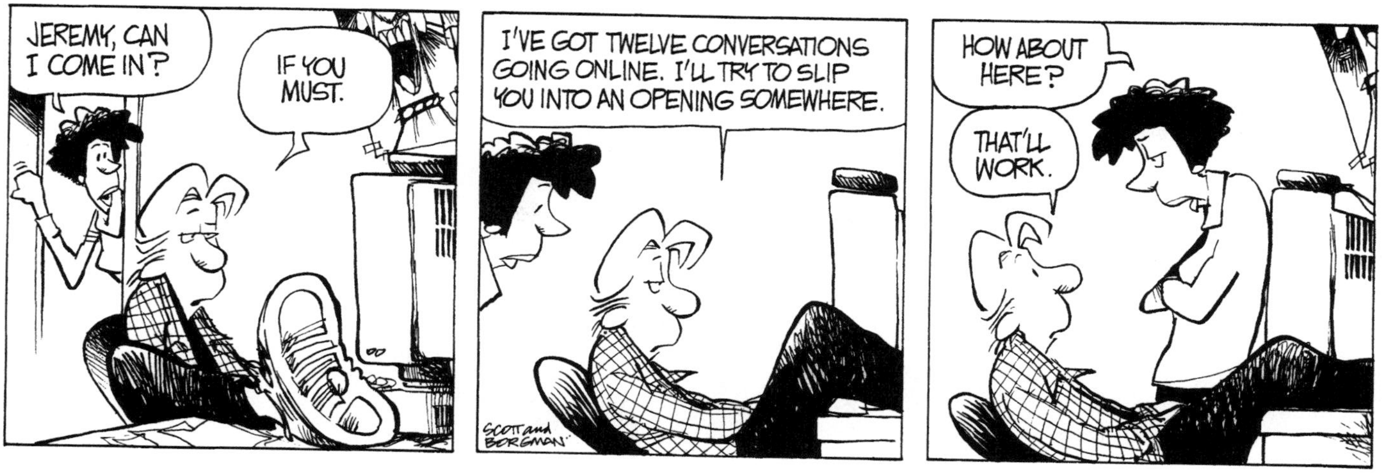
JEREMY, CAN I COME IN?
IF YOU MUST.
I'VE GOT TWELVE CONVERSATIONS GOING ONLINE. I'LL TRY TO SLIP YOU INTO AN OPENING SOMEWHERE.
SCOTT and BORGMAN
HOW ABOUT HERE?
THAT'LL WORK.

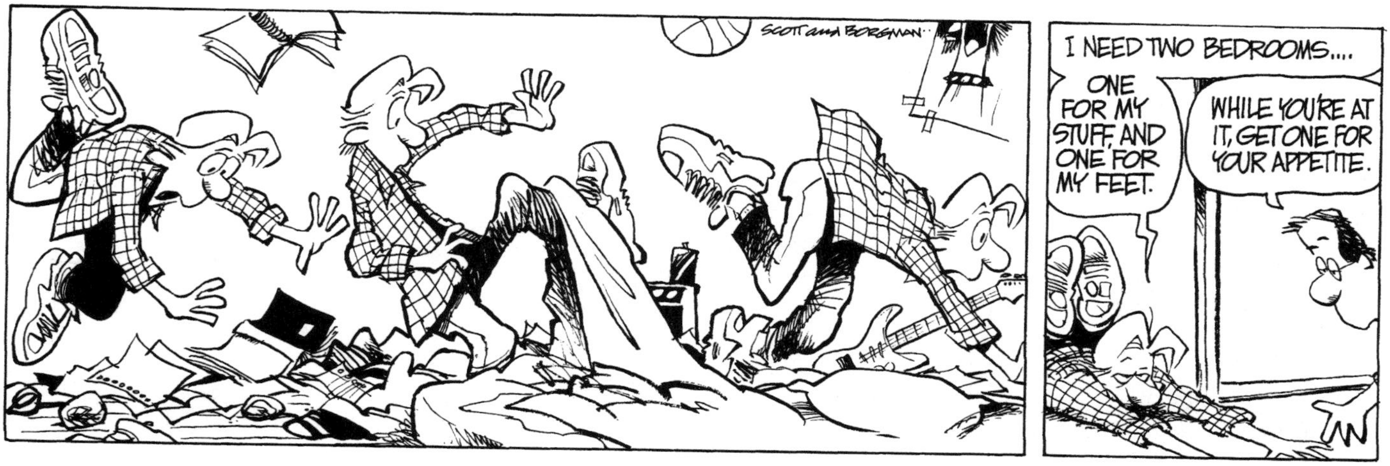
SCOTT and BORGMAN
I NEED TWO BEDROOMS....
ONE FOR MY STUFF, AND ONE FOR MY FEET.
WHILE YOU'RE AT IT, GET ONE FOR YOUR APPETITE.

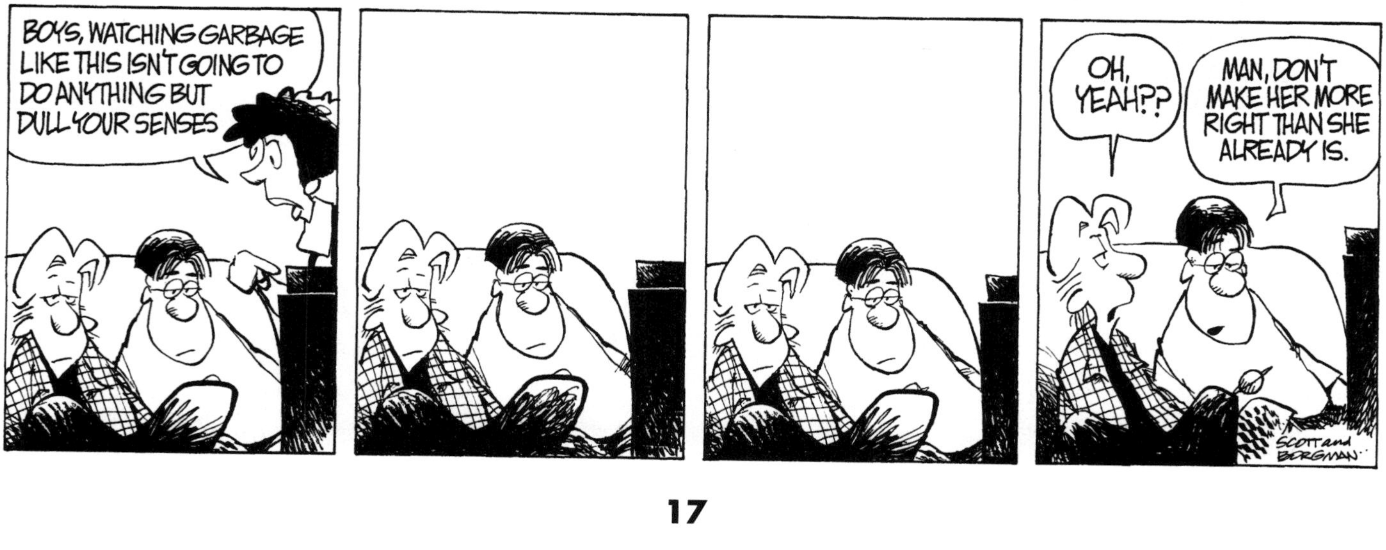
BOYS, WATCHING GARBAGE LIKE THIS ISN'T GOING TO DO ANYTHING BUT DULL YOUR SENSES
OH, YEAH??
MAN, DON'T MAKE HER MORE RIGHT THAN SHE ALREADY IS.
SCOTT and BORGMAN

Zits
by
DOUBLE CLICK
JERRY SCOTT and JIM BORGMAN

CLICK CLICK
BOOP BEEP BOOP BIP BIP BOOP BEEP
SCREEEEE!
BABONG!
BABONG!
IF THE INTERNET IS SO "CUTTING EDGE," WHY DOES IT SOUND LIKE A BUGS BUNNY CARTOON WHEN YOU LOG ON?
SCOTT and BORGMAN

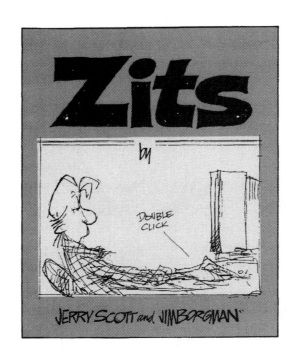

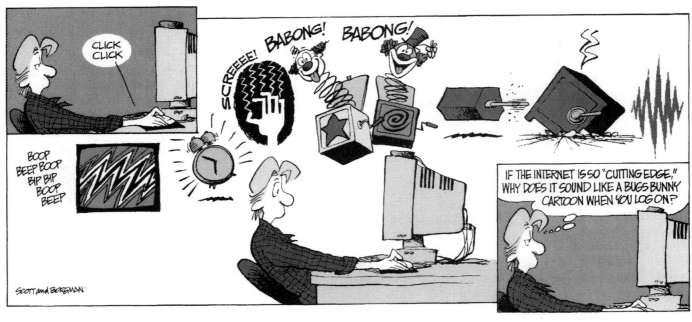

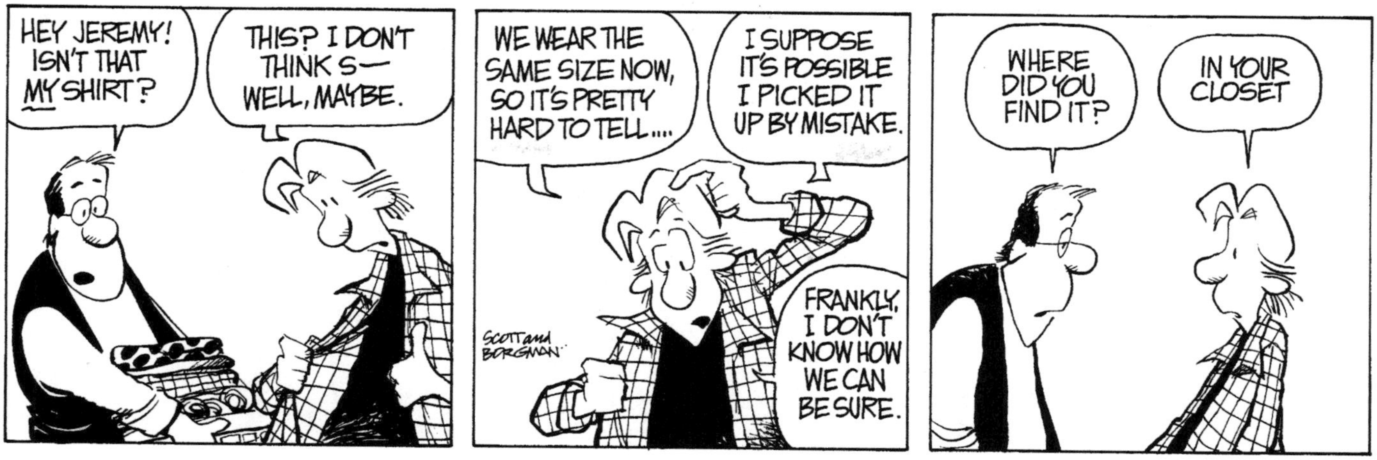
HEY JEREMY! ISN'T THAT MY SHIRT?
THIS? I DON'T THINK S— WELL, MAYBE.
WE WEAR THE SAME SIZE NOW, SO IT'S PRETTY HARD TO TELL....
I SUPPOSE IT'S POSSIBLE I PICKED IT UP BY MISTAKE.
FRANKLY, I DON'T KNOW HOW WE CAN BE SURE.
SCOTT and BORGMAN
WHERE DID YOU FIND IT?
IN YOUR CLOSET

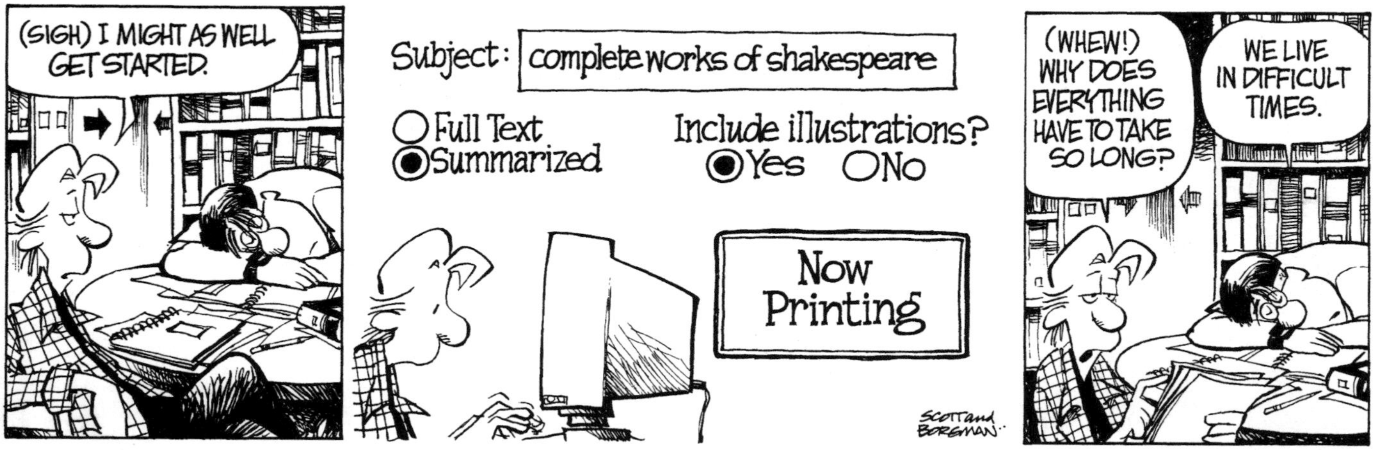
(SIGH) I MIGHT AS WELL GET STARTED.
Subject: complete works of shakespeare
Full Text
Summarized
Include illustrations?
Yes
No
Now Printing
SCOTT and BORGMAN
(WHEW!) WHY DOES EVERYTHING HAVE TO TAKE SO LONG?
WE LIVE IN DIFFICULT TIMES.

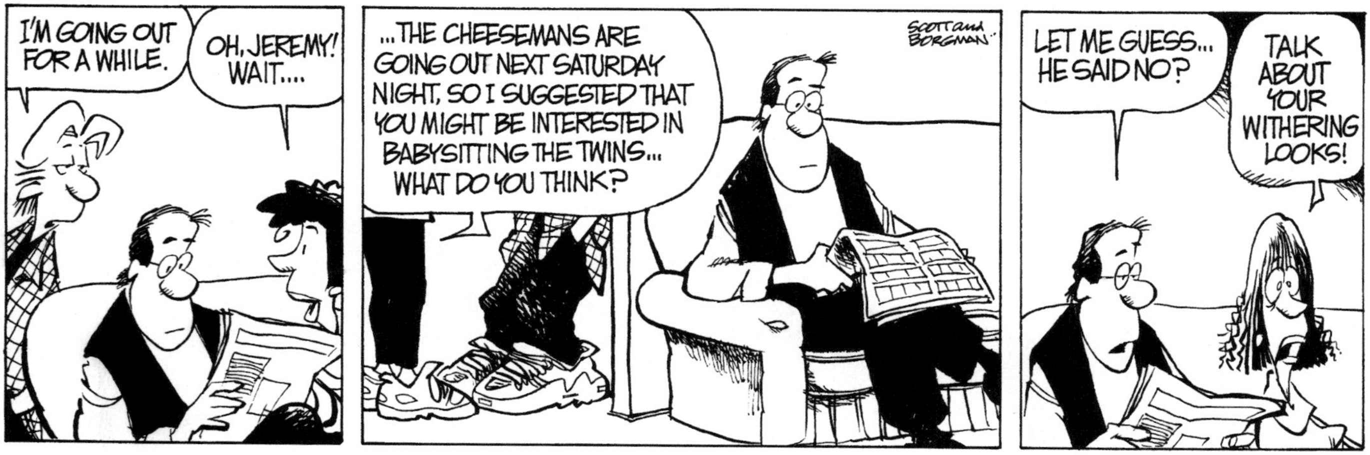
I'M GOING OUT FOR A WHILE.
OH, JEREMY! WAIT....
...THE CHEESEMANS ARE GOING OUT NEXT SATURDAY NIGHT, SO I SUGGESTED THAT YOU MIGHT BE INTERESTED IN BABYSITTING THE TWINS... WHAT DO YOU THINK?
SCOTT and BORGMAN
LET ME GUESS... HE SAID NO?
TALK ABOUT YOUR WITHERING LOOKS!

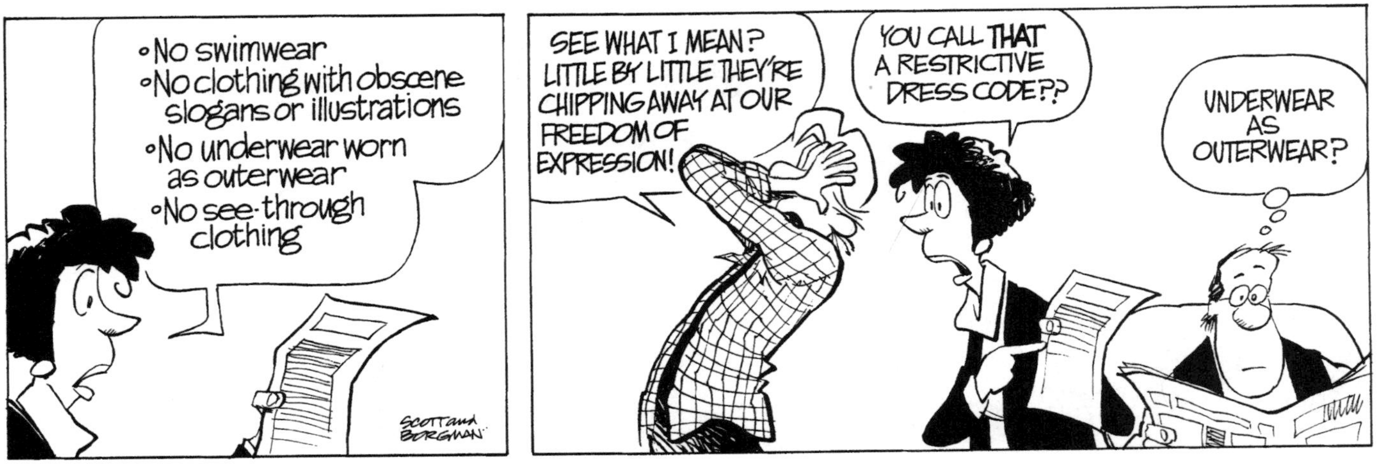

• No swimwear
• No clothing with obscene slogans or illustrations
• No underwear worn as outerwear
• No see-through clothing
SCOTT and BORGMAN
SEE WHAT I MEAN? LITTLE BY LITTLE THEY'RE CHIPPING AWAY AT OUR FREEDOM OF EXPRESSION!
YOU CALL THAT A RESTRICTIVE DRESS CODE??
UNDERWEAR AS OUTERWEAR?

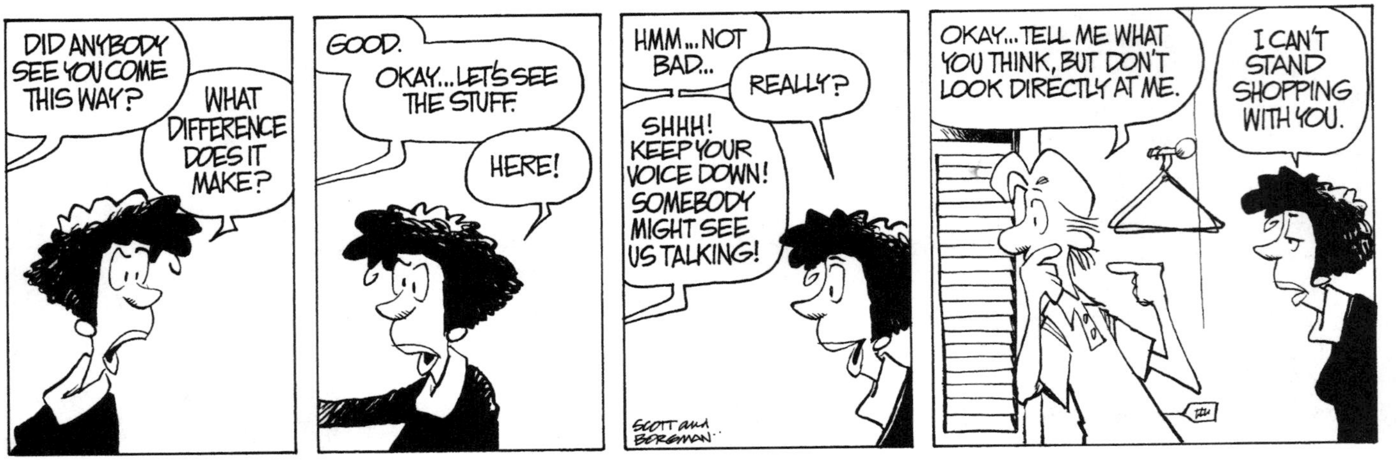

DID ANYBODY SEE YOU COME THIS WAY?
WHAT DIFFERENCE DOES IT MAKE?
GOOD.
OKAY... LET'S SEE THE STUFF.
HERE!
HMM... NOT BAD...
REALLY?
SHHH! KEEP YOUR VOICE DOWN! SOMEBODY MIGHT SEE US TALKING!
SCOTT and BORGMAN
OKAY... TELL ME WHAT YOU THINK, BUT DON'T LOOK DIRECTLY AT ME.
I CAN'T STAND SHOPPING WITH YOU.

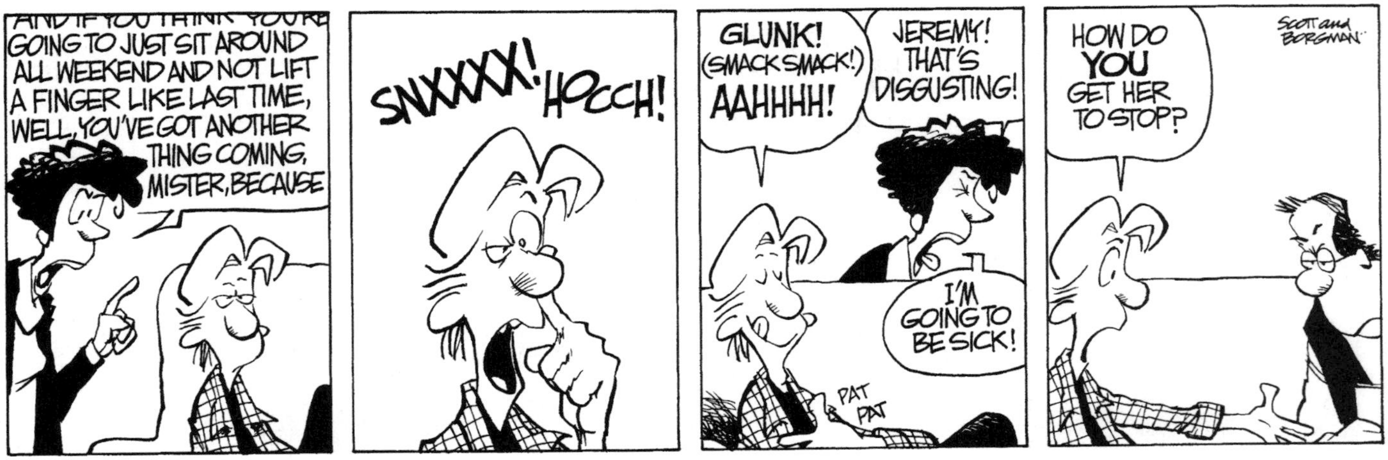

AND IF YOU THINK YOU'RE GOING TO JUST SIT AROUND ALL WEEKEND AND NOT LIFT A FINGER LIKE LAST TIME, WELL, YOU'VE GOT ANOTHER THING COMING, MISTER, BECAUSE
SNXXXX! HOCCH!
GLUNK! (SMACK SMACK!) AAHHHH!
JEREMY! THAT'S DISGUSTING!
I'M GOING TO BE SICK!
PAT PAT
HOW DO YOU GET HER TO STOP?
SCOTT and BORGMAN

Zits
by JERRY SCOTT and JIM BORGMAN

?
SCOTT and BORGMAN

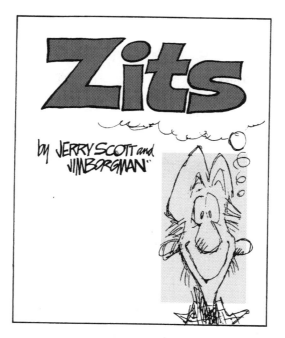

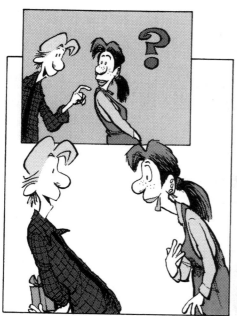

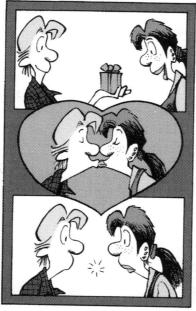

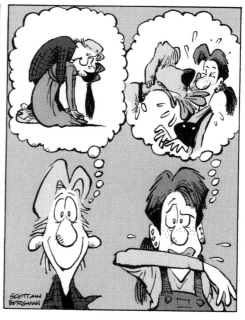

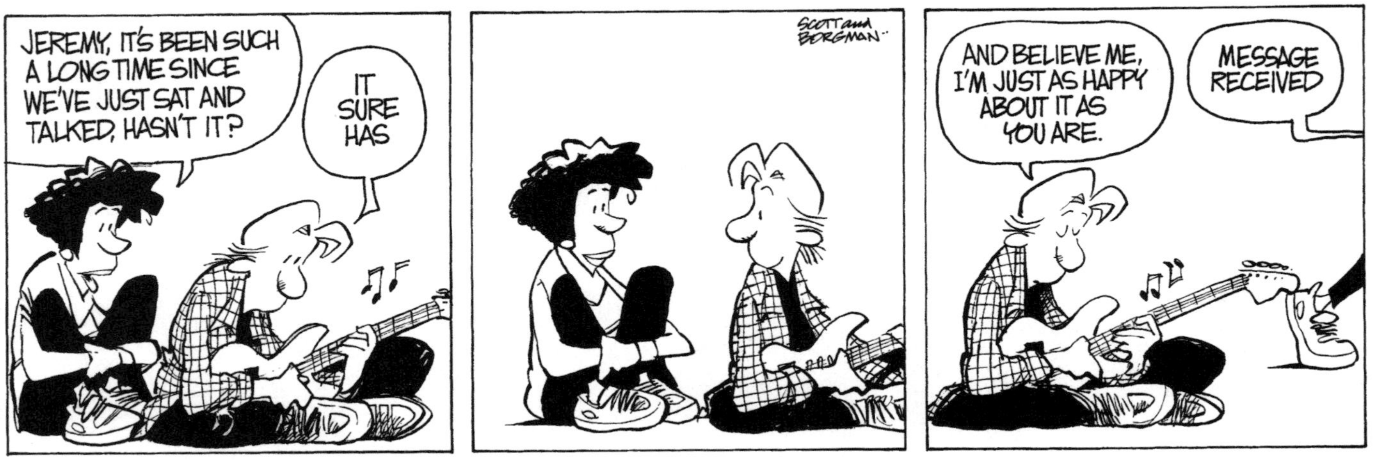
SCOTT and BORGMAN
JEREMY, IT'S BEEN SUCH A LONG TIME SINCE WE'VE JUST SAT AND TALKED, HASN'T IT?
IT SURE HAS
AND BELIEVE ME, I'M JUST AS HAPPY ABOUT IT AS YOU ARE.
MESSAGE RECEIVED

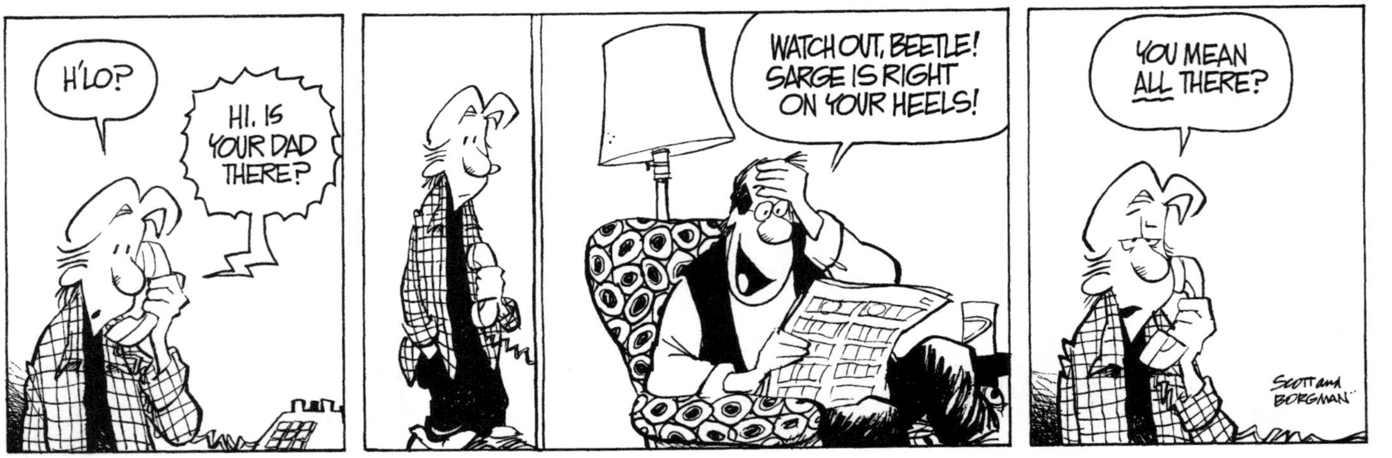
H'LO?
HI. IS YOUR DAD THERE?
WATCH OUT, BEETLE! SARGE IS RIGHT ON YOUR HEELS!
YOU MEAN ALL THERE?
SCOTT and BORGMAN

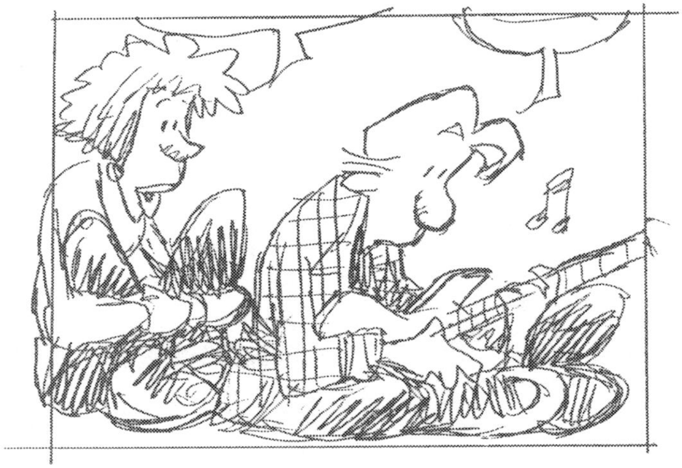

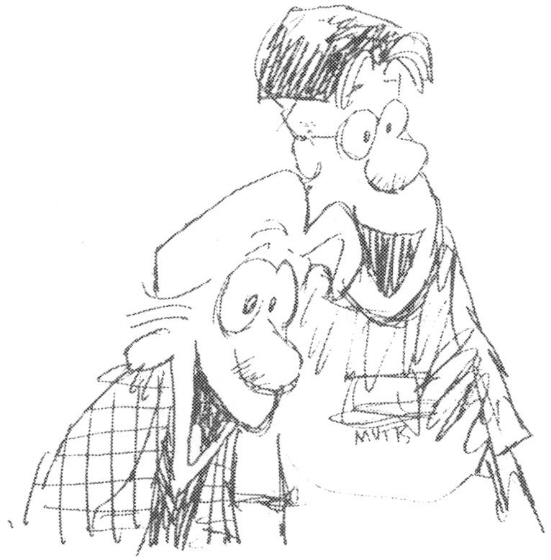
MUTTS

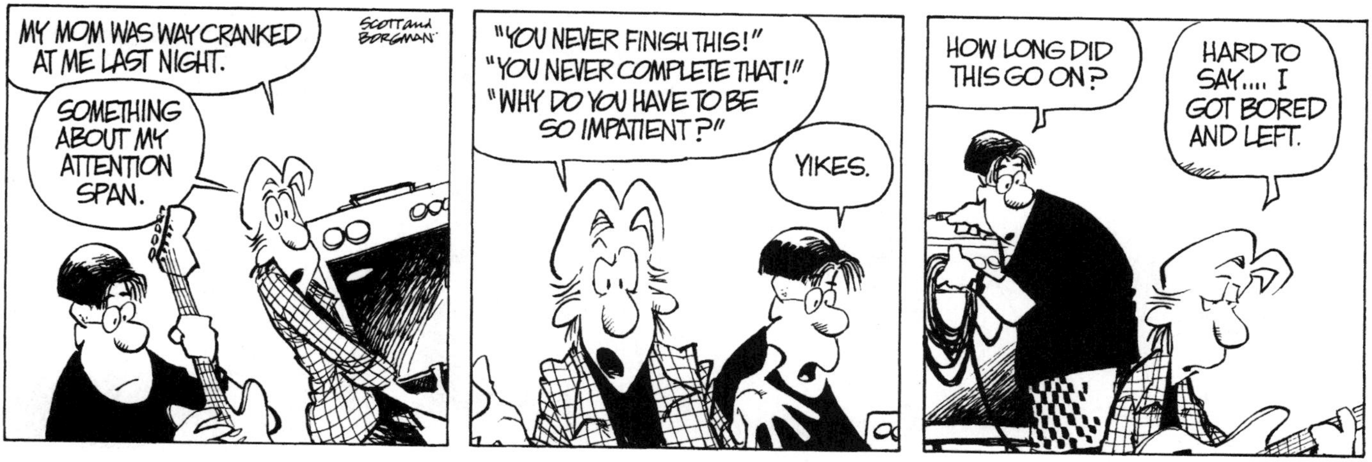
SCOTT and BORGMAN
MY MOM WAS WAY CRANKED AT ME LAST NIGHT.
SOMETHING ABOUT MY ATTENTION SPAN.
"YOU NEVER FINISH THIS!" "YOU NEVER COMPLETE THAT!" "WHY DO YOU HAVE TO BE SO IMPATIENT?"
YIKES.
HOW LONG DID THIS GO ON?
HARD TO SAY.... I GOT BORED AND LEFT.

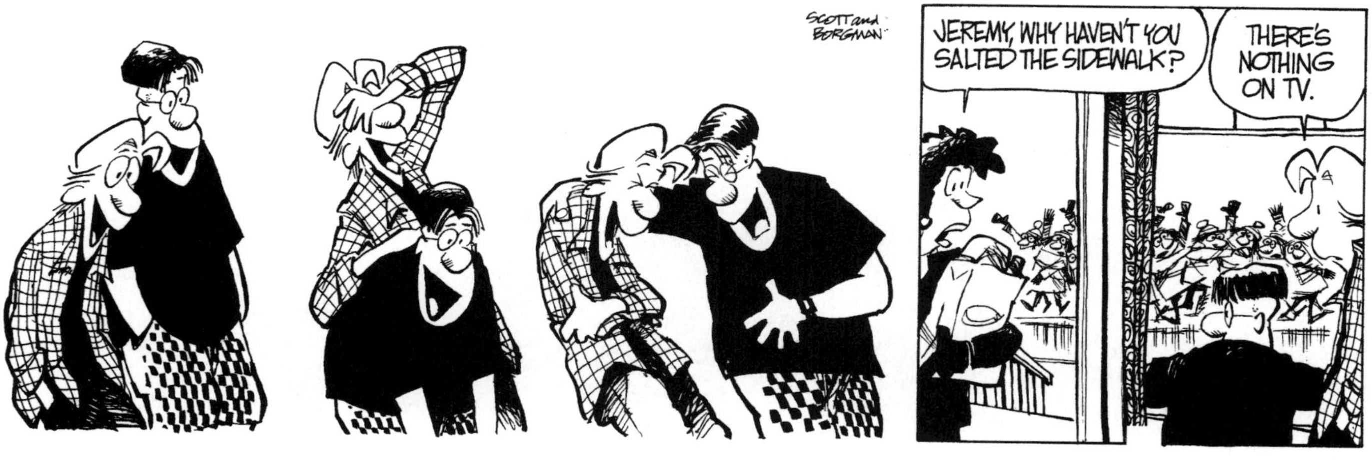
SCOTT and BORGMAN
JEREMY, WHY HAVEN'T YOU SALTED THE SIDEWALK?
THERE'S NOTHING ON TV.

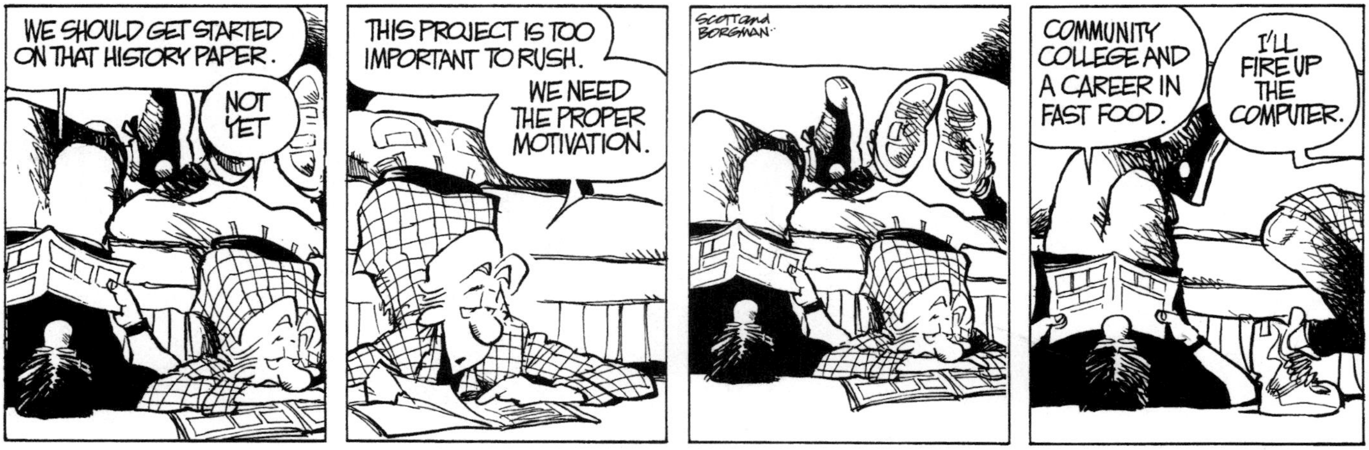
WE SHOULD GET STARTED ON THAT HISTORY PAPER.
NOT YET
THIS PROJECT IS TOO IMPORTANT TO RUSH.
WE NEED THE PROPER MOTIVATION.
SCOTT and BORGMAN
COMMUNITY COLLEGE AND A CAREER IN FAST FOOD.
I'LL FIRE UP THE COMPUTER.

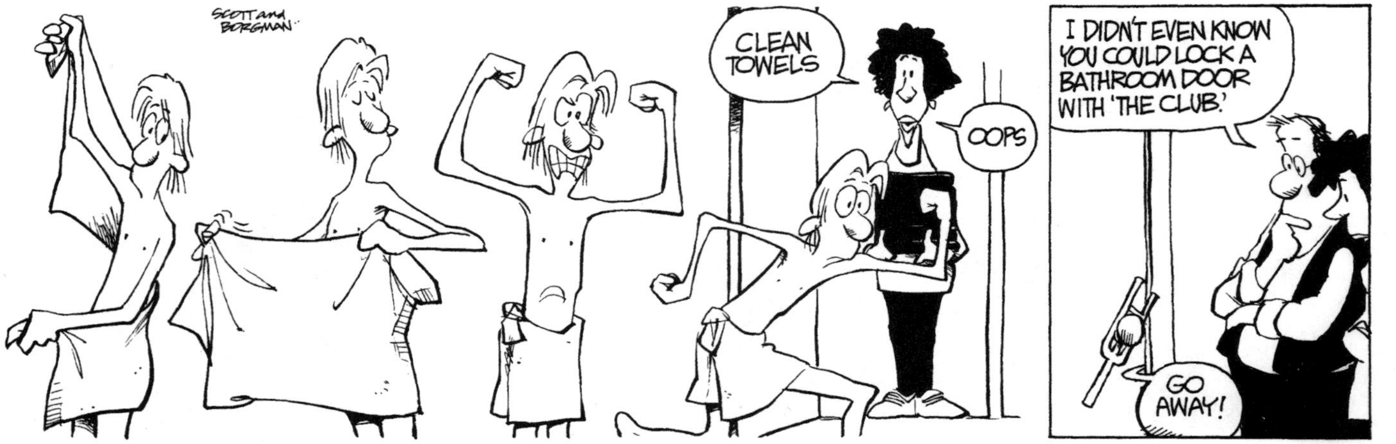
SCOTT and BORGMAN
CLEAN TOWELS
OOPS
I DIDN'T EVEN KNOW YOU COULD LOCK A BATHROOM DOOR WITH 'THE CLUB.'
GO AWAY!

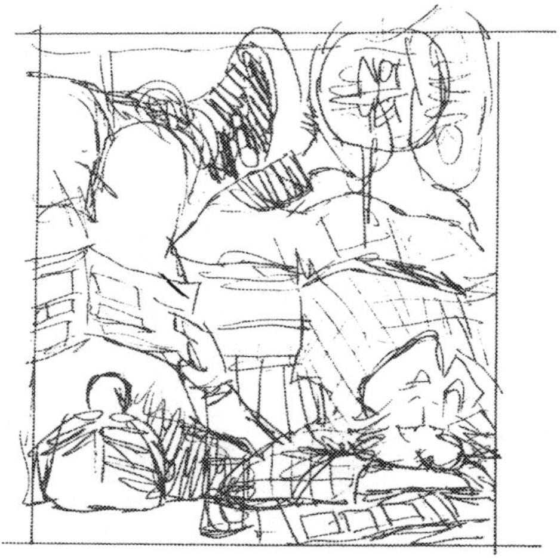

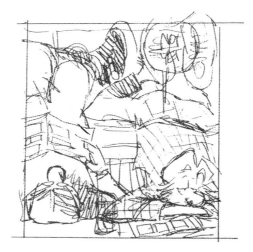

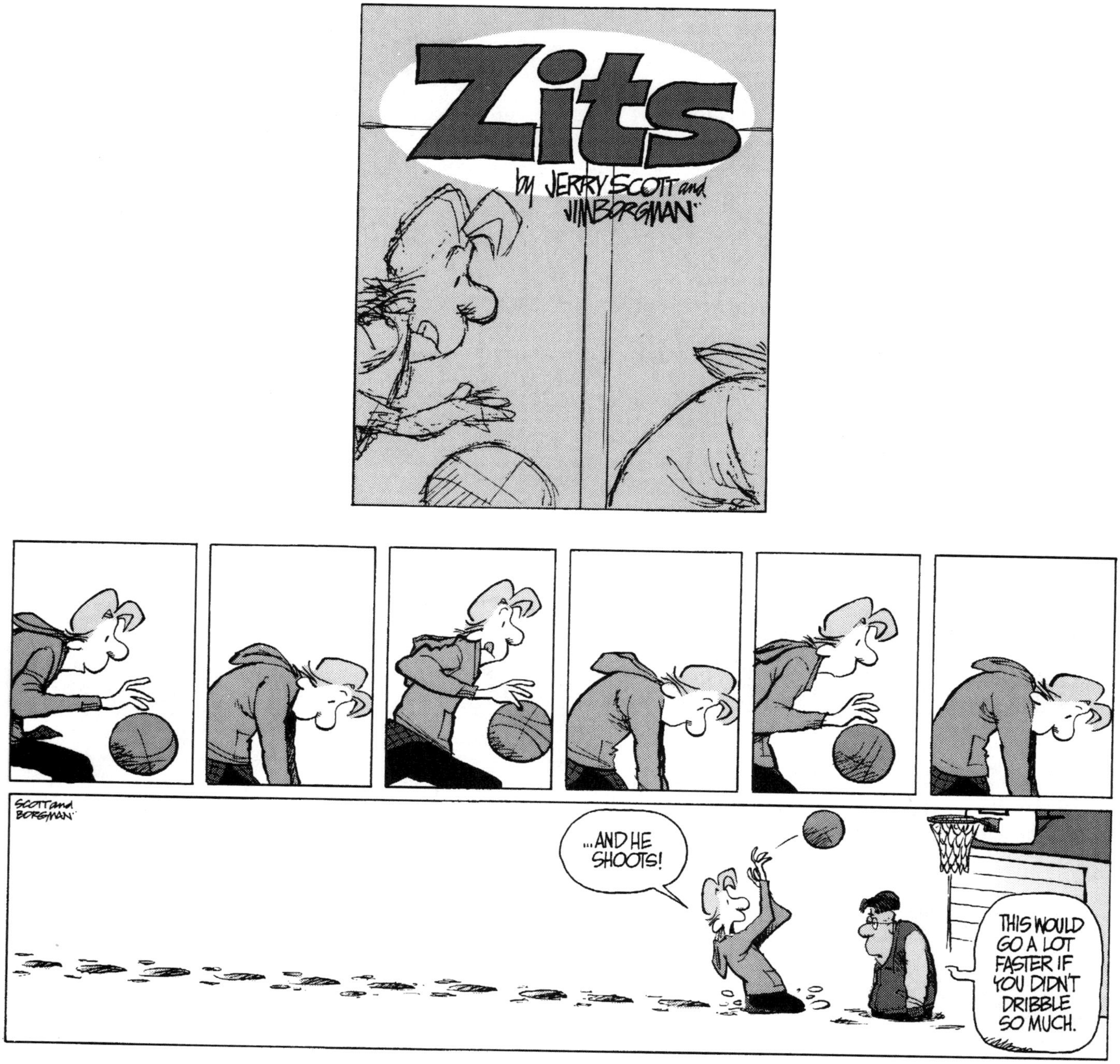
Zits
by JERRY SCOTT and JIM BORGMAN
SCOTT and BORGMAN
...AND HE SHOOTS!
THIS WOULD GO A LOT FASTER IF YOU DIDN'T DRIBBLE SO MUCH.

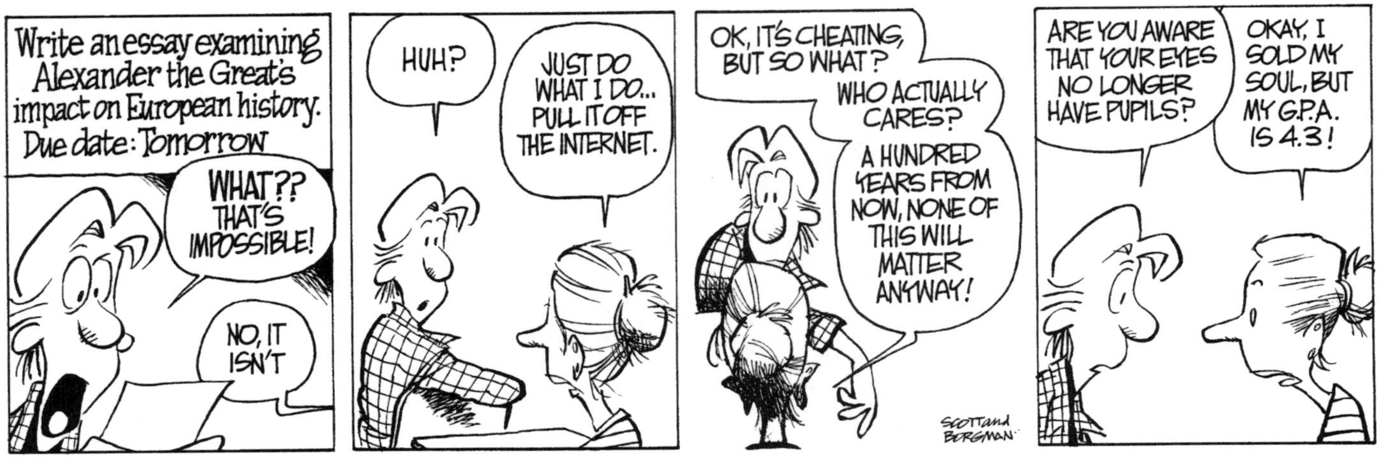
Write an essay examining Alexander the Great's impact on European history.
Due date: Tomorrow
WHAT?? THAT'S IMPOSSIBLE!
NO, IT ISN'T
HUH?
JUST DO WHAT I DO... PULL IT OFF THE INTERNET.
OK, IT'S CHEATING, BUT SO WHAT?
WHO ACTUALLY CARES?
A HUNDRED YEARS FROM NOW, NONE OF THIS WILL MATTER ANYWAY!
SCOTT and BORGMAN
ARE YOU AWARE THAT YOUR EYES NO LONGER HAVE PUPILS?
OKAY, I SOLD MY SOUL, BUT MY G.P.A. IS 4.3!

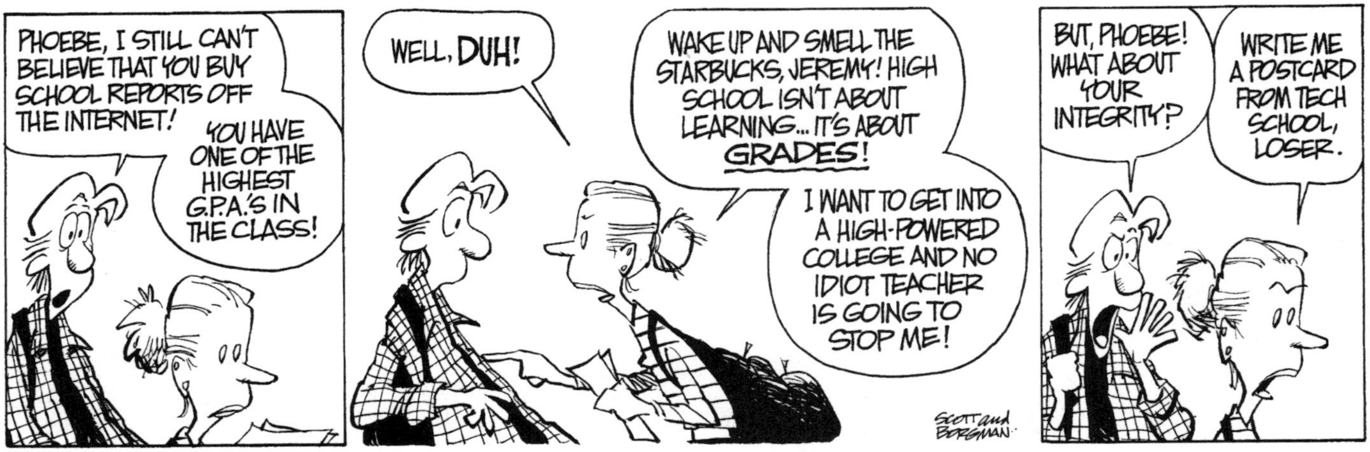
PHOEBE, I STILL CAN'T BELIEVE THAT YOU BUY SCHOOL REPORTS OFF THE INTERNET!
YOU HAVE ONE OF THE HIGHEST G.P.A.'S IN THE CLASS!
WELL, DUH!
WAKE UP AND SMELL THE STARBUCKS, JEREMY! HIGH SCHOOL ISN'T ABOUT LEARNING... IT'S ABOUT GRADES!
I WANT TO GET INTO A HIGH-POWERED COLLEGE AND NO IDIOT TEACHER IS GOING TO STOP ME!
SCOTT and BORGMAN
BUT, PHOEBE! WHAT ABOUT YOUR INTEGRITY?
WRITE ME A POSTCARD FROM TECH SCHOOL, LOSER.

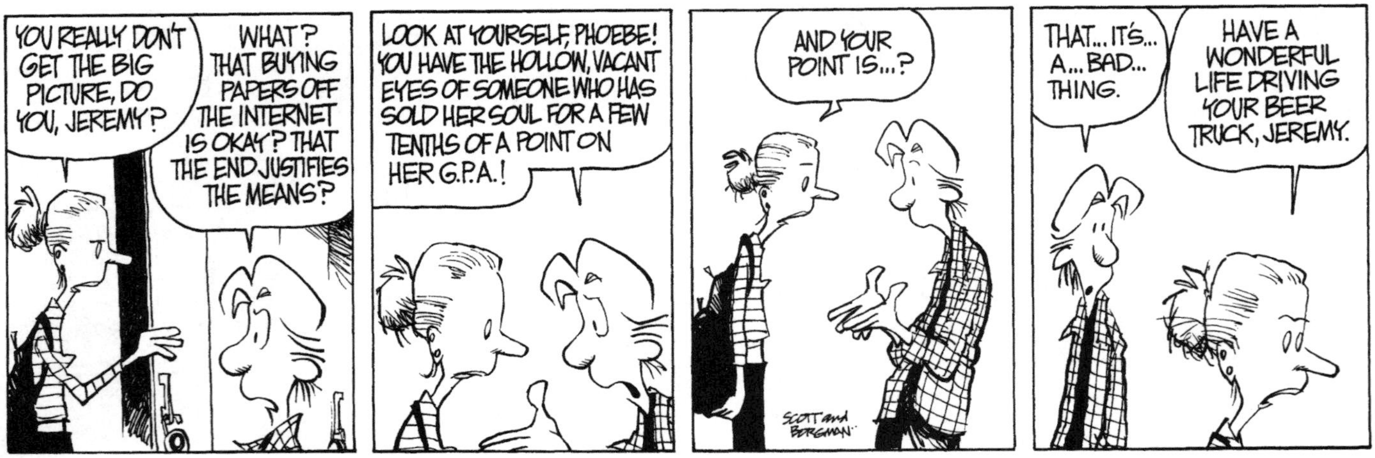
YOU REALLY DON'T GET THE BIG PICTURE, DO YOU, JEREMY?
WHAT? THAT BUYING PAPERS OFF THE INTERNET IS OKAY? THAT THE END JUSTIFIES THE MEANS?
LOOK AT YOURSELF, PHOEBE! YOU HAVE THE HOLLOW, VACANT EYES OF SOMEONE WHO HAS SOLD HER SOUL FOR A FEW TENTHS OF A POINT ON HER G.P.A.!
AND YOUR POINT IS...?
SCOTT and BORGMAN
THAT... IT'S... A... BAD... THING.
HAVE A WONDERFUL LIFE DRIVING YOUR BEER TRUCK, JEREMY.

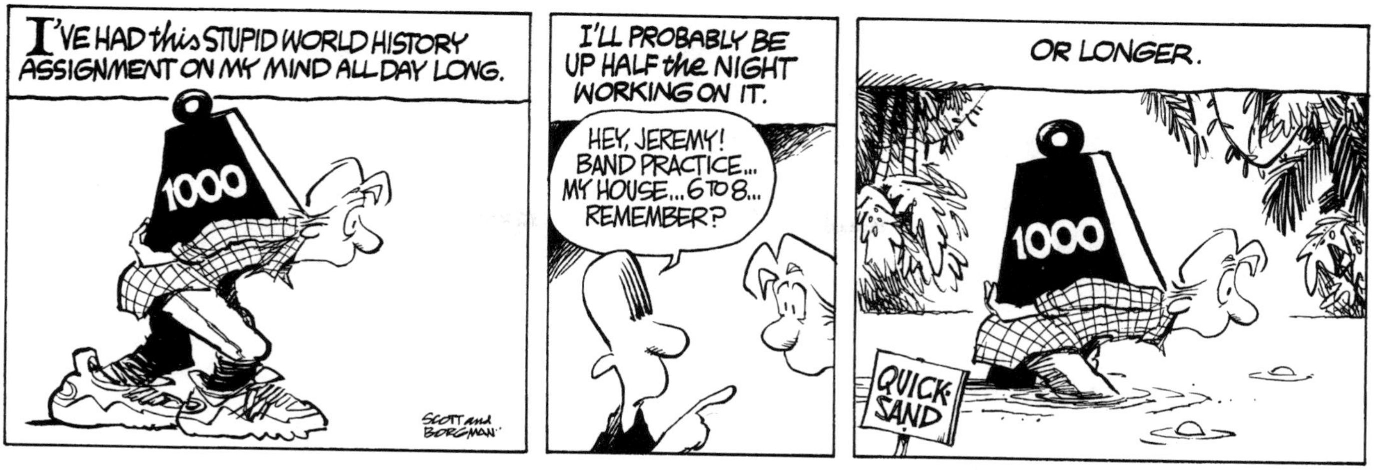
I'VE HAD this STUPID WORLD HISTORY ASSIGNMENT ON MY MIND ALL DAY LONG.
1000
SCOTT and BORGMAN
I'LL PROBABLY BE UP HALF the NIGHT WORKING ON IT.
HEY, JEREMY! BAND PRACTICE... MY HOUSE... 6 TO 8... REMEMBER?
OR LONGER.
1000
QUICK-SAND

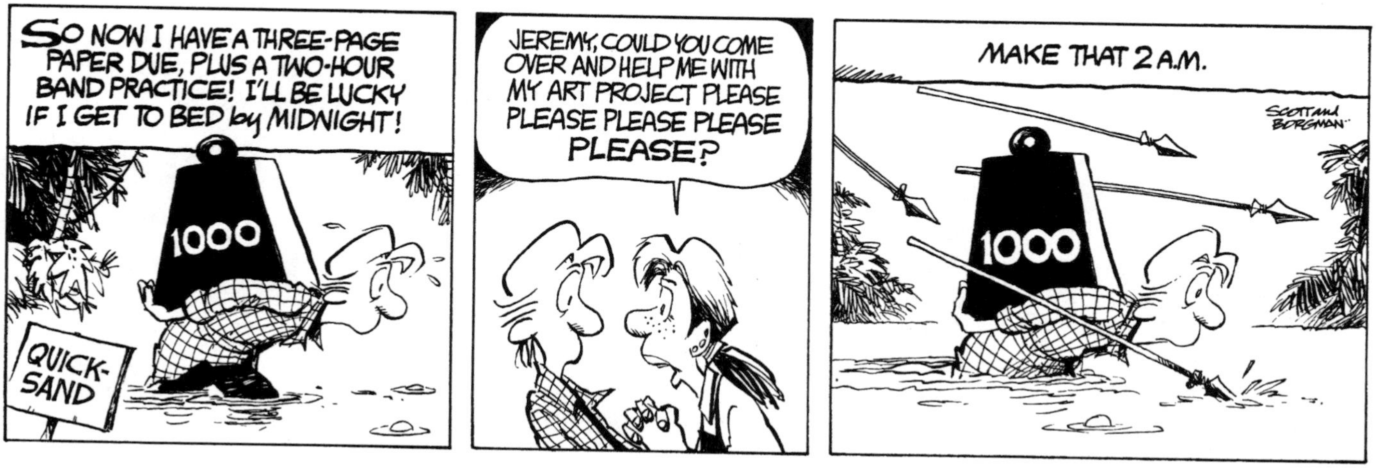
SO NOW I HAVE A THREE-PAGE PAPER DUE, PLUS A TWO-HOUR BAND PRACTICE! I'LL BE LUCKY IF I GET TO BED by MIDNIGHT!
1000
QUICK-SAND
JEREMY, COULD YOU COME OVER AND HELP ME WITH MY ART PROJECT PLEASE PLEASE PLEASE PLEASE PLEASE?
MAKE THAT 2 A.M.
SCOTT and BORGMAN
1000

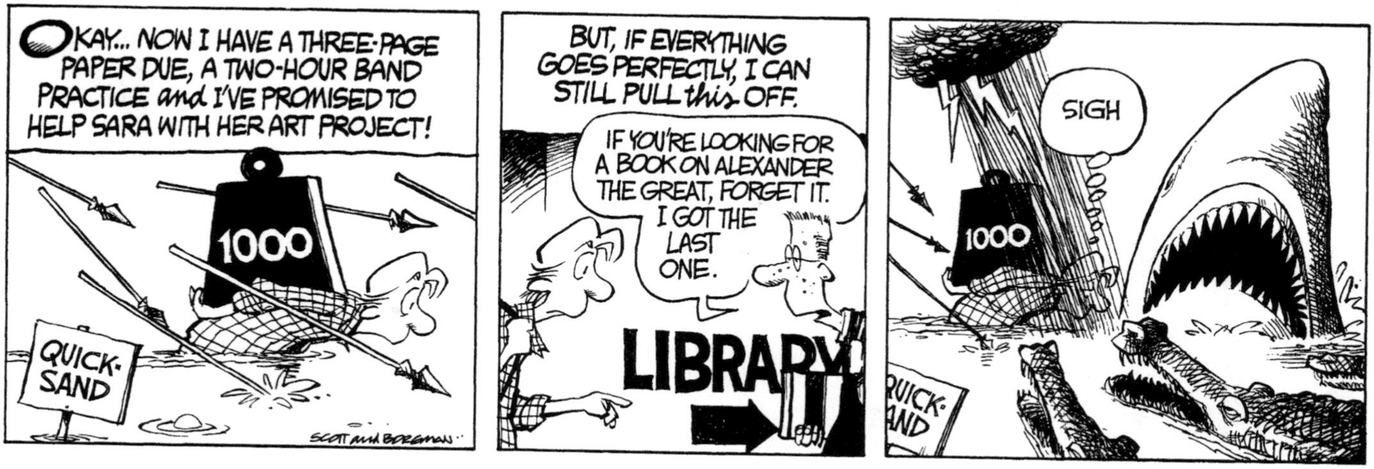
OKAY... NOW I HAVE A THREE-PAGE PAPER DUE, A TWO-HOUR BAND PRACTICE and I'VE PROMISED TO HELP SARA WITH HER ART PROJECT!
1000
QUICK-SAND
SCOTT and BORGMAN
BUT, IF EVERYTHING GOES PERFECTLY, I CAN STILL PULL this OFF.
IF YOU'RE LOOKING FOR A BOOK ON ALEXANDER THE GREAT, FORGET IT. I GOT THE LAST ONE.
LIBRARY
SIGH
1000

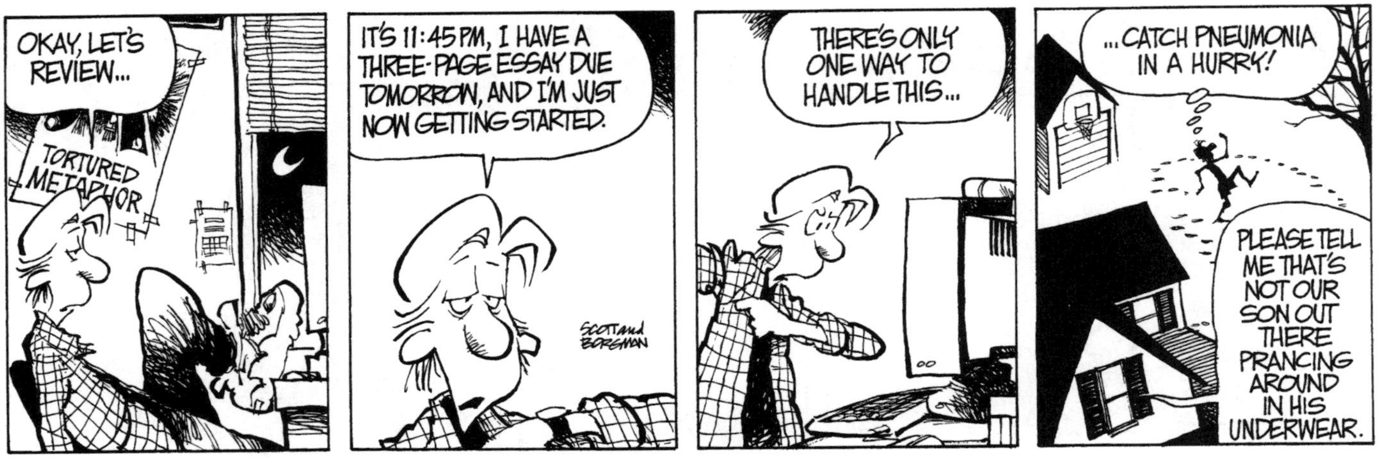
OKAY, LET'S REVIEW...
TORTURED METAPHOR
IT'S 11:45 PM, I HAVE A THREE-PAGE ESSAY DUE TOMORROW, AND I'M JUST NOW GETTING STARTED.
SCOTT and BORGMAN
THERE'S ONLY ONE WAY TO HANDLE THIS...
...CATCH PNEUMONIA IN A HURRY!
PLEASE TELL ME THAT'S NOT OUR SON OUT THERE PRANCING AROUND IN HIS UNDERWEAR.

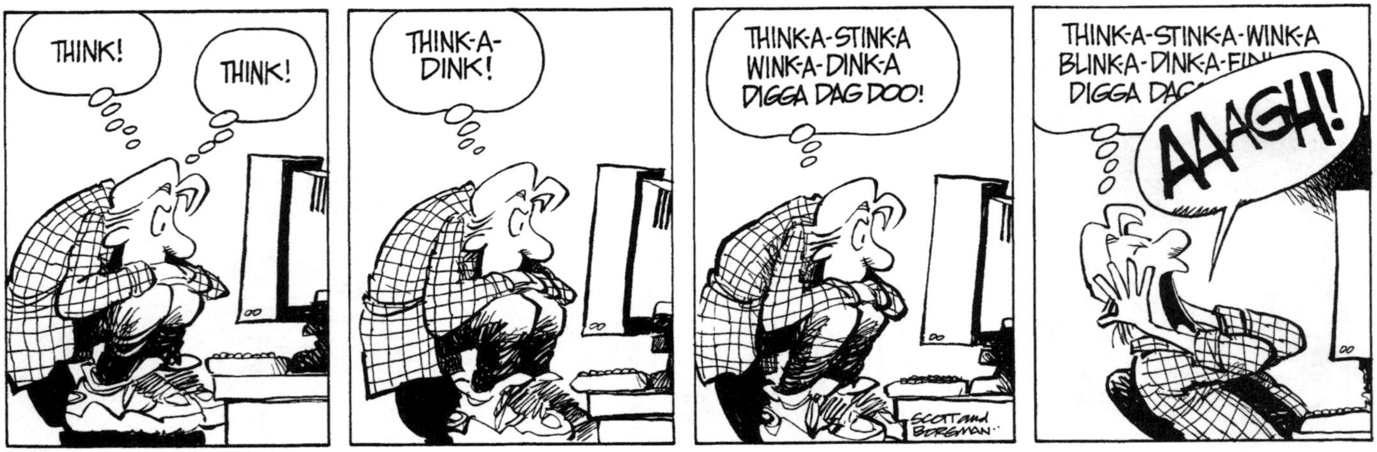
THINK!
THINK!
THINK-A-DINK!
THINK-A-STINK-A WINK-A-DINK-A DIGGA DAG DOO!
SCOTT and BORGMAN
THINK-A-STINK-A-WINK-A
BLINK-A-DINK-A-
DIGGA DA
AAAGH!

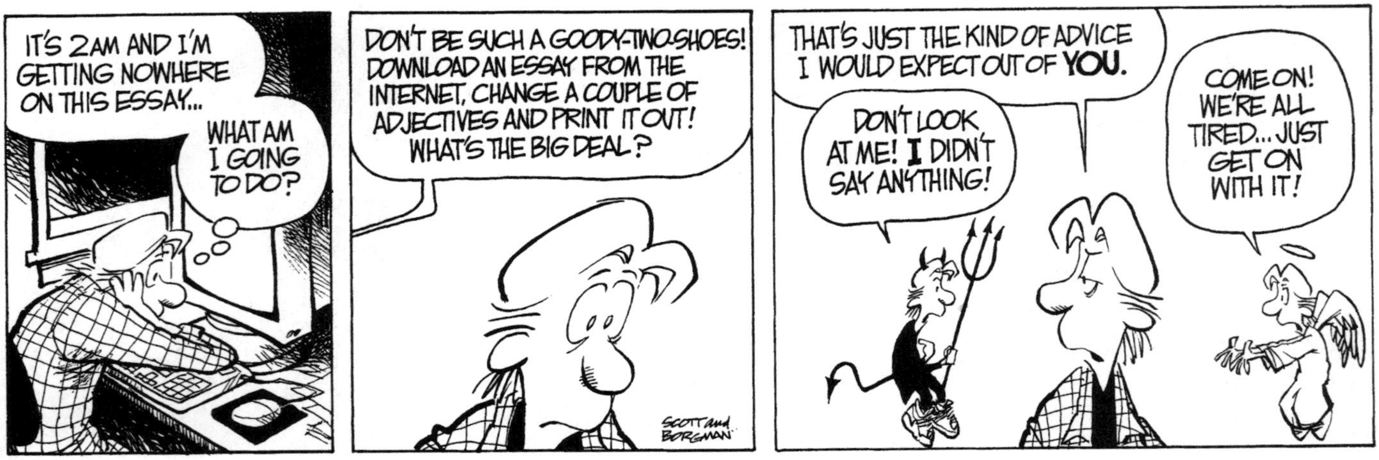
IT'S 2AM AND I'M GETTING NOWHERE ON THIS ESSAY...
WHAT AM I GOING TO DO?
DON'T BE SUCH A GOODY-TWO-SHOES! DOWNLOAD AN ESSAY FROM THE INTERNET, CHANGE A COUPLE OF ADJECTIVES AND PRINT IT OUT! WHAT'S THE BIG DEAL?
SCOTT and BORGMAN
THAT'S JUST THE KIND OF ADVICE I WOULD EXPECT OUT OF YOU.
DON'T LOOK AT ME! I DIDN'T SAY ANYTHING!
COME ON! WE'RE ALL TIRED... JUST GET ON WITH IT!

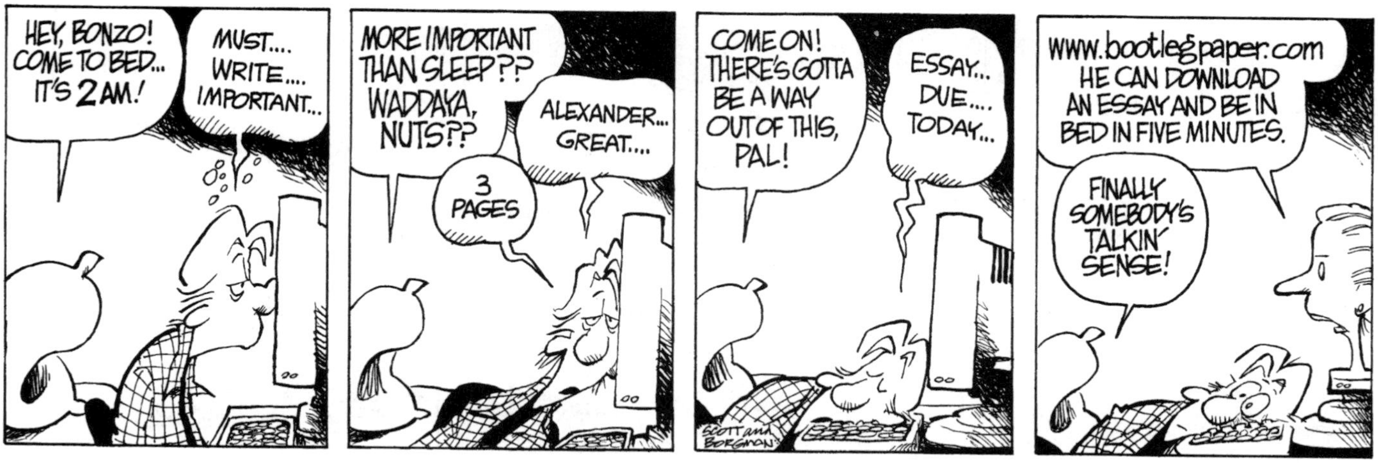
HEY, BONZO! COME TO BED... IT'S 2 AM!
MUST.... WRITE.... IMPORTANT...
MORE IMPORTANT THAN SLEEP?? WADDAYA, NUTS??
ALEXANDER... GREAT....
3 PAGES
COME ON! THERE'S GOTTA BE A WAY OUT OF THIS, PAL!
ESSAY... DUE.... TODAY...
SCOTT and BORGMAN
www.bootlegpaper.com HE CAN DOWNLOAD AN ESSAY AND BE IN BED IN FIVE MINUTES.
FINALLY SOMEBODY'S TALKIN' SENSE!

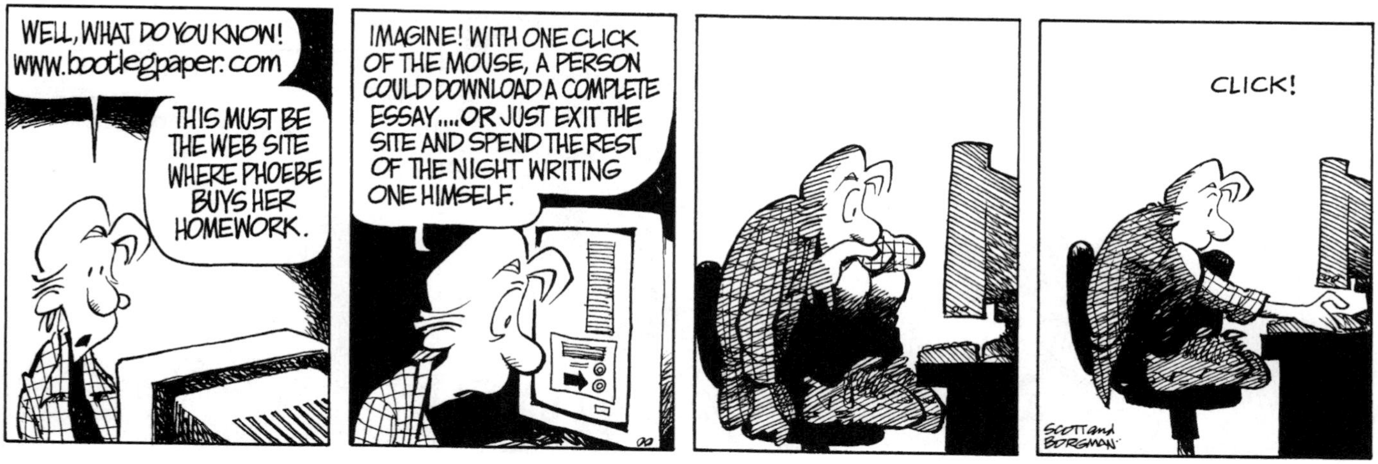
WELL, WHAT DO YOU KNOW! www.bootlegpaper.com
THIS MUST BE THE WEB SITE WHERE PHOEBE BUYS HER HOMEWORK.
IMAGINE! WITH ONE CLICK OF THE MOUSE, A PERSON COULD DOWNLOAD A COMPLETE ESSAY....OR JUST EXIT THE SITE AND SPEND THE REST OF THE NIGHT WRITING ONE HIMSELF.
CLICK!
SCOTT and BORGMAN

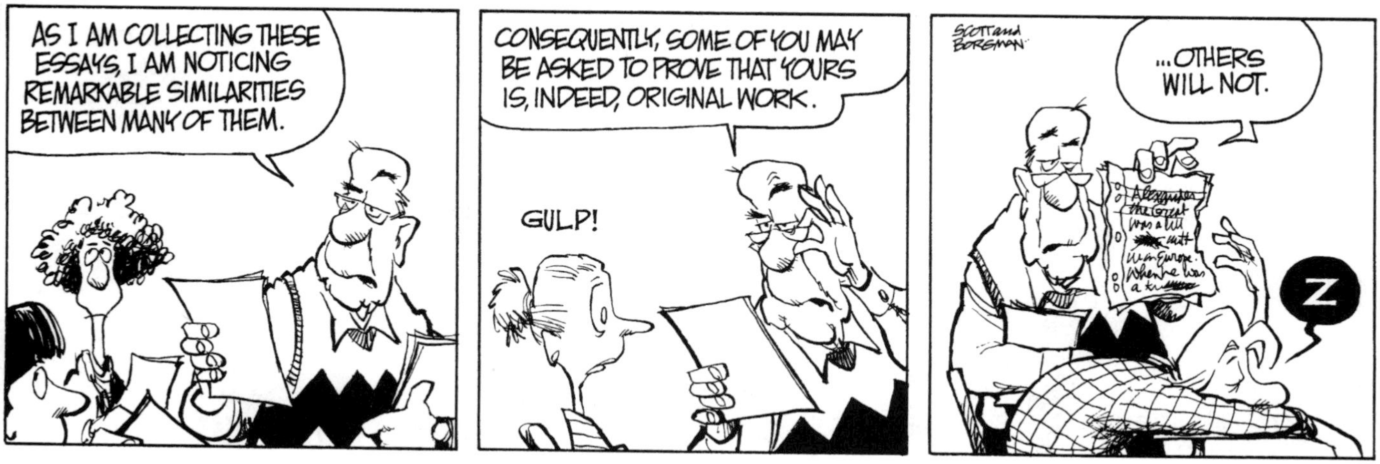
AS I AM COLLECTING THESE ESSAYS, I AM NOTICING REMARKABLE SIMILARITIES BETWEEN MANY OF THEM.
CONSEQUENTLY, SOME OF YOU MAY BE ASKED TO PROVE THAT YOURS IS, INDEED, ORIGINAL WORK.
GULP!
SCOTT and BORGMAN
...OTHERS WILL NOT.
Z

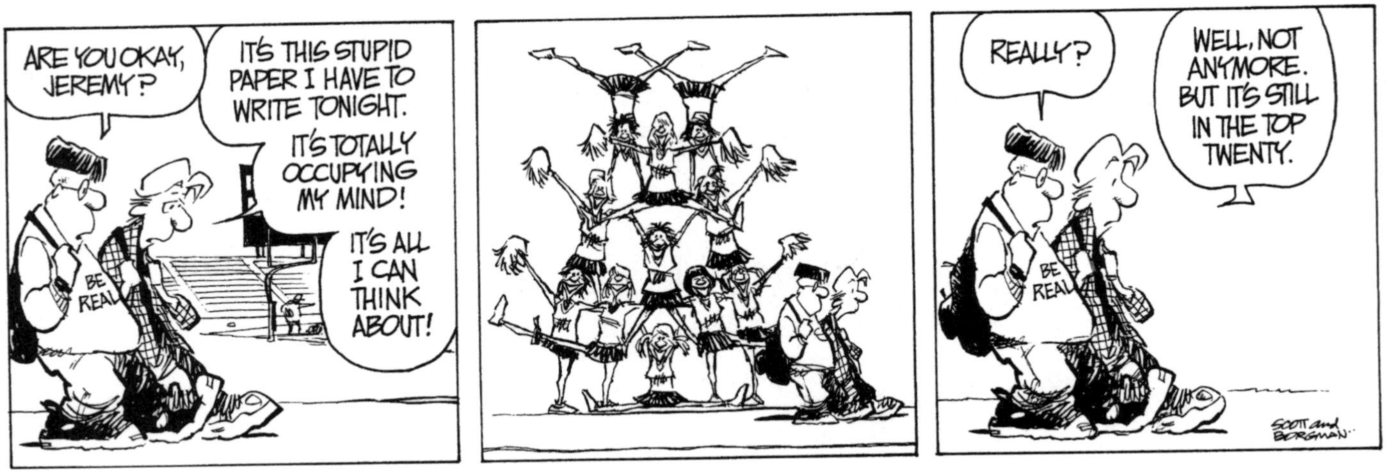
ARE YOU OKAY, JEREMY?
IT'S THIS STUPID PAPER I HAVE TO WRITE TONIGHT.
IT'S TOTALLY OCCUPYING MY MIND!
IT'S ALL I CAN THINK ABOUT!
BE REAL
REALLY?
WELL, NOT ANYMORE. BUT IT'S STILL IN THE TOP TWENTY.
SCOTT and BORGMAN

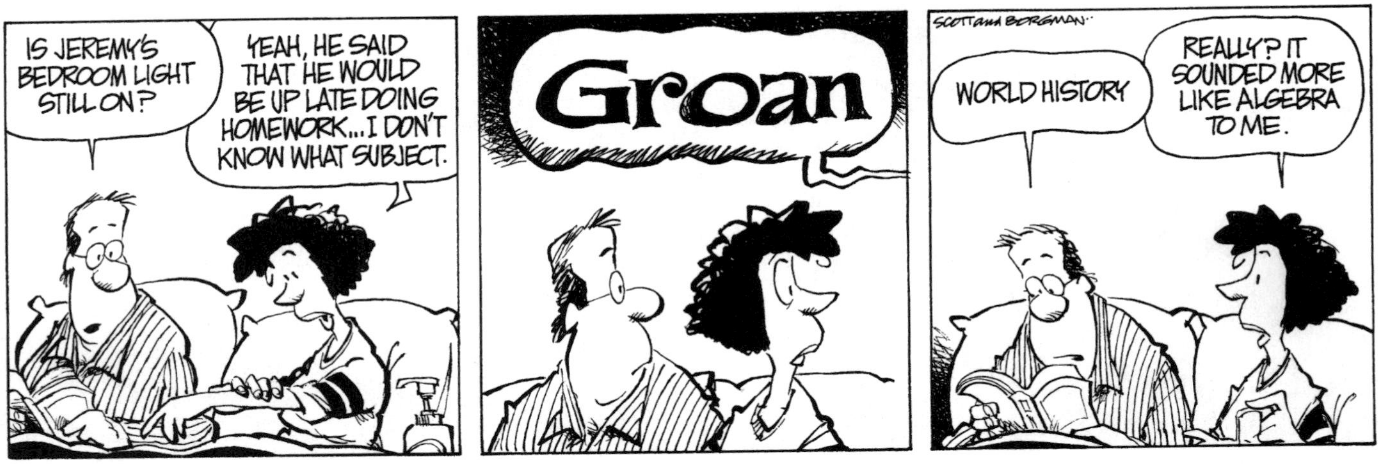
IS JEREMY'S BEDROOM LIGHT STILL ON?
YEAH, HE SAID THAT HE WOULD BE UP LATE DOING HOMEWORK...I DON'T KNOW WHAT SUBJECT.
Groan
SCOTT and BORGMAN
WORLD HISTORY
REALLY? IT SOUNDED MORE LIKE ALGEBRA TO ME.

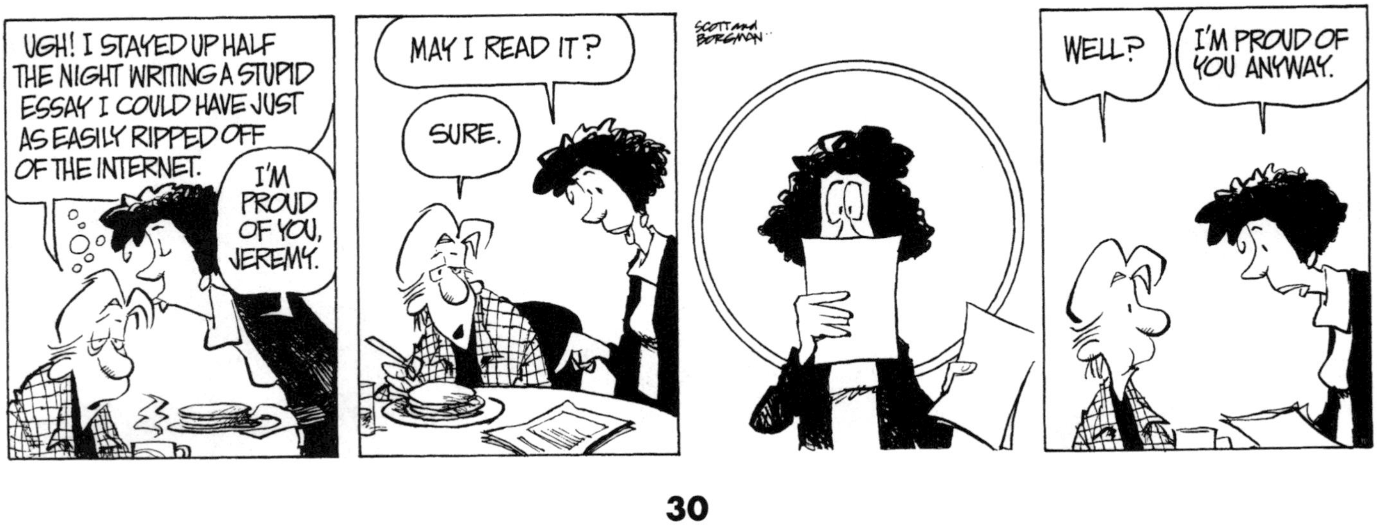
UGH! I STAYED UP HALF THE NIGHT WRITING A STUPID ESSAY I COULD HAVE JUST AS EASILY RIPPED OFF OF THE INTERNET.
I'M PROUD OF YOU, JEREMY.
MAY I READ IT?
SURE.
SCOTT and BORGMAN
WELL?
I'M PROUD OF YOU ANYWAY.

Zits
by JERRY SCOTT and JIM BORGMAN
UH-OH...

EXCUSE ME...
DO YOU HAVE MEYOW MORSELS?
WHAT?
MEYOW MORSELS! THE CAT FOOD CATS ASK FOR BY NAME.
MOTHER...
WHAT?
YOU KNOW...THEY HAVE THAT CUTE COMMERCIAL WHERE THE CATS SING!
THAT'S RIGHT!
NOT HERE.. NOT NOW..
UH-OH...
MEYOW! MEYOW! MEYOW! MEYOW! MEYOW! MEYOW! MEYOW! MEYOW! MEYOW
I THINK THEY HUMILIATE US LIKE THIS JUST TO MAKE SURE WE LEAVE HOME AT EIGHTEEN.
IN THAT CASE, IT'S WORKING.
SCOTT and BORGMAN

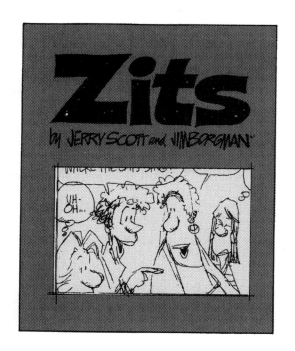

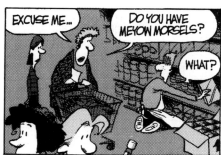

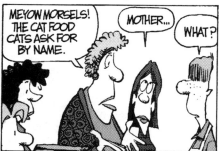

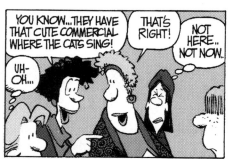

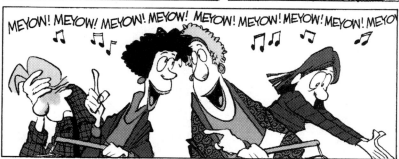

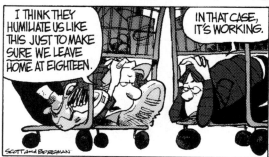

Zits by Jerry Scott and Jim Borgman

IT'S DETERGENT!

THE CROWD SITS IN HUSHED SILENCE AS WALT DUNCAN FORMULATES HIS STRATEGY.

HE'S FACING A LOAD OF PERMA-PRESS COTTONS— BUT WHAT'S THIS?? A NYLON BLEND WITH A LARGE KETCHUP STAIN!

SCOTT and BORGMAN

DUNCAN SLOWLY MOVES TO THE SHELF AND COOLLY SELECTS HIS DETERGENT.

THIS IS IT! HE'S DIALED IN THE CYCLE AND THE WASHER HAS BEGUN TO FILL!

YOU COULD CUT THE TENSION WITH A KNIFE.

WALT DUNCAN PACES LIKE A CAGED TIGER, WHEN SLOWLY... ALMOST IMPERCEPTIBLY... A LOW CHANT BUILDS FROM THE CROWD.

DUNCAN! DUNCAN!

DUNCAN! DUNCAN! DUNCAN! DUNCAN!

TESTOSTERONE AND LAUNDRY DETERGENT DON'T MIX.

YOU NEED SOME OUTSIDE INTERESTS, DAD.

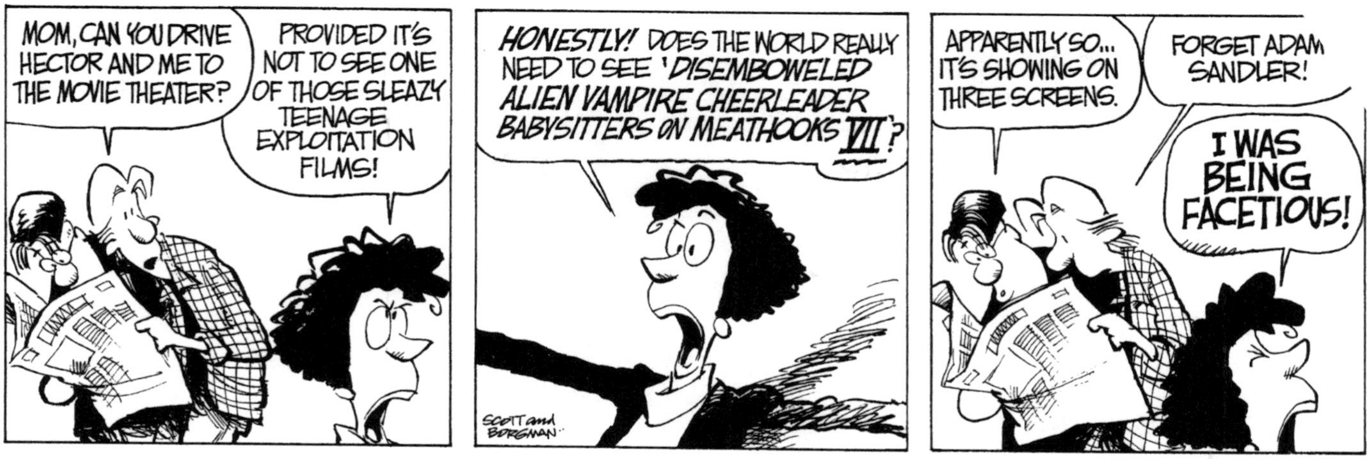
MOM, CAN YOU DRIVE HECTOR AND ME TO THE MOVIE THEATER?
PROVIDED IT'S NOT TO SEE ONE OF THOSE SLEAZY TEENAGE EXPLOITATION FILMS!
HONESTLY! DOES THE WORLD REALLY NEED TO SEE 'DISEMBOWELED ALIEN VAMPIRE CHEERLEADER BABYSITTERS ON MEATHOOKS VII'?
SCOTT and BORGMAN
APPARENTLY SO... IT'S SHOWING ON THREE SCREENS.
FORGET ADAM SANDLER!
I WAS BEING FACETIOUS!

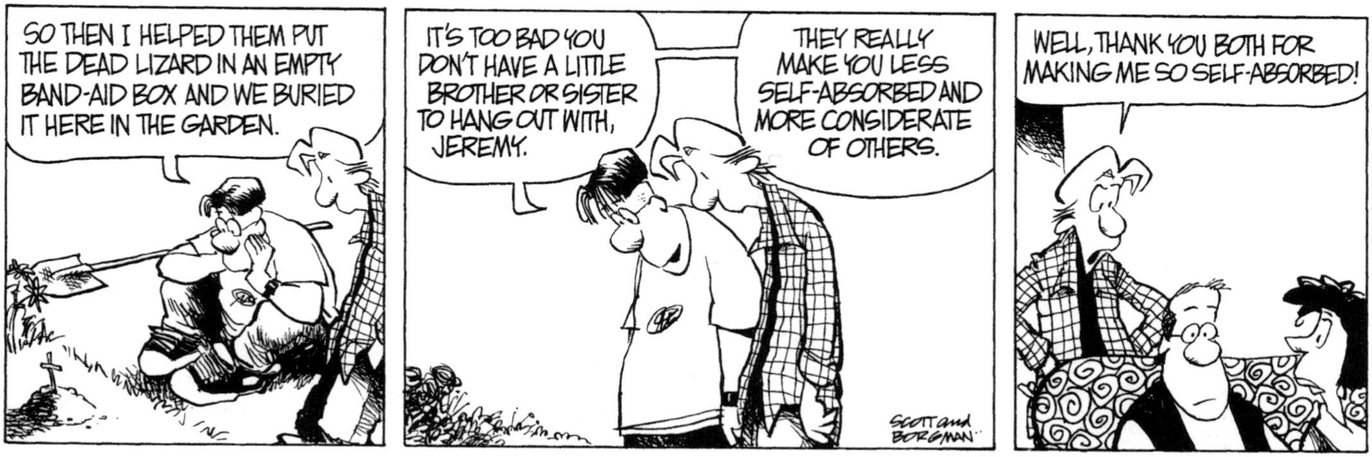
SO THEN I HELPED THEM PUT THE DEAD LIZARD IN AN EMPTY BAND-AID BOX AND WE BURIED IT HERE IN THE GARDEN.
IT'S TOO BAD YOU DON'T HAVE A LITTLE BROTHER OR SISTER TO HANG OUT WITH, JEREMY.
THEY REALLY MAKE YOU LESS SELF-ABSORBED AND MORE CONSIDERATE OF OTHERS.
SCOTT and BORGMAN
WELL, THANK YOU BOTH FOR MAKING ME SO SELF-ABSORBED!

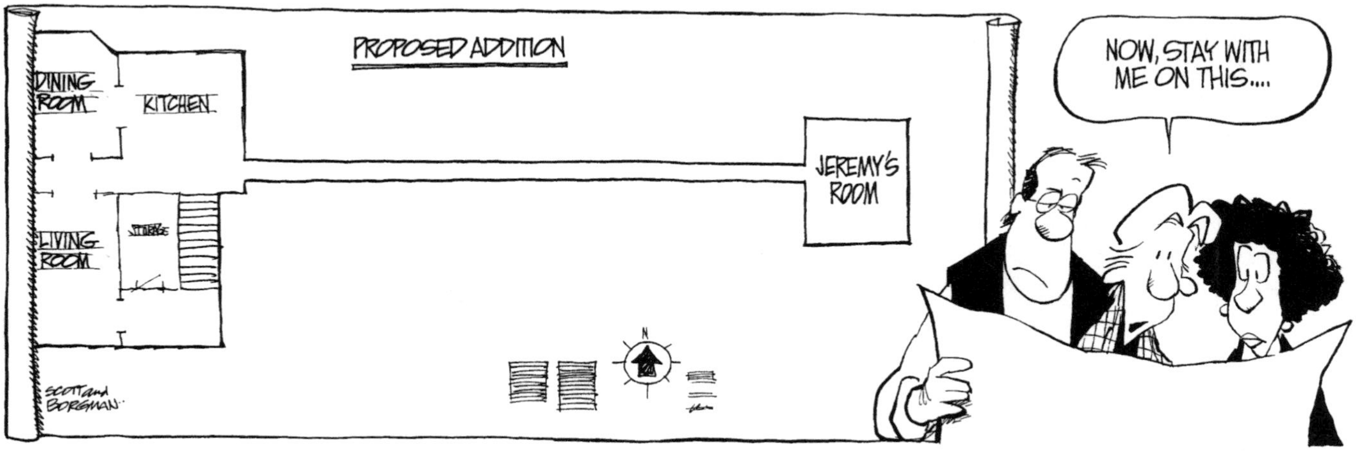
PROPOSED ADDITION
DINING ROOM
KITCHEN
LIVING ROOM
STORAGE
JEREMY'S ROOM
N
SCOTT and BORGMAN
NOW, STAY WITH ME ON THIS....

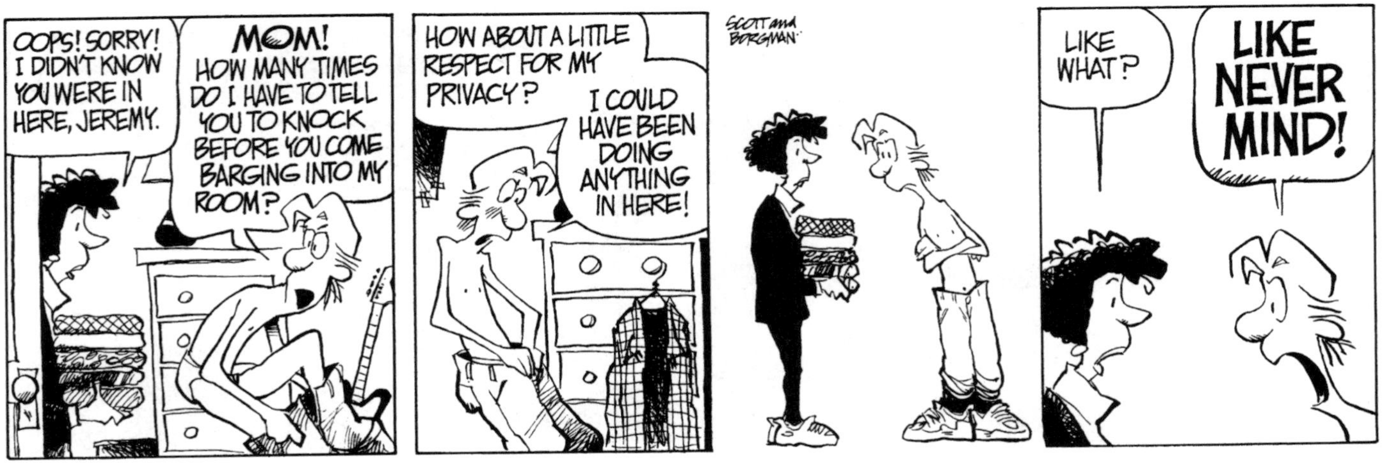
OOPS! SORRY! I DIDN'T KNOW YOU WERE IN HERE, JEREMY.
MOM! HOW MANY TIMES DO I HAVE TO TELL YOU TO KNOCK BEFORE YOU COME BARGING INTO MY ROOM?
HOW ABOUT A LITTLE RESPECT FOR MY PRIVACY?
I COULD HAVE BEEN DOING ANYTHING IN HERE!
SCOTT and BORGMAN
LIKE WHAT?
LIKE NEVER MIND!

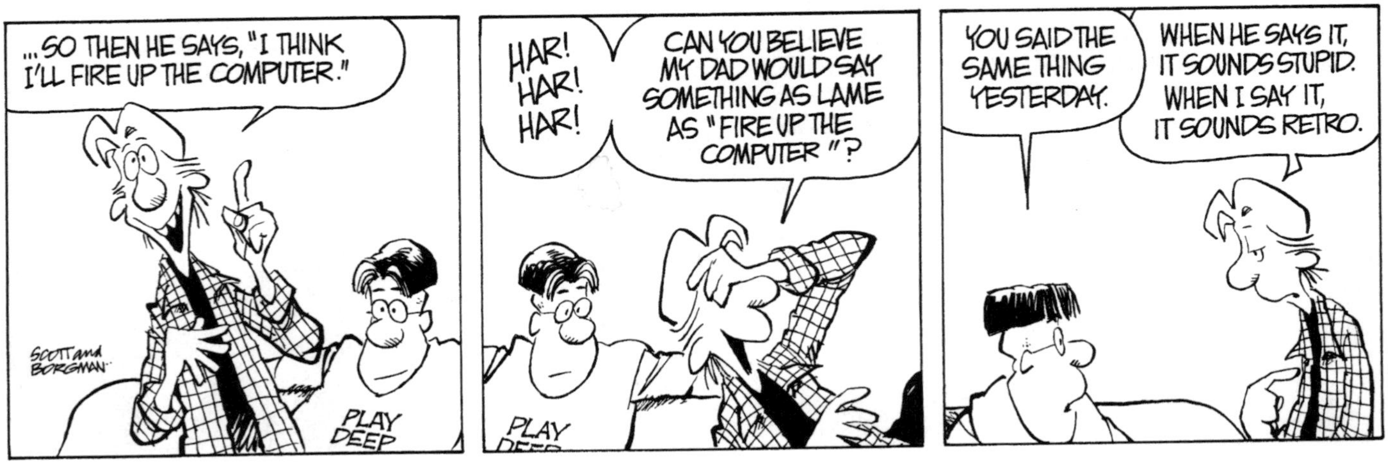
...SO THEN HE SAYS, "I THINK I'LL FIRE UP THE COMPUTER."
SCOTT and BORGMAN
PLAY DEEP
HAR! HAR! HAR!
CAN YOU BELIEVE MY DAD WOULD SAY SOMETHING AS LAME AS "FIRE UP THE COMPUTER"?
YOU SAID THE SAME THING YESTERDAY.
WHEN HE SAYS IT, IT SOUNDS STUPID. WHEN I SAY IT, IT SOUNDS RETRO.

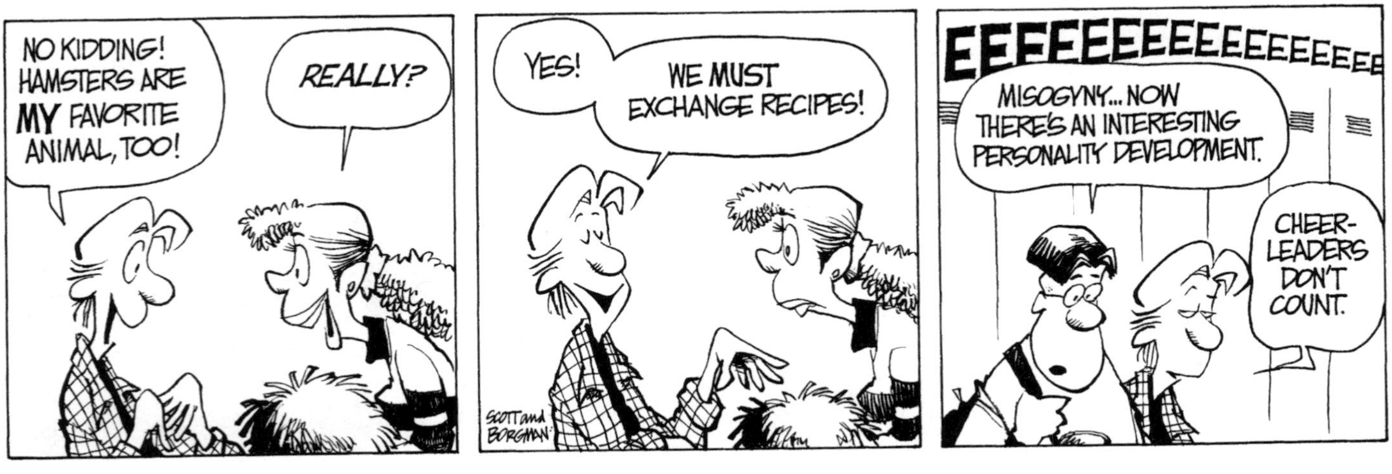
NO KIDDING! HAMSTERS ARE MY FAVORITE ANIMAL, TOO!
REALLY?
YES!
WE MUST EXCHANGE RECIPES!
SCOTT and BORGMAN
EEEEEEEEEEEEEEEEE
MISOGYNY... NOW THERE'S AN INTERESTING PERSONALITY DEVELOPMENT.
CHEER-LEADERS DON'T COUNT.

Zits
by JERRY SCOTT and JIM BORGMAN

HAS BEEN B

HEY THERE, HANDSOME!

YEEP!

WHY, MADAM! I DO BELIEVE MY HONOR HAS BEEN BESMIRCHED!

IT WOULDN'T BE THE FIRST TIME, BIG BOY!

C'MERE, YOU... IT'S TIME FOR YOUR ORAL EXAM.

(GIGGLE) ANYTHING YOU SAY, DOCTOR DUNCAN!

GLORP! SLORP! BLORG!

OOPS! I THINK JEREMY JUST CAUGHT US!

SO? KIDS **LIKE** TO SEE THEIR PARENTS DISPLAY AFFECTION TOWARD EACH OTHER.

MUST.... FIGHT.... REGURGITATION.... REFLEX....

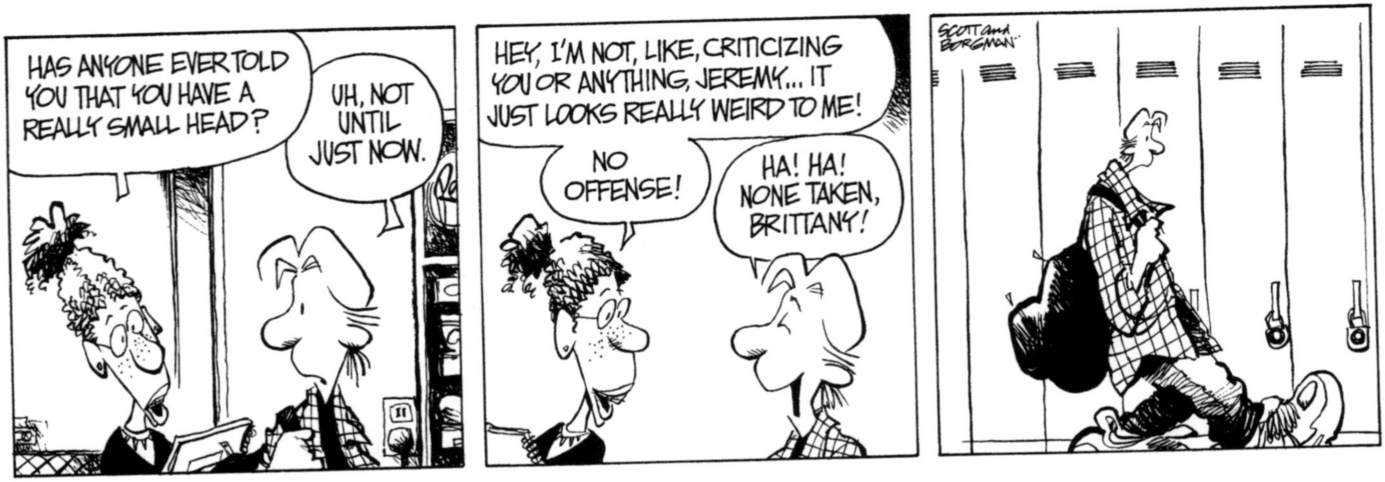
HAS ANYONE EVER TOLD YOU THAT YOU HAVE A REALLY SMALL HEAD?
UH, NOT UNTIL JUST NOW.
HEY, I'M NOT, LIKE, CRITICIZING YOU OR ANYTHING, JEREMY... IT JUST LOOKS REALLY WEIRD TO ME!
NO OFFENSE!
HA! HA! NONE TAKEN, BRITTANY!
SCOTT and BORGMAN

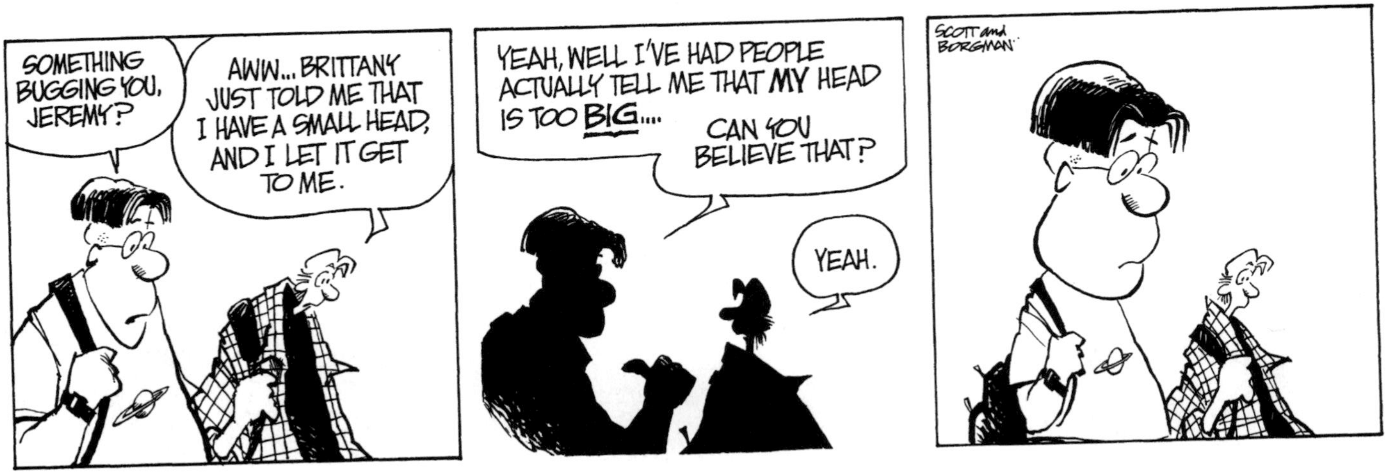
SOMETHING BUGGING YOU, JEREMY?
AWW... BRITTANY JUST TOLD ME THAT I HAVE A SMALL HEAD, AND I LET IT GET TO ME.
YEAH, WELL I'VE HAD PEOPLE ACTUALLY TELL ME THAT MY HEAD IS TOO BIG....
CAN YOU BELIEVE THAT?
YEAH.
SCOTT and BORGMAN

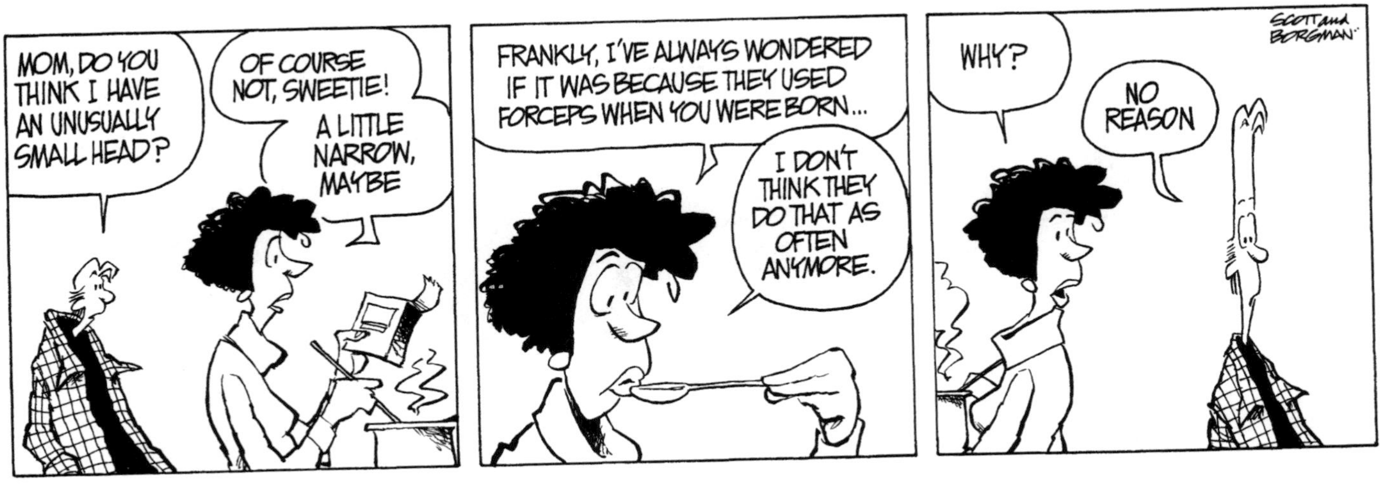
MOM, DO YOU THINK I HAVE AN UNUSUALLY SMALL HEAD?
OF COURSE NOT, SWEETIE!
A LITTLE NARROW, MAYBE
FRANKLY, I'VE ALWAYS WONDERED IF IT WAS BECAUSE THEY USED FORCEPS WHEN YOU WERE BORN...
I DON'T THINK THEY DO THAT AS OFTEN ANYMORE.
WHY?
NO REASON
SCOTT and BORGMAN

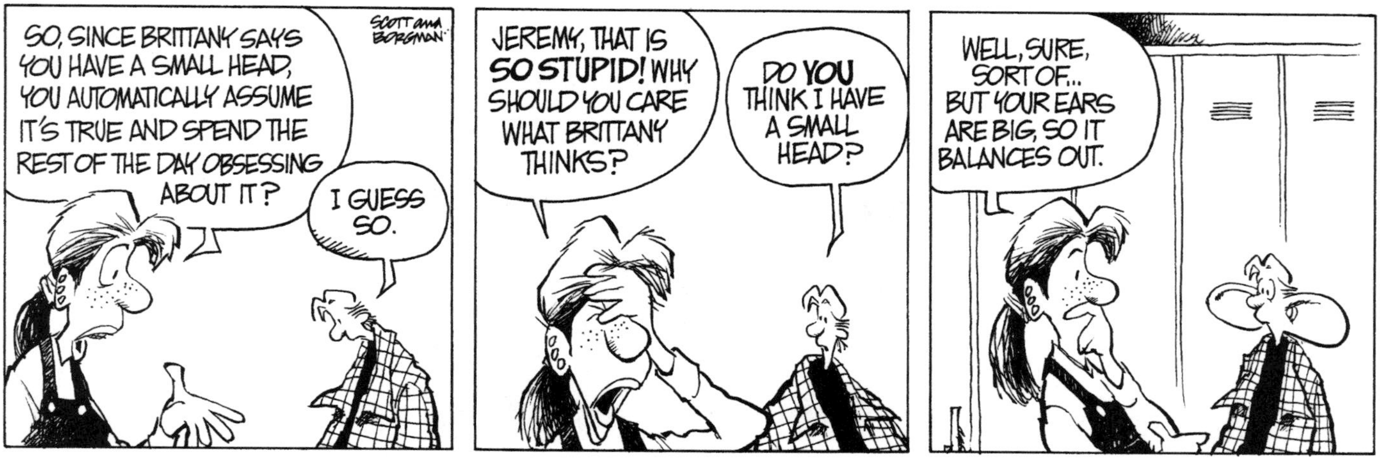
SO, SINCE BRITTANY SAYS YOU HAVE A SMALL HEAD, YOU AUTOMATICALLY ASSUME IT'S TRUE AND SPEND THE REST OF THE DAY OBSESSING ABOUT IT?
I GUESS SO.
JEREMY, THAT IS **SO STUPID!** WHY SHOULD YOU CARE WHAT BRITTANY THINKS?
DO **YOU** THINK I HAVE A SMALL HEAD?
WELL, SURE, SORT OF... BUT YOUR EARS ARE BIG, SO IT BALANCES OUT.

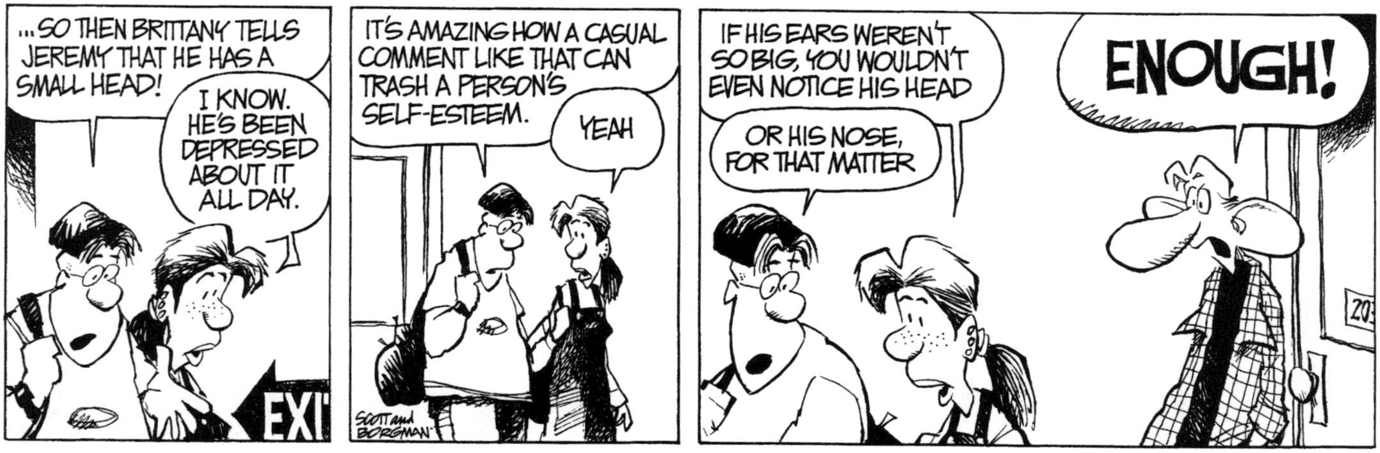
...SO THEN BRITTANY TELLS JEREMY THAT HE HAS A SMALL HEAD!
I KNOW. HE'S BEEN DEPRESSED ABOUT IT ALL DAY.
EXIT
IT'S AMAZING HOW A CASUAL COMMENT LIKE THAT CAN TRASH A PERSON'S SELF-ESTEEM.
YEAH
IF HIS EARS WEREN'T SO BIG, YOU WOULDN'T EVEN NOTICE HIS HEAD
OR HIS NOSE, FOR THAT MATTER
ENOUGH!

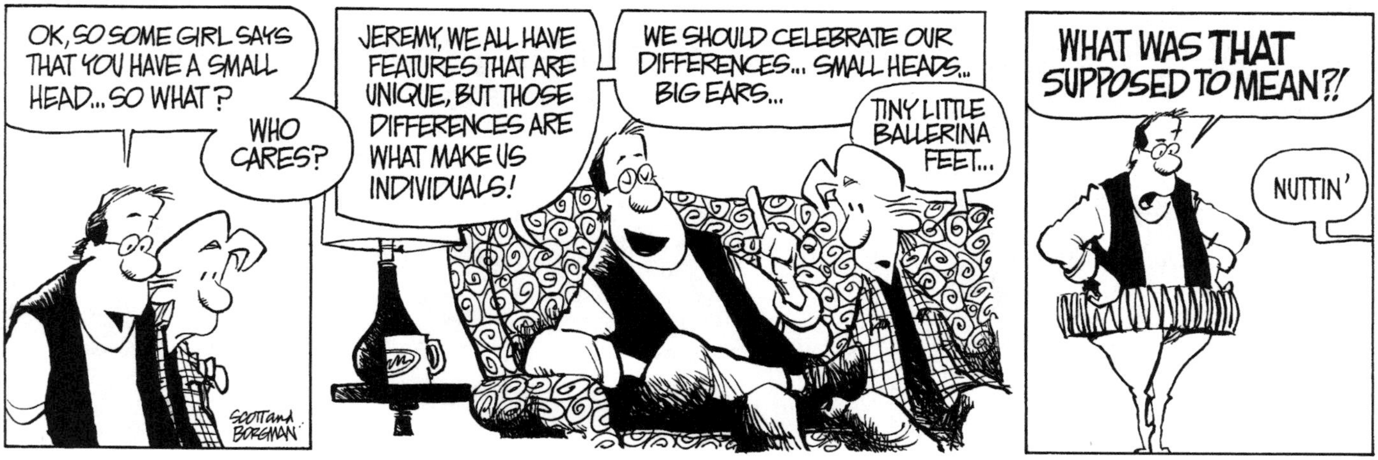
OK, SO SOME GIRL SAYS THAT YOU HAVE A SMALL HEAD... SO WHAT?
WHO CARES?
JEREMY, WE ALL HAVE FEATURES THAT ARE UNIQUE, BUT THOSE DIFFERENCES ARE WHAT MAKE US INDIVIDUALS!
WE SHOULD CELEBRATE OUR DIFFERENCES... SMALL HEADS... BIG EARS...
TINY LITTLE BALLERINA FEET...
WHAT WAS **THAT** SUPPOSED TO MEAN?!
NUTTIN'

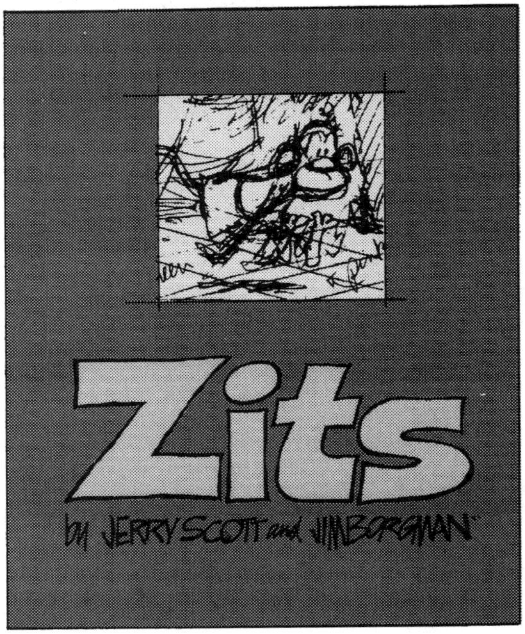
Zits
by JERRY SCOTT and JIM BORGMAN

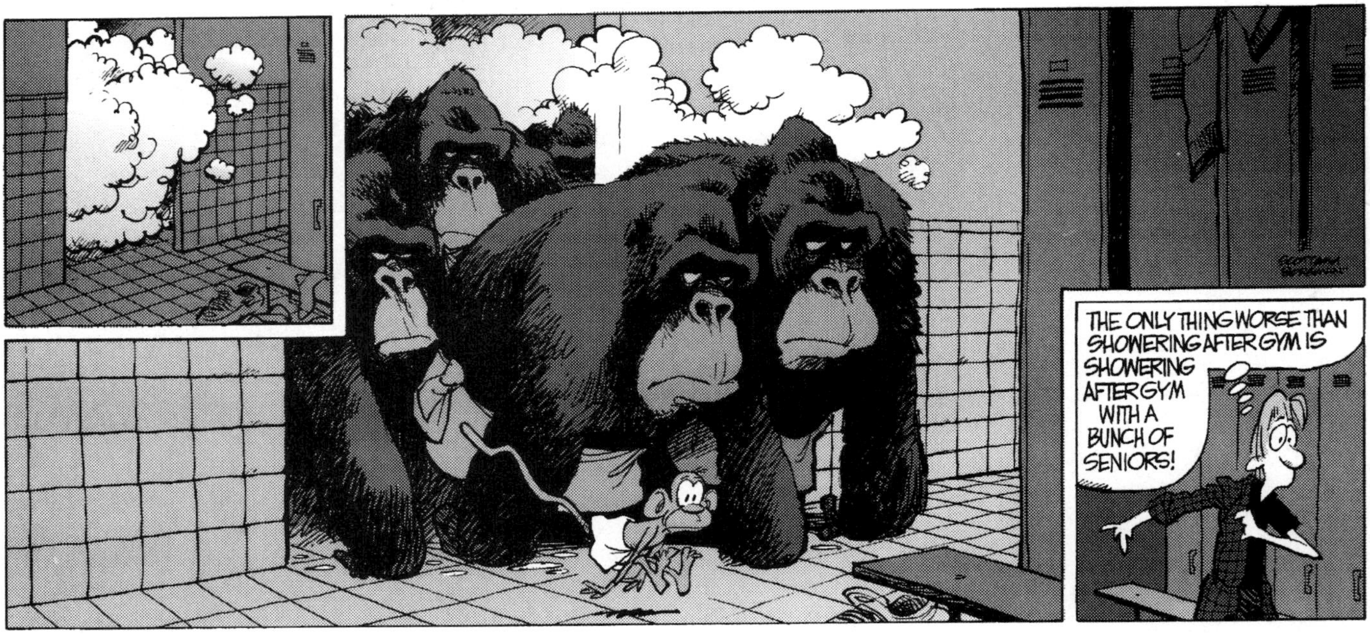
THE ONLY THING WORSE THAN SHOWERING AFTER GYM IS SHOWERING AFTER GYM WITH A BUNCH OF SENIORS!

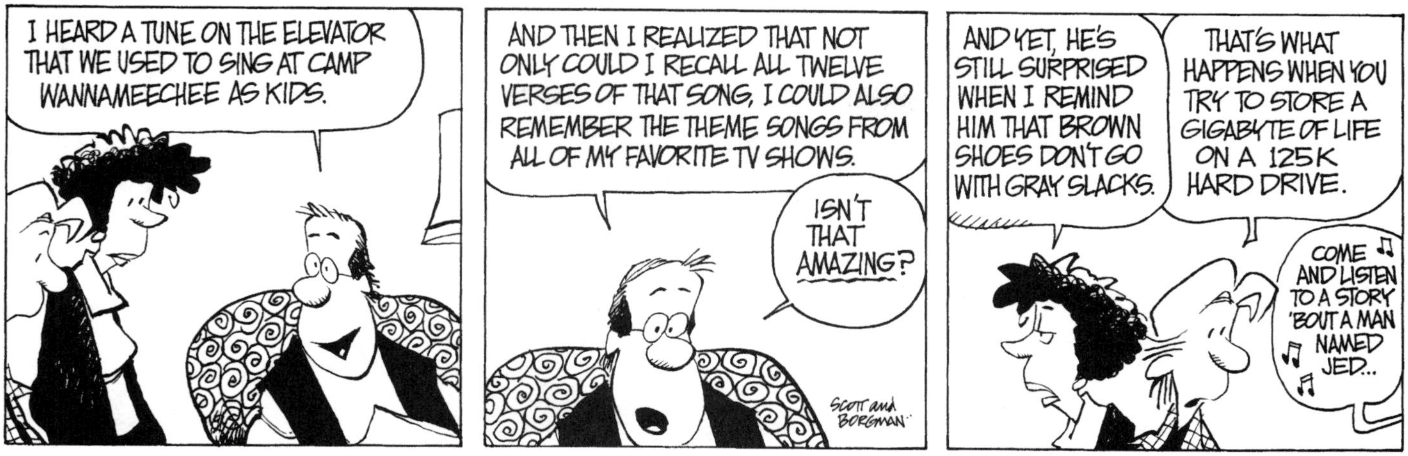
I HEARD A TUNE ON THE ELEVATOR THAT WE USED TO SING AT CAMP WANNAMEECHEE AS KIDS.
AND THEN I REALIZED THAT NOT ONLY COULD I RECALL ALL TWELVE VERSES OF THAT SONG, I COULD ALSO REMEMBER THE THEME SONGS FROM ALL OF MY FAVORITE TV SHOWS.
ISN'T THAT AMAZING?
SCOTT and BORGMAN
AND YET, HE'S STILL SURPRISED WHEN I REMIND HIM THAT BROWN SHOES DON'T GO WITH GRAY SLACKS.
THAT'S WHAT HAPPENS WHEN YOU TRY TO STORE A GIGABYTE OF LIFE ON A 125K HARD DRIVE.
COME AND LISTEN TO A STORY 'BOUT A MAN NAMED JED...

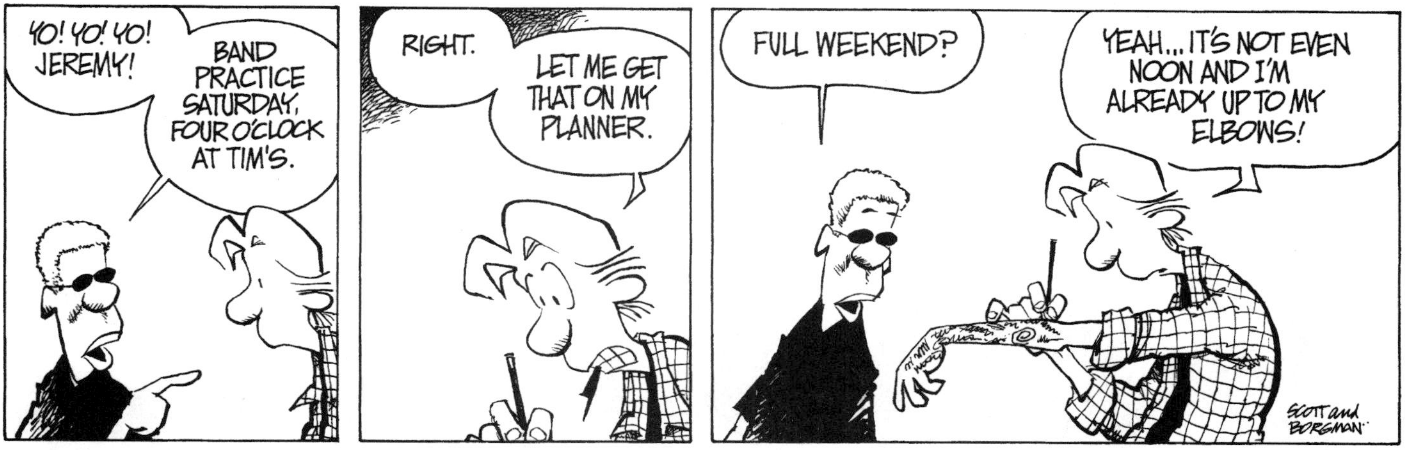
YO! YO! YO! JEREMY!
BAND PRACTICE SATURDAY, FOUR O'CLOCK AT TIM'S.
RIGHT.
LET ME GET THAT ON MY PLANNER.
FULL WEEKEND?
YEAH... IT'S NOT EVEN NOON AND I'M ALREADY UP TO MY ELBOWS!
SCOTT and BORGMAN

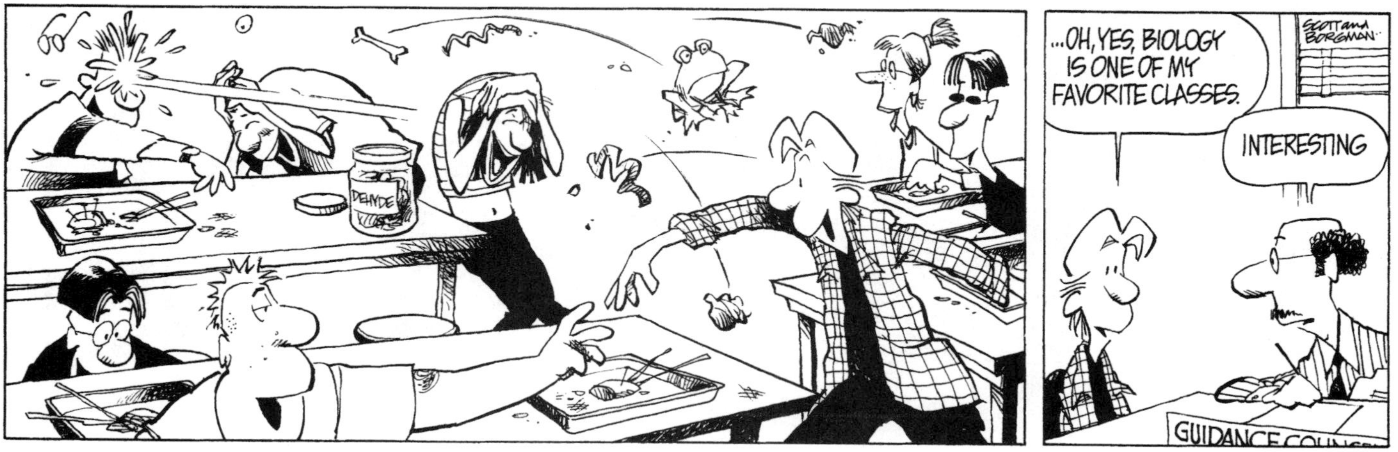
SCOTT and BORGMAN
...OH, YES, BIOLOGY IS ONE OF MY FAVORITE CLASSES.
INTERESTING
GUIDANCE

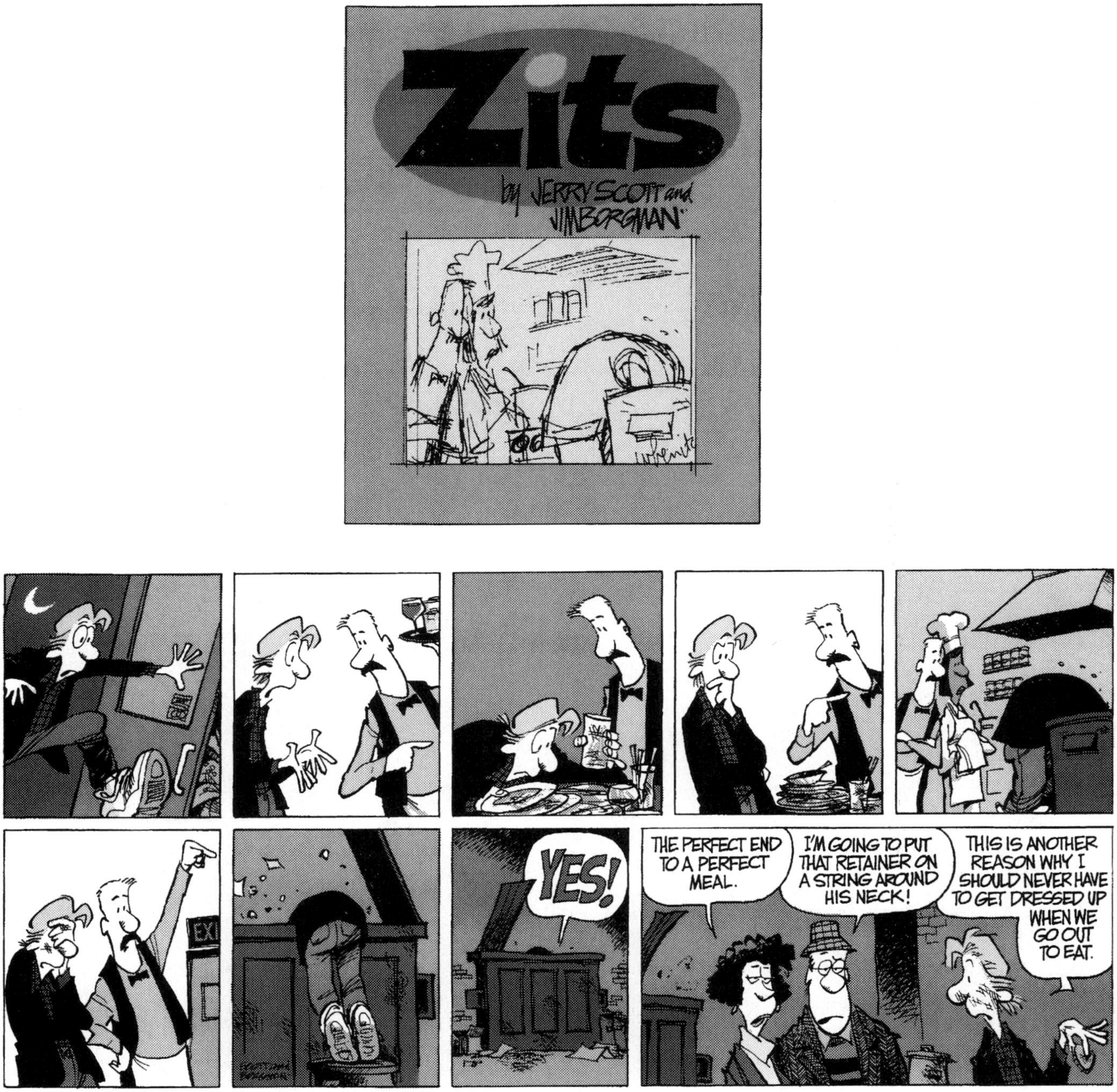
Zits
by JERRY SCOTT and JIM BORGMAN
YES!
THE PERFECT END TO A PERFECT MEAL.
I'M GOING TO PUT THAT RETAINER ON A STRING AROUND HIS NECK!
THIS IS ANOTHER REASON WHY I SHOULD NEVER HAVE TO GET DRESSED UP WHEN WE GO OUT TO EAT.

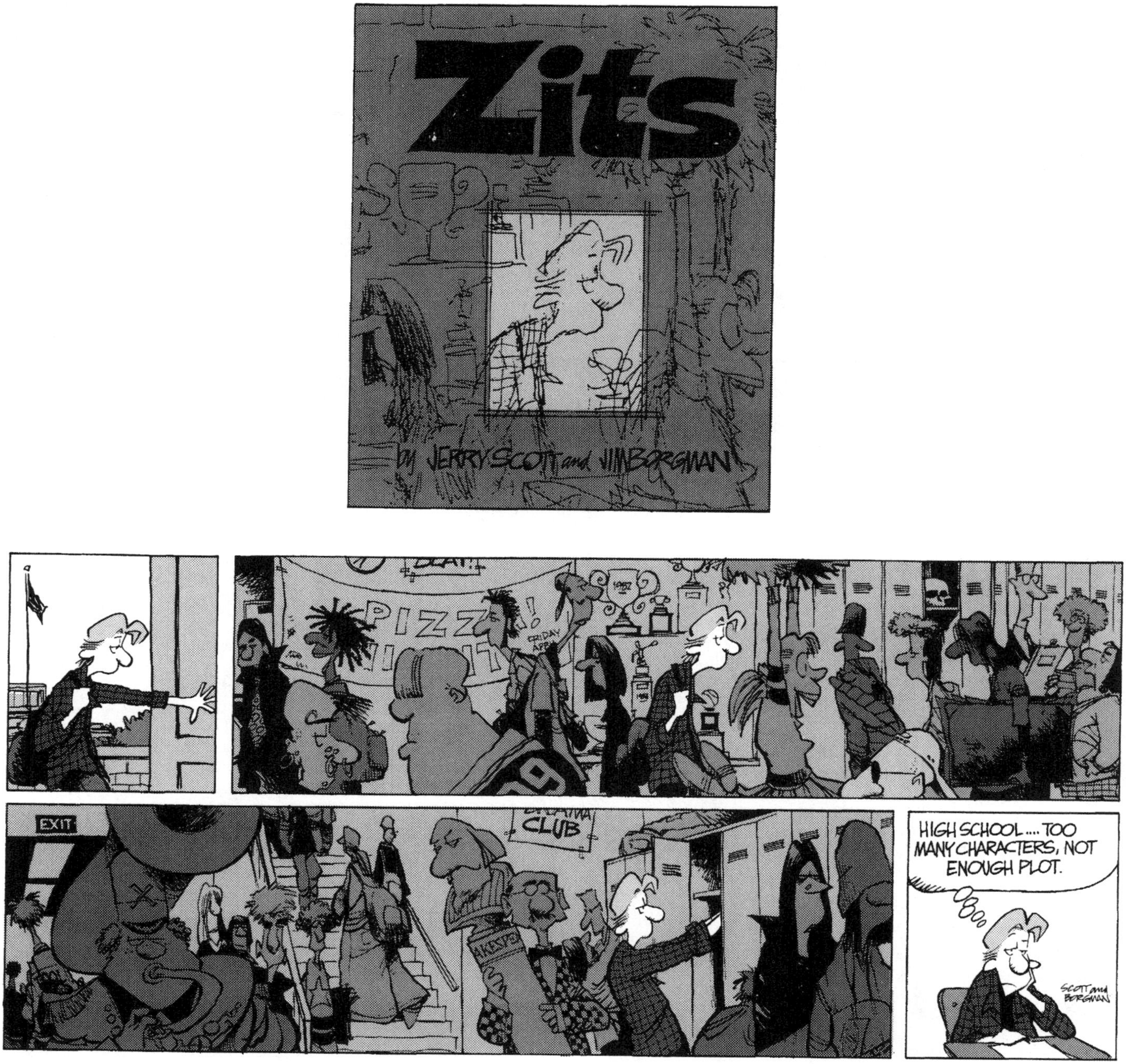
Zits
by JERRY SCOTT and JIM BORGMAN
PIZZ
EXIT
CLUB
HIGH SCHOOL.... TOO MANY CHARACTERS, NOT ENOUGH PLOT.
SCOTT and BORGMAN

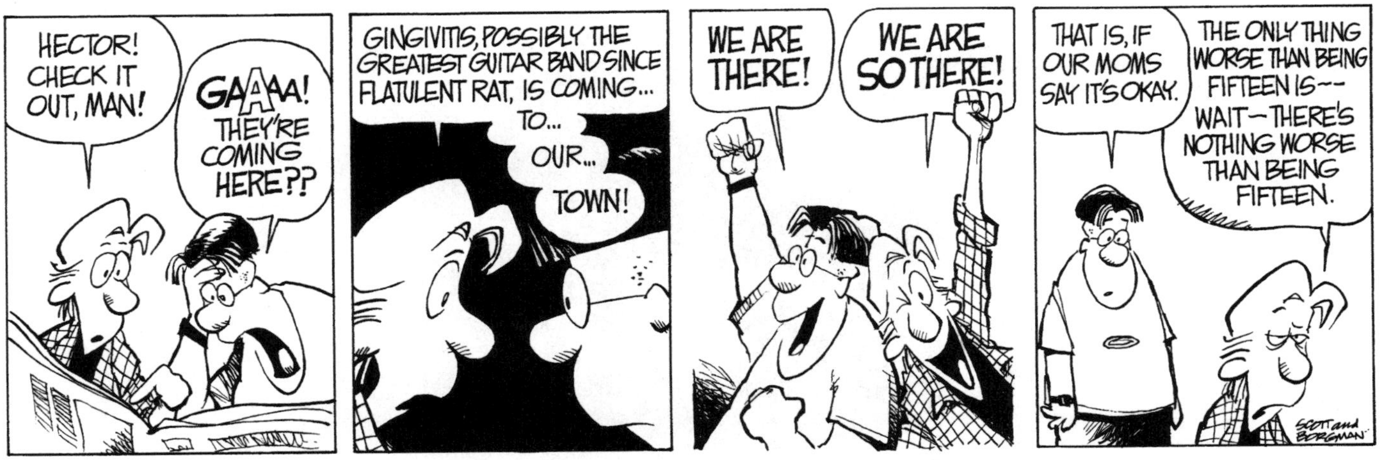
HECTOR! CHECK IT OUT, MAN!
GAAAAA! THEY'RE COMING HERE??
GINGIVITIS, POSSIBLY THE GREATEST GUITAR BAND SINCE FLATULENT RAT, IS COMING...
TO...
OUR...
TOWN!
WE ARE THERE!
WE ARE SO THERE!
THAT IS, IF OUR MOMS SAY IT'S OKAY.
THE ONLY THING WORSE THAN BEING FIFTEEN IS-- WAIT-THERE'S NOTHING WORSE THAN BEING FIFTEEN.
SCOTT and BORGMAN

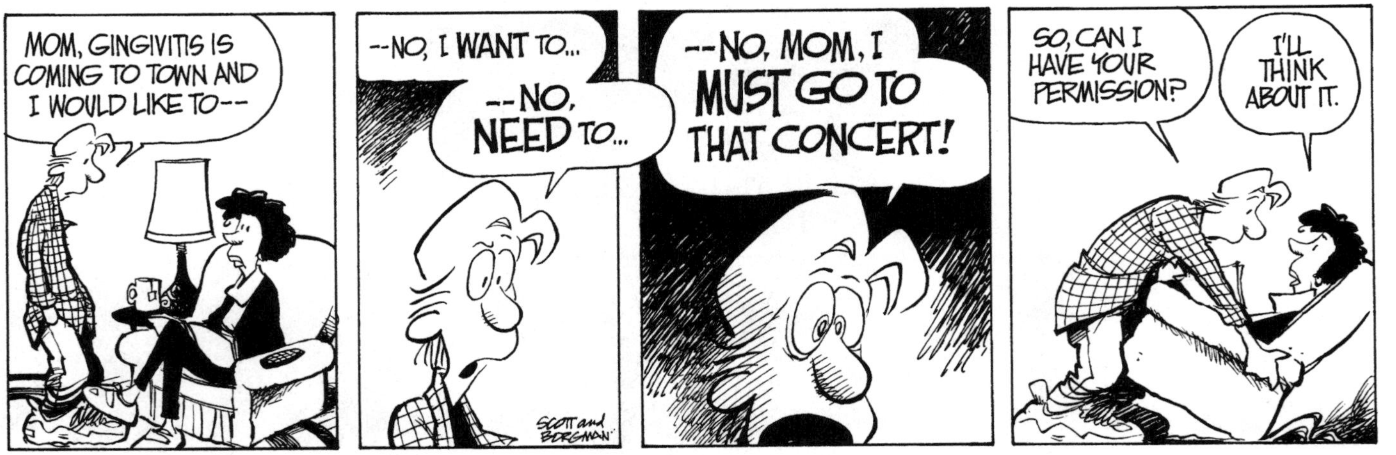
MOM, GINGIVITIS IS COMING TO TOWN AND I WOULD LIKE TO--
--NO, I WANT TO...
--NO, NEED TO...
SCOTT and BORGMAN
--NO, MOM, I MUST GO TO THAT CONCERT!
SO, CAN I HAVE YOUR PERMISSION?
I'LL THINK ABOUT IT.

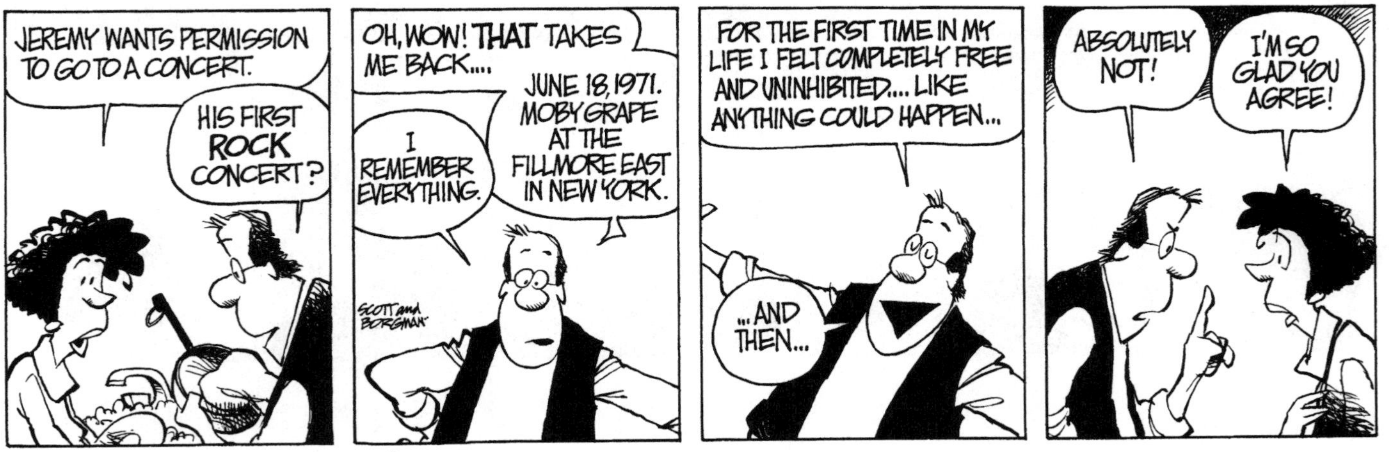
JEREMY WANTS PERMISSION TO GO TO A CONCERT.
HIS FIRST ROCK CONCERT?
OH, WOW! THAT TAKES ME BACK....
JUNE 18, 1971. MOBY GRAPE AT THE FILLMORE EAST IN NEW YORK.
I REMEMBER EVERYTHING.
SCOTT and BORGMAN
FOR THE FIRST TIME IN MY LIFE I FELT COMPLETELY FREE AND UNINHIBITED.... LIKE ANYTHING COULD HAPPEN...
...AND THEN...
ABSOLUTELY NOT!
I'M SO GLAD YOU AGREE!

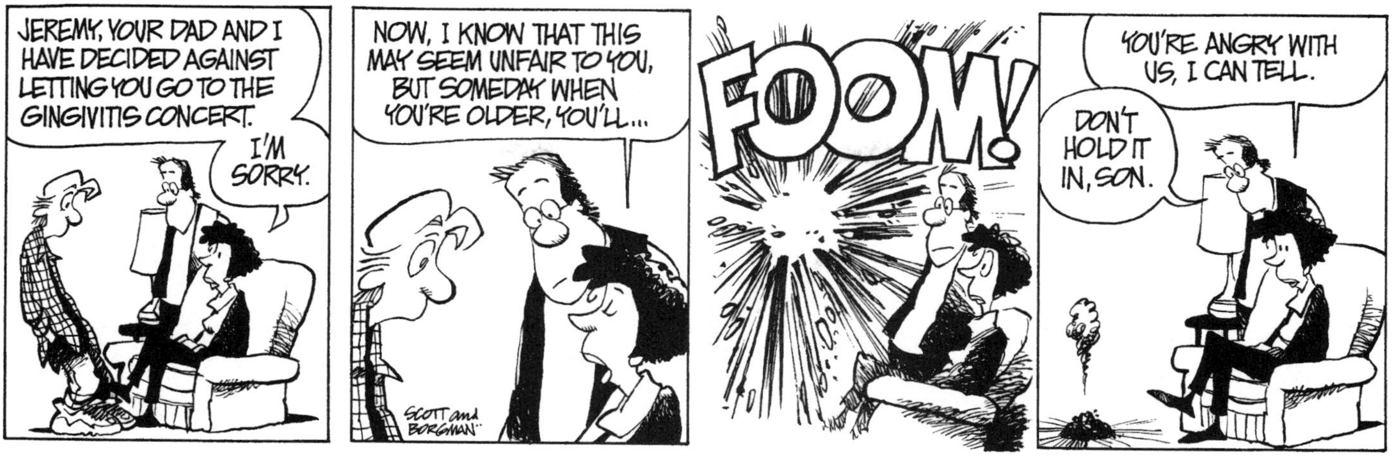
JEREMY, YOUR DAD AND I HAVE DECIDED AGAINST LETTING YOU GO TO THE GINGIVITIS CONCERT.
I'M SORRY.
NOW, I KNOW THAT THIS MAY SEEM UNFAIR TO YOU, BUT SOMEDAY WHEN YOU'RE OLDER, YOU'LL...
SCOTT and BORGMAN
FOOM!
YOU'RE ANGRY WITH US, I CAN TELL.
DON'T HOLD IT IN, SON.

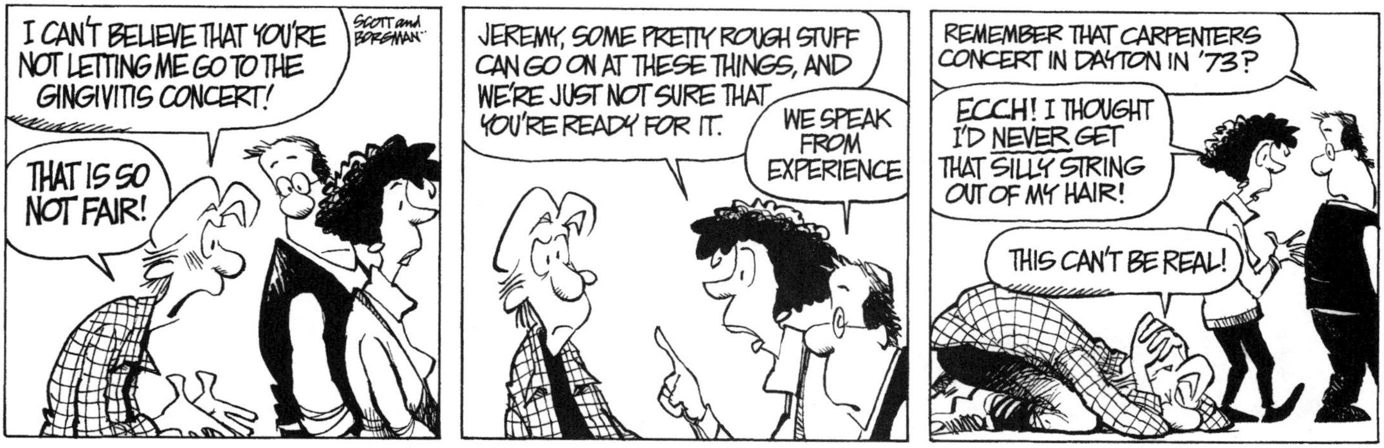
I CAN'T BELIEVE THAT YOU'RE NOT LETTING ME GO TO THE GINGIVITIS CONCERT!
SCOTT and BORGMAN
THAT IS SO NOT FAIR!
JEREMY, SOME PRETTY ROUGH STUFF CAN GO ON AT THESE THINGS, AND WE'RE JUST NOT SURE THAT YOU'RE READY FOR IT.
WE SPEAK FROM EXPERIENCE
REMEMBER THAT CARPENTERS CONCERT IN DAYTON IN '73?
ECCH! I THOUGHT I'D NEVER GET THAT SILLY STRING OUT OF MY HAIR!
THIS CAN'T BE REAL!

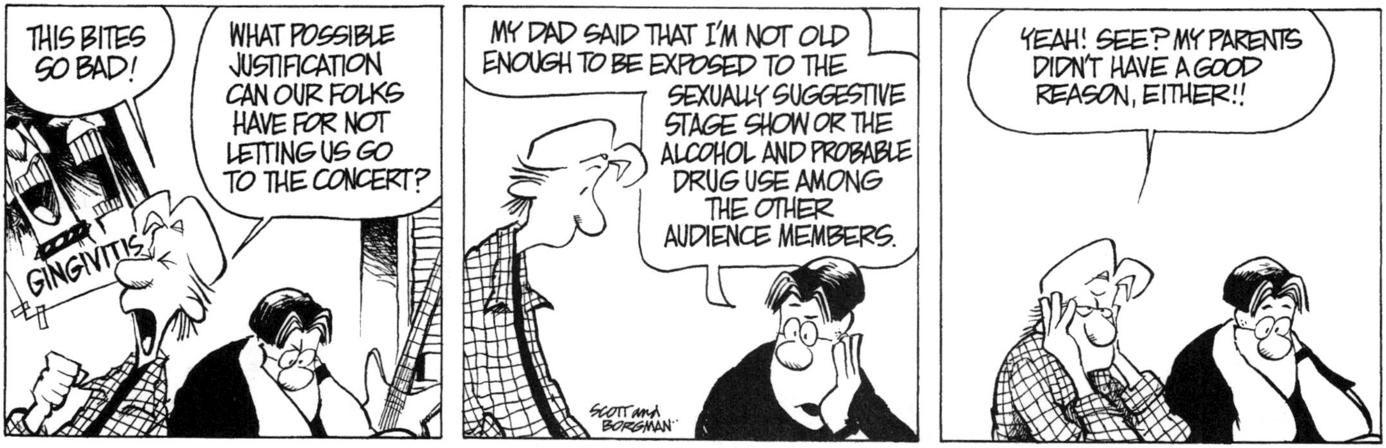
THIS BITES SO BAD!
WHAT POSSIBLE JUSTIFICATION CAN OUR FOLKS HAVE FOR NOT LETTING US GO TO THE CONCERT?
GINGIVITIS
MY DAD SAID THAT I'M NOT OLD ENOUGH TO BE EXPOSED TO THE SEXUALLY SUGGESTIVE STAGE SHOW OR THE ALCOHOL AND PROBABLE DRUG USE AMONG THE OTHER AUDIENCE MEMBERS.
SCOTT and BORGMAN
YEAH! SEE? MY PARENTS DIDN'T HAVE A GOOD REASON, EITHER!!

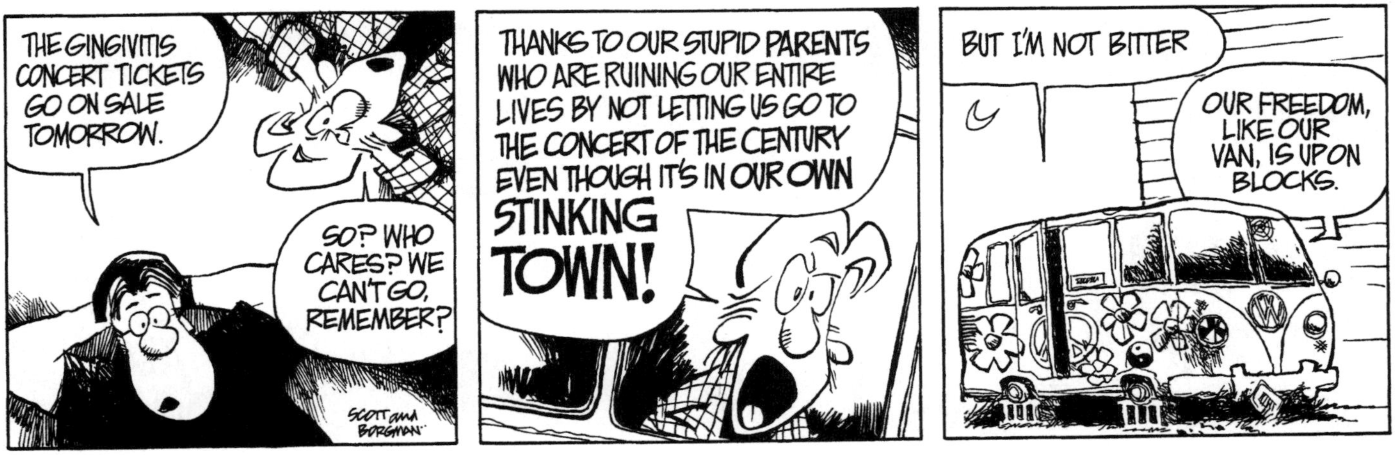
THE GINGIVITIS CONCERT TICKETS GO ON SALE TOMORROW.
SO? WHO CARES? WE CAN'T GO, REMEMBER?
SCOTT and BORGMAN
THANKS TO OUR STUPID PARENTS WHO ARE RUINING OUR ENTIRE LIVES BY NOT LETTING US GO TO THE CONCERT OF THE CENTURY EVEN THOUGH IT'S IN OUR OWN STINKING TOWN!
BUT I'M NOT BITTER
OUR FREEDOM, LIKE OUR VAN, IS UP ON BLOCKS.

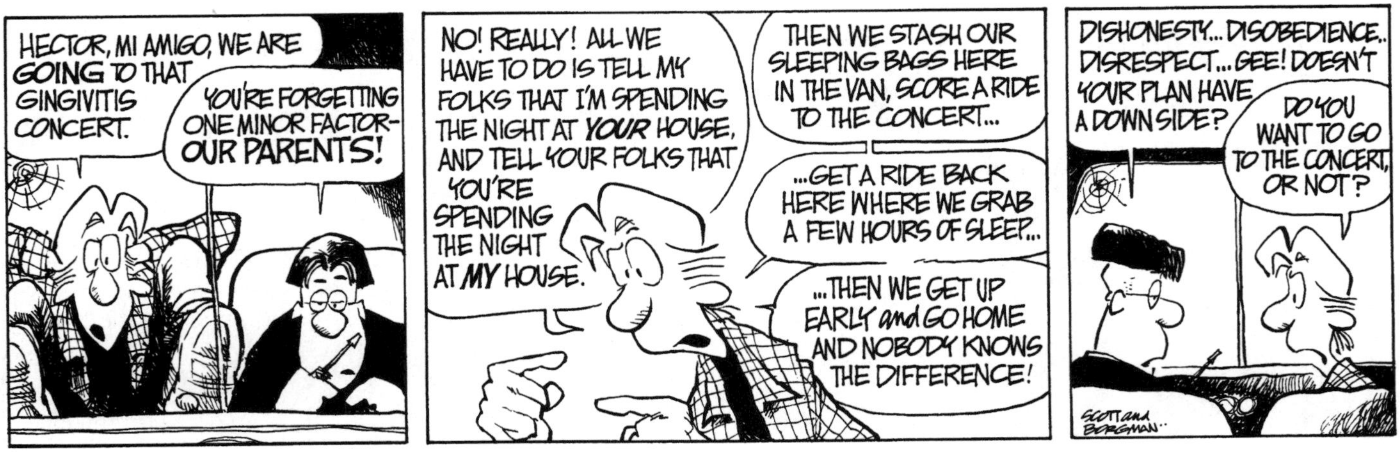
HECTOR, MI AMIGO, WE ARE GOING TO THAT GINGIVITIS CONCERT.
YOU'RE FORGETTING ONE MINOR FACTOR- OUR PARENTS!
NO! REALLY! ALL WE HAVE TO DO IS TELL MY FOLKS THAT I'M SPENDING THE NIGHT AT YOUR HOUSE, AND TELL YOUR FOLKS THAT YOU'RE SPENDING THE NIGHT AT MY HOUSE.
THEN WE STASH OUR SLEEPING BAGS HERE IN THE VAN, SCORE A RIDE TO THE CONCERT...
...GET A RIDE BACK HERE WHERE WE GRAB A FEW HOURS OF SLEEP...
...THEN WE GET UP EARLY and GO HOME AND NOBODY KNOWS THE DIFFERENCE!
DISHONESTY... DISOBEDIENCE.. DISRESPECT... GEE! DOESN'T YOUR PLAN HAVE A DOWNSIDE?
DO YOU WANT TO GO TO THE CONCERT, OR NOT?
SCOTT and BORGMAN

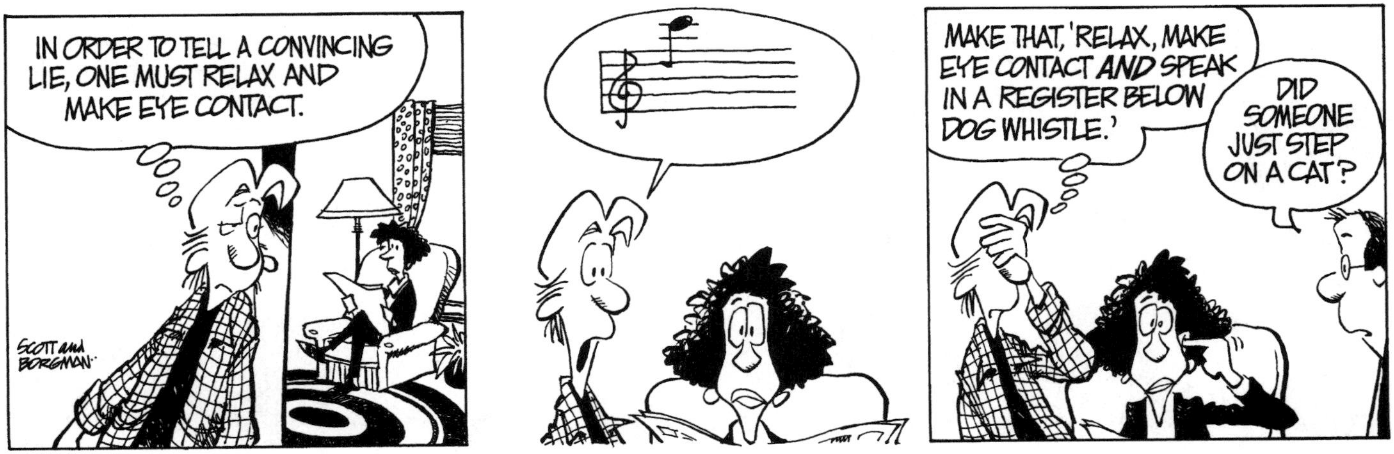
IN ORDER TO TELL A CONVINCING LIE, ONE MUST RELAX AND MAKE EYE CONTACT.
SCOTT and BORGMAN
MAKE THAT, 'RELAX, MAKE EYE CONTACT AND SPEAK IN A REGISTER BELOW DOG WHISTLE.'
DID SOMEONE JUST STEP ON A CAT?

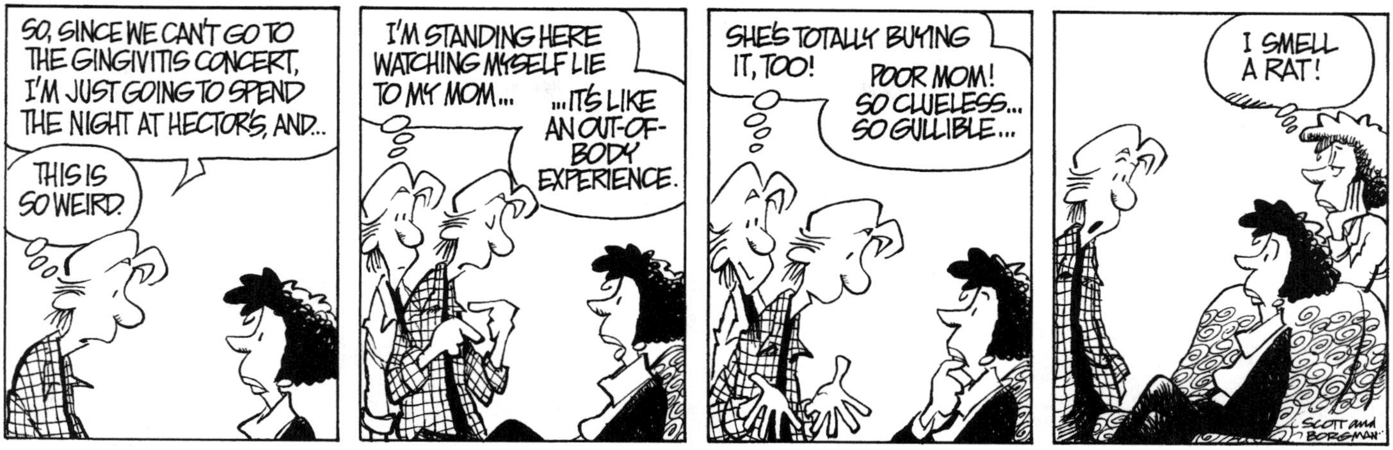
SO, SINCE WE CAN'T GO TO THE GINGIVITIS CONCERT, I'M JUST GOING TO SPEND THE NIGHT AT HECTOR'S, AND...
THIS IS SO WEIRD.
I'M STANDING HERE WATCHING MYSELF LIE TO MY MOM...
...IT'S LIKE AN OUT-OF-BODY EXPERIENCE.
SHE'S TOTALLY BUYING IT, TOO!
POOR MOM! SO CLUELESS... SO GULLIBLE...
I SMELL A RAT!
SCOTT and BORGMAN

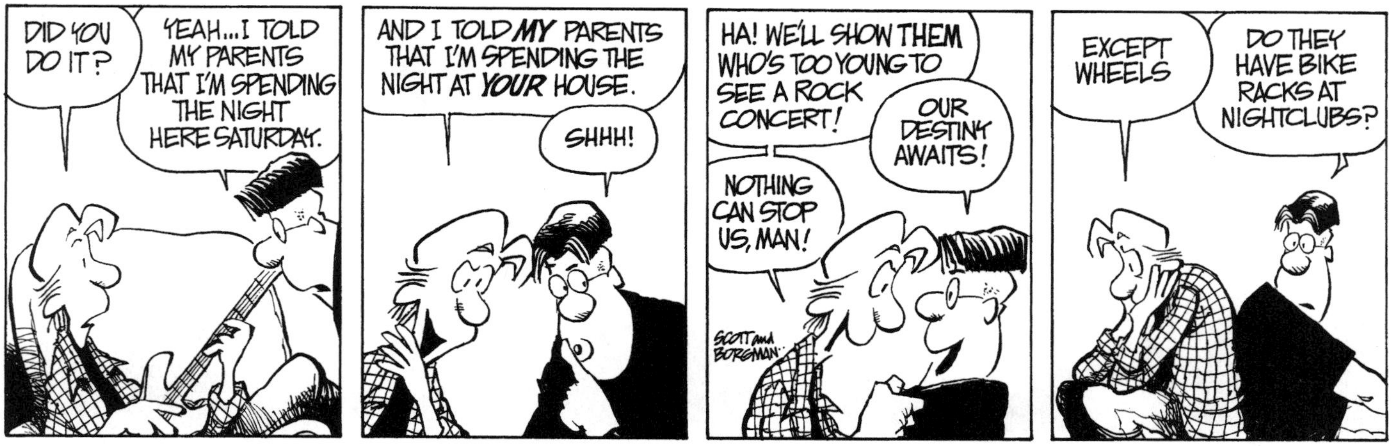
DID YOU DO IT?
YEAH... I TOLD MY PARENTS THAT I'M SPENDING THE NIGHT HERE SATURDAY.
AND I TOLD MY PARENTS THAT I'M SPENDING THE NIGHT AT YOUR HOUSE.
SHHH!
HA! WE'LL SHOW THEM WHO'S TOO YOUNG TO SEE A ROCK CONCERT!
OUR DESTINY AWAITS!
NOTHING CAN STOP US, MAN!
SCOTT and BORGMAN
EXCEPT WHEELS
DO THEY HAVE BIKE RACKS AT NIGHTCLUBS?

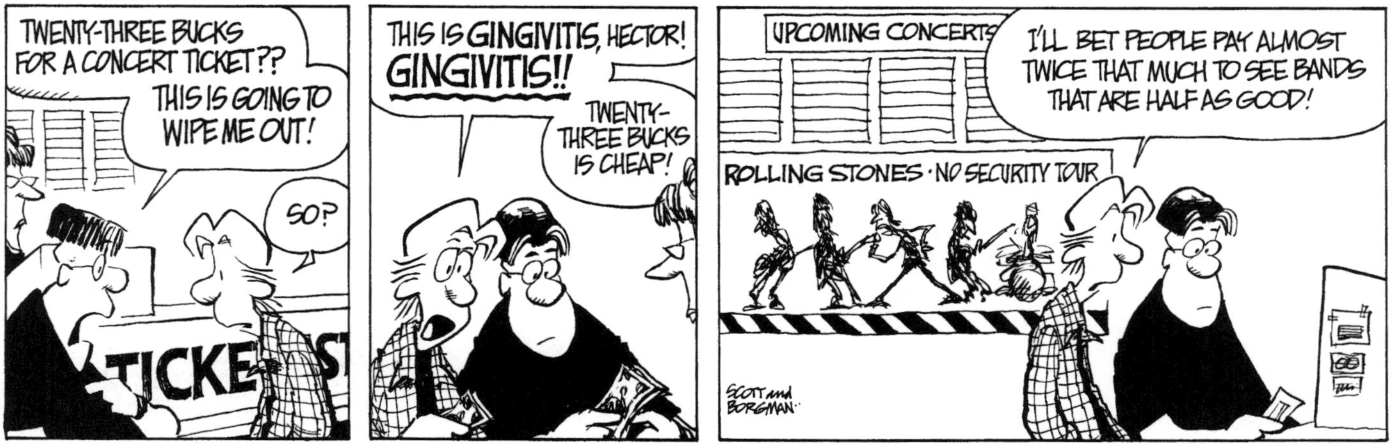
TWENTY-THREE BUCKS FOR A CONCERT TICKET??
THIS IS GOING TO WIPE ME OUT!
SO?
TICKE
THIS IS GINGIVITIS, HECTOR! GINGIVITIS!!
TWENTY-THREE BUCKS IS CHEAP!
UPCOMING CONCERTS
I'LL BET PEOPLE PAY ALMOST TWICE THAT MUCH TO SEE BANDS THAT ARE HALF AS GOOD!
ROLLING STONES · NO SECURITY TOUR
SCOTT and BORGMAN

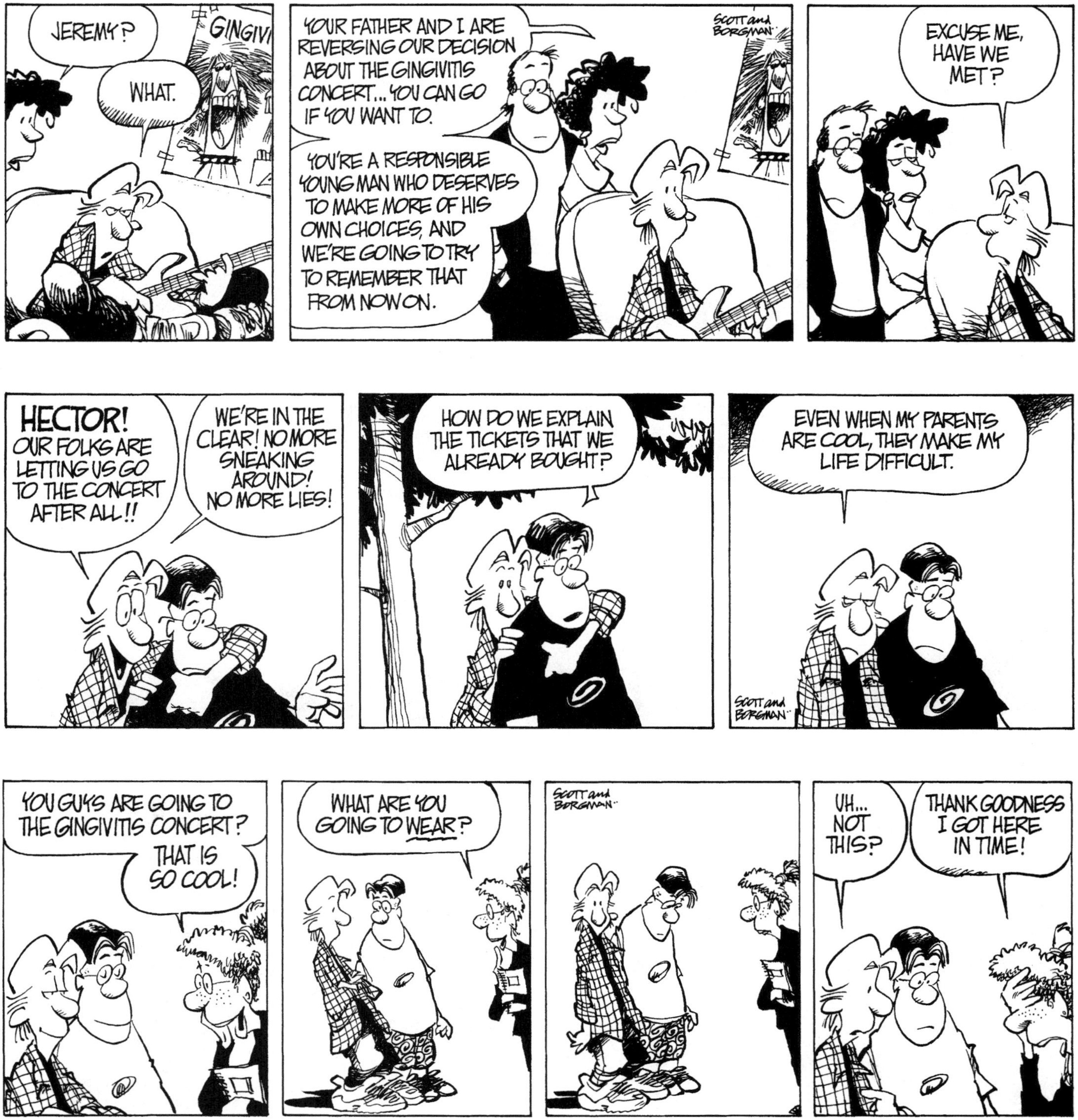
JEREMY?
WHAT.
GINGIVI
SCOTT and BORGMAN
YOUR FATHER AND I ARE REVERSING OUR DECISION ABOUT THE GINGIVITIS CONCERT... YOU CAN GO IF YOU WANT TO.
YOU'RE A RESPONSIBLE YOUNG MAN WHO DESERVES TO MAKE MORE OF HIS OWN CHOICES, AND WE'RE GOING TO TRY TO REMEMBER THAT FROM NOW ON.
EXCUSE ME, HAVE WE MET?
HECTOR! OUR FOLKS ARE LETTING US GO TO THE CONCERT AFTER ALL!!
WE'RE IN THE CLEAR! NO MORE SNEAKING AROUND! NO MORE LIES!
HOW DO WE EXPLAIN THE TICKETS THAT WE ALREADY BOUGHT?
EVEN WHEN MY PARENTS ARE COOL, THEY MAKE MY LIFE DIFFICULT.
SCOTT and BORGMAN
YOU GUYS ARE GOING TO THE GINGIVITIS CONCERT?
THAT IS SO COOL!
WHAT ARE YOU GOING TO WEAR?
SCOTT and BORGMAN
UH... NOT THIS?
THANK GOODNESS I GOT HERE IN TIME!

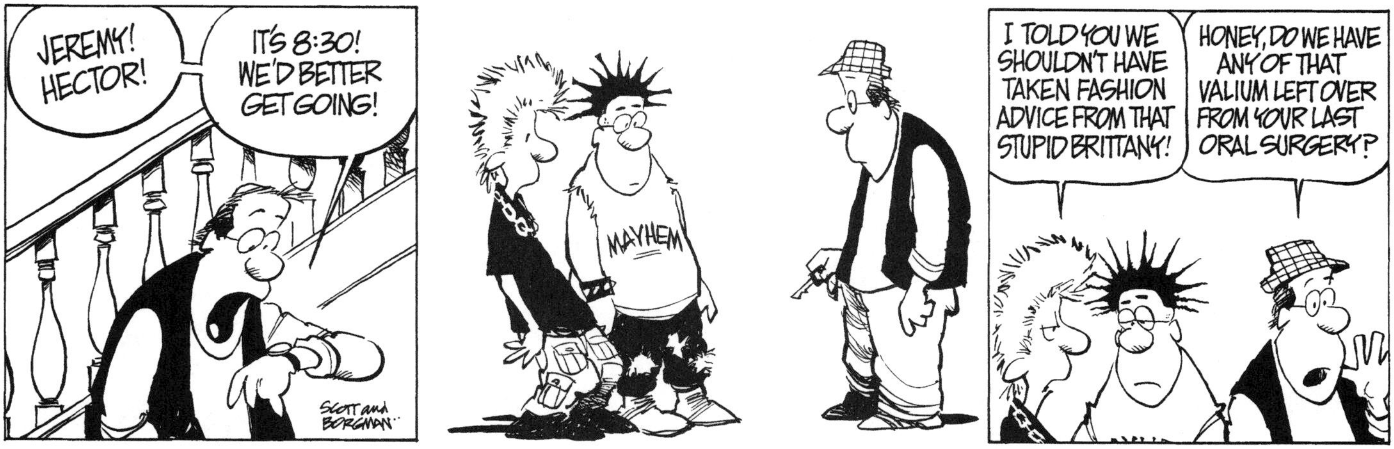
JEREMY! HECTOR!
IT'S 8:30! WE'D BETTER GET GOING!
SCOTT and BORGMAN
MAYHEM
I TOLD YOU WE SHOULDN'T HAVE TAKEN FASHION ADVICE FROM THAT STUPID BRITTANY!
HONEY, DO WE HAVE ANY OF THAT VALIUM LEFT OVER FROM YOUR LAST ORAL SURGERY?

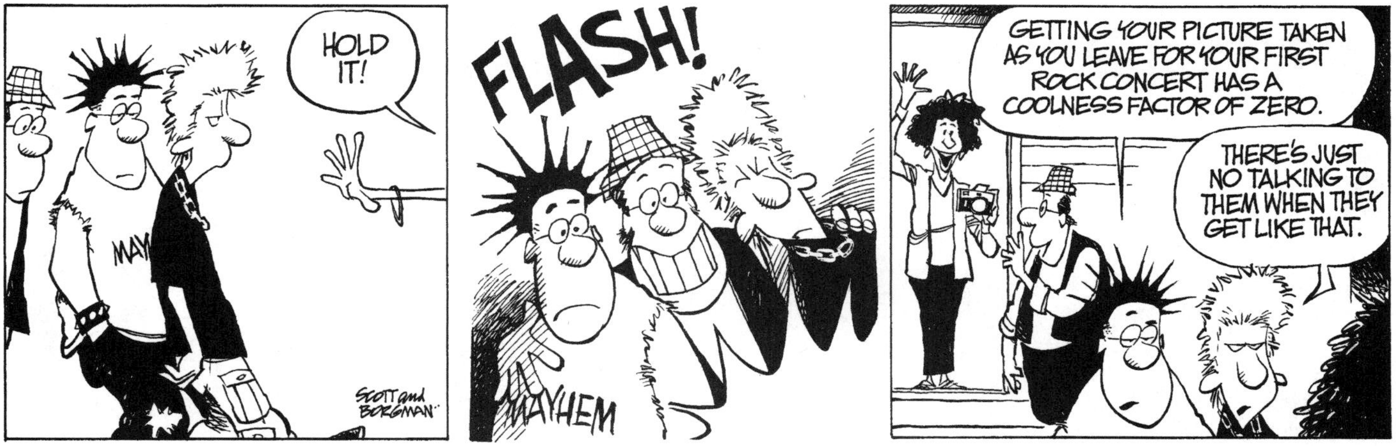
HOLD IT!
SCOTT and BORGMAN
FLASH!
MAYHEM
GETTING YOUR PICTURE TAKEN AS YOU LEAVE FOR YOUR FIRST ROCK CONCERT HAS A COOLNESS FACTOR OF ZERO.
THERE'S JUST NO TALKING TO THEM WHEN THEY GET LIKE THAT.

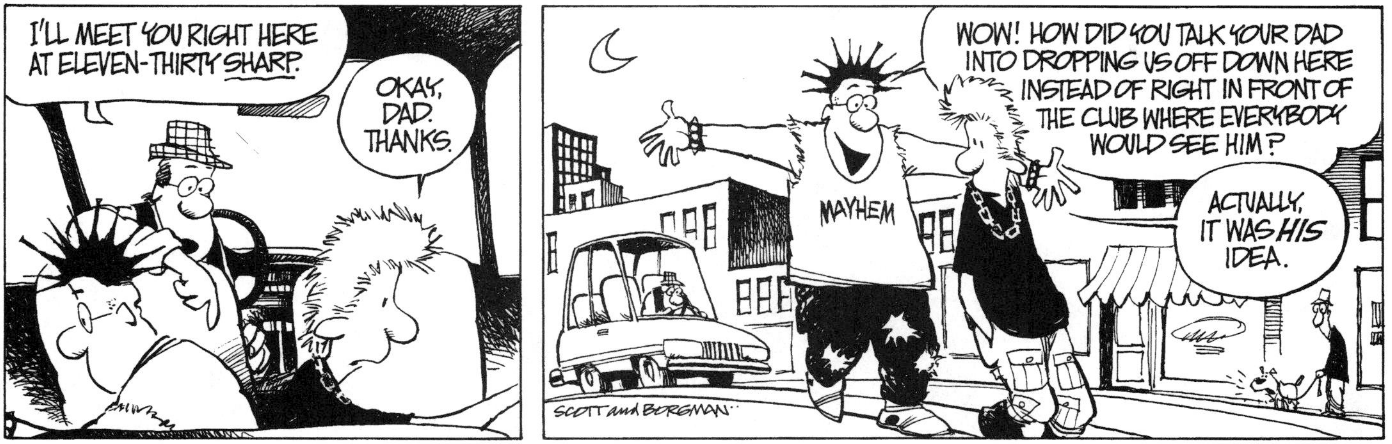
I'LL MEET YOU RIGHT HERE AT ELEVEN-THIRTY SHARP.
OKAY, DAD. THANKS.
WOW! HOW DID YOU TALK YOUR DAD INTO DROPPING US OFF DOWN HERE INSTEAD OF RIGHT IN FRONT OF THE CLUB WHERE EVERYBODY WOULD SEE HIM?
MAYHEM
ACTUALLY, IT WAS ***HIS*** IDEA.
SCOTT and BORGMAN

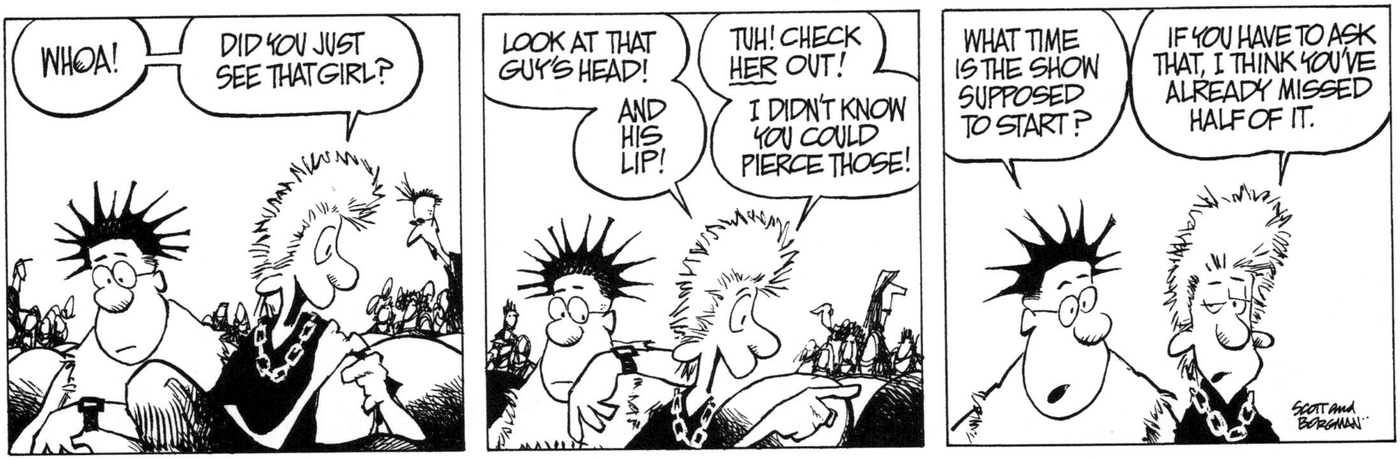
WHOA!
DID YOU JUST SEE THAT GIRL?
LOOK AT THAT GUY'S HEAD!
AND HIS LIP!
TUH! CHECK HER OUT!
I DIDN'T KNOW YOU COULD PIERCE THOSE!
WHAT TIME IS THE SHOW SUPPOSED TO START?
IF YOU HAVE TO ASK THAT, I THINK YOU'VE ALREADY MISSED HALF OF IT.
SCOTT AND BORGMAN

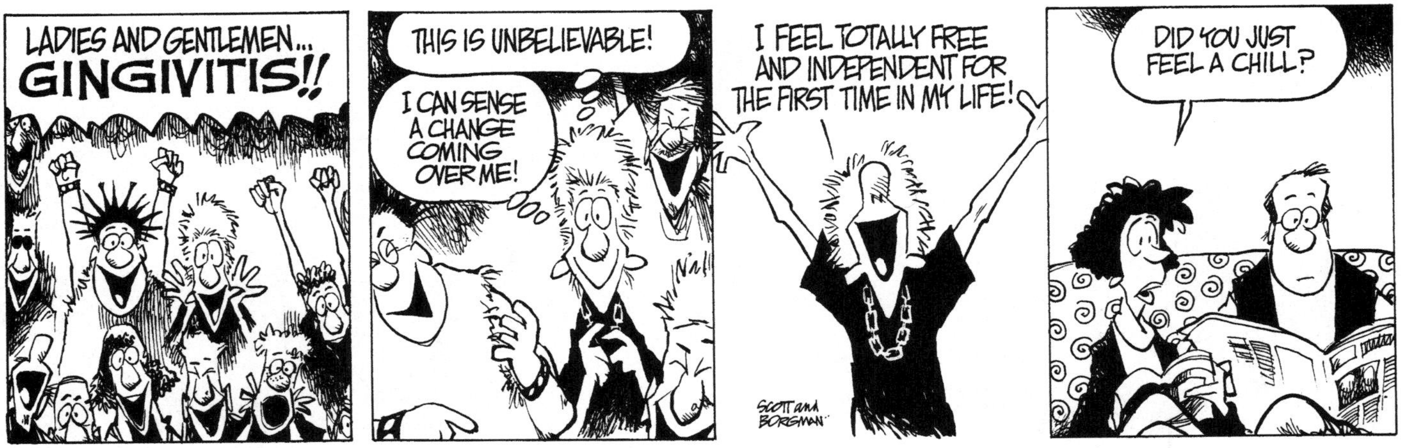
LADIES AND GENTLEMEN...
GINGIVITIS!!
THIS IS UNBELIEVABLE!
I CAN SENSE A CHANGE COMING OVER ME!
I FEEL TOTALLY FREE AND INDEPENDENT FOR THE FIRST TIME IN MY LIFE!
SCOTT AND BORGMAN
DID YOU JUST FEEL A CHILL?

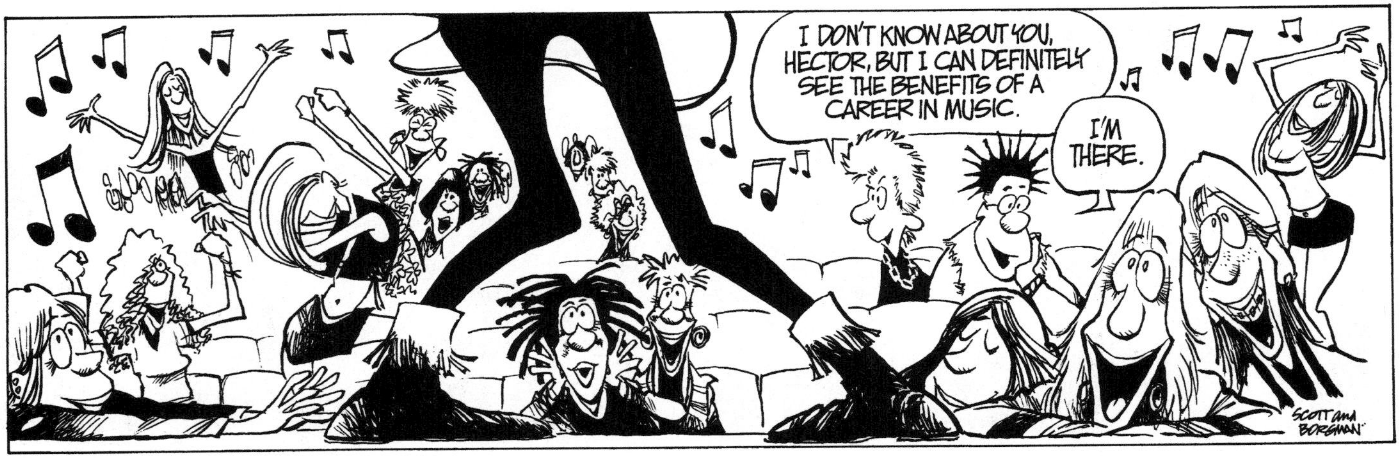
I DON'T KNOW ABOUT YOU, HECTOR, BUT I CAN DEFINITELY SEE THE BENEFITS OF A CAREER IN MUSIC.
I'M THERE.
SCOTT AND BORGMAN

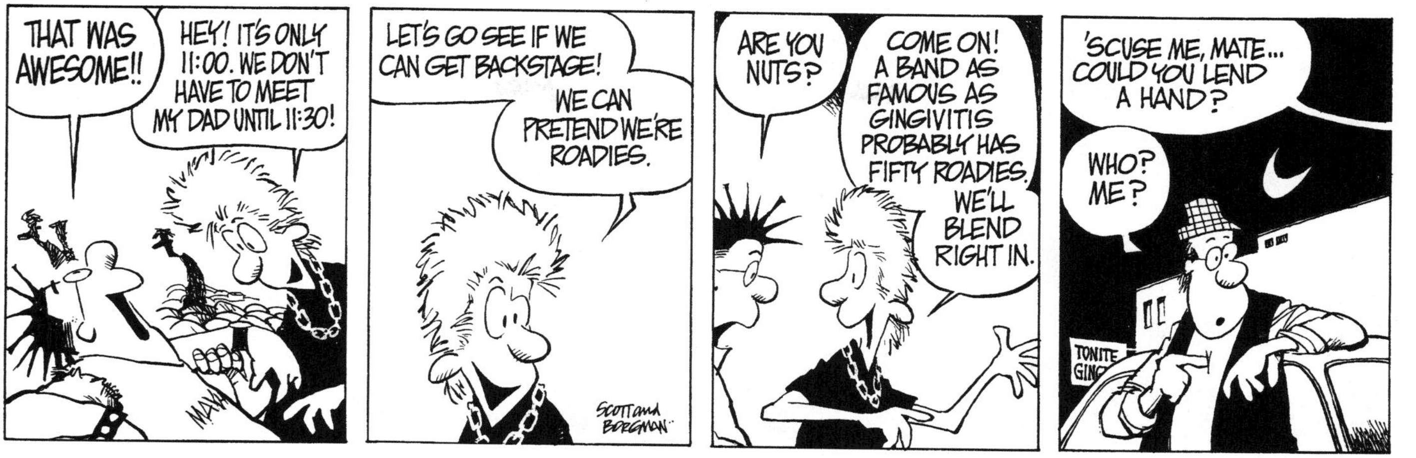
THAT WAS AWESOME!!
HEY! IT'S ONLY 11:00. WE DON'T HAVE TO MEET MY DAD UNTIL 11:30!
LET'S GO SEE IF WE CAN GET BACKSTAGE!
WE CAN PRETEND WE'RE ROADIES.
SCOTT and BORGMAN
ARE YOU NUTS?
COME ON! A BAND AS FAMOUS AS GINGIVITIS PROBABLY HAS FIFTY ROADIES.
WE'LL BLEND RIGHT IN.
'SCUSE ME, MATE... COULD YOU LEND A HAND?
WHO? ME?
TONITE

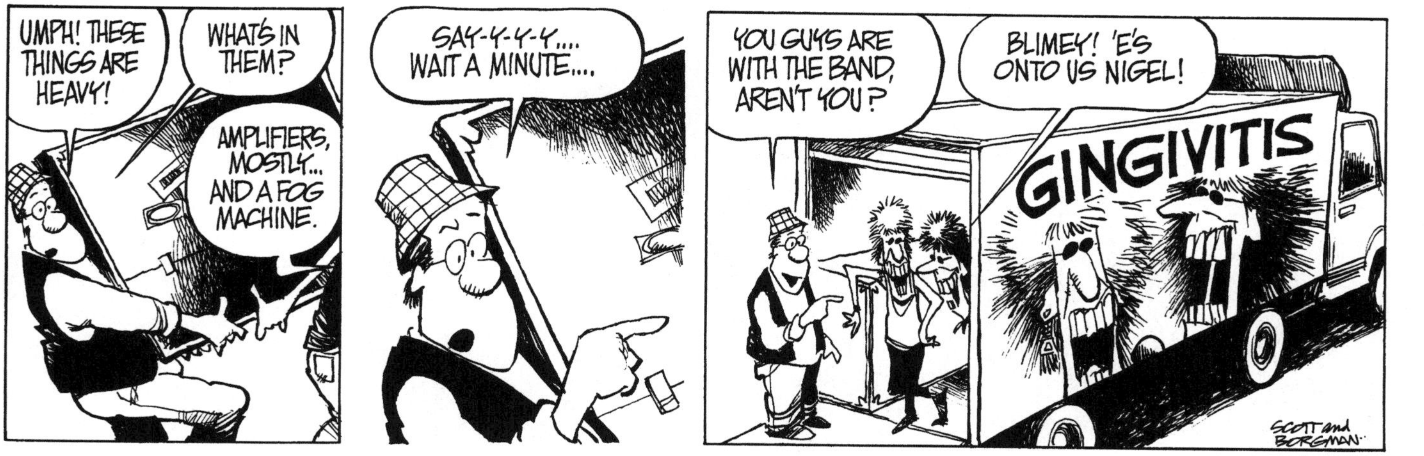
UMPH! THESE THINGS ARE HEAVY!
WHAT'S IN THEM?
AMPLIFIERS, MOSTLY... AND A FOG MACHINE.
SAY-Y-Y-Y.... WAIT A MINUTE....
YOU GUYS ARE WITH THE BAND, AREN'T YOU?
BLIMEY! 'E'S ONTO US NIGEL!
GINGIVITIS
SCOTT and BORGMAN

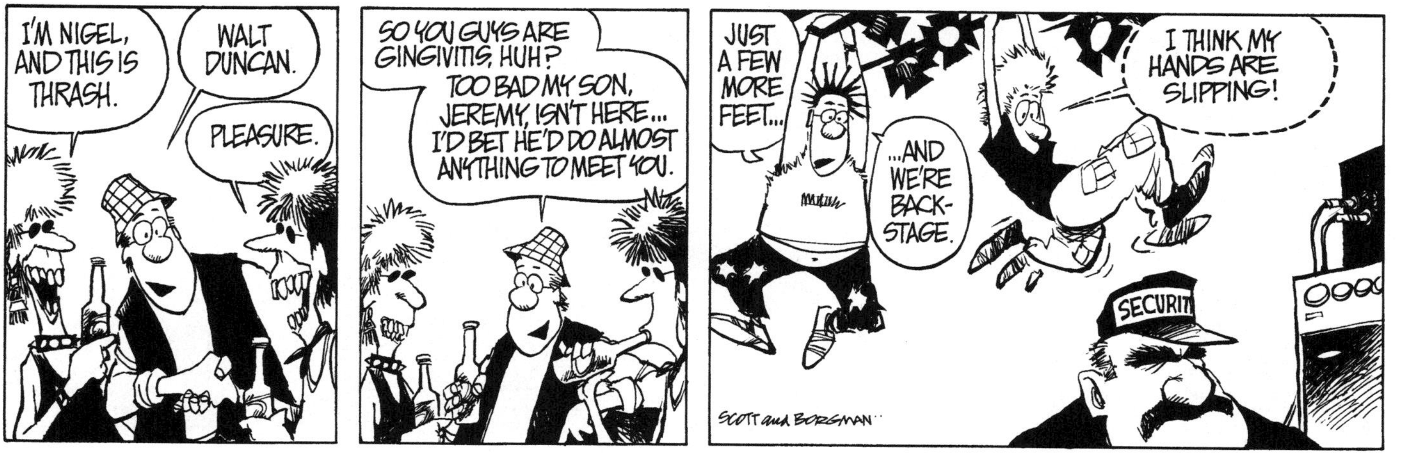
I'M NIGEL, AND THIS IS THRASH.
WALT DUNCAN.
PLEASURE.
SO YOU GUYS ARE GINGIVITIS, HUH?
TOO BAD MY SON, JEREMY, ISN'T HERE... I'D BET HE'D DO ALMOST ANYTHING TO MEET YOU.
JUST A FEW MORE FEET...
...AND WE'RE BACK-STAGE.
I THINK MY HANDS ARE SLIPPING!
SCOTT and BORGMAN

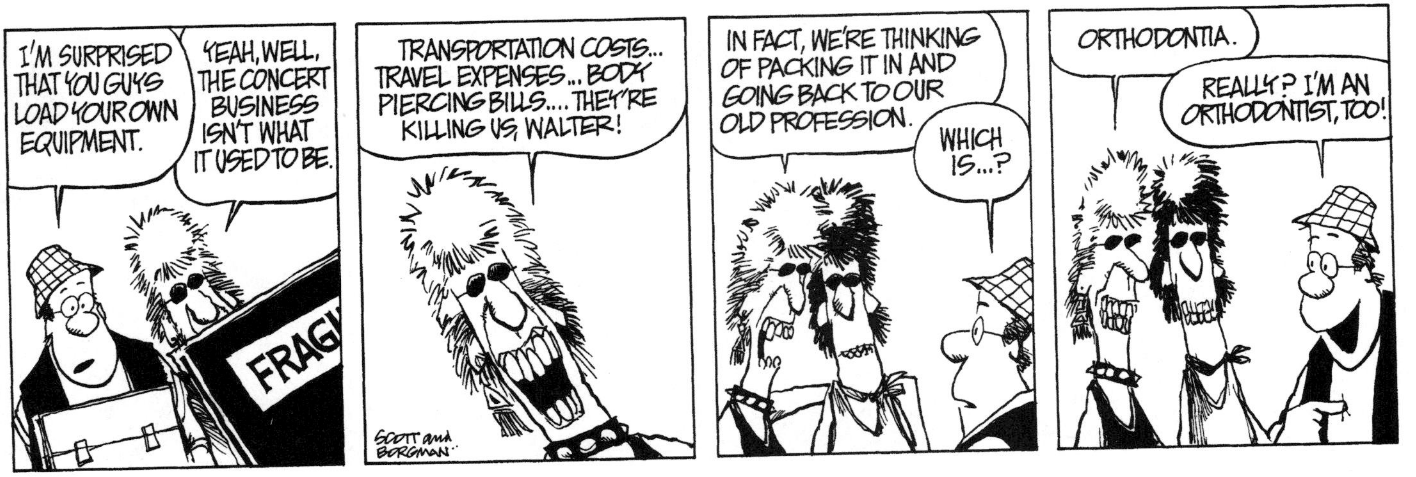
I'M SURPRISED THAT YOU GUYS LOAD YOUR OWN EQUIPMENT.
YEAH, WELL, THE CONCERT BUSINESS ISN'T WHAT IT USED TO BE.
FRAG
TRANSPORTATION COSTS... TRAVEL EXPENSES... BODY PIERCING BILLS.... THEY'RE KILLING US, WALTER!
SCOTT and BORGMAN
IN FACT, WE'RE THINKING OF PACKING IT IN AND GOING BACK TO OUR OLD PROFESSION.
WHICH IS...?
ORTHODONTIA.
REALLY? I'M AN ORTHODONTIST, TOO!

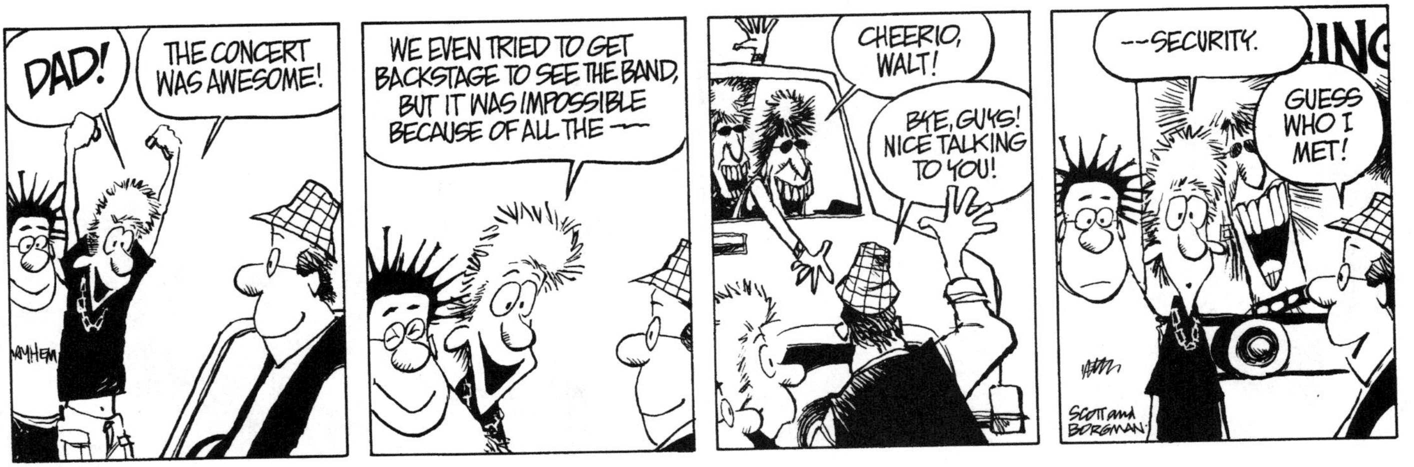
DAD!
THE CONCERT WAS AWESOME!
WE EVEN TRIED TO GET BACKSTAGE TO SEE THE BAND, BUT IT WAS IMPOSSIBLE BECAUSE OF ALL THE ---
CHEERIO, WALT!
BYE, GUYS! NICE TALKING TO YOU!
--SECURITY.
GUESS WHO I MET!
SCOTT and BORGMAN

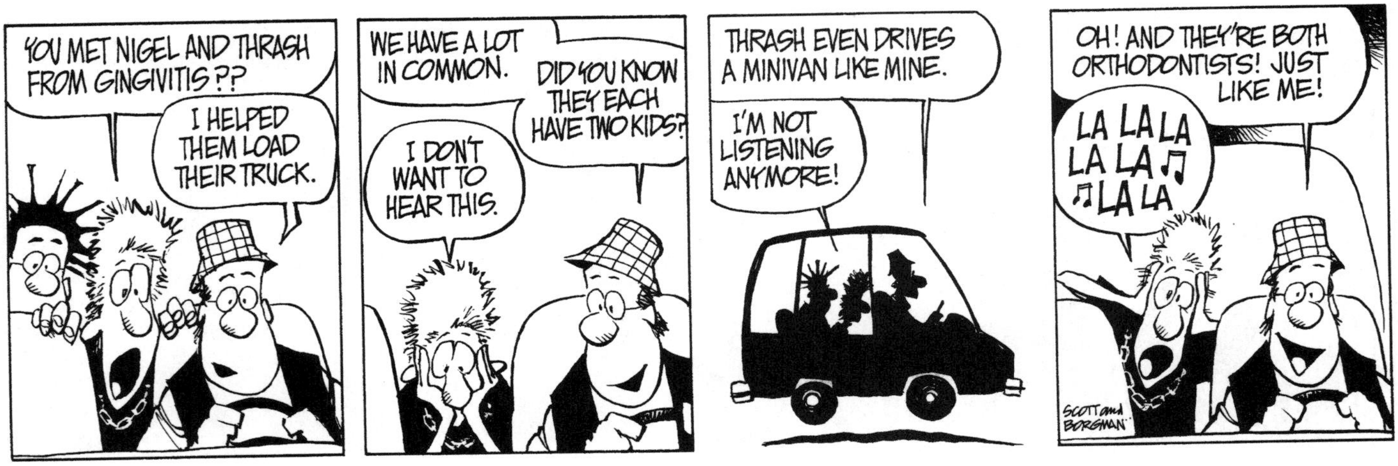
YOU MET NIGEL AND THRASH FROM GINGIVITIS??
I HELPED THEM LOAD THEIR TRUCK.
WE HAVE A LOT IN COMMON.
DID YOU KNOW THEY EACH HAVE TWO KIDS?
I DON'T WANT TO HEAR THIS.
THRASH EVEN DRIVES A MINIVAN LIKE MINE.
I'M NOT LISTENING ANYMORE!
OH! AND THEY'RE BOTH ORTHODONTISTS! JUST LIKE ME!
LA LA LA LA LA ♫ ♫ LA LA
SCOTT and BORGMAN

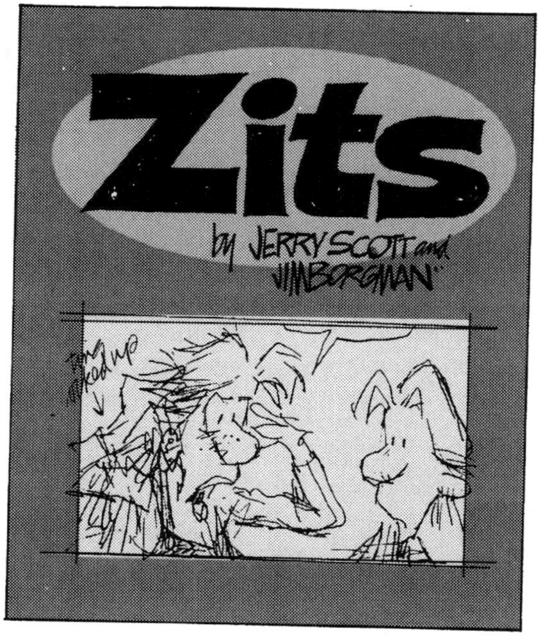
Zits
by JERRY SCOTT and JIM BORGMAN

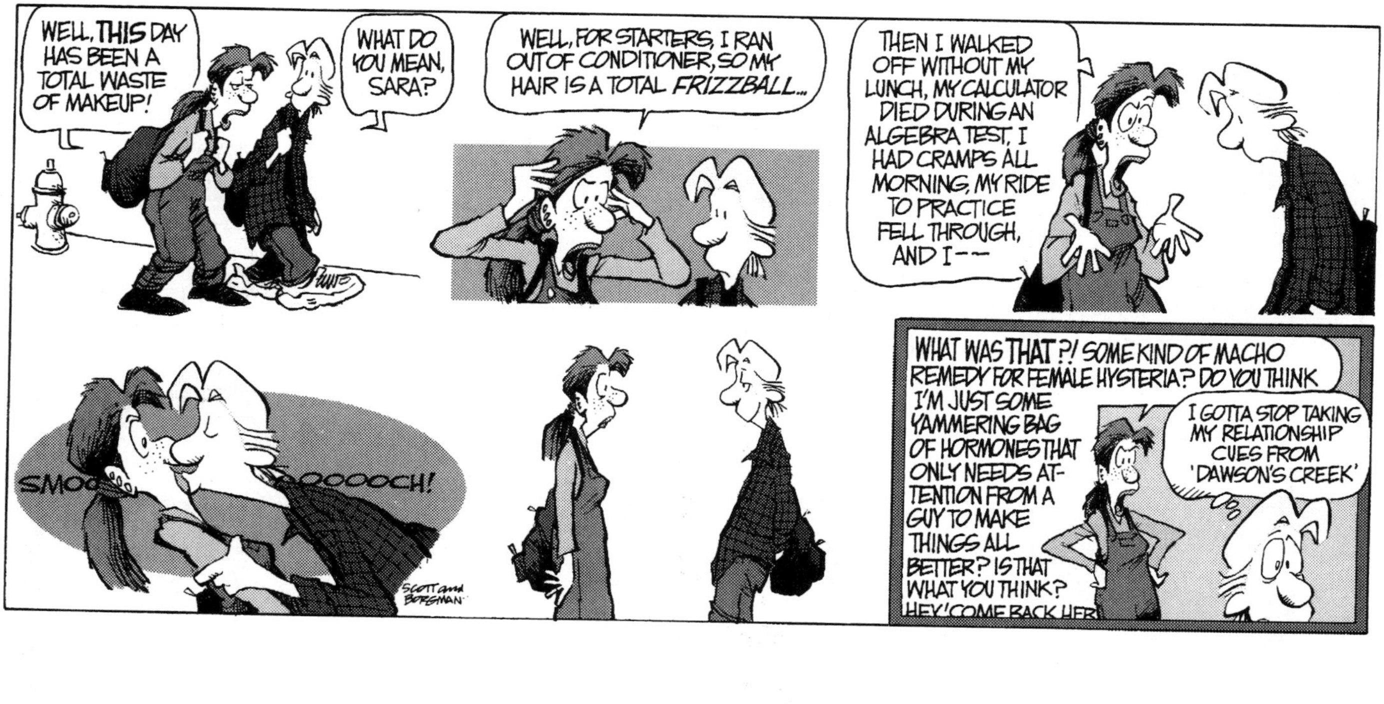
WELL, THIS DAY HAS BEEN A TOTAL WASTE OF MAKEUP!
WHAT DO YOU MEAN, SARA?
WELL, FOR STARTERS, I RAN OUT OF CONDITIONER, SO MY HAIR IS A TOTAL FRIZZBALL...
THEN I WALKED OFF WITHOUT MY LUNCH, MY CALCULATOR DIED DURING AN ALGEBRA TEST, I HAD CRAMPS ALL MORNING, MY RIDE TO PRACTICE FELL THROUGH, AND I---
SMOOOOOOOCH!
SCOTT and BORGMAN
WHAT WAS THAT?! SOME KIND OF MACHO REMEDY FOR FEMALE HYSTERIA? DO YOU THINK I'M JUST SOME YAMMERING BAG OF HORMONES THAT ONLY NEEDS ATTENTION FROM A GUY TO MAKE THINGS ALL BETTER? IS THAT WHAT YOU THINK? HEY! COME BACK HER
I GOTTA STOP TAKING MY RELATIONSHIP CUES FROM 'DAWSON'S CREEK'

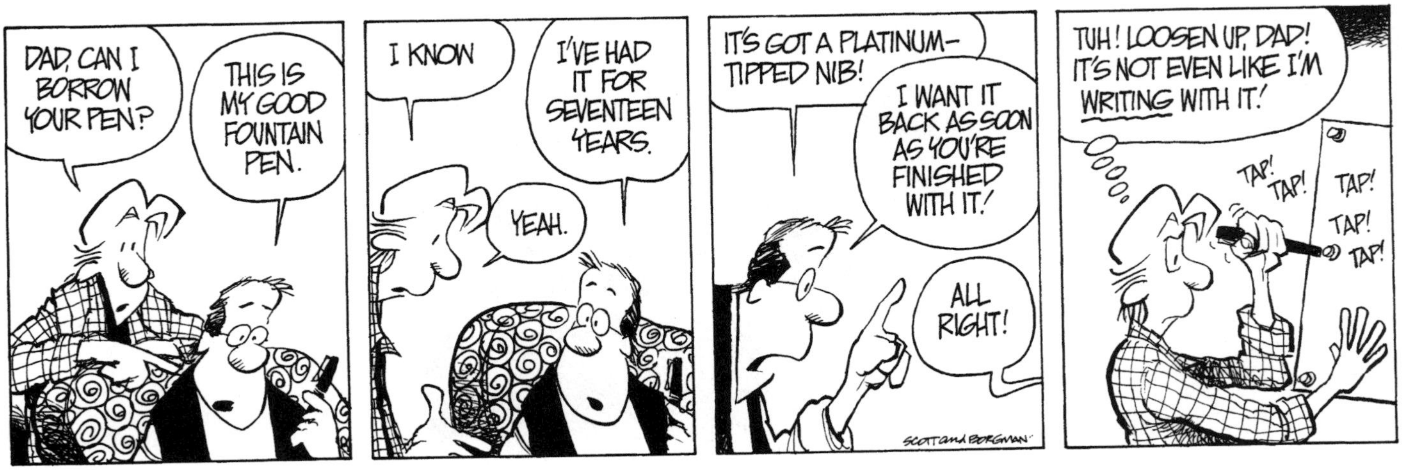
DAD, CAN I BORROW YOUR PEN?
THIS IS MY GOOD FOUNTAIN PEN.
I KNOW
I'VE HAD IT FOR SEVENTEEN YEARS.
YEAH.
IT'S GOT A PLATINUM-TIPPED NIB!
I WANT IT BACK AS SOON AS YOU'RE FINISHED WITH IT!
ALL RIGHT!
SCOTT and BORGMAN
TUH! LOOSEN UP, DAD! IT'S NOT EVEN LIKE I'M WRITING WITH IT!
TAP! TAP!
TAP! TAP! TAP!

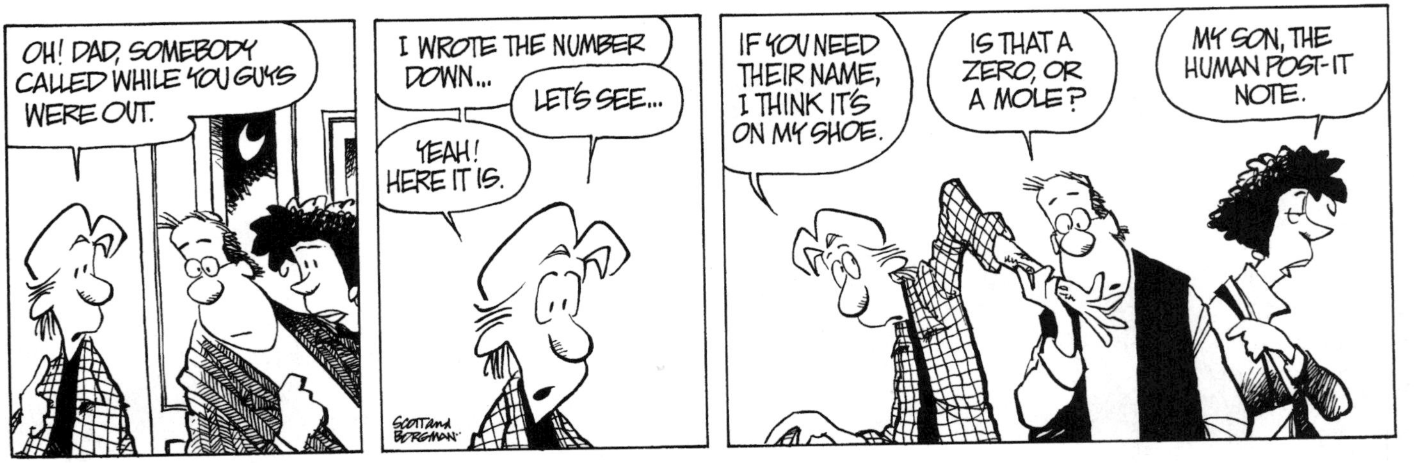
OH! DAD, SOMEBODY CALLED WHILE YOU GUYS WERE OUT.
I WROTE THE NUMBER DOWN...
LET'S SEE...
YEAH! HERE IT IS.
SCOTT and BORGMAN
IF YOU NEED THEIR NAME, I THINK IT'S ON MY SHOE.
IS THAT A ZERO, OR A MOLE?
MY SON, THE HUMAN POST-IT NOTE.

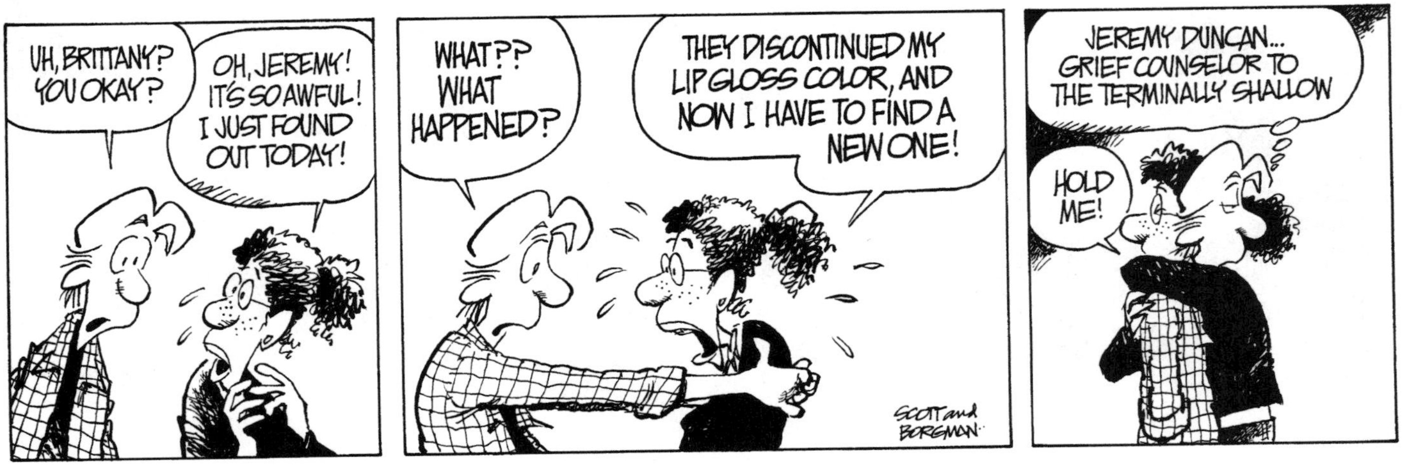
UH, BRITTANY? YOU OKAY?
OH, JEREMY! IT'S SO AWFUL! I JUST FOUND OUT TODAY!
WHAT?? WHAT HAPPENED?
THEY DISCONTINUED MY LIP GLOSS COLOR, AND NOW I HAVE TO FIND A NEW ONE!
SCOTT and BORGMAN
JEREMY DUNCAN... GRIEF COUNSELOR TO THE TERMINALLY SHALLOW
HOLD ME!

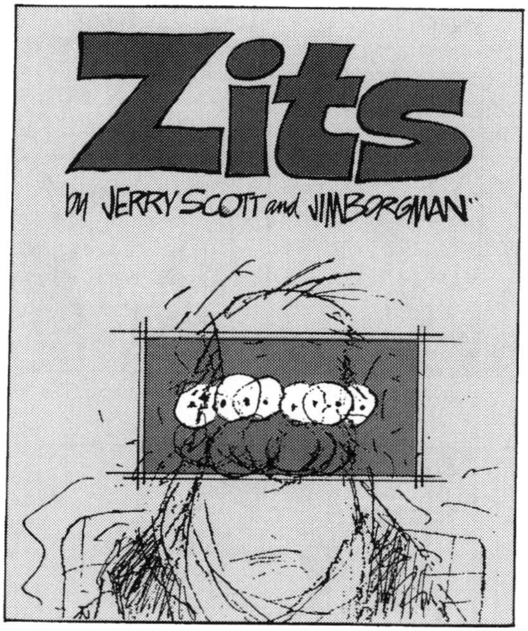
Zits
by JERRY SCOTT and JIM BORGMAN

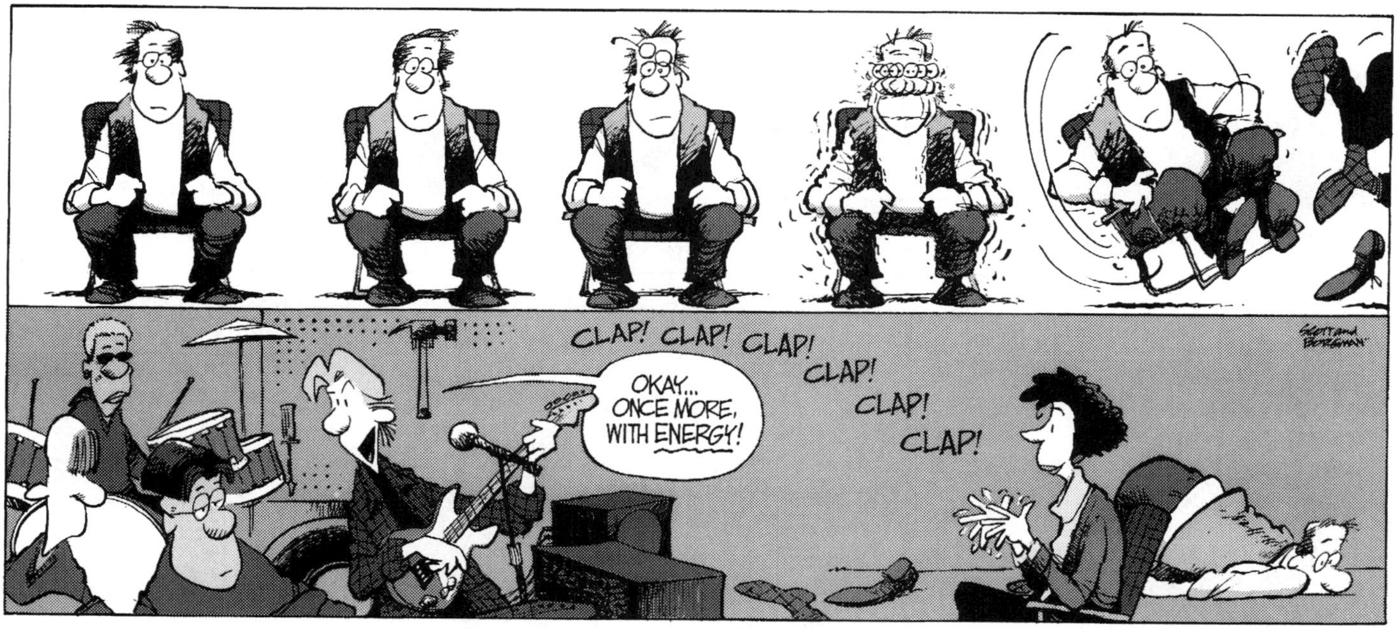
SCOTT and BORGMAN
CLAP! CLAP! CLAP!
CLAP!
CLAP!
CLAP!
OKAY... ONCE MORE, WITH ENERGY!

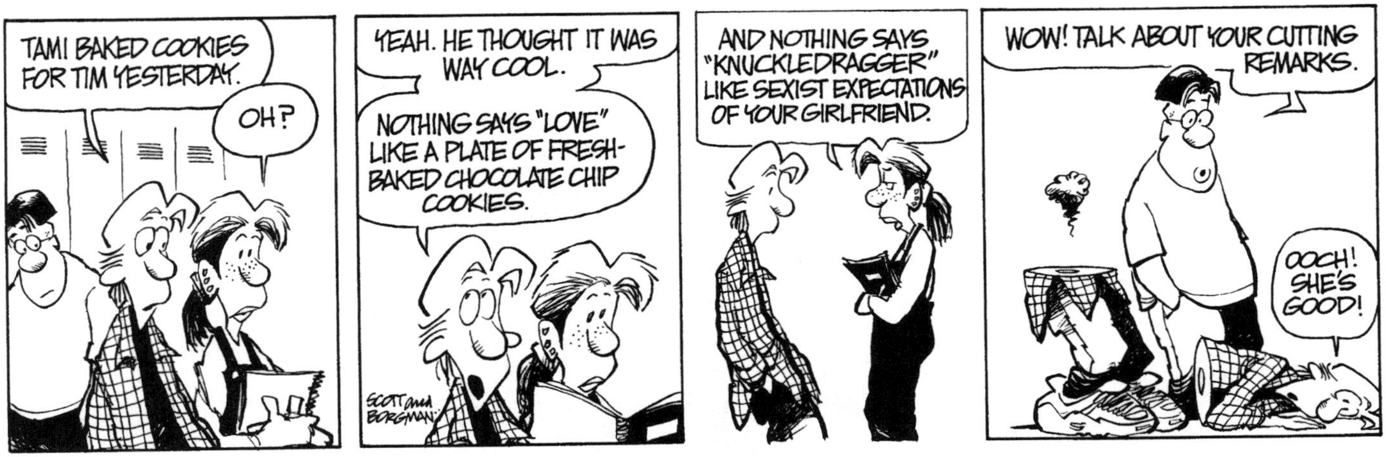
TAMI BAKED COOKIES FOR TIM YESTERDAY.
OH?
YEAH. HE THOUGHT IT WAS WAY COOL.
NOTHING SAYS "LOVE" LIKE A PLATE OF FRESH-BAKED CHOCOLATE CHIP COOKIES.
SCOTT and BORGMAN
AND NOTHING SAYS "KNUCKLEDRAGGER" LIKE SEXIST EXPECTATIONS OF YOUR GIRLFRIEND.
WOW! TALK ABOUT YOUR CUTTING REMARKS.
OOCH! SHE'S GOOD!

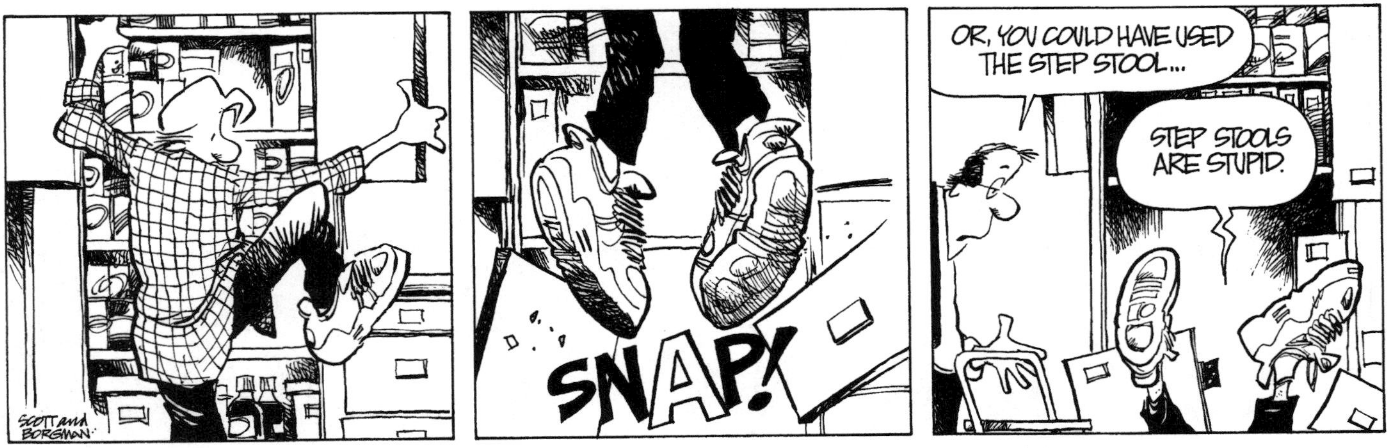
SCOTT and BORGMAN
SNAP!
OR, YOU COULD HAVE USED THE STEP STOOL...
STEP STOOLS ARE STUPID.

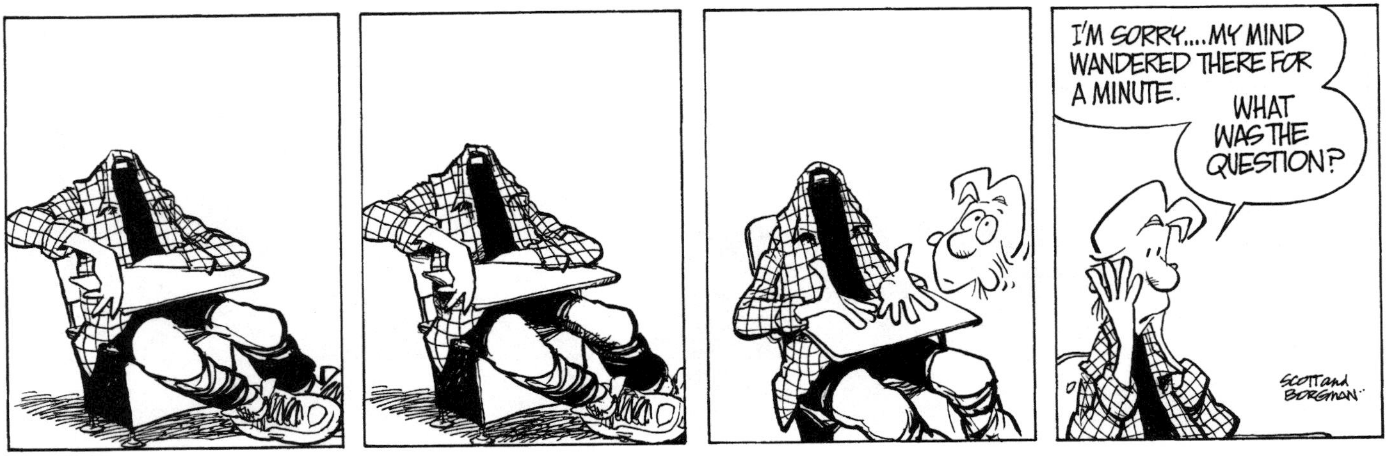
I'M SORRY....MY MIND WANDERED THERE FOR A MINUTE.
WHAT WAS THE QUESTION?
SCOTT and BORGMAN

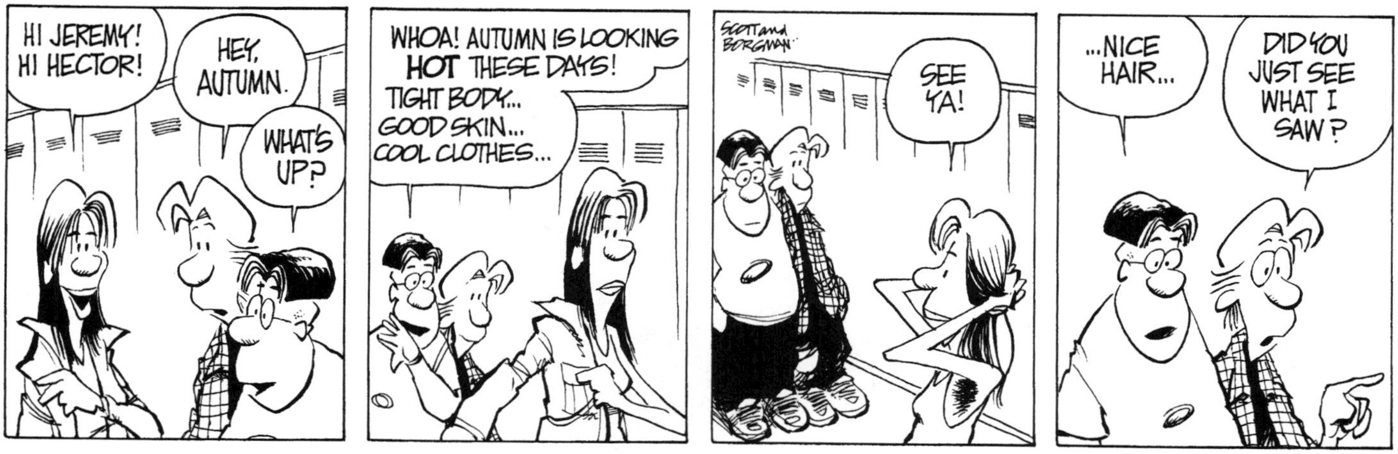
HI JEREMY! HI HECTOR!
HEY, AUTUMN.
WHAT'S UP?
WHOA! AUTUMN IS LOOKING **HOT** THESE DAYS!
TIGHT BODY... GOOD SKIN... COOL CLOTHES...
SCOTT and BORGMAN
SEE YA!
...NICE HAIR...
DID YOU JUST SEE WHAT I SAW?

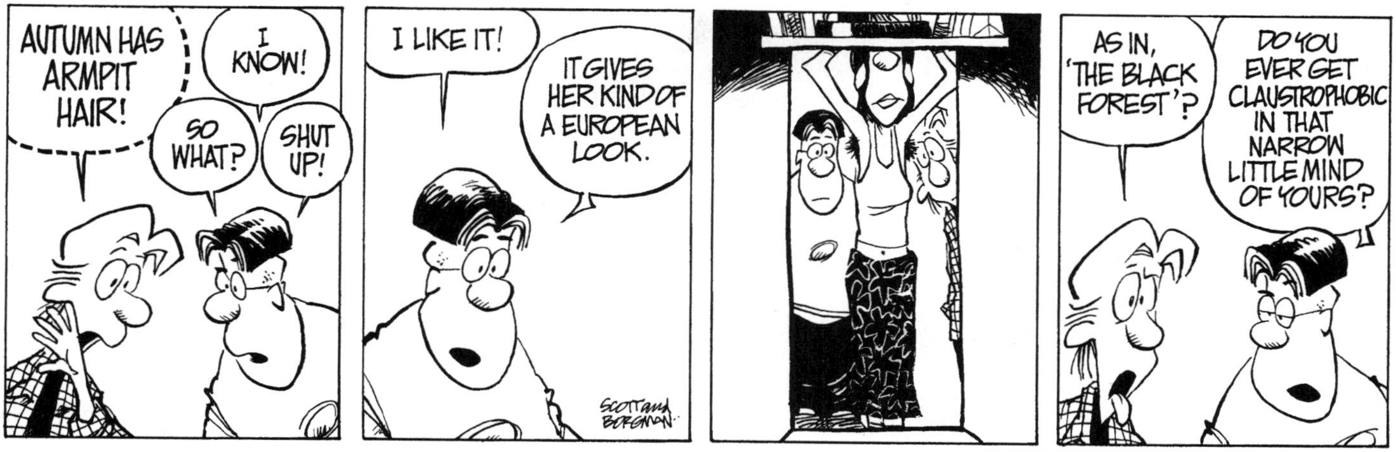
AUTUMN HAS ARMPIT HAIR!
I KNOW!
SO WHAT?
SHUT UP!
I LIKE IT!
IT GIVES HER KIND OF A EUROPEAN LOOK.
SCOTT and BORGMAN
AS IN, 'THE BLACK FOREST'?
DO YOU EVER GET CLAUSTROPHOBIC IN THAT NARROW LITTLE MIND OF YOURS?

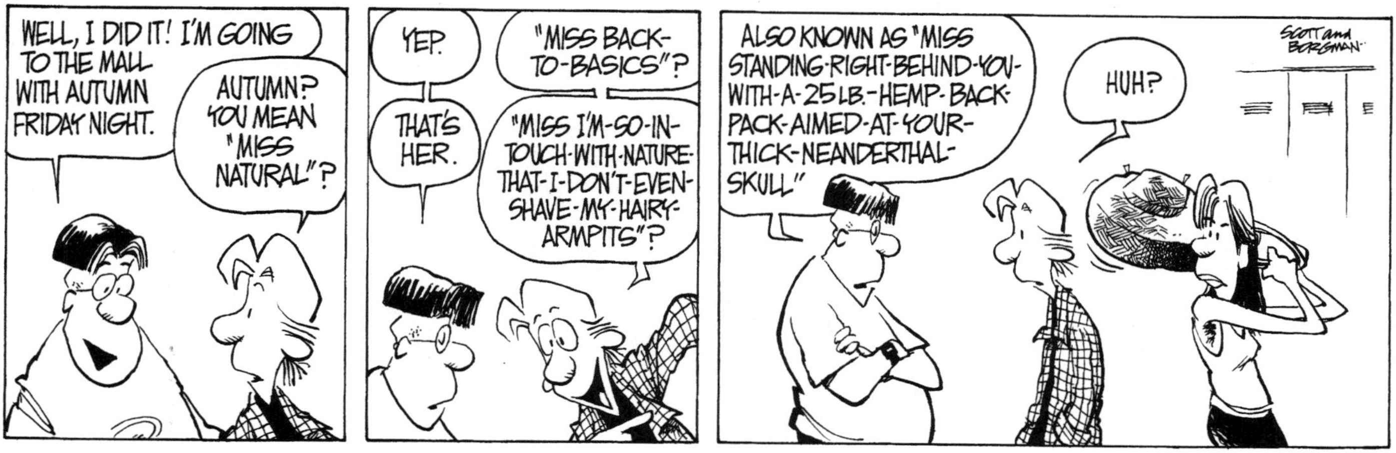
WELL, I DID IT! I'M GOING TO THE MALL WITH AUTUMN FRIDAY NIGHT.
AUTUMN? YOU MEAN "MISS NATURAL"?
YEP.
"MISS BACK-TO-BASICS"?
THAT'S HER.
"MISS I'M-SO-IN-TOUCH-WITH-NATURE-THAT-I-DON'T-EVEN-SHAVE-MY-HAIRY-ARMPITS"?
SCOTT and BORGMAN
ALSO KNOWN AS "MISS STANDING-RIGHT-BEHIND-YOU-WITH-A-25 LB.-HEMP-BACK-PACK-AIMED-AT-YOUR-THICK-NEANDERTHAL-SKULL"
HUH?

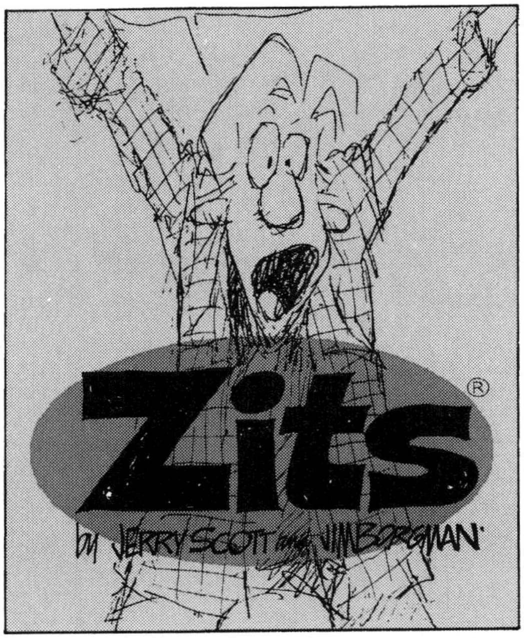
Zits®
by JERRY SCOTT and JIM BORGMAN

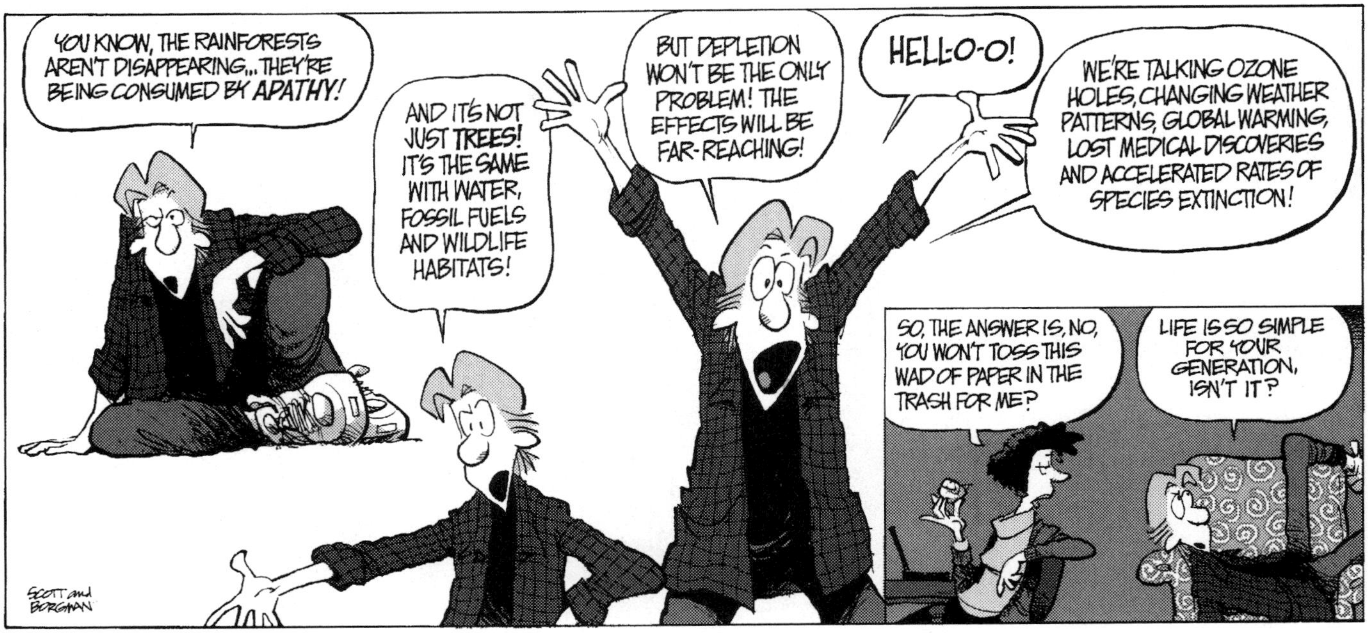
YOU KNOW, THE RAINFORESTS AREN'T DISAPPEARING... THEY'RE BEING CONSUMED BY APATHY!
AND IT'S NOT JUST TREES! IT'S THE SAME WITH WATER, FOSSIL FUELS AND WILDLIFE HABITATS!
BUT DEPLETION WON'T BE THE ONLY PROBLEM! THE EFFECTS WILL BE FAR-REACHING!
HELL-O-O!
WE'RE TALKING OZONE HOLES, CHANGING WEATHER PATTERNS, GLOBAL WARMING, LOST MEDICAL DISCOVERIES AND ACCELERATED RATES OF SPECIES EXTINCTION!
SCOTT and BORGMAN
SO, THE ANSWER IS, NO, YOU WON'T TOSS THIS WAD OF PAPER IN THE TRASH FOR ME?
LIFE IS SO SIMPLE FOR YOUR GENERATION, ISN'T IT?

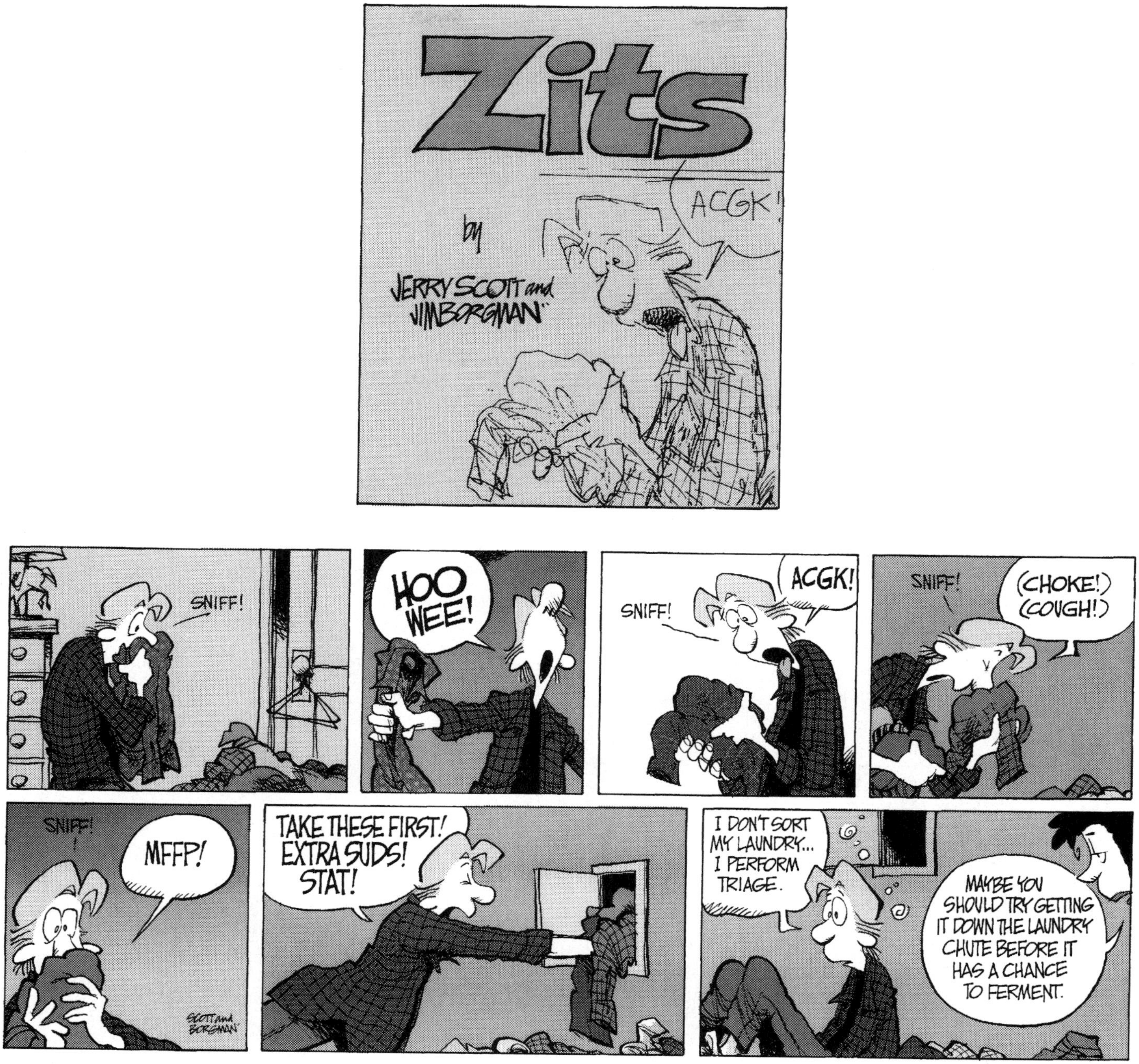
Zits
by
JERRY SCOTT and JIM BORGMAN
ACGK!
SNIFF!
HOO WEE!
SNIFF!
ACGK!
SNIFF!
(CHOKE!) (COUGH!)
SNIFF!
MFFP!
SCOTT and BORGMAN
TAKE THESE FIRST! EXTRA SUDS! STAT!
I DON'T SORT MY LAUNDRY... I PERFORM TRIAGE.
MAYBE YOU SHOULD TRY GETTING IT DOWN THE LAUNDRY CHUTE BEFORE IT HAS A CHANCE TO FERMENT.

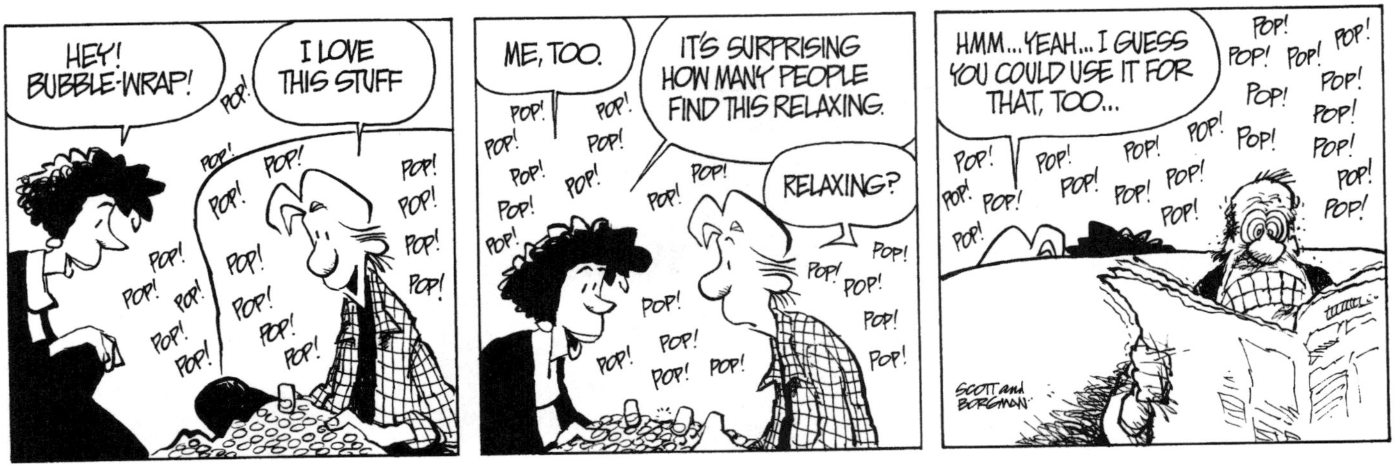
HEY! BUBBLE-WRAP!
POP!
I LOVE THIS STUFF
POP! POP! POP! POP! POP! POP! POP! POP! POP! POP! POP! POP! POP! POP! POP!
ME, TOO.
IT'S SURPRISING HOW MANY PEOPLE FIND THIS RELAXING.
POP! POP! POP! POP! POP! POP! POP! POP! POP! POP!
RELAXING?
POP! POP! POP! POP! POP! POP! POP! POP! POP!
HMM... YEAH... I GUESS YOU COULD USE IT FOR THAT, TOO...
POP! POP! POP! POP! POP! POP! POP! POP! POP! POP! POP! POP! POP! POP! POP! POP! POP! POP! POP! POP! POP!
SCOTT and BORGMAN

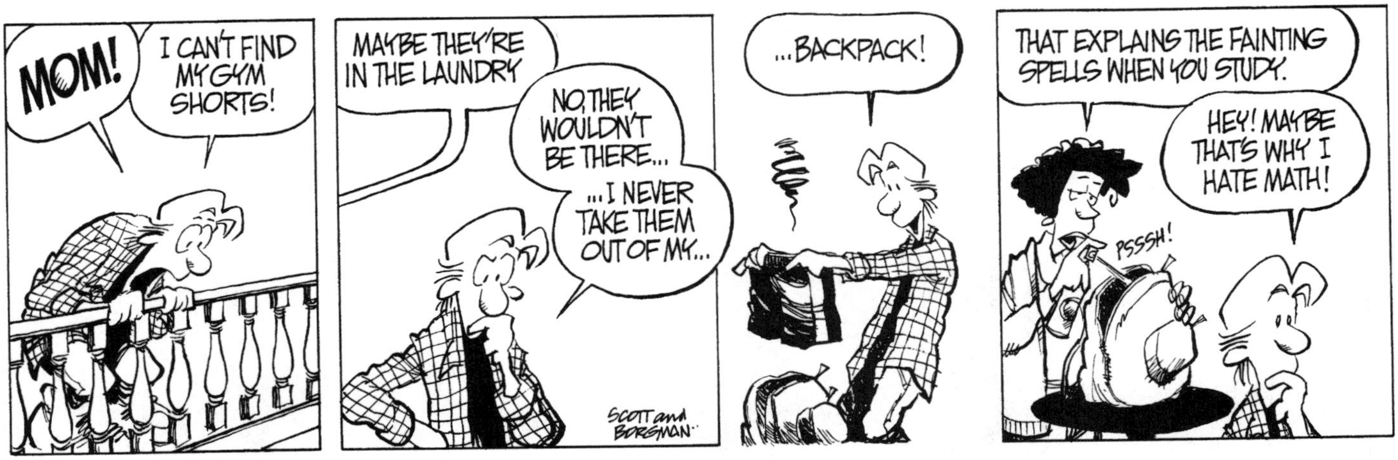
MOM!
I CAN'T FIND MY GYM SHORTS!
MAYBE THEY'RE IN THE LAUNDRY
NO, THEY WOULDN'T BE THERE...
...I NEVER TAKE THEM OUT OF MY...
SCOTT and BORGMAN
...BACKPACK!
THAT EXPLAINS THE FAINTING SPELLS WHEN YOU STUDY.
PSSSH!
HEY! MAYBE THAT'S WHY I HATE MATH!

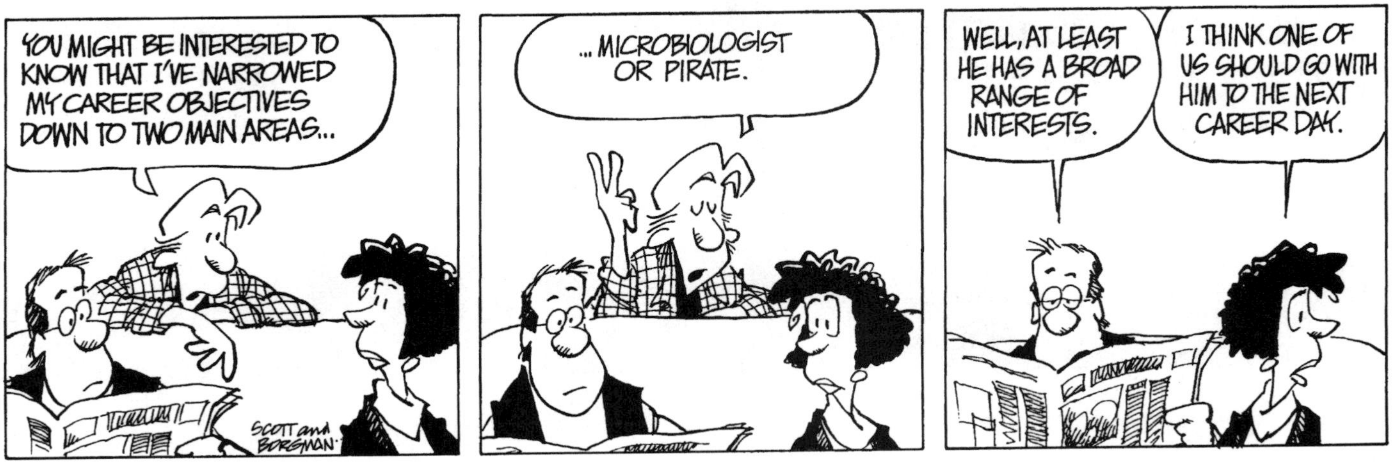
YOU MIGHT BE INTERESTED TO KNOW THAT I'VE NARROWED MY CAREER OBJECTIVES DOWN TO TWO MAIN AREAS...
SCOTT and BORGMAN
...MICROBIOLOGIST OR PIRATE.
WELL, AT LEAST HE HAS A BROAD RANGE OF INTERESTS.
I THINK ONE OF US SHOULD GO WITH HIM TO THE NEXT CAREER DAY.

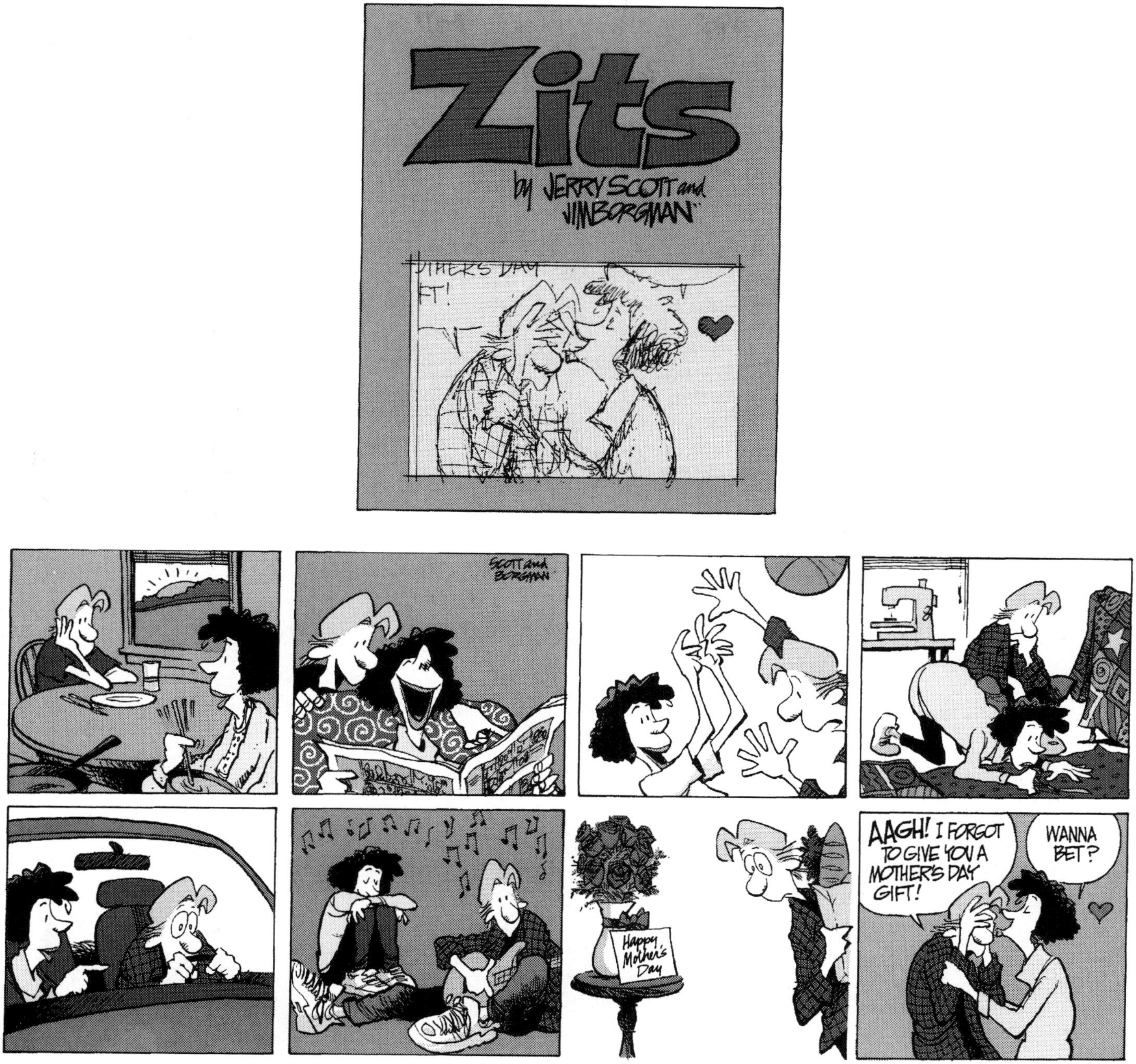
Zits
by JERRY SCOTT and JIM BORGMAN
SCOTT and BORGMAN
Happy Mother's Day
AAGH! I FORGOT TO GIVE YOU A MOTHER'S DAY GIFT!
WANNA BET?

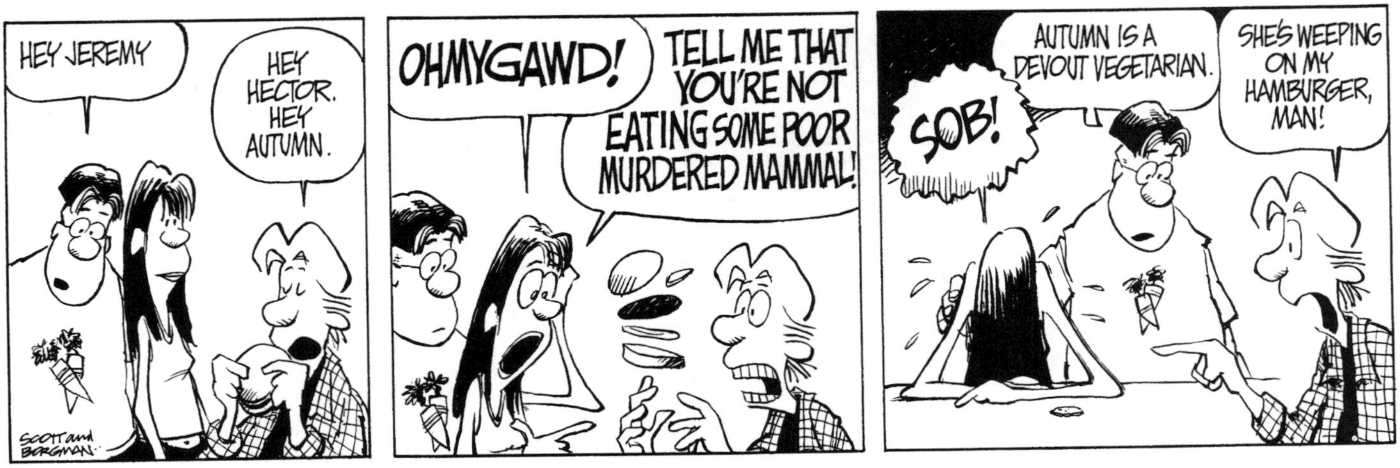
HEY JEREMY
HEY HECTOR. HEY AUTUMN.
SCOTT and BORGMAN
OHMYGAWD!
TELL ME THAT YOU'RE NOT EATING SOME POOR MURDERED MAMMAL!
SOB!
AUTUMN IS A DEVOUT VEGETARIAN.
SHE'S WEEPING ON MY HAMBURGER, MAN!

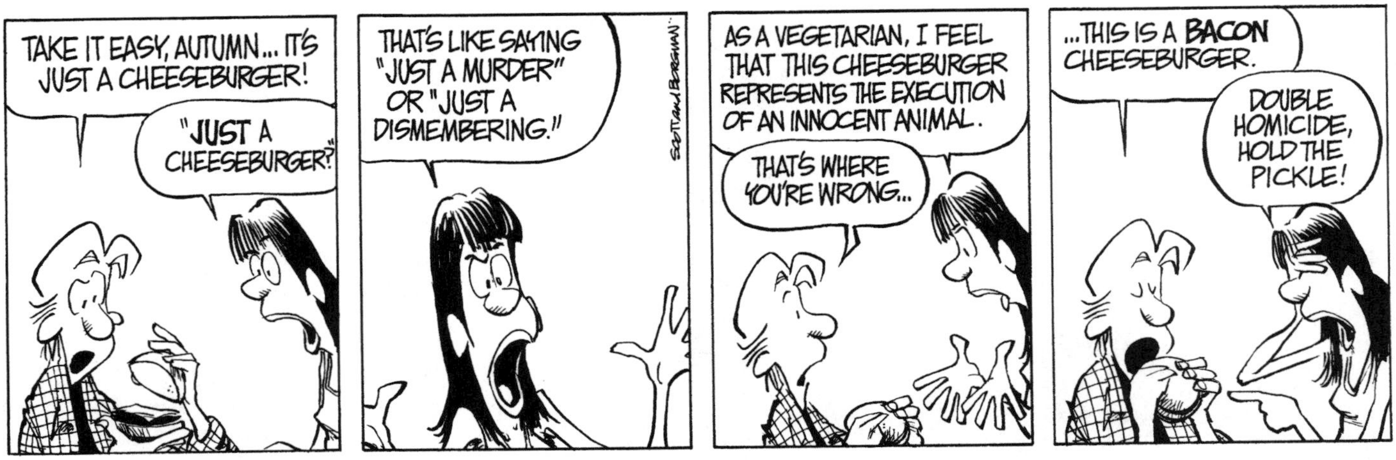
TAKE IT EASY, AUTUMN... IT'S JUST A CHEESEBURGER!
"**JUST** A CHEESEBURGER?"
THAT'S LIKE SAYING "JUST A MURDER" OR "JUST A DISMEMBERING."
SCOTT and BORGMAN
AS A VEGETARIAN, I FEEL THAT THIS CHEESEBURGER REPRESENTS THE EXECUTION OF AN INNOCENT ANIMAL.
THAT'S WHERE YOU'RE WRONG...
...THIS IS A **BACON** CHEESEBURGER.
DOUBLE HOMICIDE, HOLD THE PICKLE!

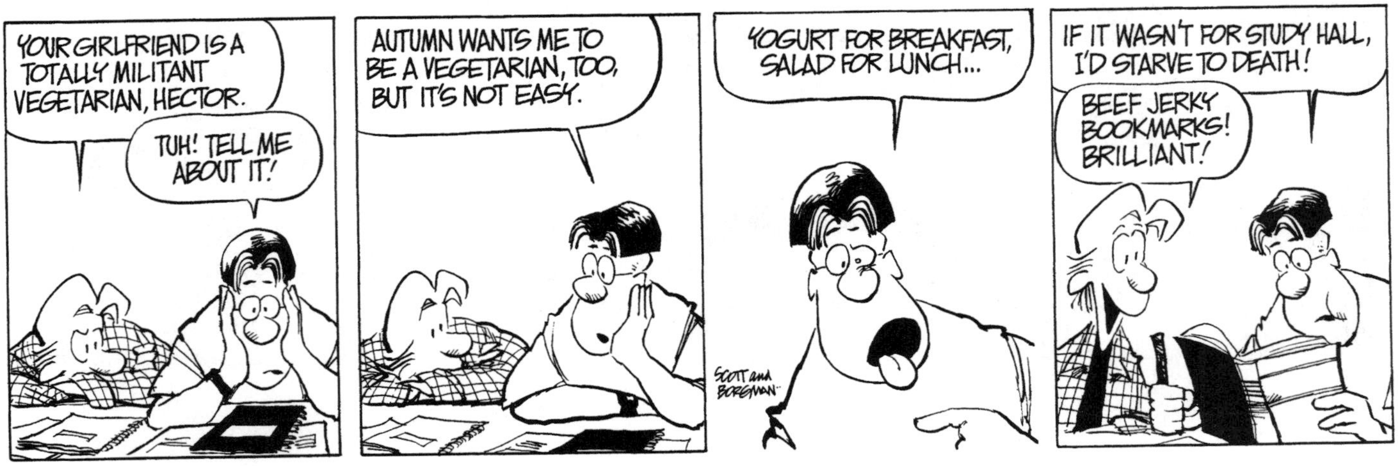
YOUR GIRLFRIEND IS A TOTALLY MILITANT VEGETARIAN, HECTOR.
TUH! TELL ME ABOUT IT!
AUTUMN WANTS ME TO BE A VEGETARIAN, TOO, BUT IT'S NOT EASY.
YOGURT FOR BREAKFAST, SALAD FOR LUNCH...
SCOTT and BORGMAN
IF IT WASN'T FOR STUDY HALL, I'D STARVE TO DEATH!
BEEF JERKY BOOKMARKS! BRILLIANT!

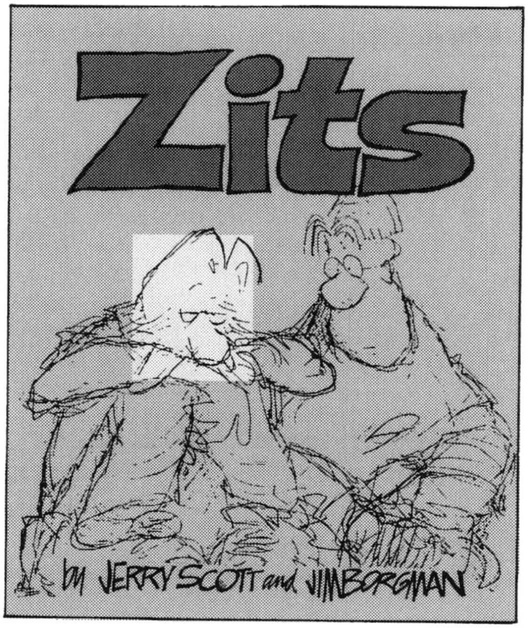
Zits
by JERRY SCOTT and JIM BORGMAN

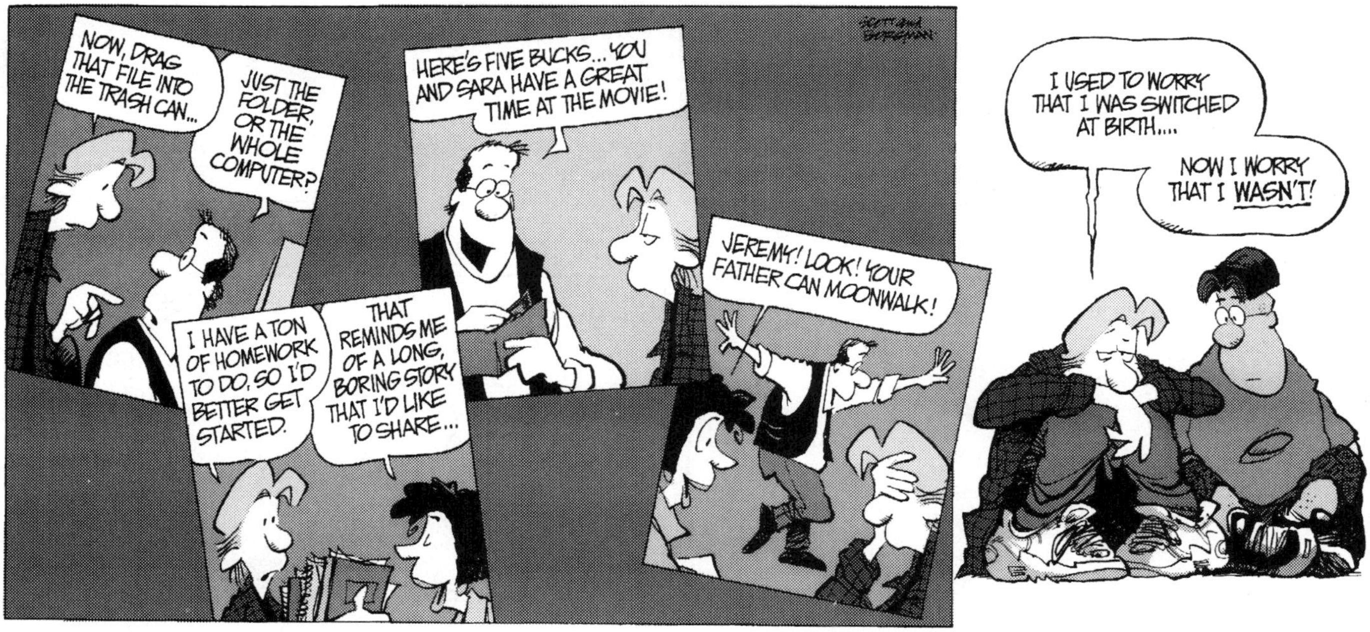
SCOTT and BORGMAN
NOW, DRAG THAT FILE INTO THE TRASH CAN...
JUST THE FOLDER, OR THE WHOLE COMPUTER?
HERE'S FIVE BUCKS... YOU AND SARA HAVE A GREAT TIME AT THE MOVIE!
I HAVE A TON OF HOMEWORK TO DO, SO I'D BETTER GET STARTED.
THAT REMINDS ME OF A LONG, BORING STORY THAT I'D LIKE TO SHARE...
JEREMY! LOOK! YOUR FATHER CAN MOONWALK!
I USED TO WORRY THAT I WAS SWITCHED AT BIRTH....
NOW I WORRY THAT I WASN'T!

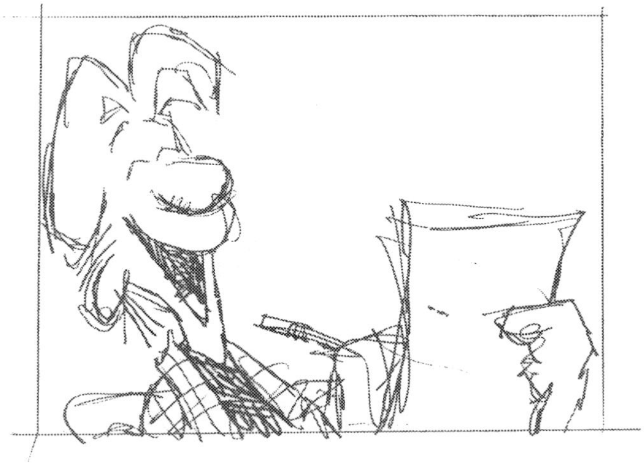

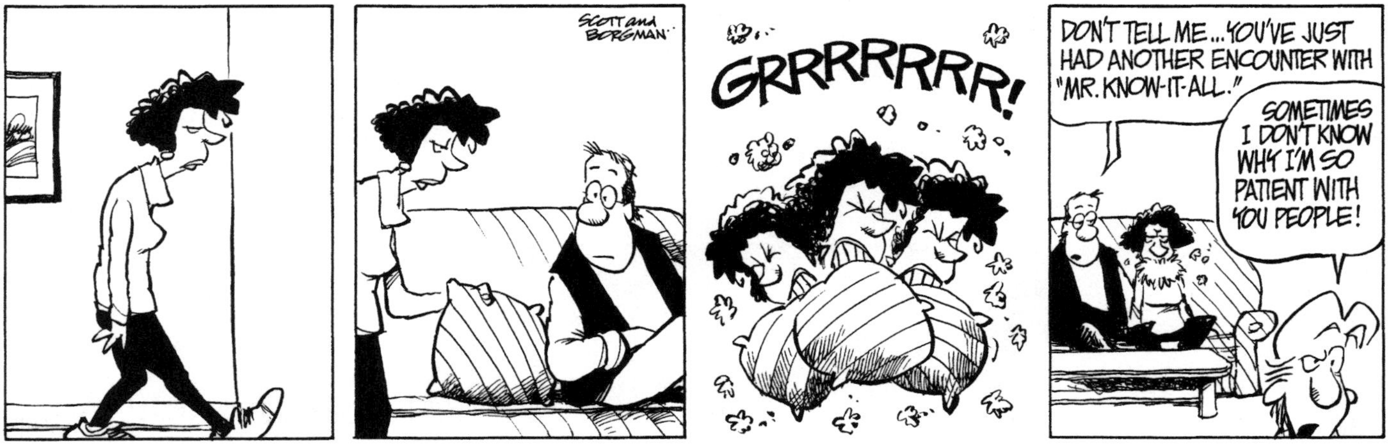

SCOTT AND BORGMAN
GRRRRRRR!
DON'T TELL ME...YOU'VE JUST HAD ANOTHER ENCOUNTER WITH "MR. KNOW-IT-ALL."
SOMETIMES I DON'T KNOW WHY I'M SO PATIENT WITH YOU PEOPLE!

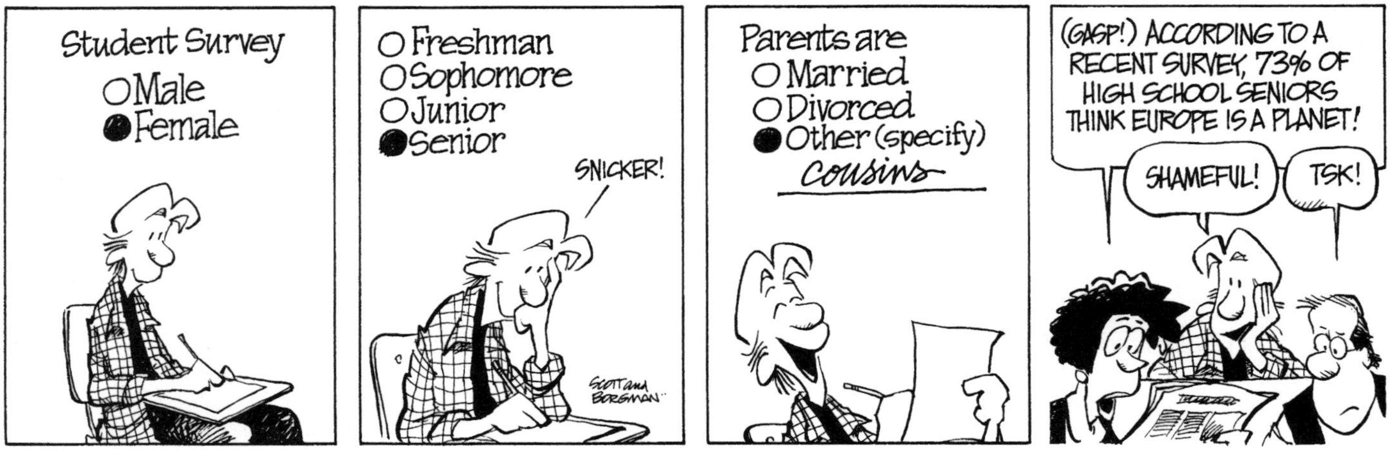

Student Survey
Male
Female
Freshman
Sophomore
Junior
Senior
SNICKER!
SCOTT AND BORGMAN
Parents are
Married
Divorced
Other (specify)
Cousins
(GASP!) ACCORDING TO A RECENT SURVEY, 73% OF HIGH SCHOOL SENIORS THINK EUROPE IS A PLANET!
SHAMEFUL!
TSK!

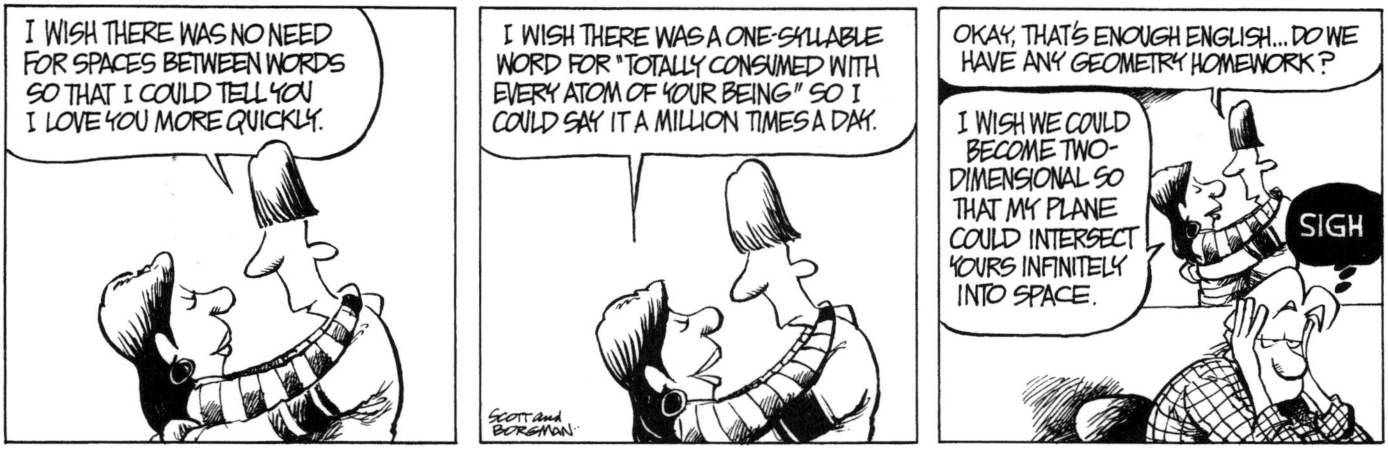
I WISH THERE WAS NO NEED FOR SPACES BETWEEN WORDS SO THAT I COULD TELL YOU I LOVE YOU MORE QUICKLY.
I WISH THERE WAS A ONE-SYLLABLE WORD FOR "TOTALLY CONSUMED WITH EVERY ATOM OF YOUR BEING" SO I COULD SAY IT A MILLION TIMES A DAY.
SCOTT and BORGMAN
OKAY, THAT'S ENOUGH ENGLISH... DO WE HAVE ANY GEOMETRY HOMEWORK?
I WISH WE COULD BECOME TWO-DIMENSIONAL SO THAT MY PLANE COULD INTERSECT YOURS INFINITELY INTO SPACE.
SIGH

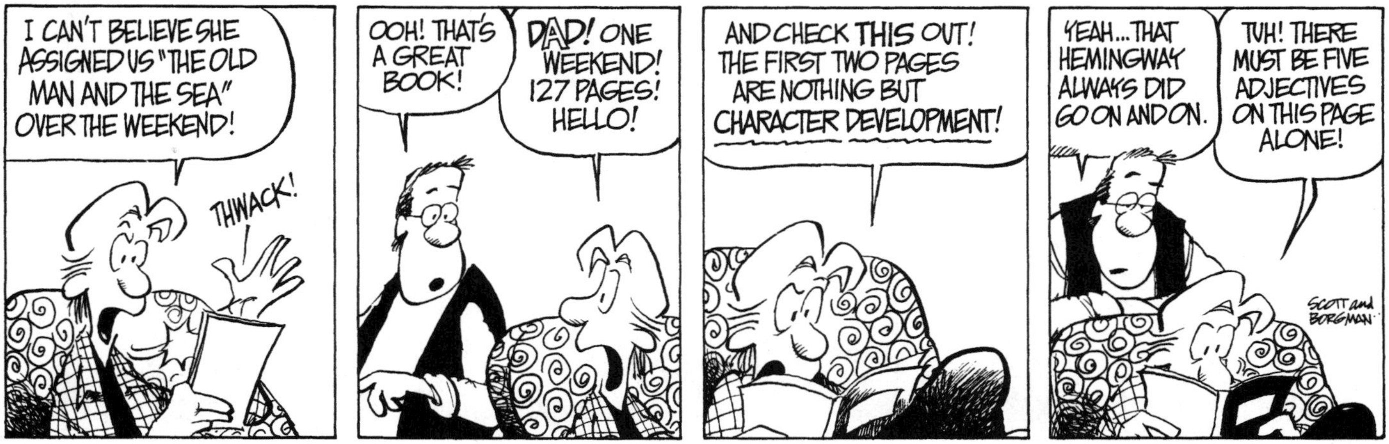
I CAN'T BELIEVE SHE ASSIGNED US "THE OLD MAN AND THE SEA" OVER THE WEEKEND!
THWACK!
OOH! THAT'S A GREAT BOOK!
DAD! ONE WEEKEND! 127 PAGES! HELLO!
AND CHECK THIS OUT! THE FIRST TWO PAGES ARE NOTHING BUT CHARACTER DEVELOPMENT!
YEAH... THAT HEMINGWAY ALWAYS DID GO ON AND ON.
TUH! THERE MUST BE FIVE ADJECTIVES ON THIS PAGE ALONE!
SCOTT and BORGMAN

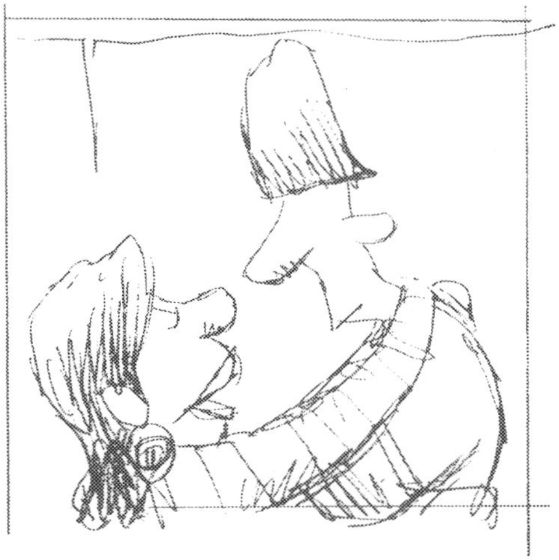

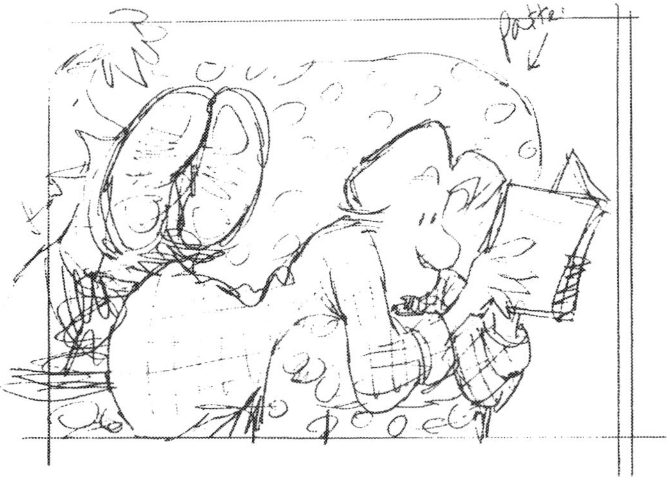

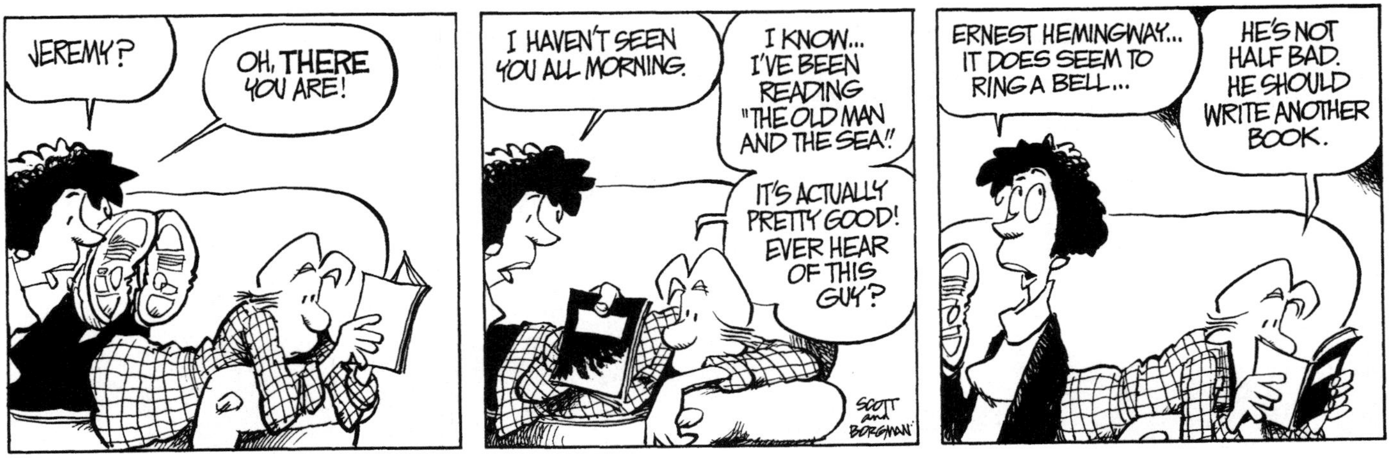
JEREMY?
OH, THERE YOU ARE!
I HAVEN'T SEEN YOU ALL MORNING.
I KNOW... I'VE BEEN READING "THE OLD MAN AND THE SEA!"
IT'S ACTUALLY PRETTY GOOD! EVER HEAR OF THIS GUY?
SCOTT and BORGMAN
ERNEST HEMINGWAY... IT DOES SEEM TO RING A BELL...
HE'S NOT HALF BAD. HE SHOULD WRITE ANOTHER BOOK.

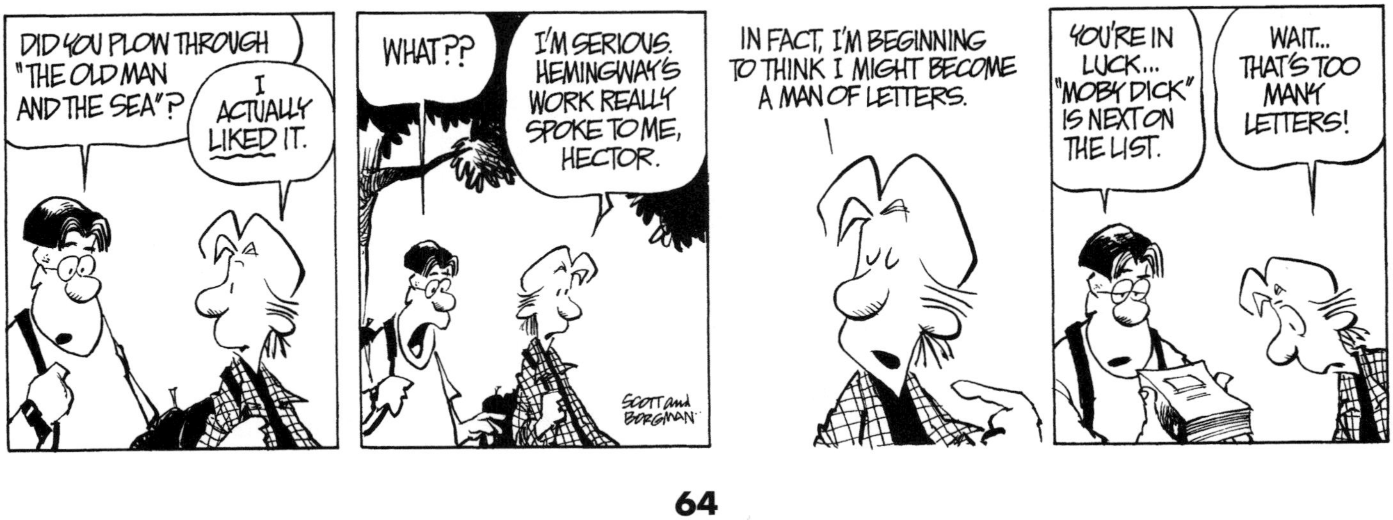
DID YOU PLOW THROUGH "THE OLD MAN AND THE SEA"?
I ACTUALLY LIKED IT.
WHAT??
I'M SERIOUS. HEMINGWAY'S WORK REALLY SPOKE TO ME, HECTOR.
SCOTT and BORGMAN
IN FACT, I'M BEGINNING TO THINK I MIGHT BECOME A MAN OF LETTERS.
YOU'RE IN LUCK... "MOBY DICK" IS NEXT ON THE LIST.
WAIT... THAT'S TOO MANY LETTERS!

Zits
by JERRY SCOTT and JIM BORGMAN
SLAM!

CLICK!
WHEEE!
SLAM!
SCOTT and BORGMAN
KA-CHUNK!
THERE WILL BE A FINAL EXAM ON WEDNESDAY, SO I WOULD RECOMMEND THAT YOU NOT LET YOUR BRAINS START SUMMER VACATION QUITE YET.
TOO LATE.
HEY! DO ME A FAVOR AND RUB A LITTLE OF THIS ON MY BALD SPOT!

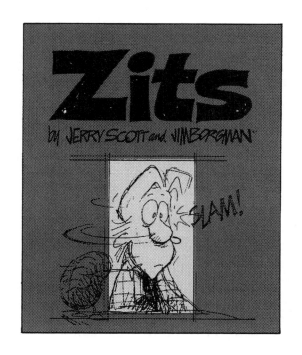

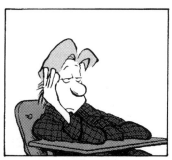

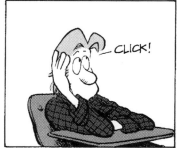

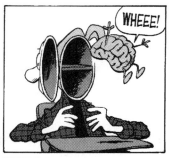

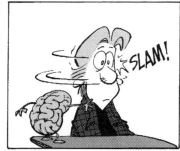

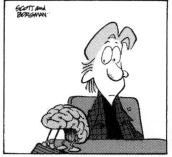

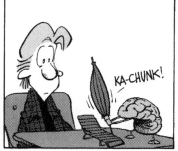

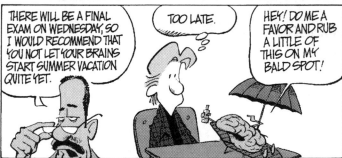

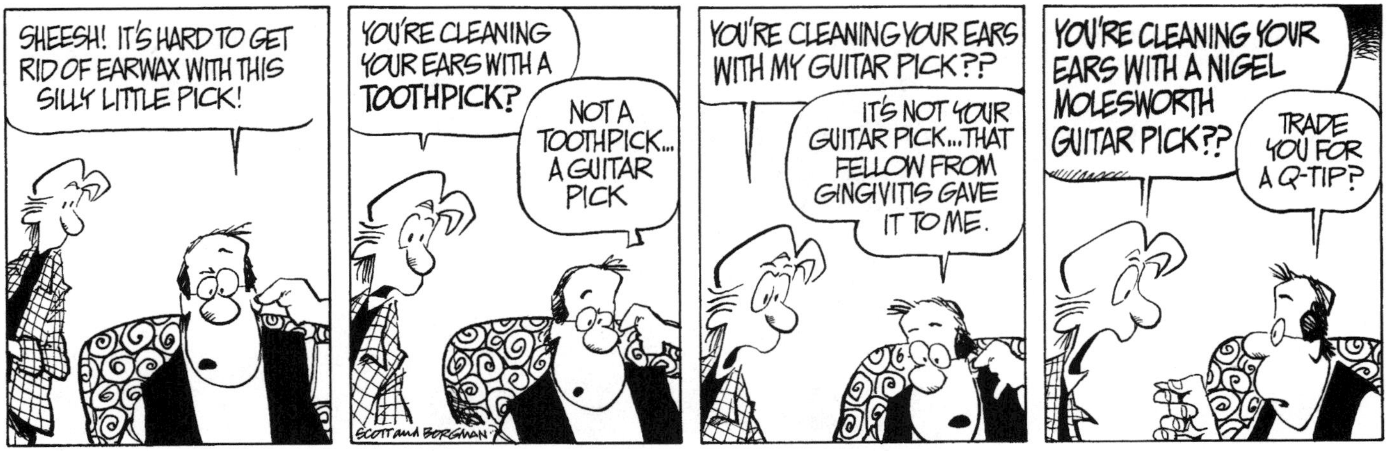
SHEESH! IT'S HARD TO GET RID OF EARWAX WITH THIS SILLY LITTLE PICK!
YOU'RE CLEANING YOUR EARS WITH A TOOTHPICK?
NOT A TOOTHPICK... A GUITAR PICK
YOU'RE CLEANING YOUR EARS WITH MY GUITAR PICK??
IT'S NOT YOUR GUITAR PICK...THAT FELLOW FROM GINGIVITIS GAVE IT TO ME.
YOU'RE CLEANING YOUR EARS WITH A NIGEL MOLESWORTH GUITAR PICK??
TRADE YOU FOR A Q-TIP?
SCOTT AND BORGMAN

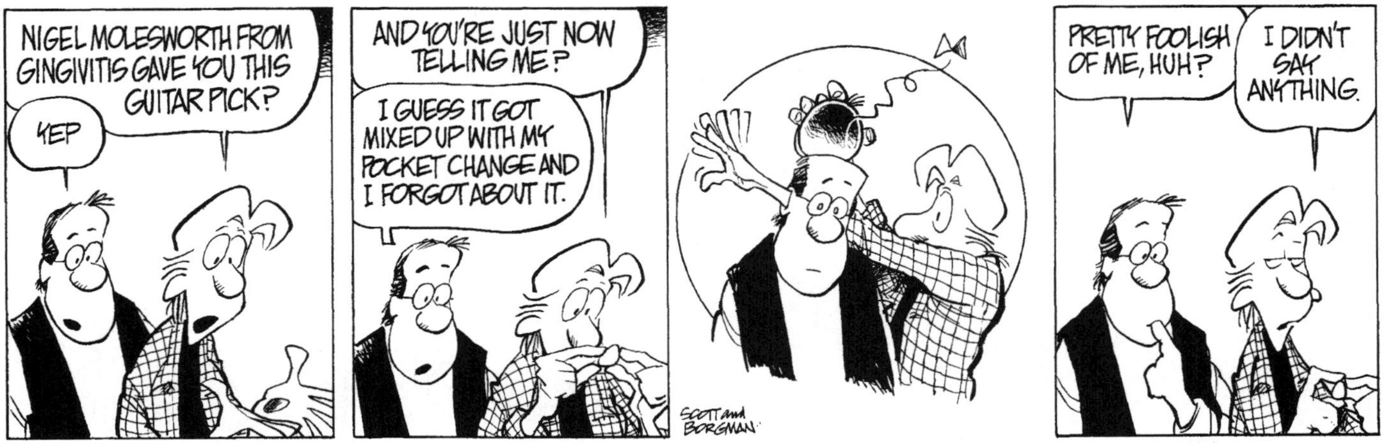
NIGEL MOLESWORTH FROM GINGIVITIS GAVE YOU THIS GUITAR PICK?
YEP
AND YOU'RE JUST NOW TELLING ME?
I GUESS IT GOT MIXED UP WITH MY POCKET CHANGE AND I FORGOT ABOUT IT.
PRETTY FOOLISH OF ME, HUH?
I DIDN'T SAY ANYTHING.
SCOTT AND BORGMAN

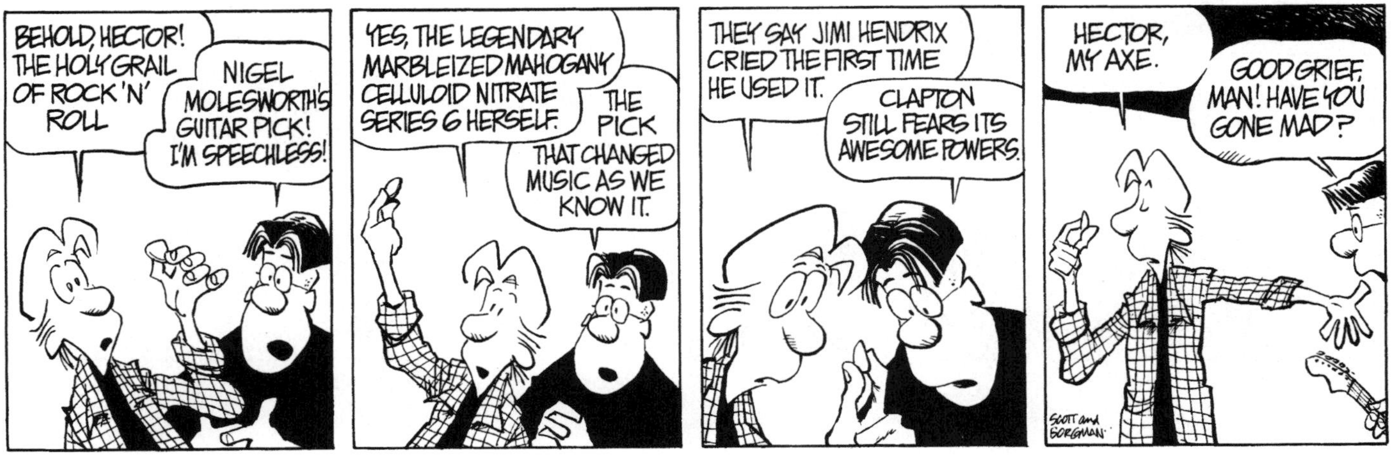
BEHOLD, HECTOR! THE HOLY GRAIL OF ROCK 'N' ROLL
NIGEL MOLESWORTH'S GUITAR PICK! I'M SPEECHLESS!
YES, THE LEGENDARY MARBLEIZED MAHOGANY CELLULOID NITRATE SERIES 6 HERSELF.
THE PICK THAT CHANGED MUSIC AS WE KNOW IT.
THEY SAY JIMI HENDRIX CRIED THE FIRST TIME HE USED IT.
CLAPTON STILL FEARS ITS AWESOME POWERS.
HECTOR, MY AXE.
GOOD GRIEF, MAN! HAVE YOU GONE MAD?
SCOTT AND BORGMAN

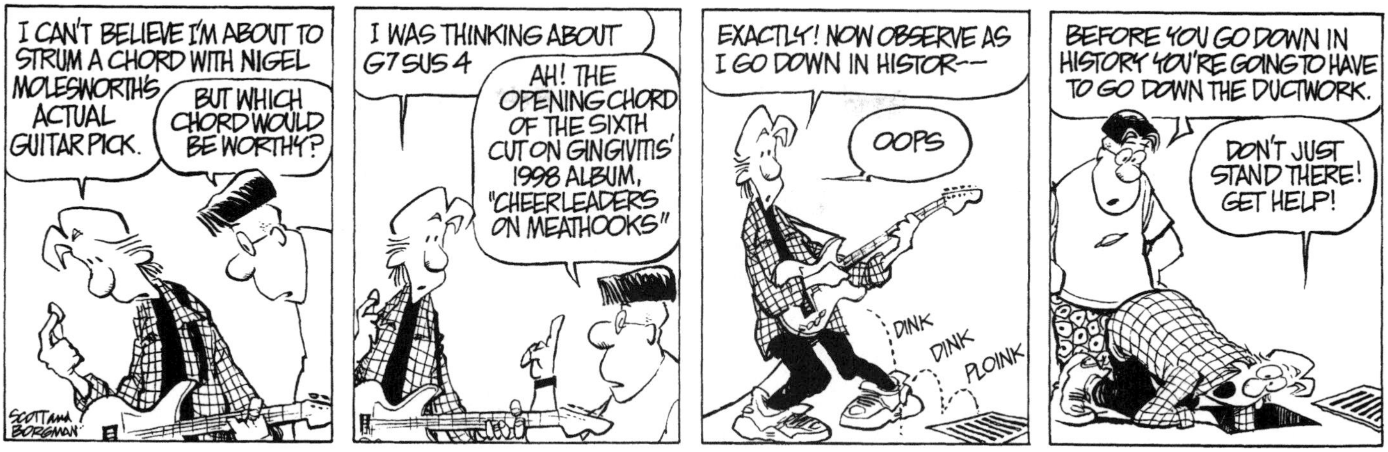
I CAN'T BELIEVE I'M ABOUT TO STRUM A CHORD WITH NIGEL MOLESWORTH'S ACTUAL GUITAR PICK.
BUT WHICH CHORD WOULD BE WORTHY?
I WAS THINKING ABOUT G7 SUS 4
AH! THE OPENING CHORD OF THE SIXTH CUT ON GINGIVITIS' 1998 ALBUM, "CHEERLEADERS ON MEATHOOKS"
EXACTLY! NOW OBSERVE AS I GO DOWN IN HISTOR--
OOPS
DINK
DINK
PLOINK
BEFORE YOU GO DOWN IN HISTORY YOU'RE GOING TO HAVE TO GO DOWN THE DUCTWORK.
DON'T JUST STAND THERE! GET HELP!
SCOTT AND BORGMAN

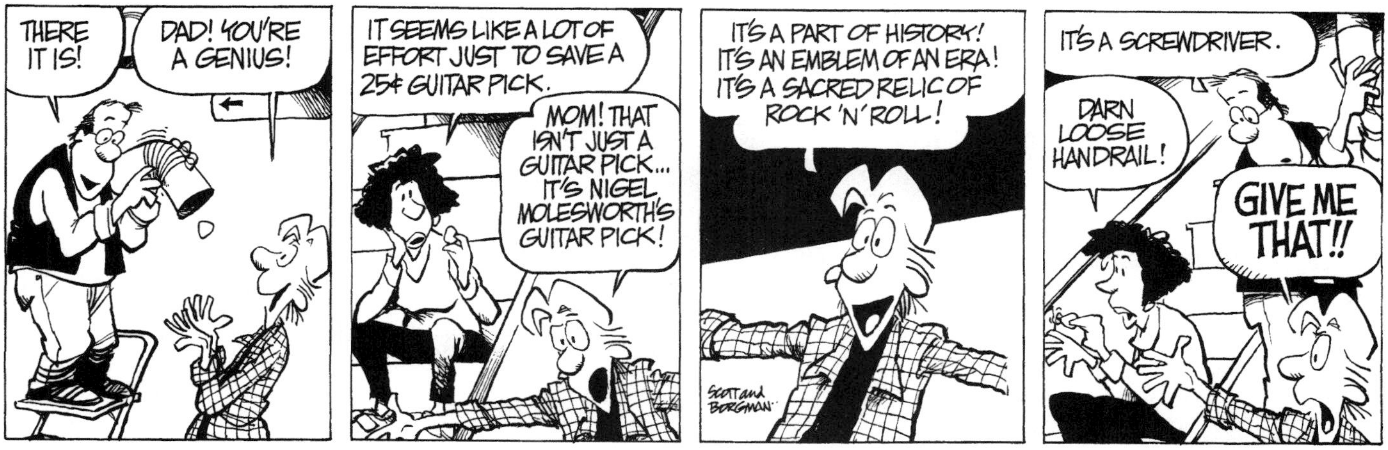
THERE IT IS!
DAD! YOU'RE A GENIUS!
IT SEEMS LIKE A LOT OF EFFORT JUST TO SAVE A 25¢ GUITAR PICK.
MOM! THAT ISN'T JUST A GUITAR PICK... IT'S NIGEL MOLESWORTH'S GUITAR PICK!
IT'S A PART OF HISTORY! IT'S AN EMBLEM OF AN ERA! IT'S A SACRED RELIC OF ROCK 'N' ROLL!
SCOTT AND BORGMAN
IT'S A SCREWDRIVER.
DARN LOOSE HANDRAIL!
GIVE ME THAT!!

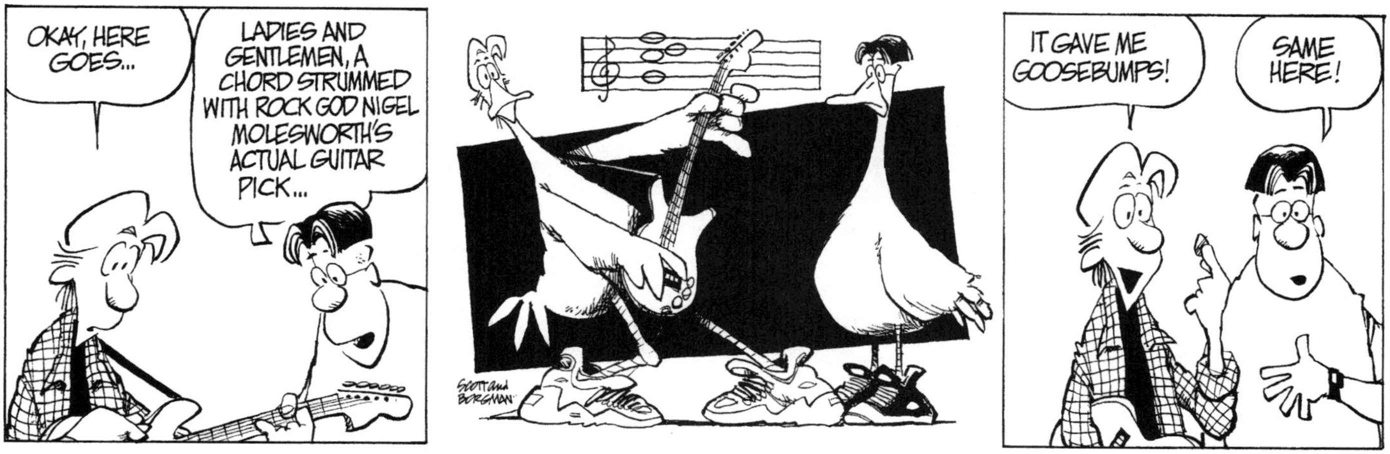
OKAY, HERE GOES...
LADIES AND GENTLEMEN, A CHORD STRUMMED WITH ROCK GOD NIGEL MOLESWORTH'S ACTUAL GUITAR PICK...
SCOTT AND BORGMAN
IT GAVE ME GOOSEBUMPS!
SAME HERE!

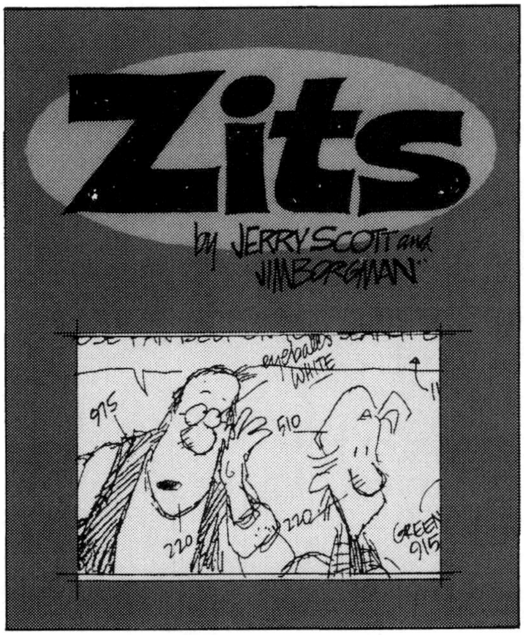
Zits
by JERRY SCOTT and JIM BORGMAN

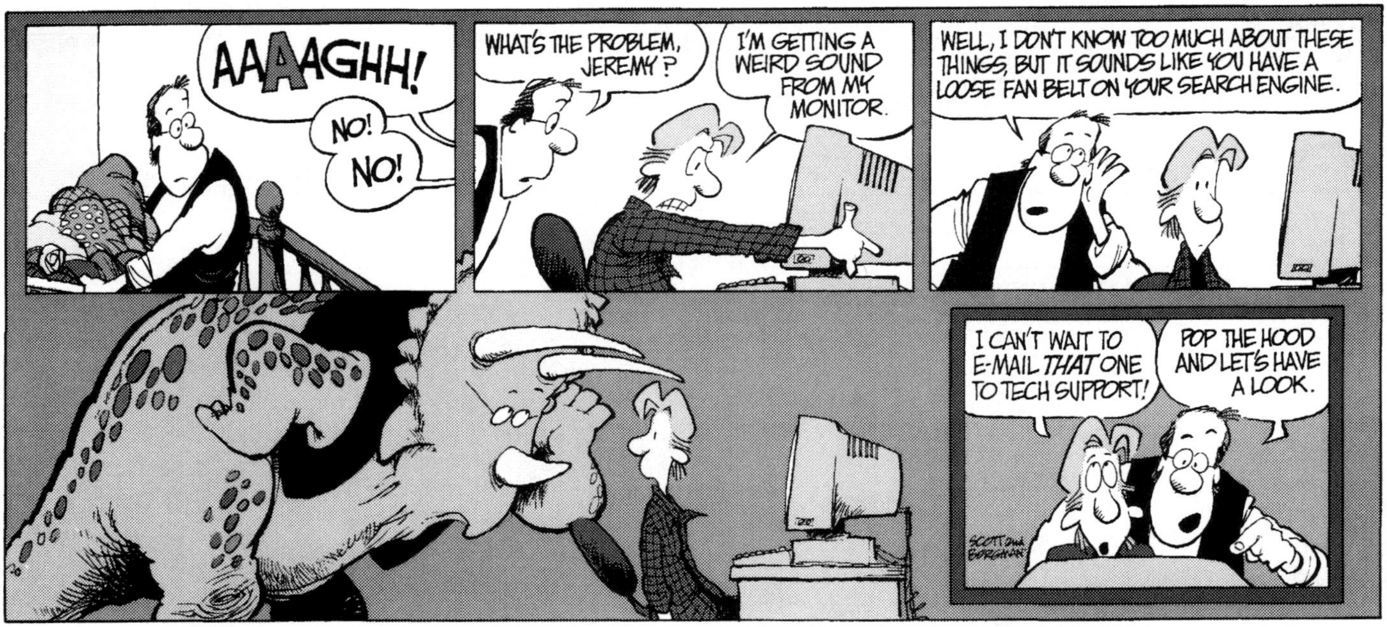
AAAAGHH!
NO! NO!
WHAT'S THE PROBLEM, JEREMY?
I'M GETTING A WEIRD SOUND FROM MY MONITOR.
WELL, I DON'T KNOW TOO MUCH ABOUT THESE THINGS, BUT IT SOUNDS LIKE YOU HAVE A LOOSE FAN BELT ON YOUR SEARCH ENGINE.
POP THE HOOD AND LET'S HAVE A LOOK.
I CAN'T WAIT TO E-MAIL *THAT* ONE TO TECH SUPPORT!
SCOTT and BORGMAN

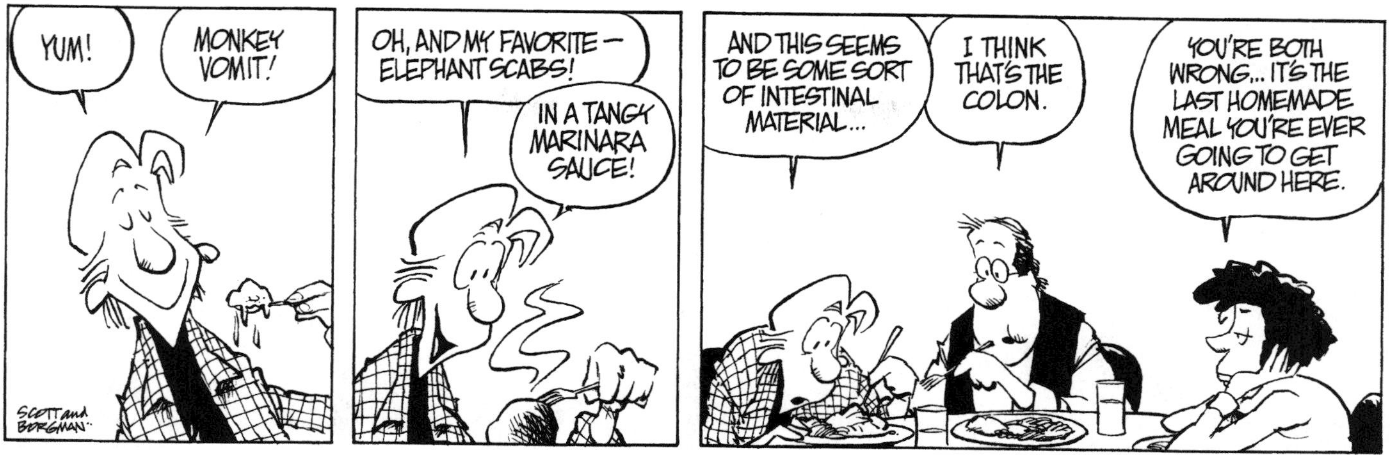
YUM!
MONKEY VOMIT!
SCOTT and BORGMAN
OH, AND MY FAVORITE — ELEPHANT SCABS!
IN A TANGY MARINARA SAUCE!
AND THIS SEEMS TO BE SOME SORT OF INTESTINAL MATERIAL...
I THINK THAT'S THE COLON.
YOU'RE BOTH WRONG... IT'S THE LAST HOMEMADE MEAL YOU'RE EVER GOING TO GET AROUND HERE.

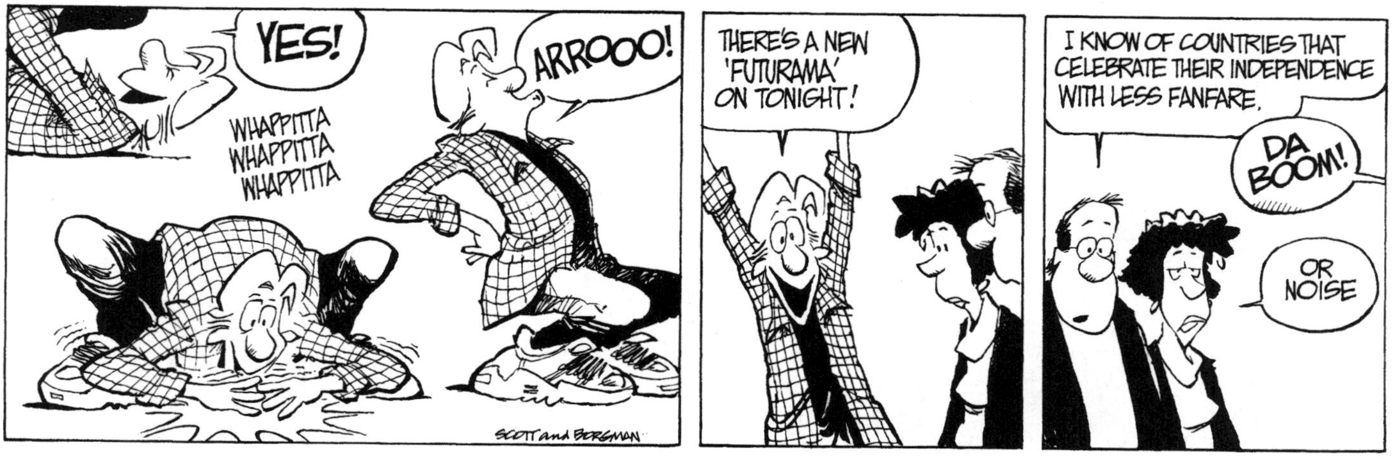
YES!
WHAPPITTA WHAPPITTA WHAPPITTA
ARROOO!
SCOTT and BORGMAN
THERE'S A NEW 'FUTURAMA' ON TONIGHT!
I KNOW OF COUNTRIES THAT CELEBRATE THEIR INDEPENDENCE WITH LESS FANFARE.
DA BOOM!
OR NOISE

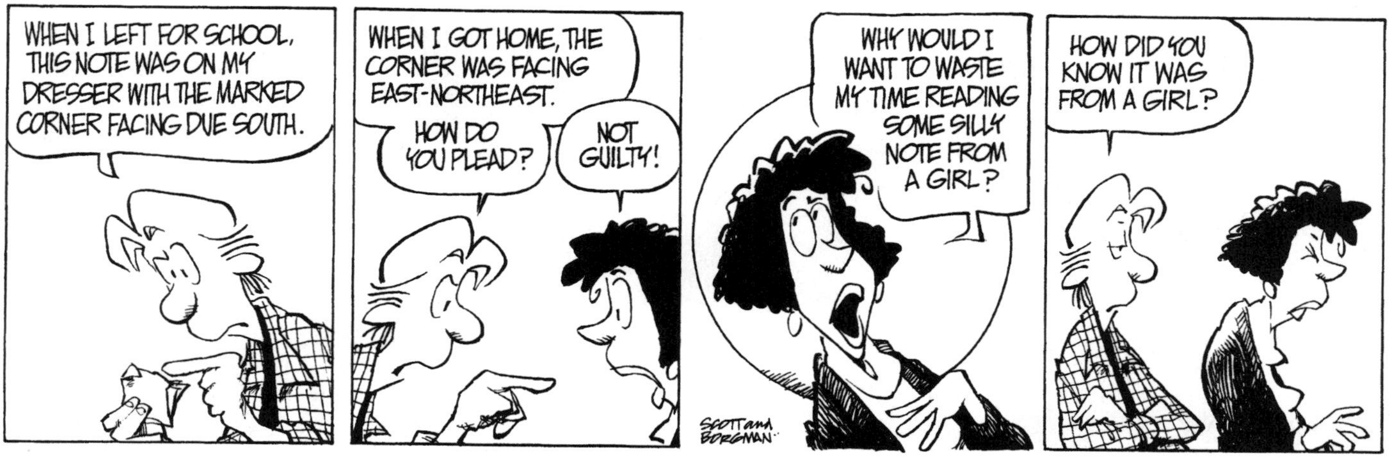
WHEN I LEFT FOR SCHOOL, THIS NOTE WAS ON MY DRESSER WITH THE MARKED CORNER FACING DUE SOUTH.
WHEN I GOT HOME, THE CORNER WAS FACING EAST-NORTHEAST.
HOW DO YOU PLEAD?
NOT GUILTY!
WHY WOULD I WANT TO WASTE MY TIME READING SOME SILLY NOTE FROM A GIRL?
SCOTT and BORGMAN
HOW DID YOU KNOW IT WAS FROM A GIRL?

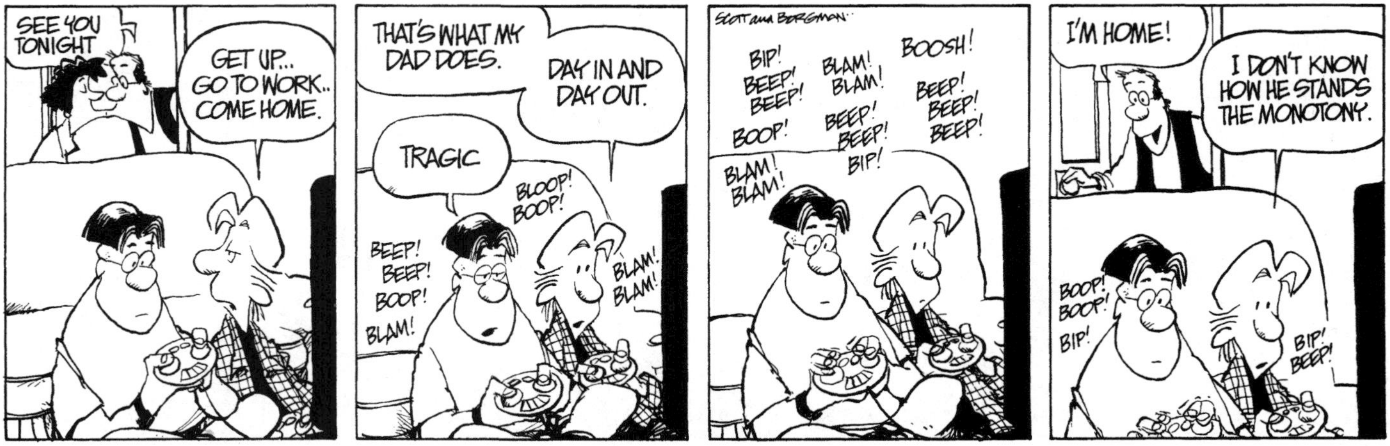
SEE YOU TONIGHT
GET UP... GO TO WORK... COME HOME.
THAT'S WHAT MY DAD DOES.
DAY IN AND DAY OUT.
TRAGIC
BLOOP! BOOP!
BEEP! BEEP! BOOP! BLAM!
BLAM! BLAM!
SCOTT and BORGMAN
BIP! BEEP! BEEP!
BLAM! BLAM!
BOOSH!
BEEP! BEEP! BEEP!
BOOP!
BEEP! BEEP! BIP!
BLAM! BLAM!
I'M HOME!
I DON'T KNOW HOW HE STANDS THE MONOTONY.
BOOP! BOOP! BIP!
BIP! BEEP!

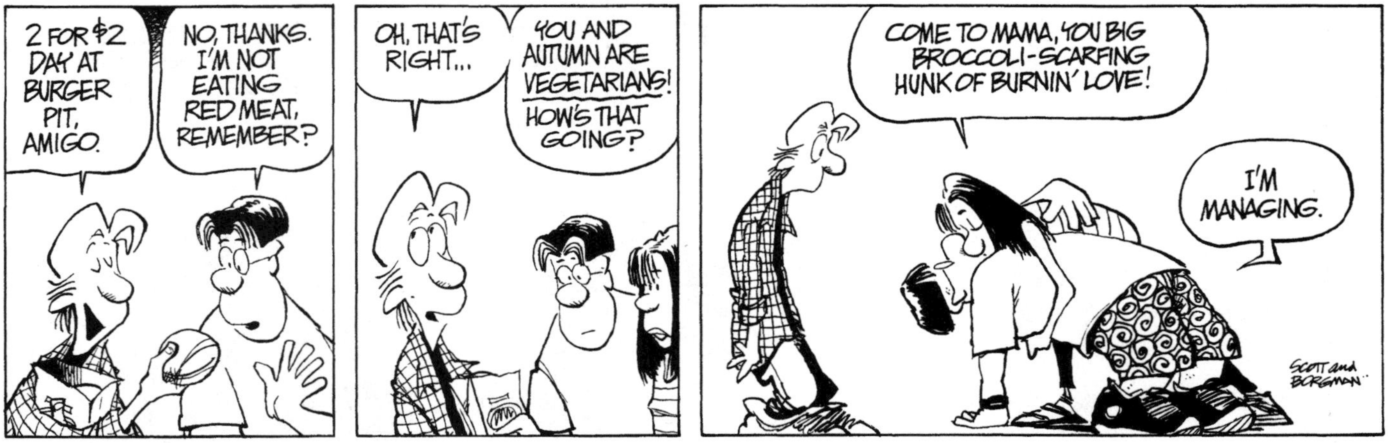
2 FOR $2 DAY AT BURGER PIT, AMIGO.
NO, THANKS. I'M NOT EATING RED MEAT, REMEMBER?
OH, THAT'S RIGHT...
YOU AND AUTUMN ARE VEGETARIANS! HOW'S THAT GOING?
COME TO MAMA, YOU BIG BROCCOLI-SCARFING HUNK OF BURNIN' LOVE!
I'M MANAGING.
SCOTT and BORGMAN

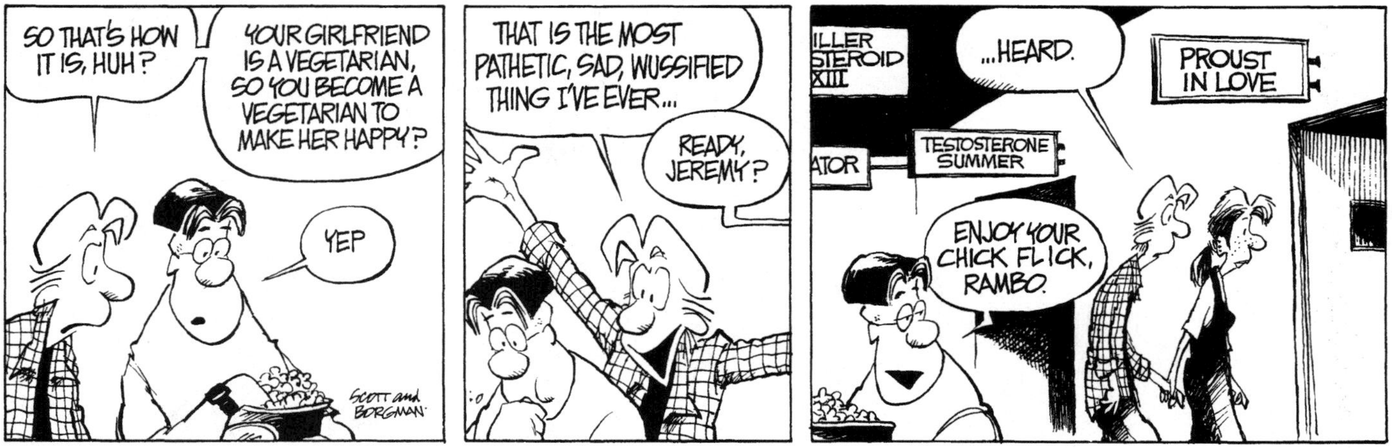
SO THAT'S HOW IT IS, HUH?
YOUR GIRLFRIEND IS A VEGETARIAN, SO YOU BECOME A VEGETARIAN TO MAKE HER HAPPY?
YEP
SCOTT and BORGMAN
THAT IS THE MOST PATHETIC, SAD, WUSSIFIED THING I'VE EVER...
READY, JEREMY?
...HEARD.
ILLER
STEROID
XIII
PROUST IN LOVE
TESTOSTERONE SUMMER
ATOR
ENJOY YOUR CHICK FLICK, RAMBO.

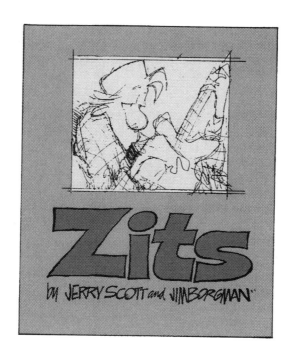

Zits

by JERRY SCOTT and JIM BORGMAN

DID YOU ASK SARA IF SHE WANTED TO GO SEE `PHANTOM MENACE' AGAIN TONIGHT?

ESSENTIALLY....

I MEAN, I SAW AMBER IN FIRST PERIOD TODAY AND SHE WAS GOING TO SEE BRITTANY IN GEOMETRY CLASS.

IF BRITTANY HADN'T SEEN SARA BY LUNCHTIME, SHE WAS GOING TO HAVE LA'RONDA PASS HER A NOTE DURING BIO LAB.

EITHER WAY, LECK ALWAYS SEES HER ON THE BUS, AND I'M SURE MAX WOULD HAVE TOLD HIM TO TELL HER BECAUSE MAX TELLS EVERYBODY EVERYTHING.

SO, BASICALLY, YES, I DID ASK HER.

AND THEY SAY GUYS CAN'T COMMUNICATE.

RING!

WHAT TOOK YOU SO LONG?

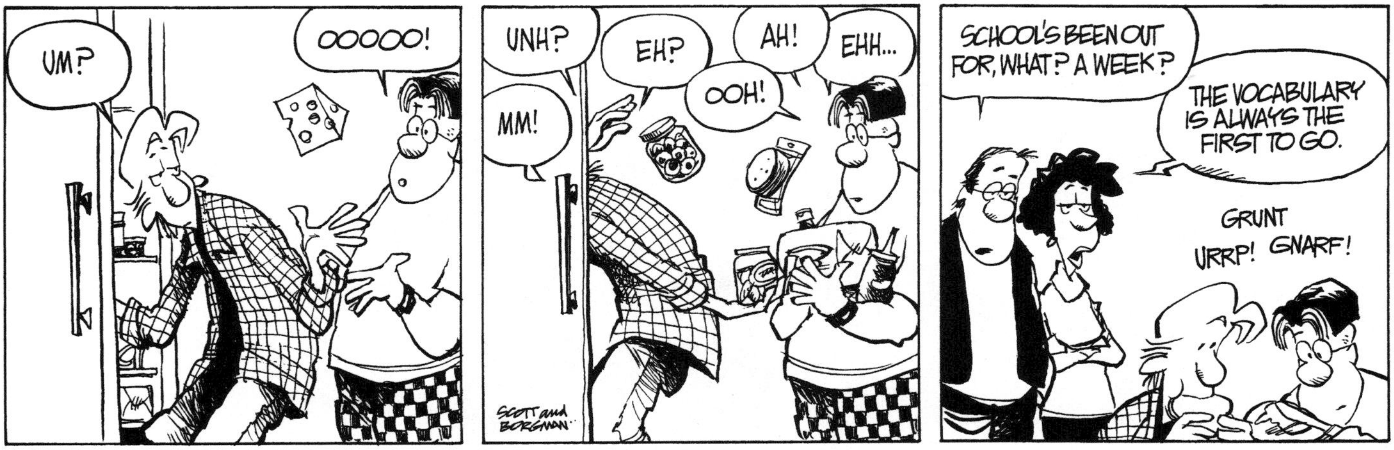
UM?
OOOOO!
UNH?
MM!
EH?
AH!
OOH!
EHH...
SCOTT and BORGMAN
SCHOOL'S BEEN OUT FOR, WHAT? A WEEK?
THE VOCABULARY IS ALWAYS THE FIRST TO GO.
GRUNT
URRP! GNARF!

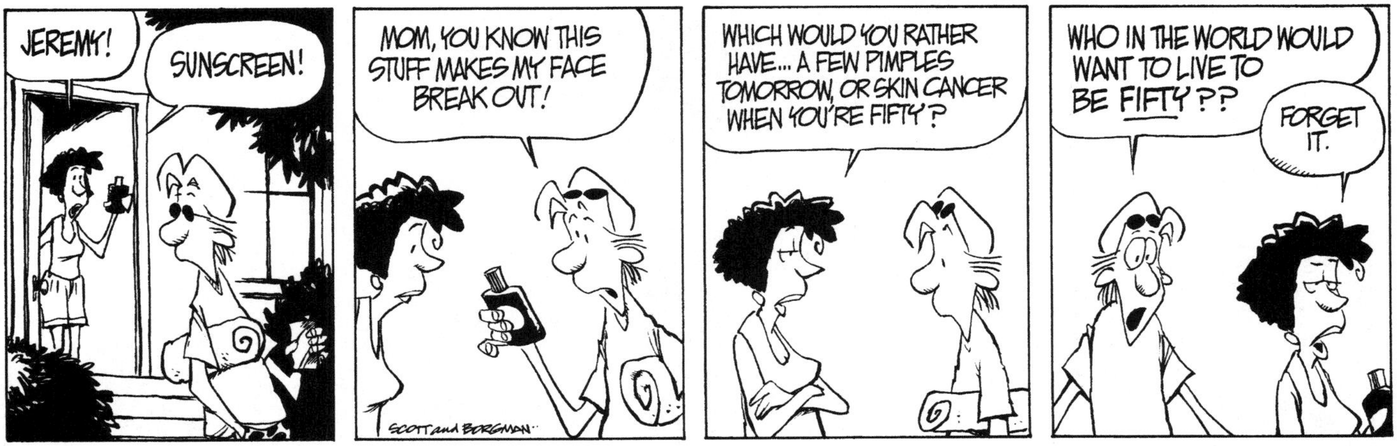
JEREMY!
SUNSCREEN!
MOM, YOU KNOW THIS STUFF MAKES MY FACE BREAK OUT!
SCOTT and BORGMAN
WHICH WOULD YOU RATHER HAVE... A FEW PIMPLES TOMORROW, OR SKIN CANCER WHEN YOU'RE FIFTY?
WHO IN THE WORLD WOULD WANT TO LIVE TO BE FIFTY??
FORGET IT.

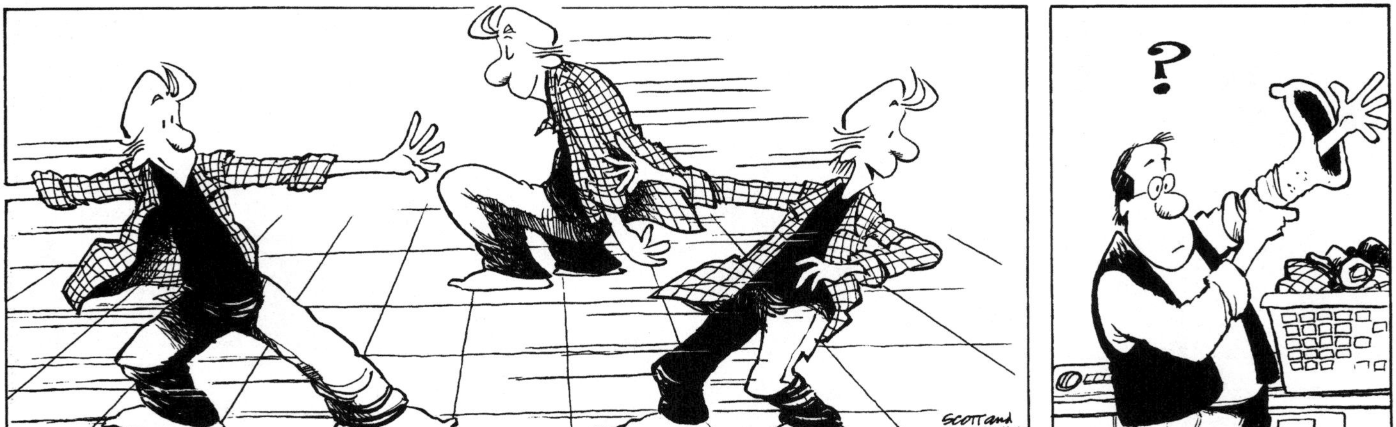
SCOTT and BORGMAN
?

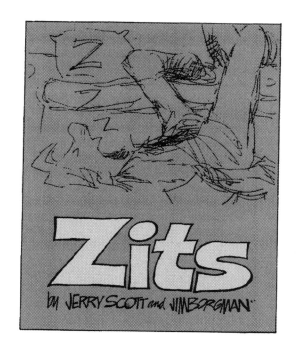

Zits

by JERRY SCOTT and JIM BORGMAN

DON'T FORGET TO PUT YOUR DIRTY DISHES IN THE SINK, JEREMY.

TALK ABOUT SCREWING UP YOUR FLOW!

THEY JUST DON'T GRASP THE ART OF SUMMER VACATION.

KATHY ASKED FOR A FEW DAYS OFF THIS WEEK, SO I NEED SOMEONE TO FILL IN FOR HER.

I DON'T SUPPOSE THAT YOU COULD --

I'LL DO IT.

YOU?? A RECEPTIONIST?

WHY NOT? I CAN ANSWER THE PHONE, PLUS I NEED THE MONEY.

THAT'S JUST CRAZY ENOUGH TO WORK!

I'LL AGREE WITH THE FIRST THREE WORDS OF THAT SENTENCE.

SCOTT and BORGMAN

I'M READY TO ROLL, DAD.

YOU CAN'T WEAR THAT TO WORK IN MY OFFICE, JEREMY!

WHY NOT?

PEOPLE WHO WORK IN AN ORTHODONTIST'S OFFICE ARE EXPECTED TO WEAR CLOTHING THAT REFLECTS THE DIGNITY OF THE DENTAL ARTS.

OKAY, I'LL BE RIGHT BACK.

WHAT???

BITE ME

THIS IS YOUR DESK, JEREMY.

WHEN A PATIENT COMES IN, I WANT YOU TO SAY, "WELCOME TO DUNCAN DENTAL. THE DOCTOR WILL BE RIGHT WITH YOU."

SCOTT and BORGMAN

WELCOME TO DUNCAN DENTAL! THE DOCTOR WILL BE RIGHT WITH YOU!

WITHOUT THE NOVELTY TEETH, PLEASE.

JUST TRYING TO LIGHTEN UP THE MOOD AROUND HERE, DAD. WHAT'S WITH THE ELEVATOR MUSIC?

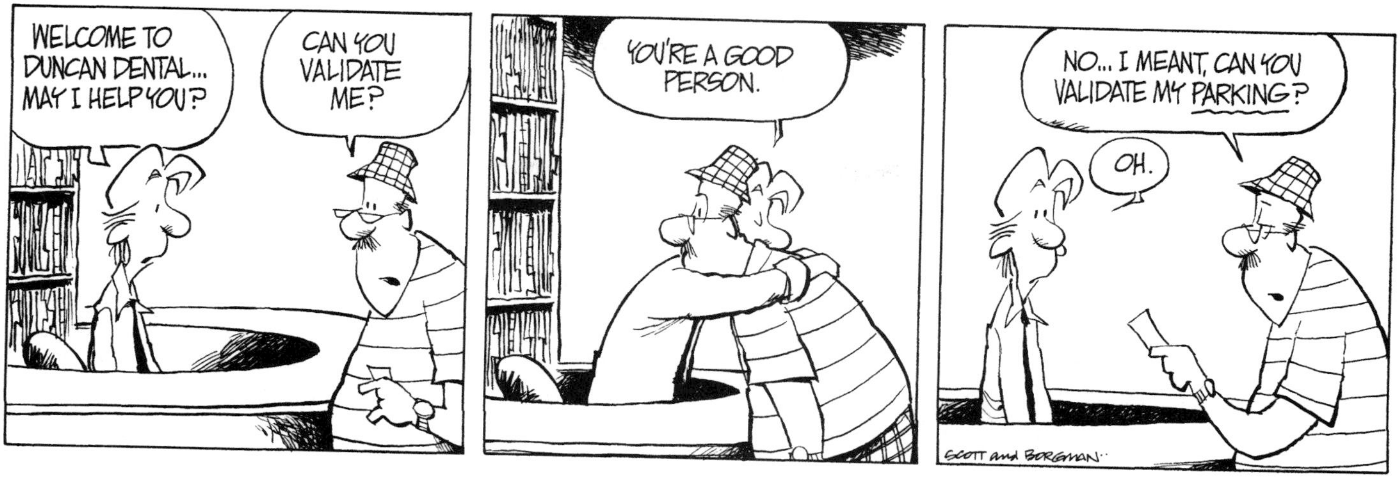
WELCOME TO DUNCAN DENTAL... MAY I HELP YOU?
CAN YOU VALIDATE ME?
YOU'RE A GOOD PERSON.
NO... I MEANT, CAN YOU VALIDATE MY PARKING?
OH.
SCOTT and BORGMAN

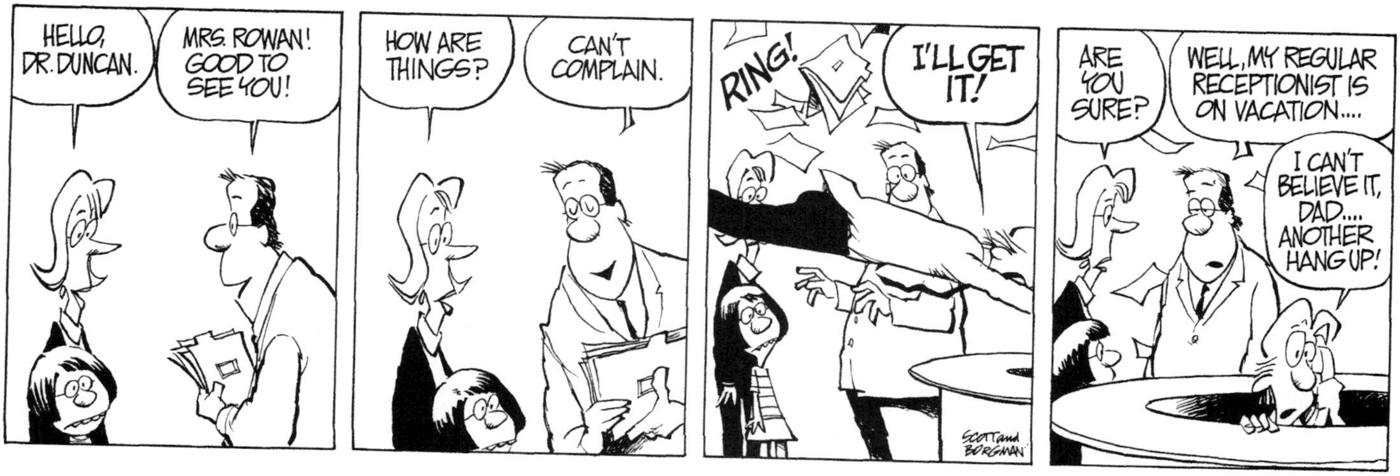
HELLO, DR. DUNCAN.
MRS. ROWAN! GOOD TO SEE YOU!
HOW ARE THINGS?
CAN'T COMPLAIN.
RING!
I'LL GET IT!
SCOTT and BORGMAN
ARE YOU SURE?
WELL, MY REGULAR RECEPTIONIST IS ON VACATION....
I CAN'T BELIEVE IT, DAD.... ANOTHER HANG UP!

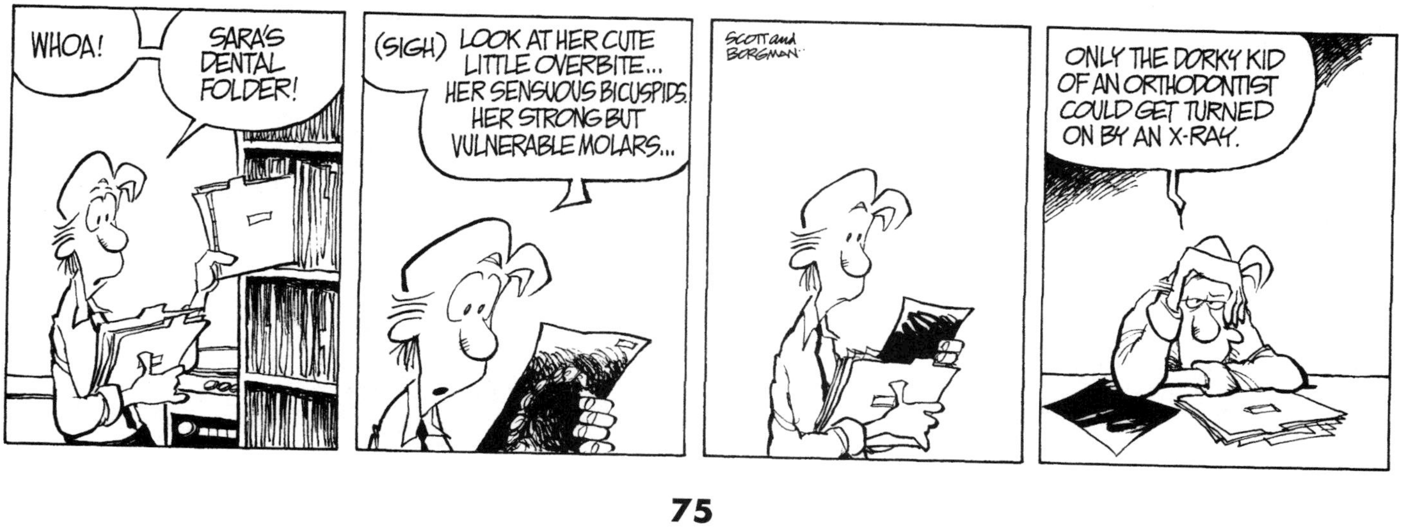
WHOA!
SARA'S DENTAL FOLDER!
(SIGH)
LOOK AT HER CUTE LITTLE OVERBITE... HER SENSUOUS BICUSPIDS. HER STRONG BUT VULNERABLE MOLARS...
SCOTT and BORGMAN
ONLY THE DORKY KID OF AN ORTHODONTIST COULD GET TURNED ON BY AN X-RAY.

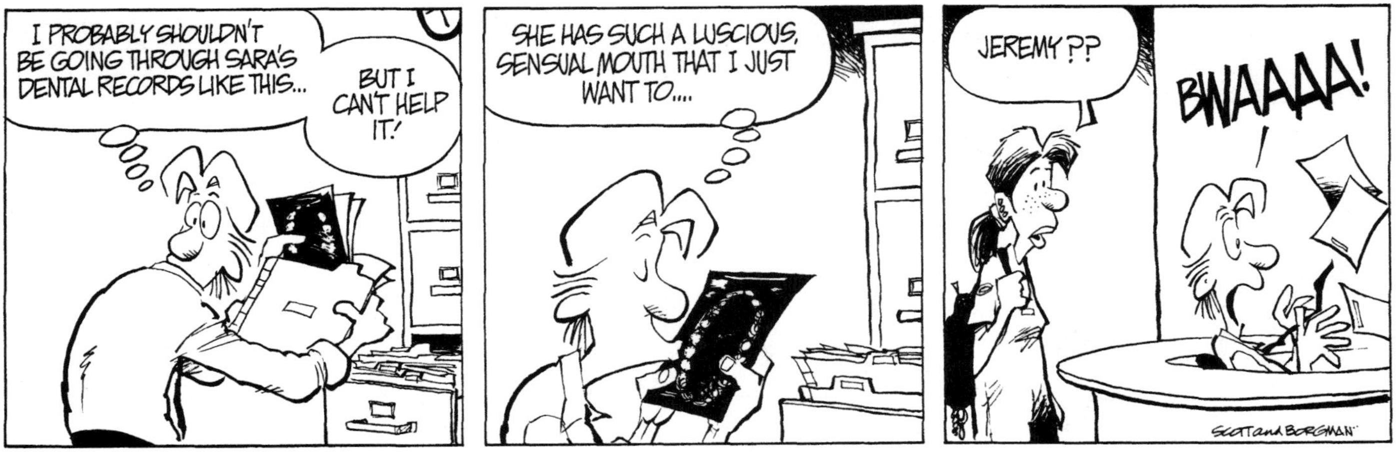
I PROBABLY SHOULDN'T BE GOING THROUGH SARA'S DENTAL RECORDS LIKE THIS...
BUT I CAN'T HELP IT!
SHE HAS SUCH A LUSCIOUS, SENSUAL MOUTH THAT I JUST WANT TO....
JEREMY??
BWAAAA!
SCOTT and BORGMAN

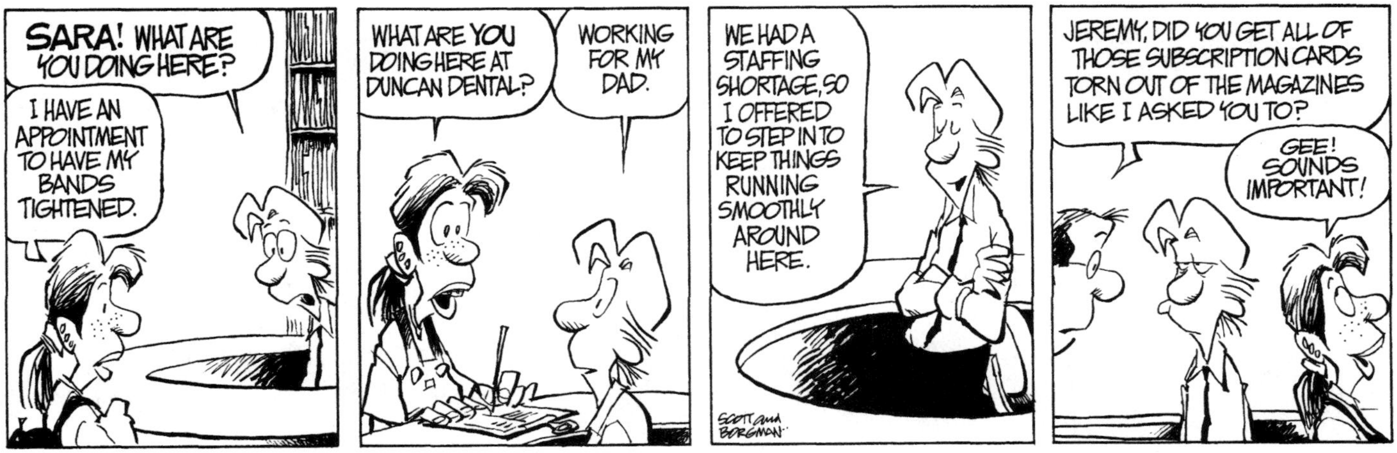
SARA! WHAT ARE YOU DOING HERE?
I HAVE AN APPOINTMENT TO HAVE MY BANDS TIGHTENED.
WHAT ARE YOU DOING HERE AT DUNCAN DENTAL?
WORKING FOR MY DAD.
WE HAD A STAFFING SHORTAGE, SO I OFFERED TO STEP IN TO KEEP THINGS RUNNING SMOOTHLY AROUND HERE.
SCOTT and BORGMAN
JEREMY, DID YOU GET ALL OF THOSE SUBSCRIPTION CARDS TORN OUT OF THE MAGAZINES LIKE I ASKED YOU TO?
GEE! SOUNDS IMPORTANT!

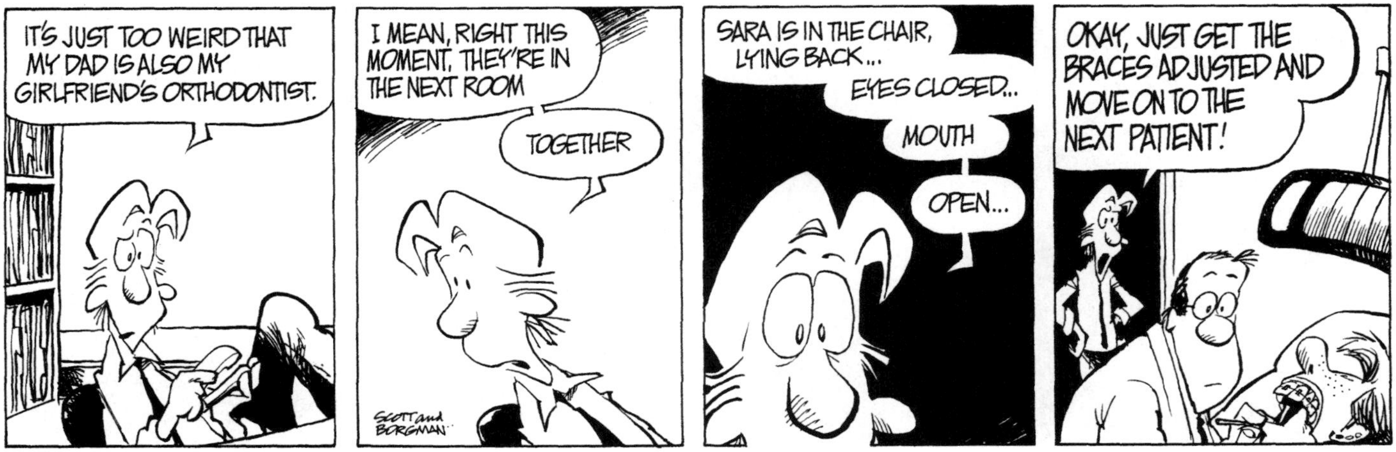
IT'S JUST TOO WEIRD THAT MY DAD IS ALSO MY GIRLFRIEND'S ORTHODONTIST.
I MEAN, RIGHT THIS MOMENT, THEY'RE IN THE NEXT ROOM
TOGETHER
SCOTT and BORGMAN
SARA IS IN THE CHAIR, LYING BACK...
EYES CLOSED...
MOUTH
OPEN...
OKAY, JUST GET THE BRACES ADJUSTED AND MOVE ON TO THE NEXT PATIENT!

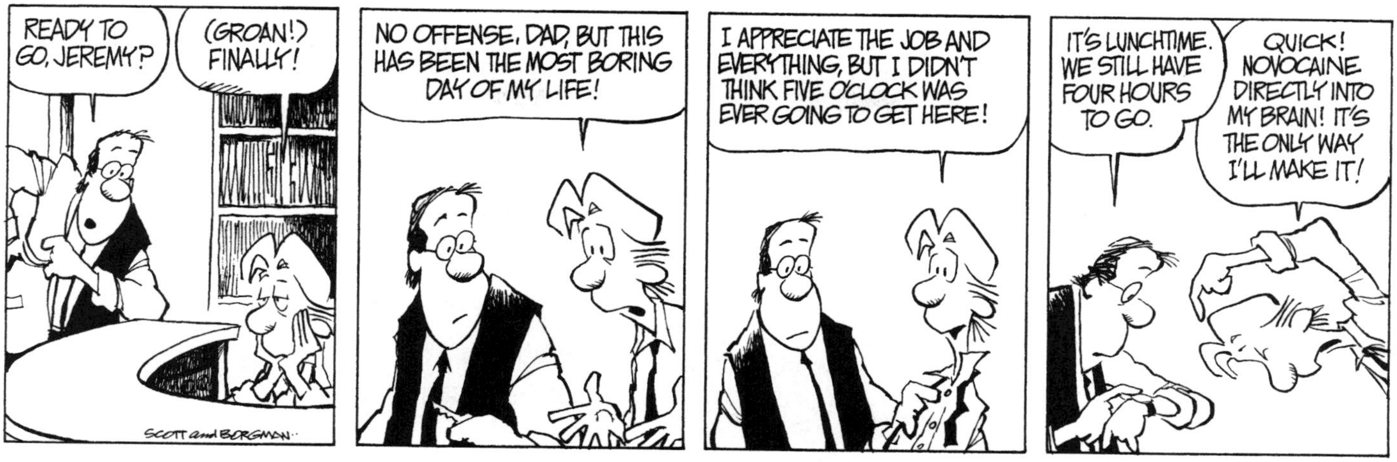
READY TO GO, JEREMY?
(GROAN!) FINALLY!
SCOTT and BORGMAN
NO OFFENSE, DAD, BUT THIS HAS BEEN THE MOST BORING DAY OF MY LIFE!
I APPRECIATE THE JOB AND EVERYTHING, BUT I DIDN'T THINK FIVE O'CLOCK WAS EVER GOING TO GET HERE!
IT'S LUNCHTIME. WE STILL HAVE FOUR HOURS TO GO.
QUICK! NOVOCAINE DIRECTLY INTO MY BRAIN! IT'S THE ONLY WAY I'LL MAKE IT!

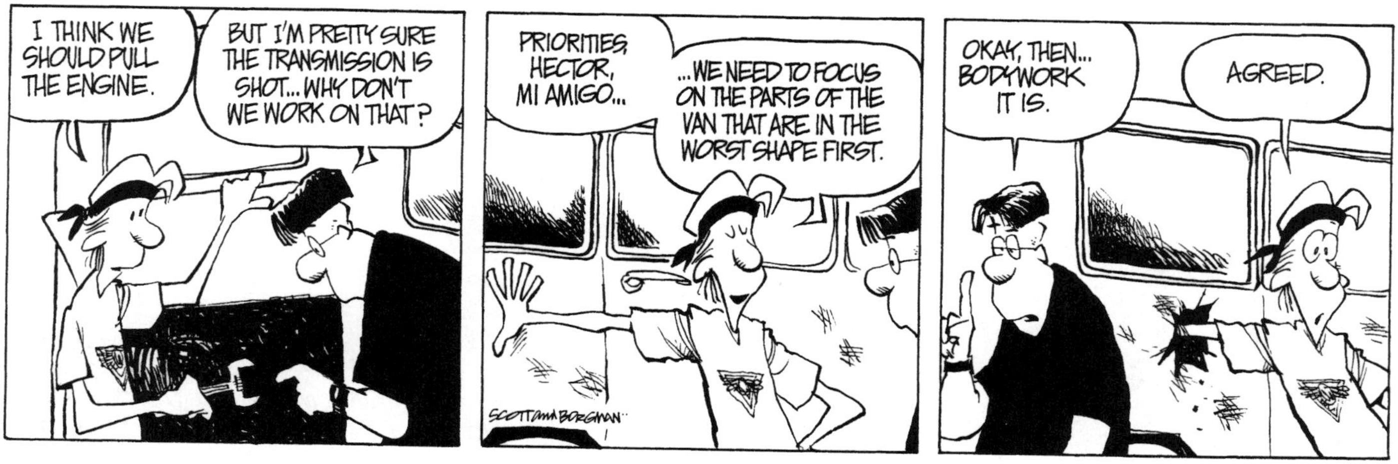
I THINK WE SHOULD PULL THE ENGINE.
BUT I'M PRETTY SURE THE TRANSMISSION IS SHOT... WHY DON'T WE WORK ON THAT?
PRIORITIES, HECTOR, MI AMIGO...
...WE NEED TO FOCUS ON THE PARTS OF THE VAN THAT ARE IN THE WORST SHAPE FIRST.
SCOTT and BORGMAN
OKAY, THEN... BODYWORK IT IS.
AGREED.

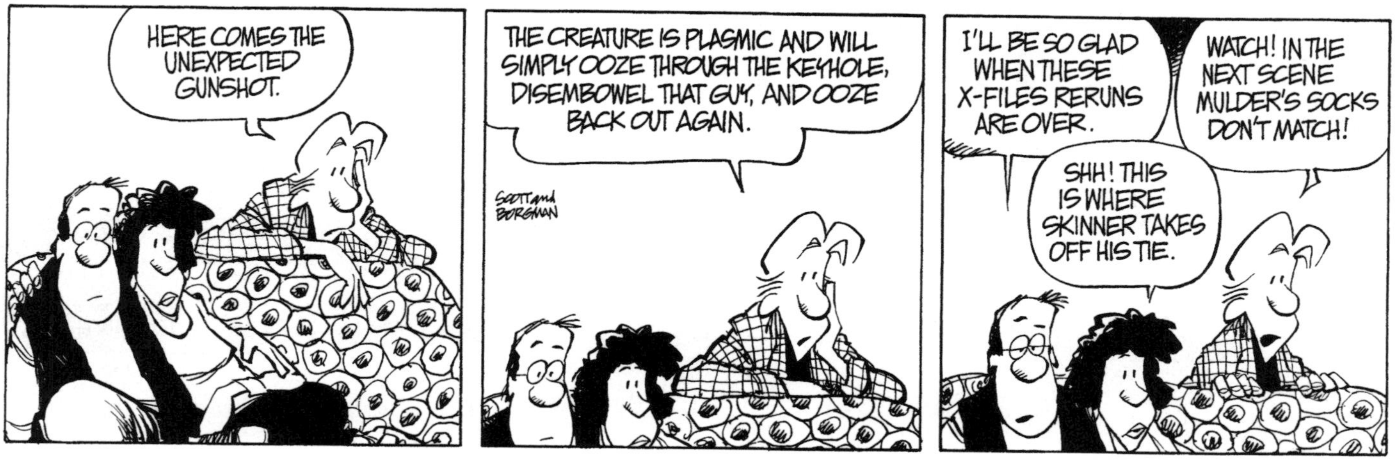
HERE COMES THE UNEXPECTED GUNSHOT.
THE CREATURE IS PLASMIC AND WILL SIMPLY OOZE THROUGH THE KEYHOLE, DISEMBOWEL THAT GUY, AND OOZE BACK OUT AGAIN.
SCOTT and BORGMAN
I'LL BE SO GLAD WHEN THESE X-FILES RERUNS ARE OVER.
WATCH! IN THE NEXT SCENE MULDER'S SOCKS DON'T MATCH!
SHH! THIS IS WHERE SKINNER TAKES OFF HIS TIE.

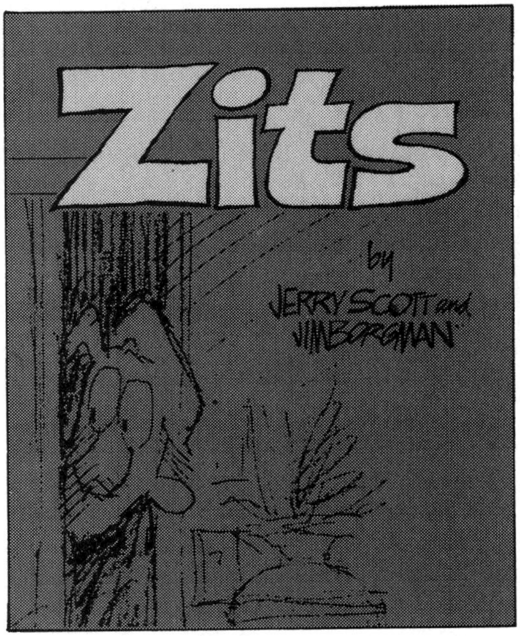
Zits
by
JERRY SCOTT and
JIM BORGMAN

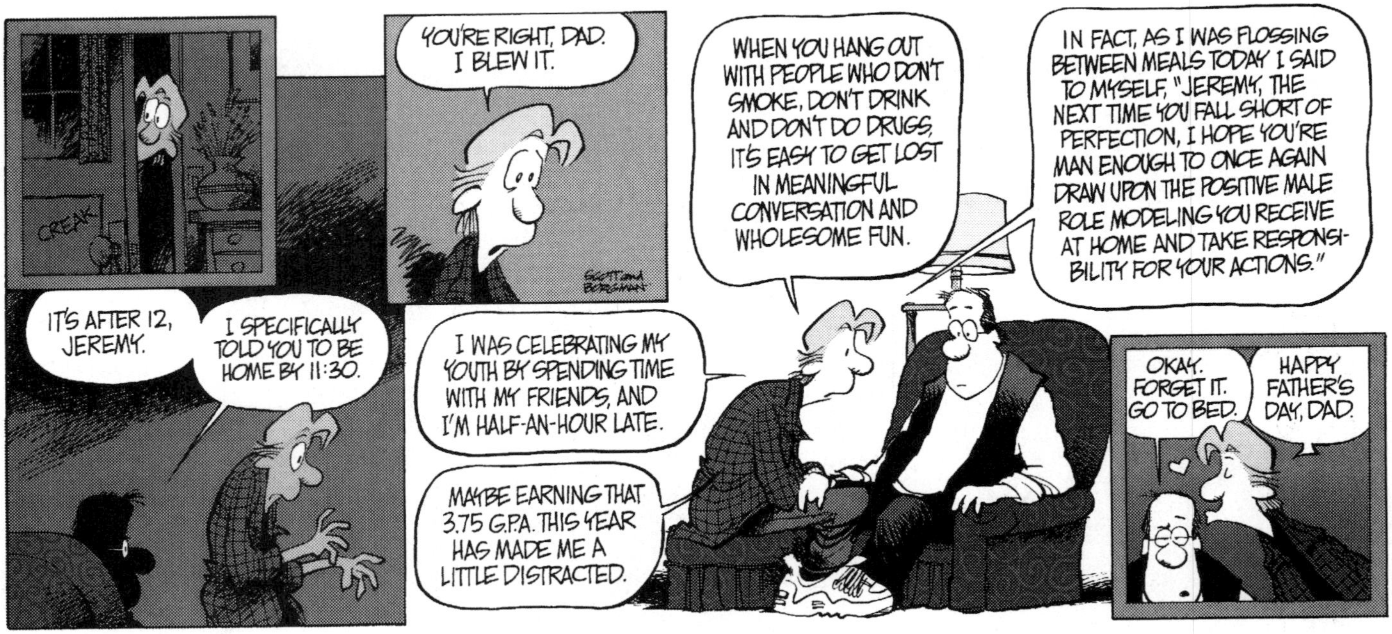
CREAK
IT'S AFTER 12, JEREMY.
I SPECIFICALLY TOLD YOU TO BE HOME BY 11:30.
YOU'RE RIGHT, DAD. I BLEW IT.
I WAS CELEBRATING MY YOUTH BY SPENDING TIME WITH MY FRIENDS, AND I'M HALF-AN-HOUR LATE.
MAYBE EARNING THAT 3.75 G.P.A. THIS YEAR HAS MADE ME A LITTLE DISTRACTED.
WHEN YOU HANG OUT WITH PEOPLE WHO DON'T SMOKE, DON'T DRINK AND DON'T DO DRUGS, IT'S EASY TO GET LOST IN MEANINGFUL CONVERSATION AND WHOLESOME FUN.
IN FACT, AS I WAS FLOSSING BETWEEN MEALS TODAY I SAID TO MYSELF, "JEREMY, THE NEXT TIME YOU FALL SHORT OF PERFECTION, I HOPE YOU'RE MAN ENOUGH TO ONCE AGAIN DRAW UPON THE POSITIVE MALE ROLE MODELING YOU RECEIVE AT HOME AND TAKE RESPONSIBILITY FOR YOUR ACTIONS."
OKAY. FORGET IT. GO TO BED.
HAPPY FATHER'S DAY, DAD.
SCOTT and BORGMAN

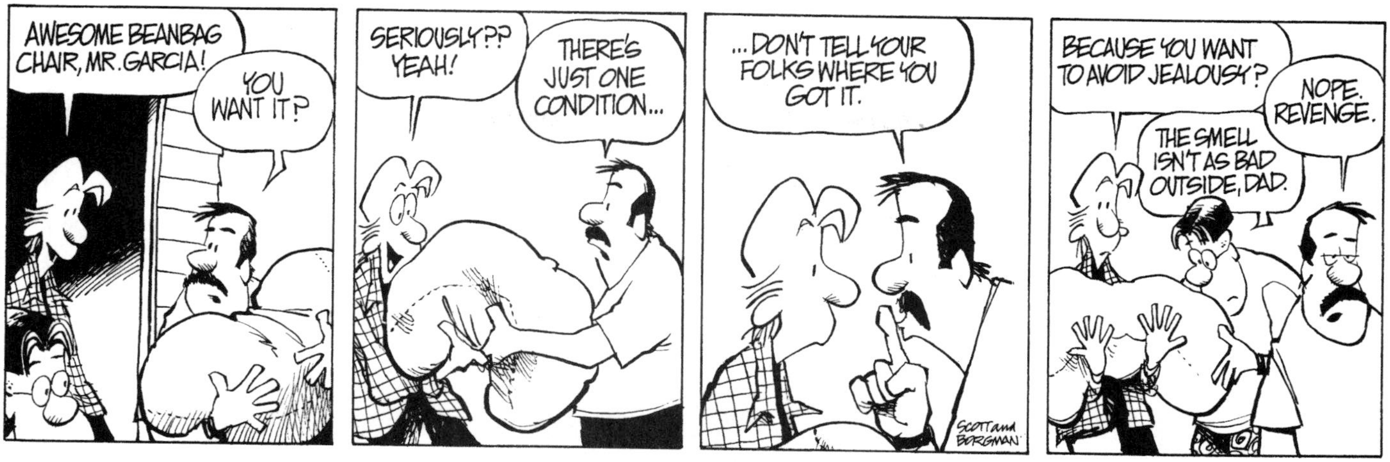
AWESOME BEANBAG CHAIR, MR. GARCIA!
YOU WANT IT?
SERIOUSLY?? YEAH!
THERE'S JUST ONE CONDITION...
...DON'T TELL YOUR FOLKS WHERE YOU GOT IT.
BECAUSE YOU WANT TO AVOID JEALOUSY?
NOPE. REVENGE.
THE SMELL ISN'T AS BAD OUTSIDE, DAD.

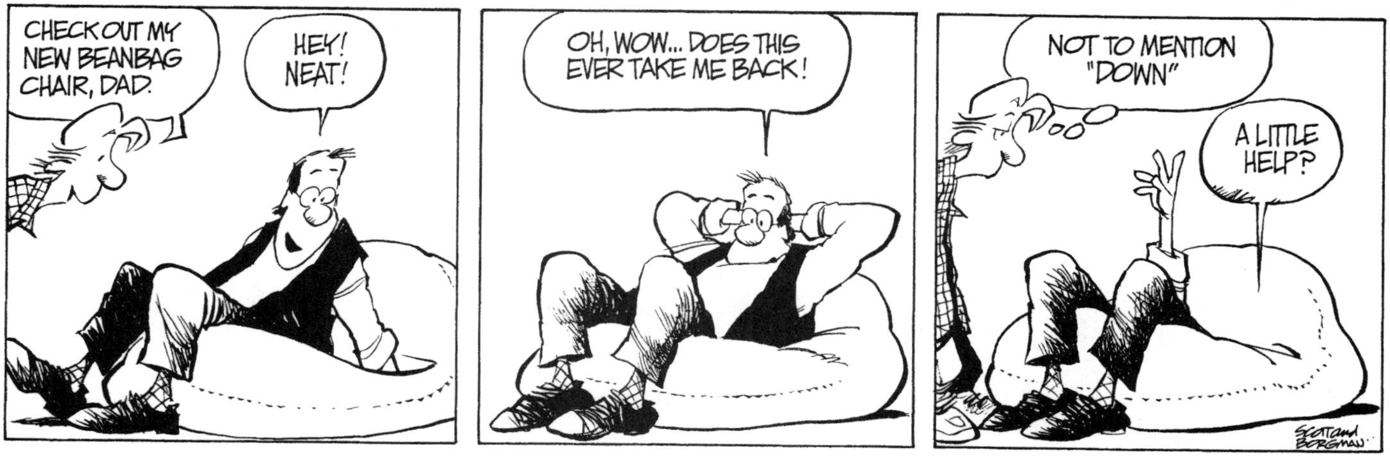
CHECK OUT MY NEW BEANBAG CHAIR, DAD.
HEY! NEAT!
OH, WOW... DOES THIS EVER TAKE ME BACK!
NOT TO MENTION "DOWN"
A LITTLE HELP?

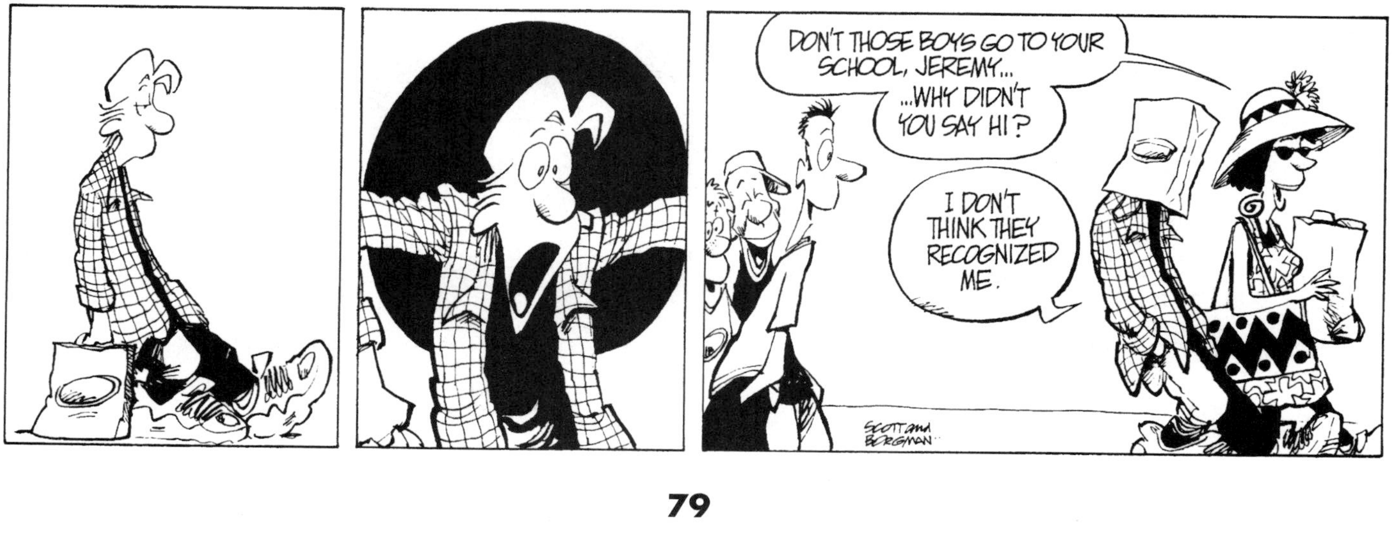
DON'T THOSE BOYS GO TO YOUR SCHOOL, JEREMY...
...WHY DIDN'T YOU SAY HI?
I DON'T THINK THEY RECOGNIZED ME.

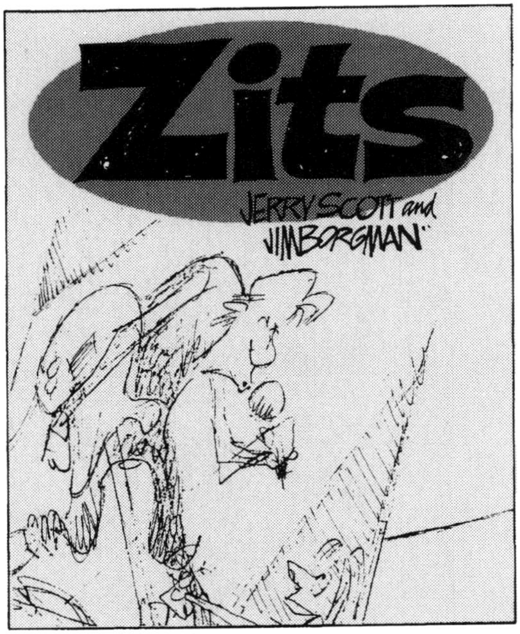
Zits
JERRY SCOTT and JIM BORGMAN

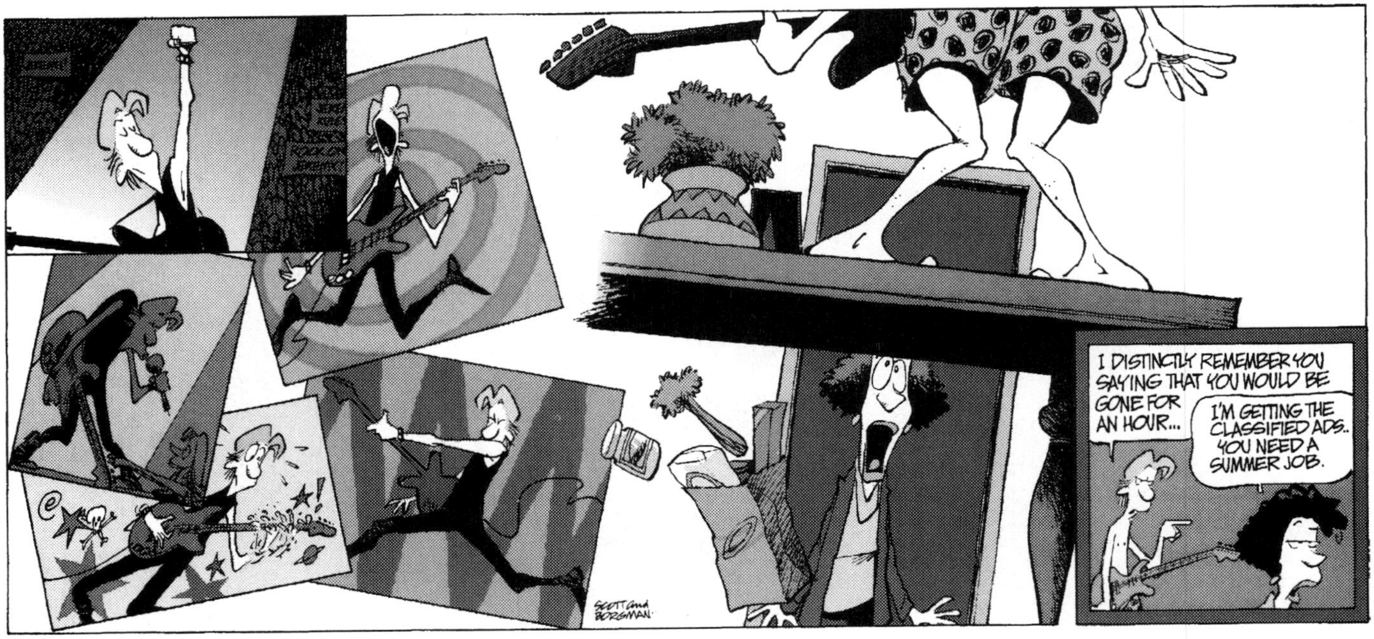
I DISTINCTLY REMEMBER YOU SAYING THAT YOU WOULD BE GONE FOR AN HOUR...
I'M GETTING THE CLASSIFIED ADS.. YOU NEED A SUMMER JOB.
SCOTT and BORGMAN

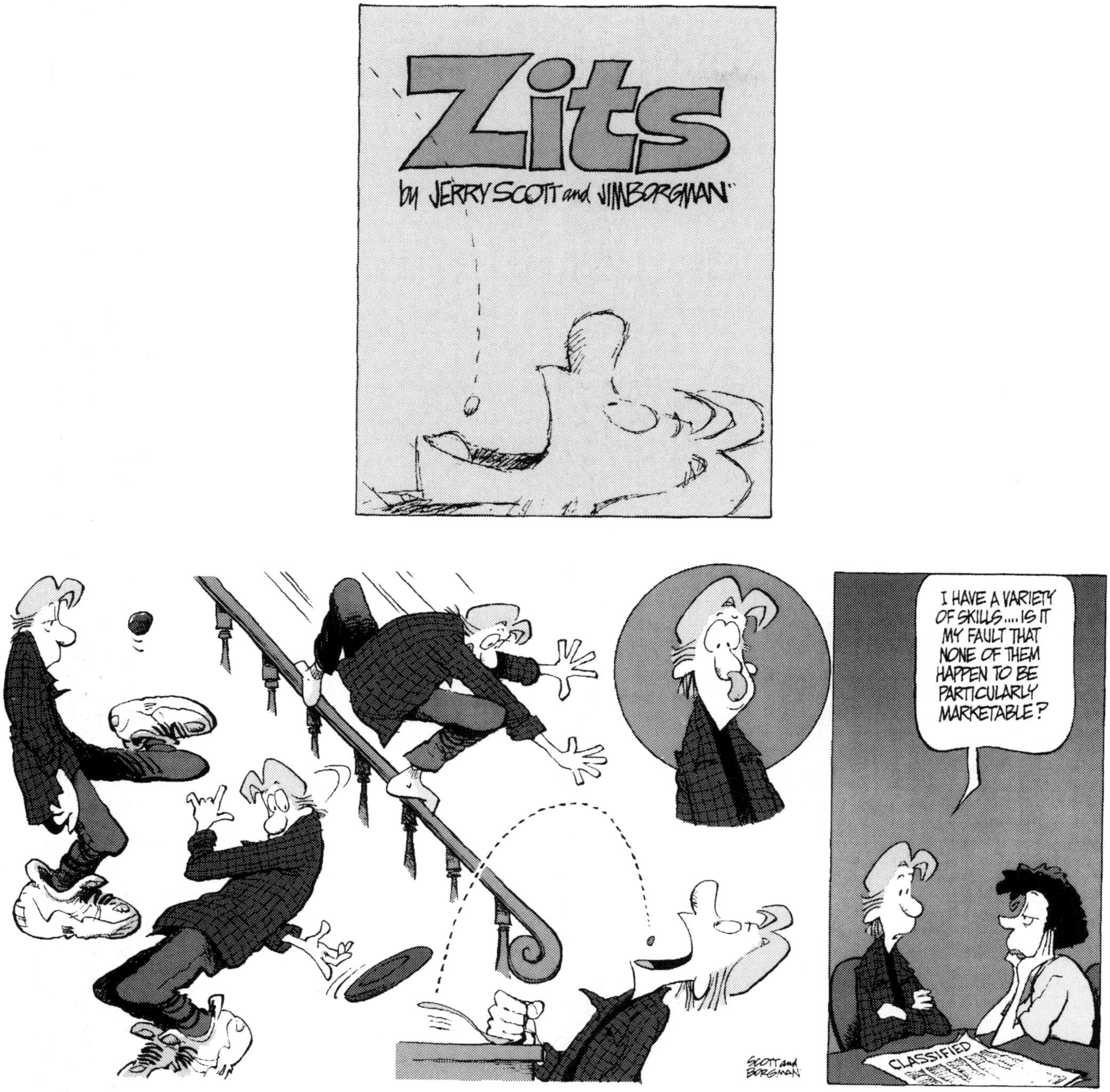
Zits
by JERRY SCOTT and JIM BORGMAN
I HAVE A VARIETY OF SKILLS.... IS IT MY FAULT THAT NONE OF THEM HAPPEN TO BE PARTICULARLY MARKETABLE?
CLASSIFIED
SCOTT and BORGMAN

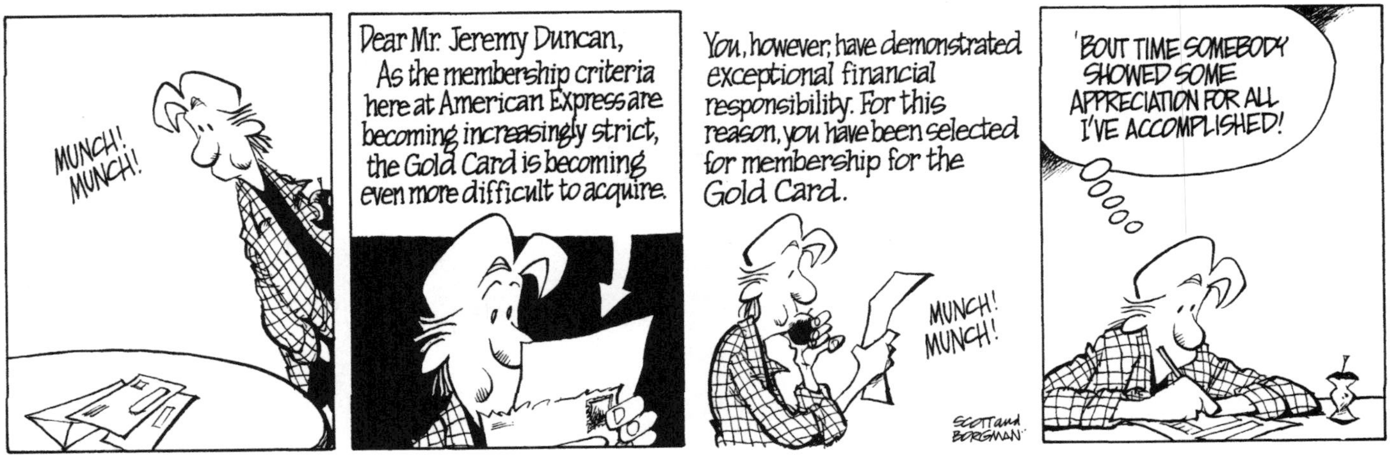
MUNCH! MUNCH!
Dear Mr. Jeremy Duncan,
As the membership criteria here at American Express are becoming increasingly strict, the Gold Card is becoming even more difficult to acquire.
You, however, have demonstrated exceptional financial responsibility. For this reason, you have been selected for membership for the Gold Card.
MUNCH! MUNCH!
SCOTT and BORGMAN
'BOUT TIME SOMEBODY SHOWED SOME APPRECIATION FOR ALL I'VE ACCOMPLISHED!

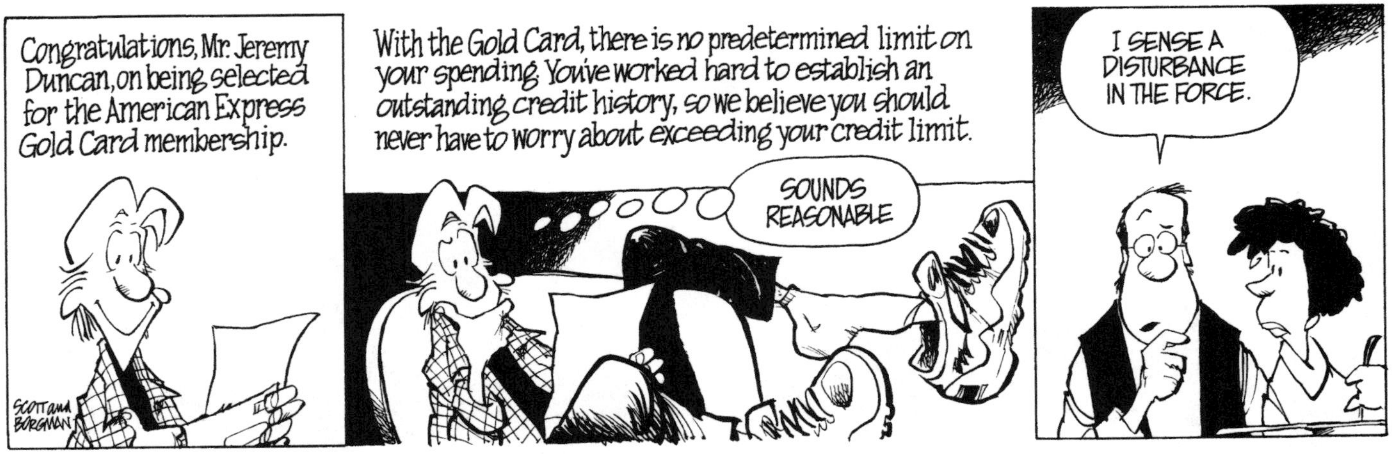
Congratulations, Mr. Jeremy Duncan, on being selected for the American Express Gold Card membership.
SCOTT and BORGMAN
With the Gold Card, there is no predetermined limit on your spending. You've worked hard to establish an outstanding credit history, so we believe you should never have to worry about exceeding your credit limit.
SOUNDS REASONABLE
I SENSE A DISTURBANCE IN THE FORCE.

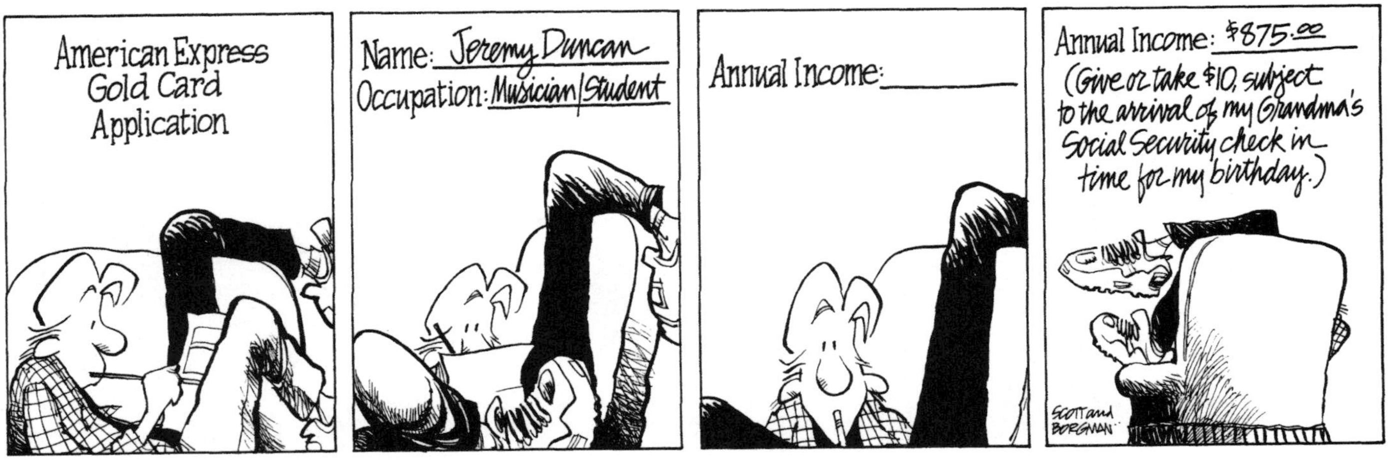
American Express Gold Card Application
Name: Jeremy Duncan
Occupation: Musician/Student
Annual Income:
Annual Income: $875.00
(Give or take $10, subject to the arrival of my Grandma's Social Security check in time for my birthday.)
SCOTT and BORGMAN

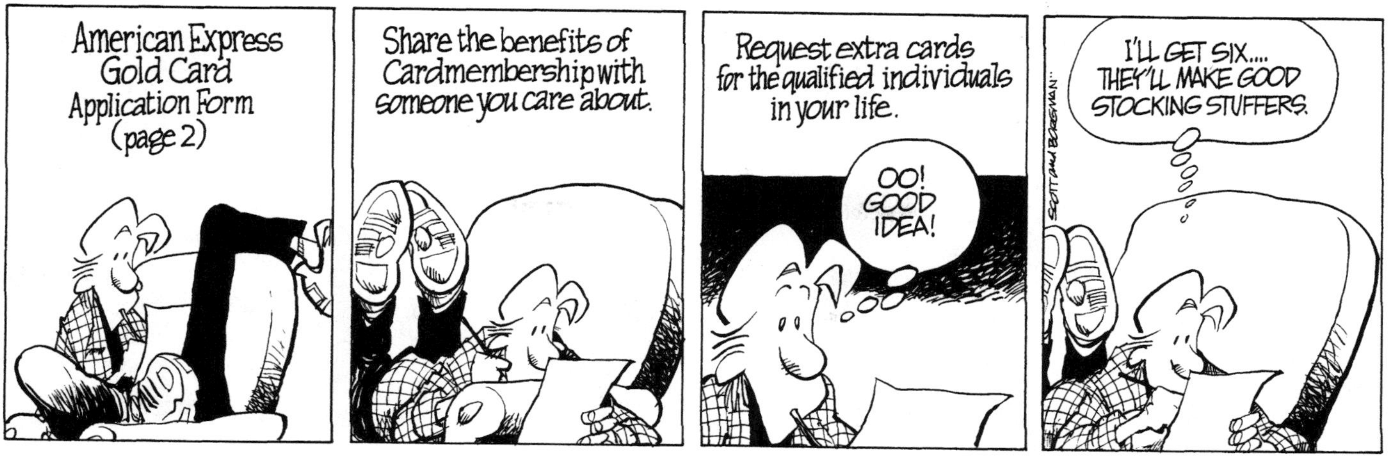
American Express Gold Card Application Form (page 2)
Share the benefits of Cardmembership with someone you care about.
Request extra cards for the qualified individuals in your life.
OO! GOOD IDEA!
SCOTT and BORGMAN
I'LL GET SIX.... THEY'LL MAKE GOOD STOCKING STUFFERS.

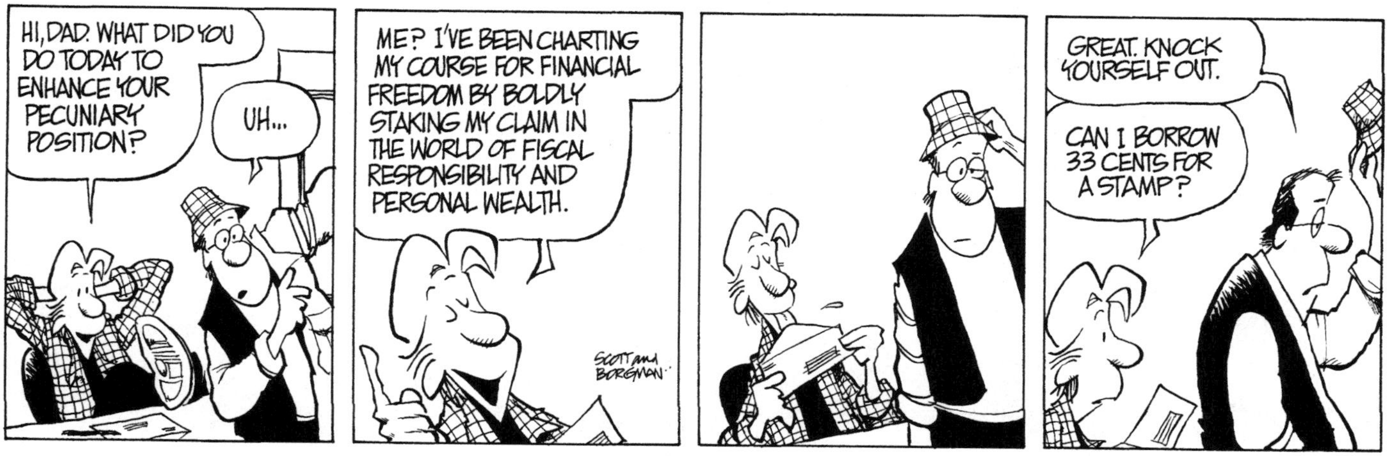
HI, DAD. WHAT DID YOU DO TODAY TO ENHANCE YOUR PECUNIARY POSITION?
UH...
ME? I'VE BEEN CHARTING MY COURSE FOR FINANCIAL FREEDOM BY BOLDLY STAKING MY CLAIM IN THE WORLD OF FISCAL RESPONSIBILITY AND PERSONAL WEALTH.
SCOTT and BORGMAN
GREAT. KNOCK YOURSELF OUT.
CAN I BORROW 33 CENTS FOR A STAMP?

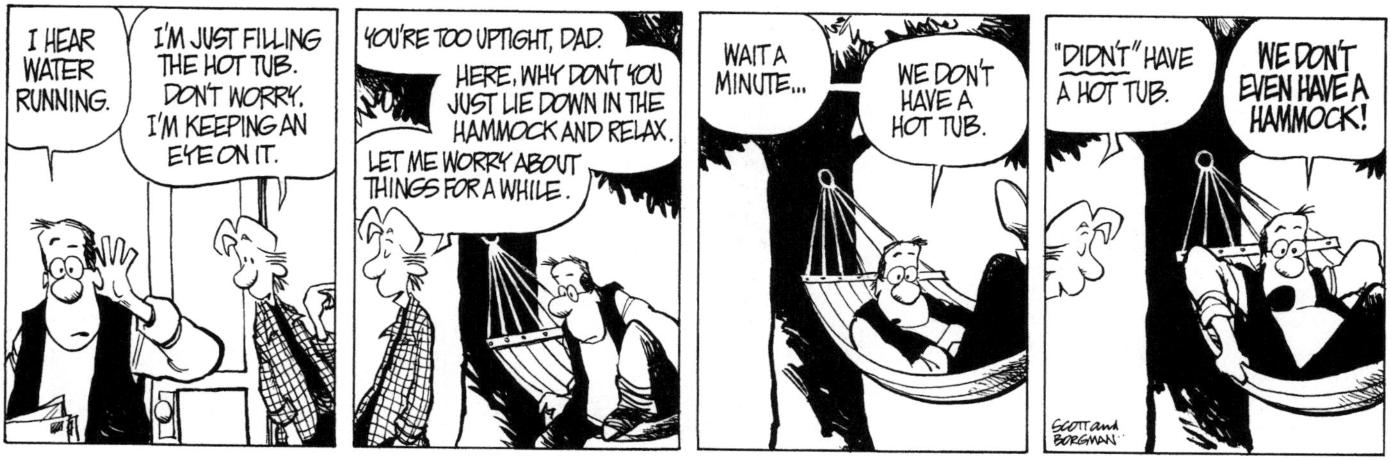
I HEAR WATER RUNNING.
I'M JUST FILLING THE HOT TUB. DON'T WORRY. I'M KEEPING AN EYE ON IT.
YOU'RE TOO UPTIGHT, DAD.
HERE, WHY DON'T YOU JUST LIE DOWN IN THE HAMMOCK AND RELAX.
LET ME WORRY ABOUT THINGS FOR A WHILE.
WAIT A MINUTE...
WE DON'T HAVE A HOT TUB.
"DIDN'T" HAVE A HOT TUB.
WE DON'T EVEN HAVE A HAMMOCK!
SCOTT and BORGMAN

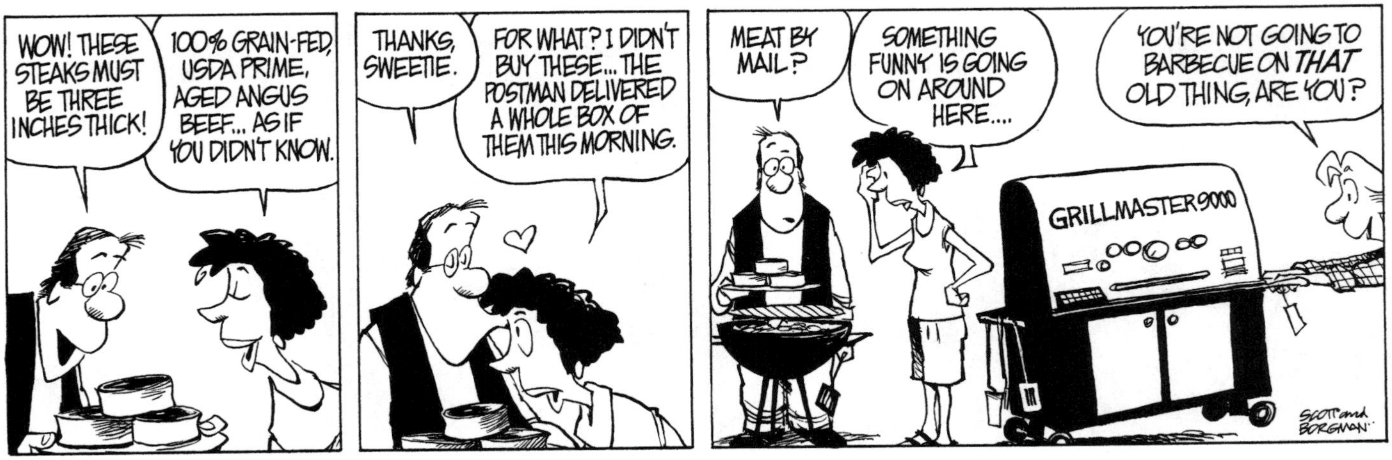
WOW! THESE STEAKS MUST BE THREE INCHES THICK!
100% GRAIN-FED, USDA PRIME, AGED ANGUS BEEF... AS IF YOU DIDN'T KNOW.
THANKS, SWEETIE.
FOR WHAT? I DIDN'T BUY THESE... THE POSTMAN DELIVERED A WHOLE BOX OF THEM THIS MORNING.
MEAT BY MAIL?
SOMETHING FUNNY IS GOING ON AROUND HERE....
YOU'RE NOT GOING TO BARBECUE ON *THAT* OLD THING, ARE YOU?
GRILLMASTER 9000
SCOTT and BORGMAN

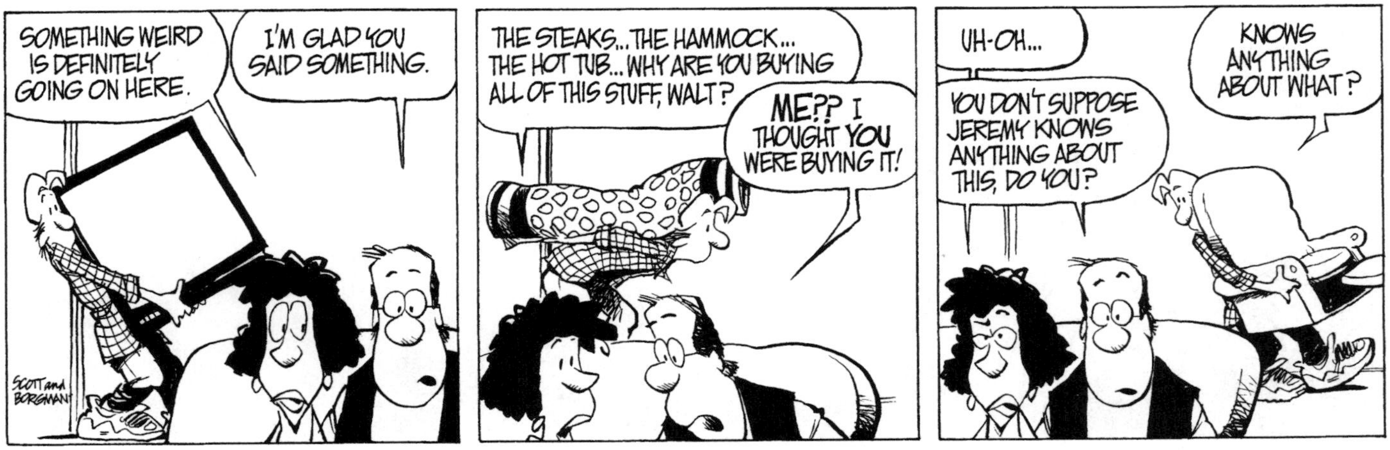
SOMETHING WEIRD IS DEFINITELY GOING ON HERE.
I'M GLAD YOU SAID SOMETHING.
SCOTT and BORGMAN
THE STEAKS... THE HAMMOCK... THE HOT TUB... WHY ARE YOU BUYING ALL OF THIS STUFF, WALT?
ME?? I THOUGHT **YOU** WERE BUYING IT!
UH-OH...
YOU DON'T SUPPOSE JEREMY KNOWS ANYTHING ABOUT THIS, DO YOU?
KNOWS ANYTHING ABOUT WHAT?

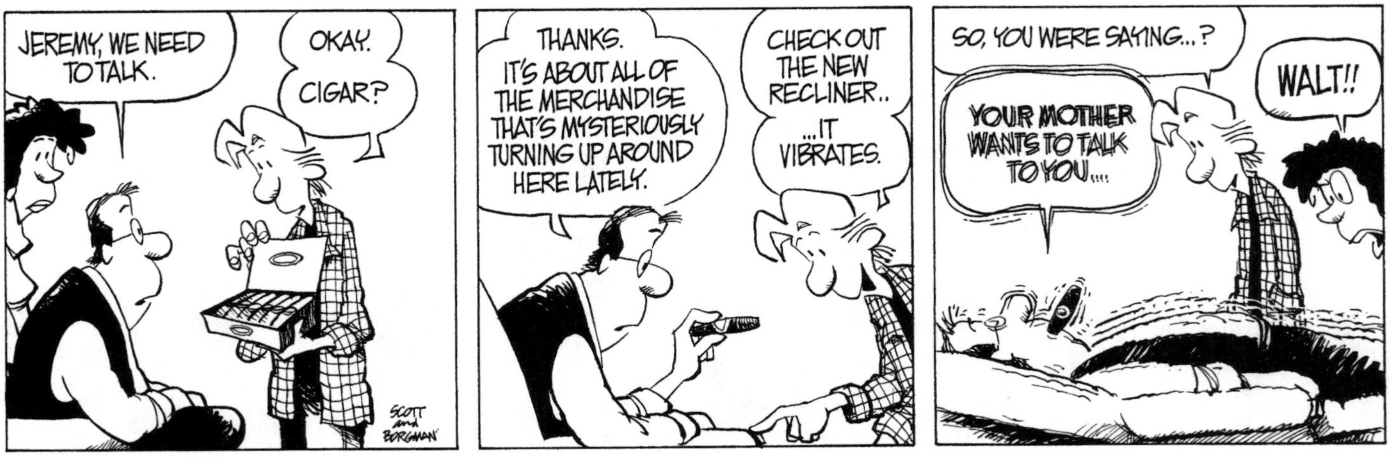
JEREMY, WE NEED TO TALK.
OKAY.
CIGAR?
SCOTT and BORGMAN
THANKS.
IT'S ABOUT ALL OF THE MERCHANDISE THAT'S MYSTERIOUSLY TURNING UP AROUND HERE LATELY.
CHECK OUT THE NEW RECLINER..
...IT VIBRATES.
SO, YOU WERE SAYING...?
YOUR MOTHER WANTS TO TALK TO YOU....
WALT!!

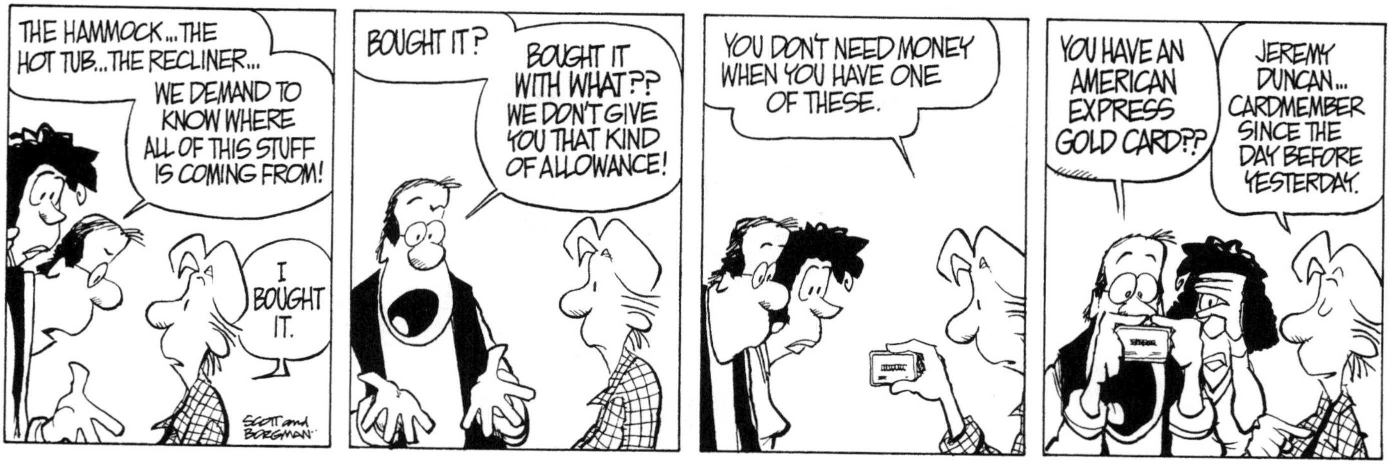
THE HAMMOCK...THE HOT TUB...THE RECLINER...
WE DEMAND TO KNOW WHERE ALL OF THIS STUFF IS COMING FROM!
I BOUGHT IT.
SCOTT and BORGMAN
BOUGHT IT?
BOUGHT IT WITH WHAT?? WE DON'T GIVE YOU THAT KIND OF ALLOWANCE!
YOU DON'T NEED MONEY WHEN YOU HAVE ONE OF THESE.
YOU HAVE AN AMERICAN EXPRESS GOLD CARD??
JEREMY DUNCAN... CARDMEMBER SINCE THE DAY BEFORE YESTERDAY.

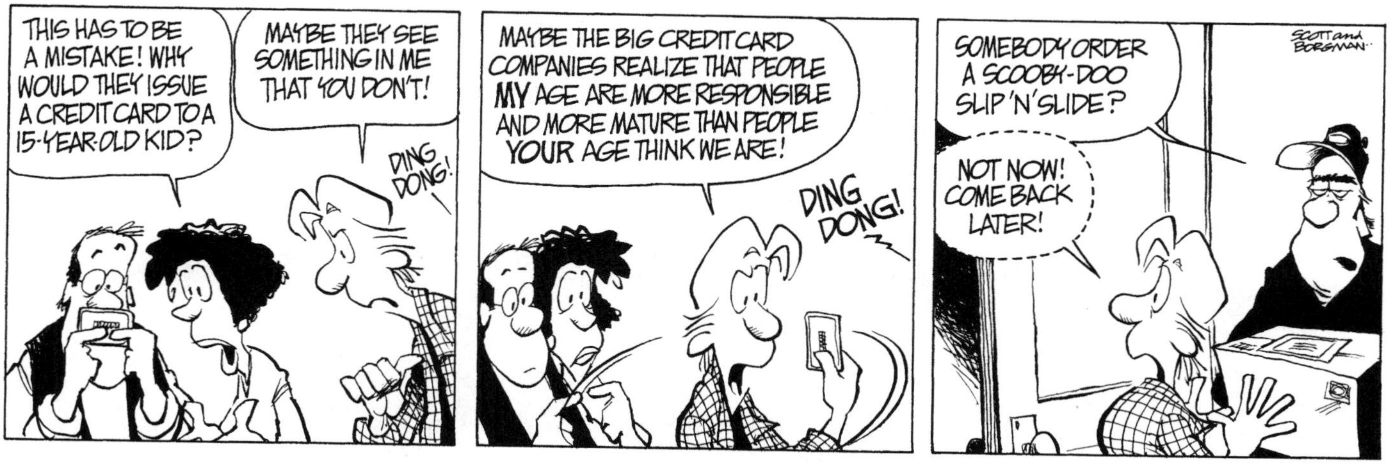
THIS HAS TO BE A MISTAKE! WHY WOULD THEY ISSUE A CREDIT CARD TO A 15-YEAR-OLD KID?
MAYBE THEY SEE SOMETHING IN ME THAT YOU DON'T!
DING DONG!
MAYBE THE BIG CREDIT CARD COMPANIES REALIZE THAT PEOPLE MY AGE ARE MORE RESPONSIBLE AND MORE MATURE THAN PEOPLE YOUR AGE THINK WE ARE!
DING DONG!
SCOTT and BORGMAN
SOMEBODY ORDER A SCOOBY-DOO SLIP 'N' SLIDE?
NOT NOW! COME BACK LATER!

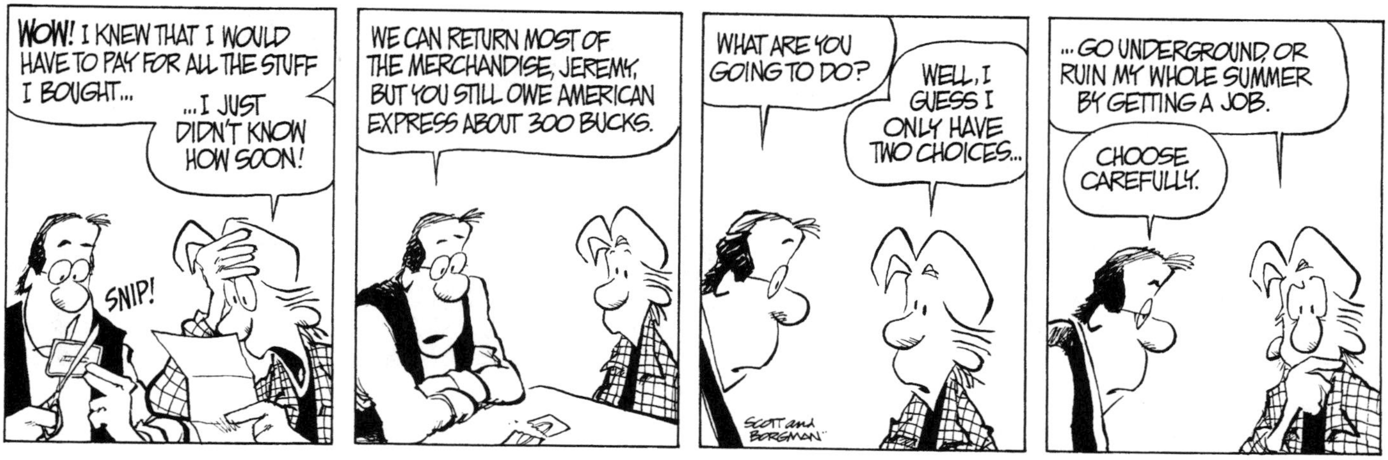
WOW! I KNEW THAT I WOULD HAVE TO PAY FOR ALL THE STUFF I BOUGHT...
...I JUST DIDN'T KNOW HOW SOON!
SNIP!
WE CAN RETURN MOST OF THE MERCHANDISE, JEREMY, BUT YOU STILL OWE AMERICAN EXPRESS ABOUT 300 BUCKS.
WHAT ARE YOU GOING TO DO?
WELL, I GUESS I ONLY HAVE TWO CHOICES...
SCOTT and BORGMAN
...GO UNDERGROUND, OR RUIN MY WHOLE SUMMER BY GETTING A JOB.
CHOOSE CAREFULLY.

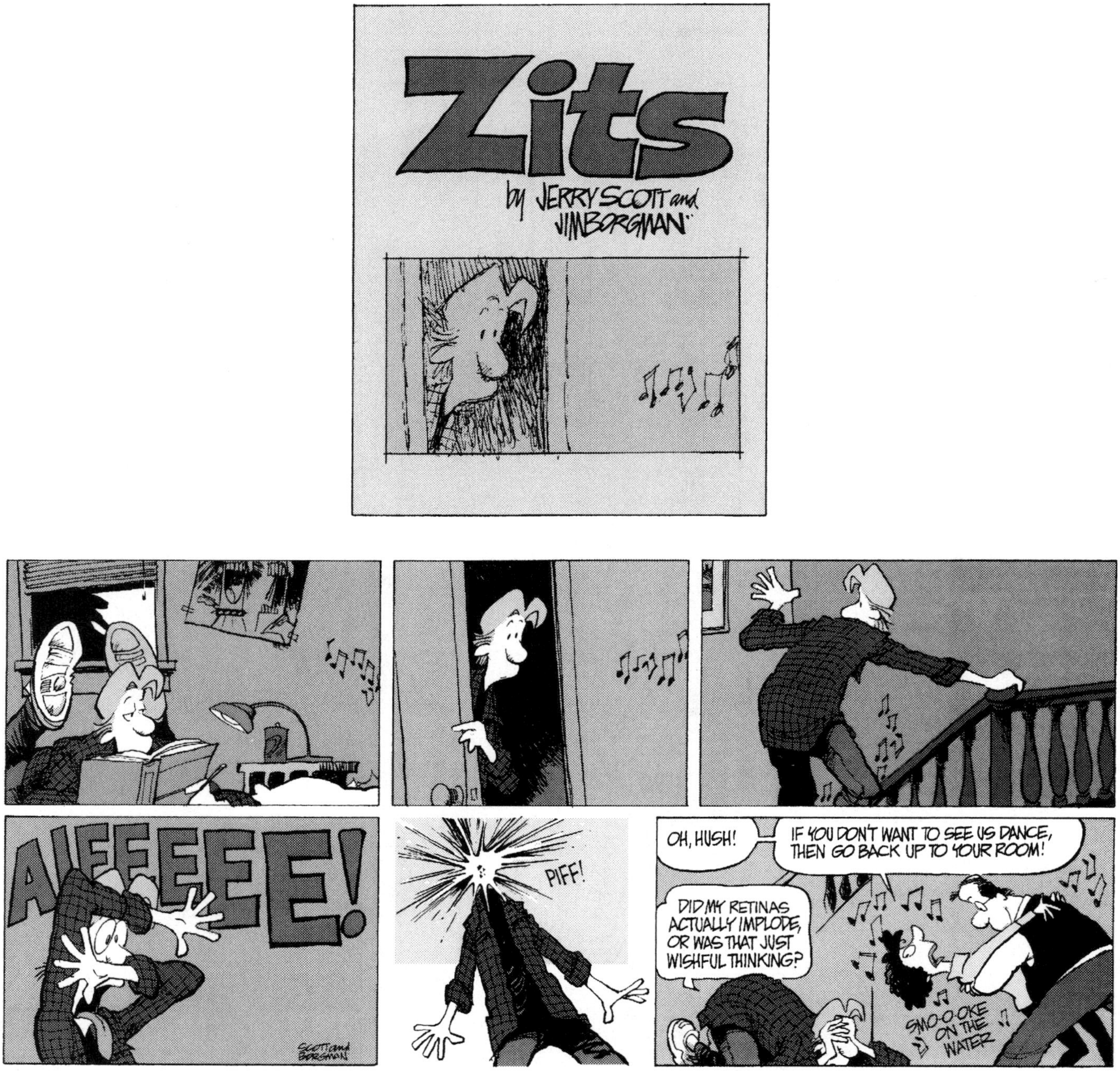
Zits
by JERRY SCOTT and JIM BORGMAN
AIEEEEE!
SCOTT and BORGMAN
PIFF!
OH, HUSH!
IF YOU DON'T WANT TO SEE US DANCE, THEN GO BACK UP TO YOUR ROOM!
DID MY RETINAS ACTUALLY IMPLODE, OR WAS THAT JUST WISHFUL THINKING?
SMO-O-OKE ON THE WATER

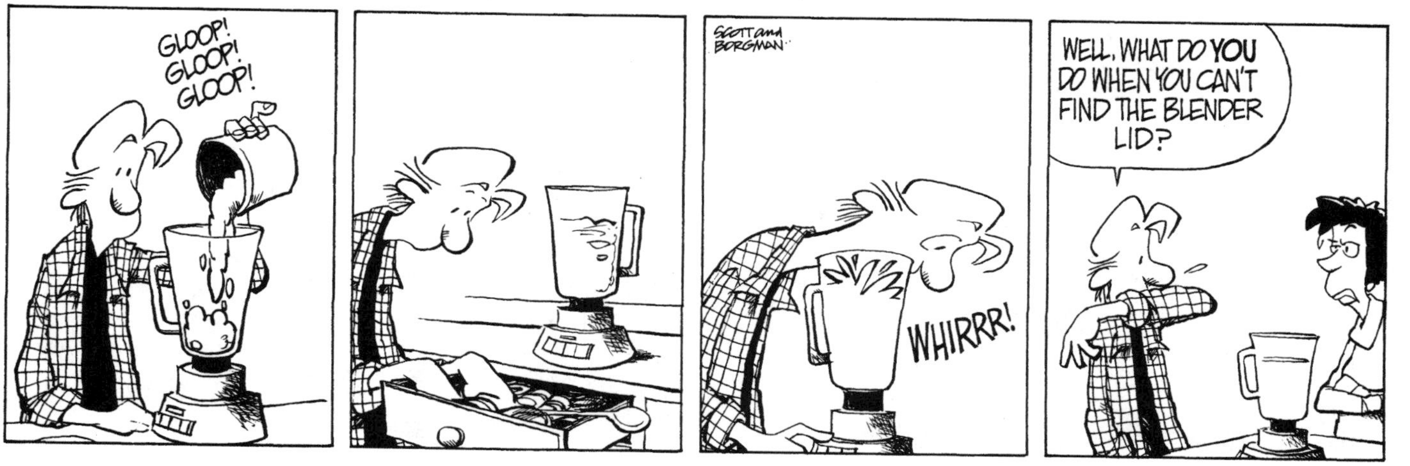
GLOOP! GLOOP! GLOOP!
SCOTT and BORGMAN
WHIRRR!
WELL, WHAT DO **YOU** DO WHEN YOU CAN'T FIND THE BLENDER LID?

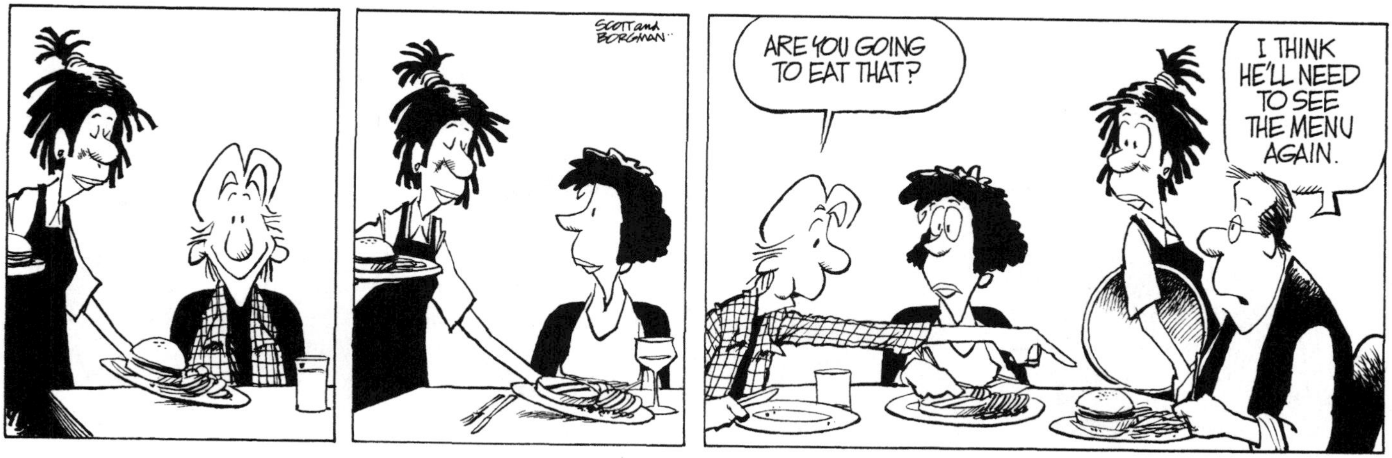
SCOTT and BORGMAN
ARE YOU GOING TO EAT THAT?
I THINK HE'LL NEED TO SEE THE MENU AGAIN.

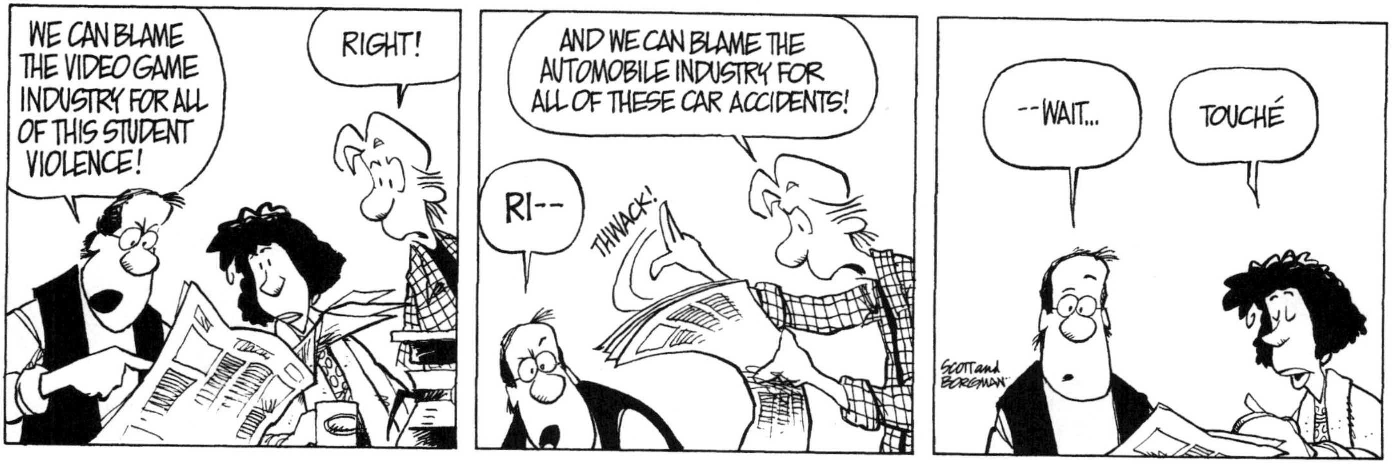
WE CAN BLAME THE VIDEO GAME INDUSTRY FOR ALL OF THIS STUDENT VIOLENCE!
RIGHT!
AND WE CAN BLAME THE AUTOMOBILE INDUSTRY FOR ALL OF THESE CAR ACCIDENTS!
RI--
THWACK!
--WAIT...
TOUCHÉ
SCOTT and BORGMAN

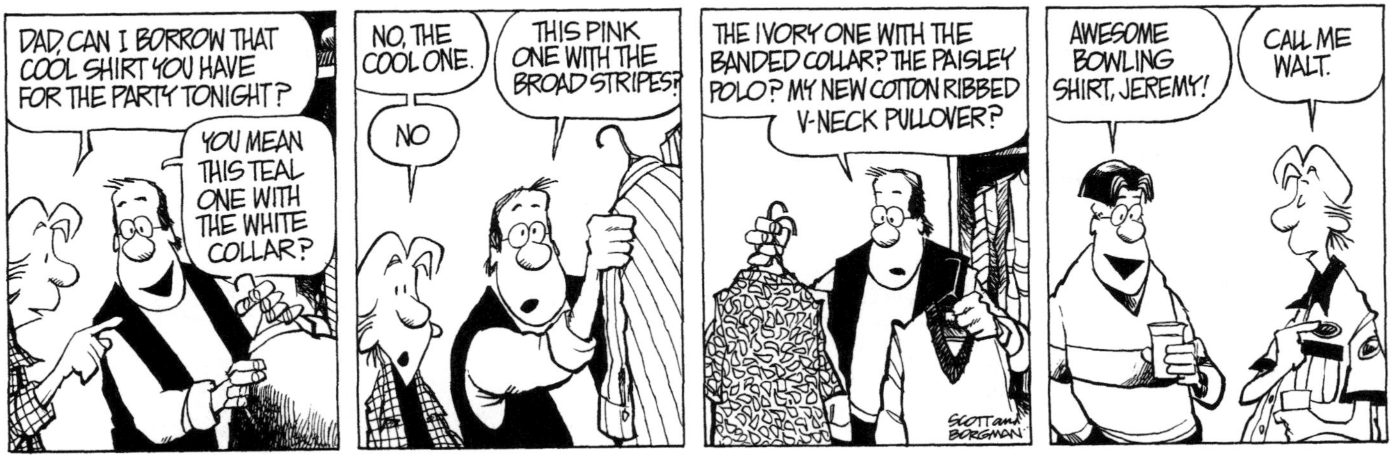
DAD, CAN I BORROW THAT COOL SHIRT YOU HAVE FOR THE PARTY TONIGHT?
YOU MEAN THIS TEAL ONE WITH THE WHITE COLLAR?
NO, THE COOL ONE.
THIS PINK ONE WITH THE BROAD STRIPES?
NO
THE IVORY ONE WITH THE BANDED COLLAR? THE PAISLEY POLO? MY NEW COTTON RIBBED V-NECK PULLOVER?
SCOTT and BORGMAN
AWESOME BOWLING SHIRT, JEREMY!
CALL ME WALT.

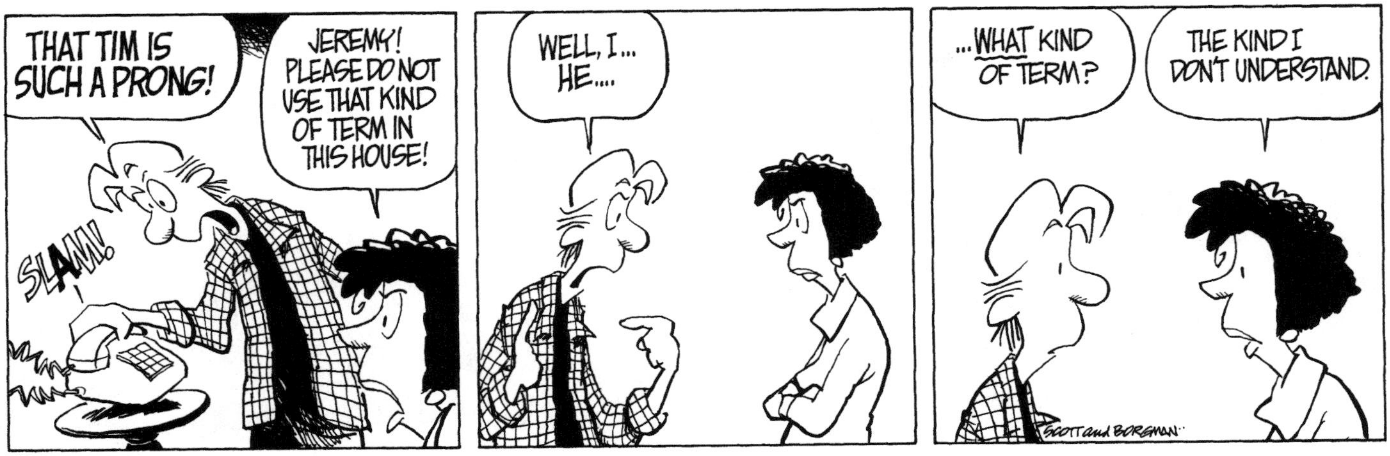
THAT TIM IS SUCH A PRONG!
SLAM!
JEREMY! PLEASE DO NOT USE THAT KIND OF TERM IN THIS HOUSE!
WELL, I... HE....
...WHAT KIND OF TERM?
THE KIND I DON'T UNDERSTAND.
SCOTT and BORGMAN

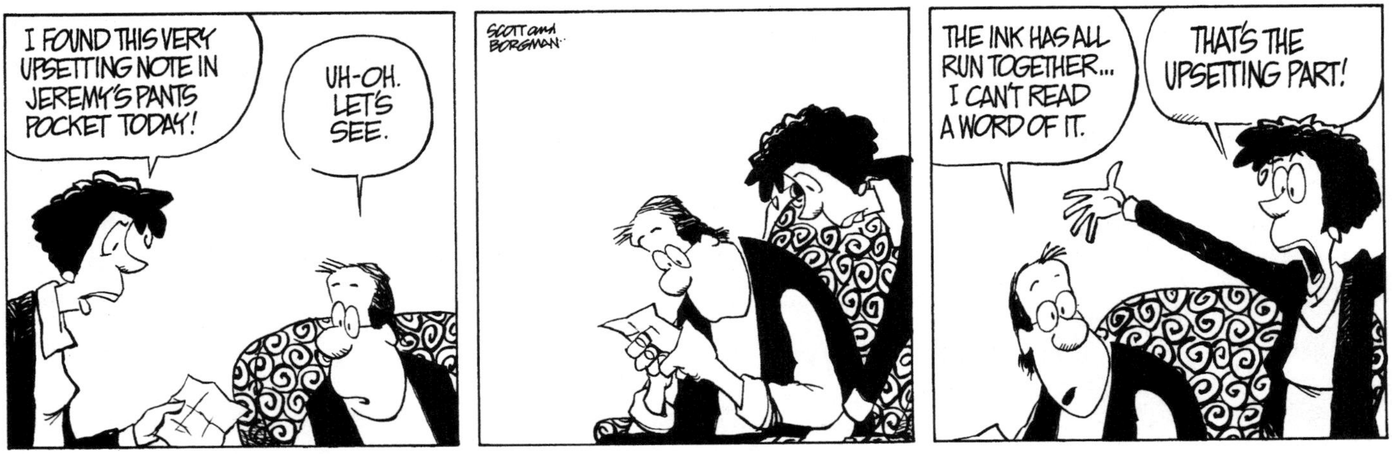
I FOUND THIS VERY UPSETTING NOTE IN JEREMY'S PANTS POCKET TODAY!
UH-OH. LET'S SEE.
SCOTT and BORGMAN
THE INK HAS ALL RUN TOGETHER... I CAN'T READ A WORD OF IT.
THAT'S THE UPSETTING PART!

Zits by Jerry Scott and Jim Borgman

DARN! THAT CAR IN FRONT OF US SURE IS POKEY!

SO, WHY DON'T YOU PASS HIM?

WELL, I — — SAY! WOULD YOU DO IT FOR ME?

WHAT?? HOW? YOU'RE DRIVING!

OPEN THE GLOVE-BOX AND PUSH THE RED BUTTON.

WHOA!

SPROING!

SURPRISED? I HAD IT INSTALLED JUST FOR YOU.

AWESOME!

NOW YOU TAKE OVER WHILE I CATCH A FEW WINKS.

EASY ON THE TURBOTHRUSTER, JEREMY... WE WANT TO STAY INSIDE THE EARTH'S GRAVITATIONAL PULL.

RIGHT, DAD!

VROOOOOOM!

"DO NOT PASS NEXT 26 MILES"

WELL, THAT JUST GIVES US MORE TIME TO SPEND TOGETHER.

SIGH

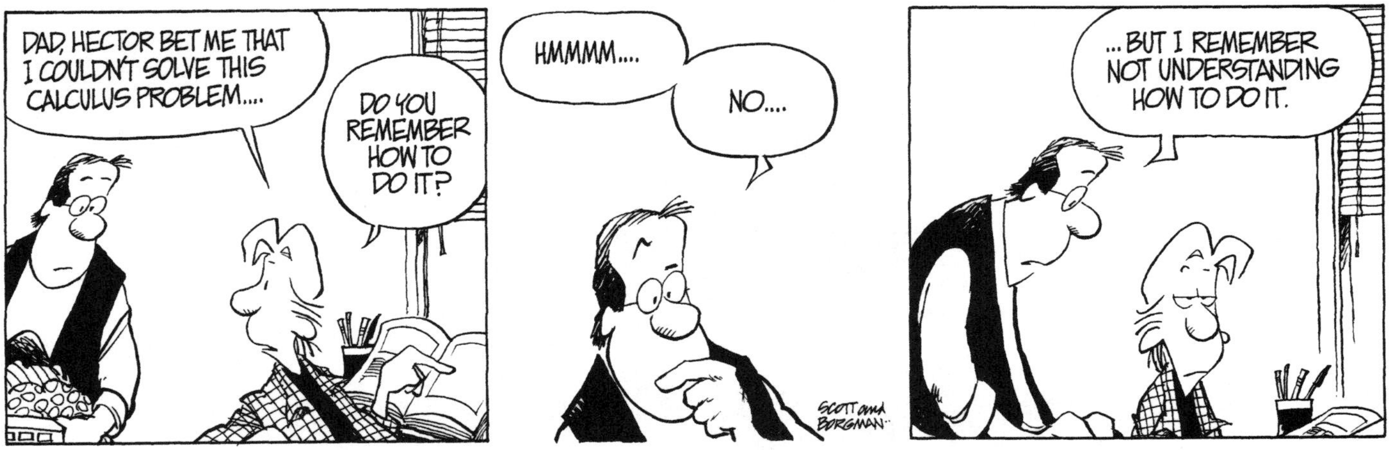
DAD, HECTOR BET ME THAT I COULDN'T SOLVE THIS CALCULUS PROBLEM....
DO YOU REMEMBER HOW TO DO IT?
HMMMM....
NO....
...BUT I REMEMBER NOT UNDERSTANDING HOW TO DO IT.
SCOTT and BORGMAN

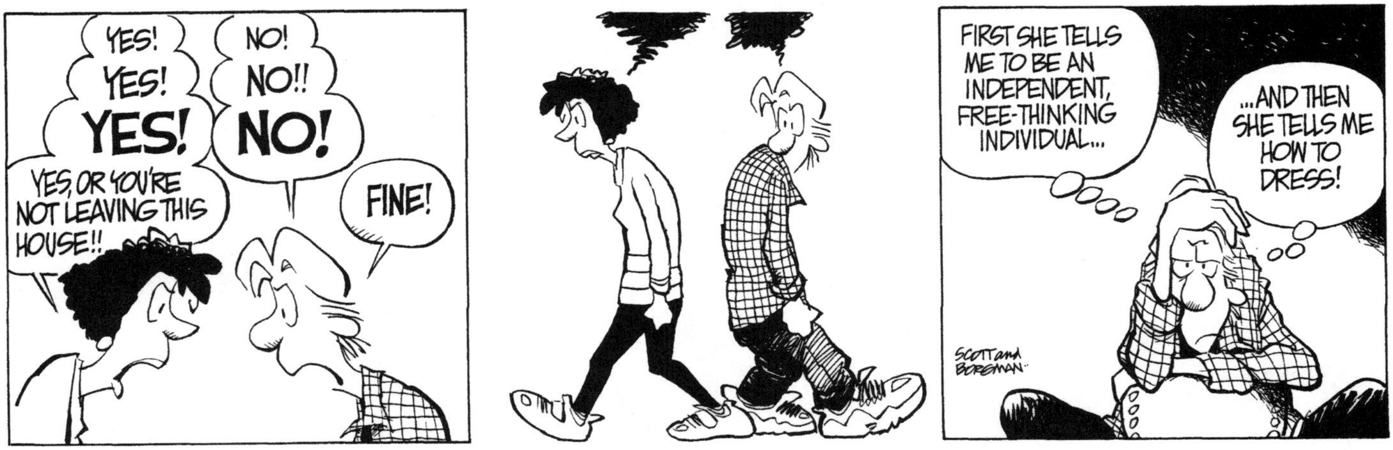
YES! YES! YES!
NO! NO!! NO!
YES, OR YOU'RE NOT LEAVING THIS HOUSE!!
FINE!
FIRST SHE TELLS ME TO BE AN INDEPENDENT, FREE-THINKING INDIVIDUAL...
...AND THEN SHE TELLS ME HOW TO DRESS!
SCOTT and BORGMAN

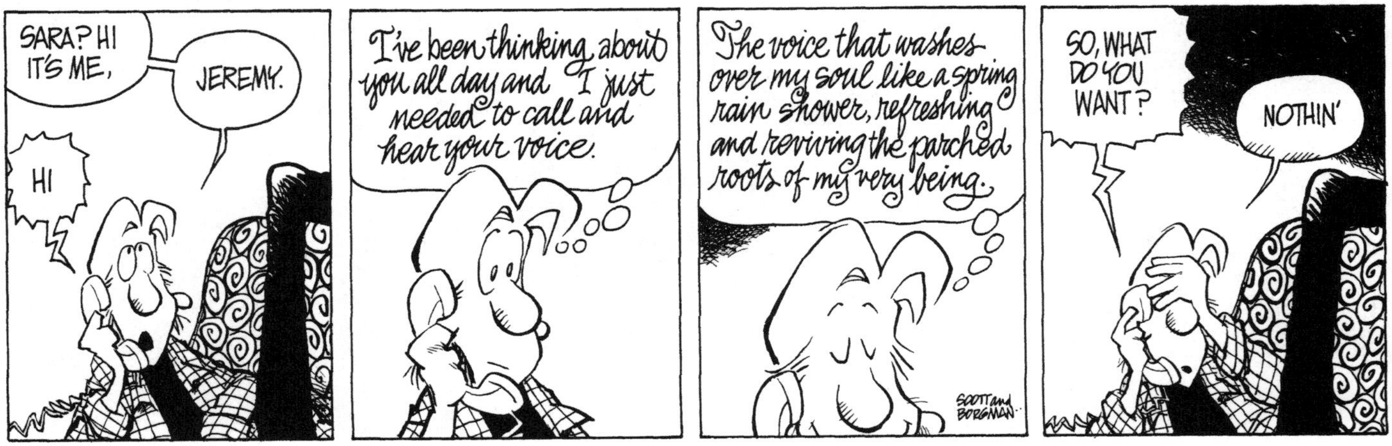
SARA? HI IT'S ME,
JEREMY.
HI
I've been thinking about you all day and I just needed to call and hear your voice.
The voice that washes over my soul like a spring rain shower, refreshing and reviving the parched roots of my very being.
SCOTT and BORGMAN
SO, WHAT DO YOU WANT?
NOTHIN'

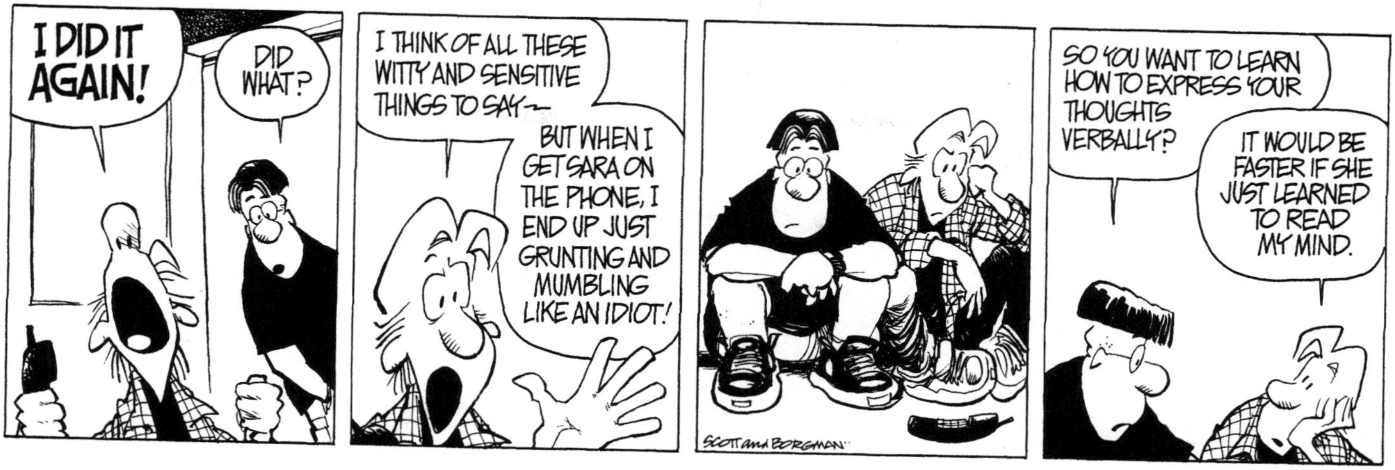
I DID IT AGAIN!
DID WHAT?
I THINK OF ALL THESE WITTY AND SENSITIVE THINGS TO SAY--
BUT WHEN I GET SARA ON THE PHONE, I END UP JUST GRUNTING AND MUMBLING LIKE AN IDIOT!
SCOTT and BORGMAN
SO YOU WANT TO LEARN HOW TO EXPRESS YOUR THOUGHTS VERBALLY?
IT WOULD BE FASTER IF SHE JUST LEARNED TO READ MY MIND.

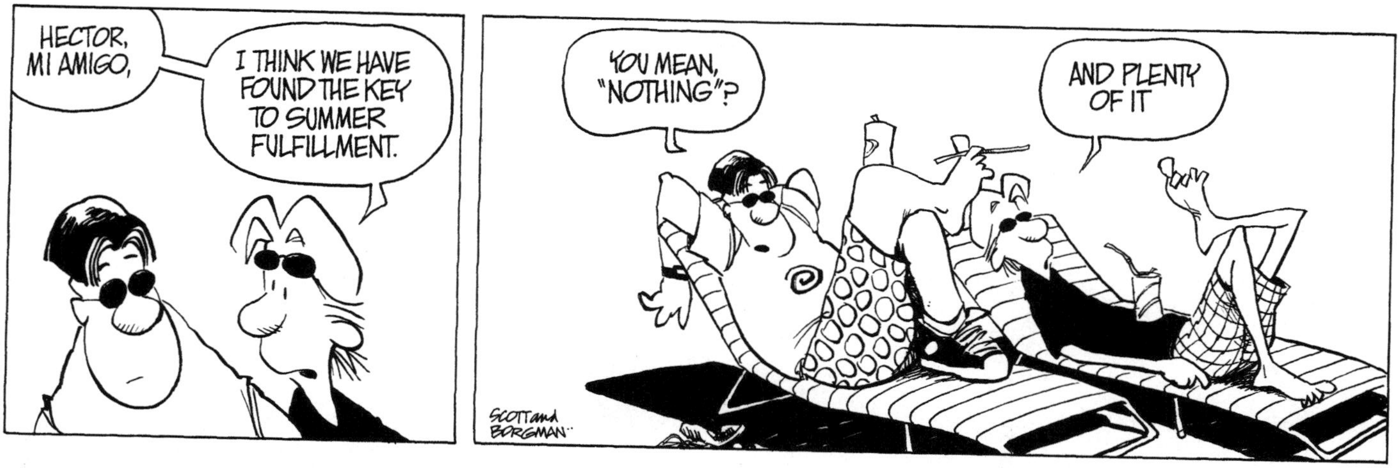
HECTOR, MI AMIGO,
I THINK WE HAVE FOUND THE KEY TO SUMMER FULFILLMENT.
SCOTT and BORGMAN
YOU MEAN, "NOTHING"?
AND PLENTY OF IT

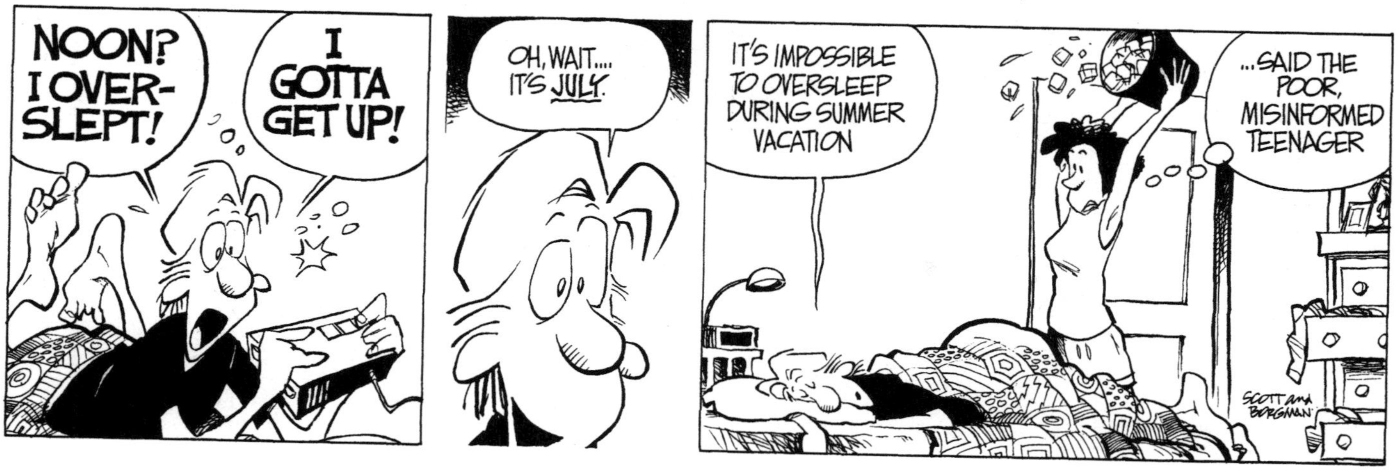
NOON? I OVER-SLEPT!
I GOTTA GET UP!
OH, WAIT.... IT'S JULY.
IT'S IMPOSSIBLE TO OVERSLEEP DURING SUMMER VACATION
...SAID THE POOR, MISINFORMED TEENAGER
SCOTT and BORGMAN

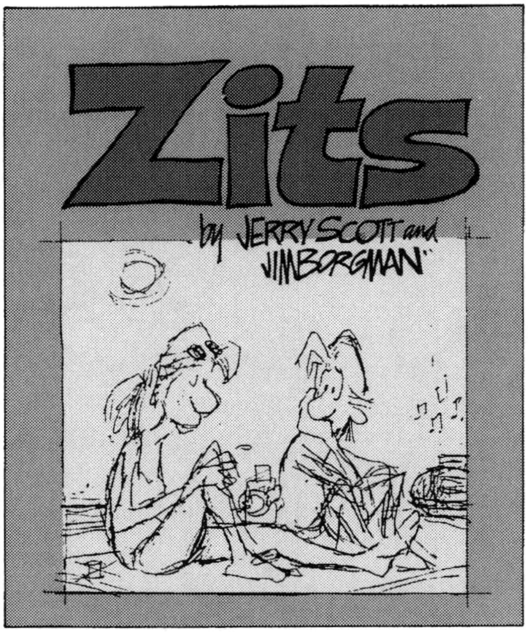
Zits
by JERRY SCOTT and JIM BORGMAN

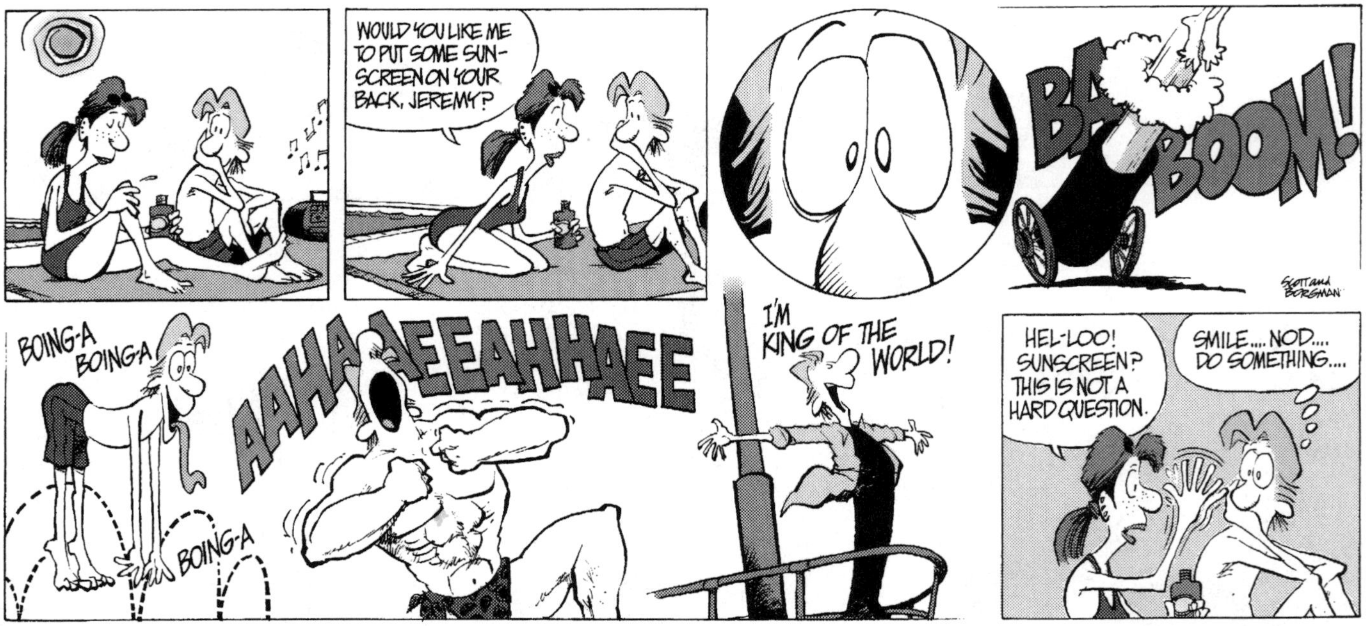
WOULD YOU LIKE ME TO PUT SOME SUN-SCREEN ON YOUR BACK, JEREMY?
BA BOOM!
SCOTT and BORGMAN
BOING-A BOING-A
BOING-A
AAHAAEEEAHHAEE
I'M KING OF THE WORLD!
HEL-LOO! SUNSCREEN? THIS IS NOT A HARD QUESTION.
SMILE.... NOD.... DO SOMETHING....

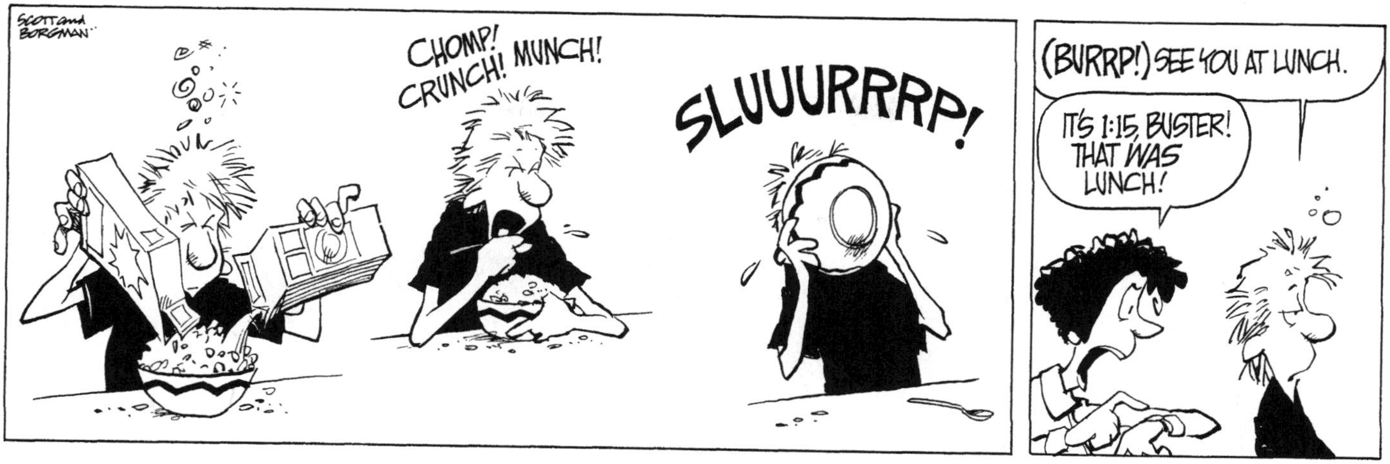
CHOMP! CRUNCH! MUNCH!
SLUUURRRP!
(BURRP!) SEE YOU AT LUNCH.
IT'S 1:15, BUSTER! THAT *WAS* LUNCH!

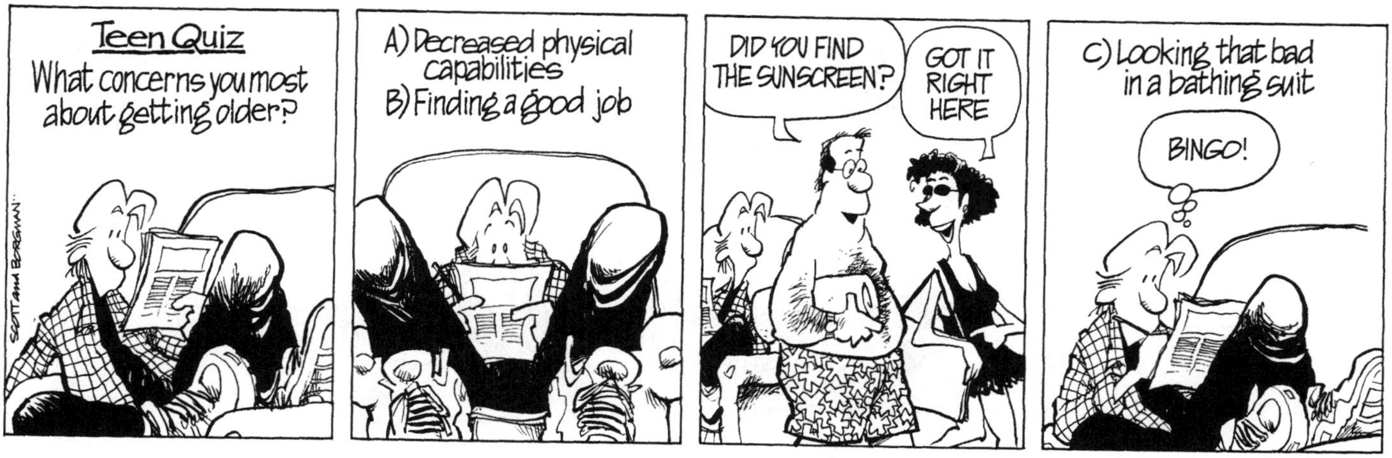
Teen Quiz
What concerns you most about getting older?
A) Decreased physical capabilities
B) Finding a good job
DID YOU FIND THE SUNSCREEN?
GOT IT RIGHT HERE
C) Looking that bad in a bathing suit
BINGO!

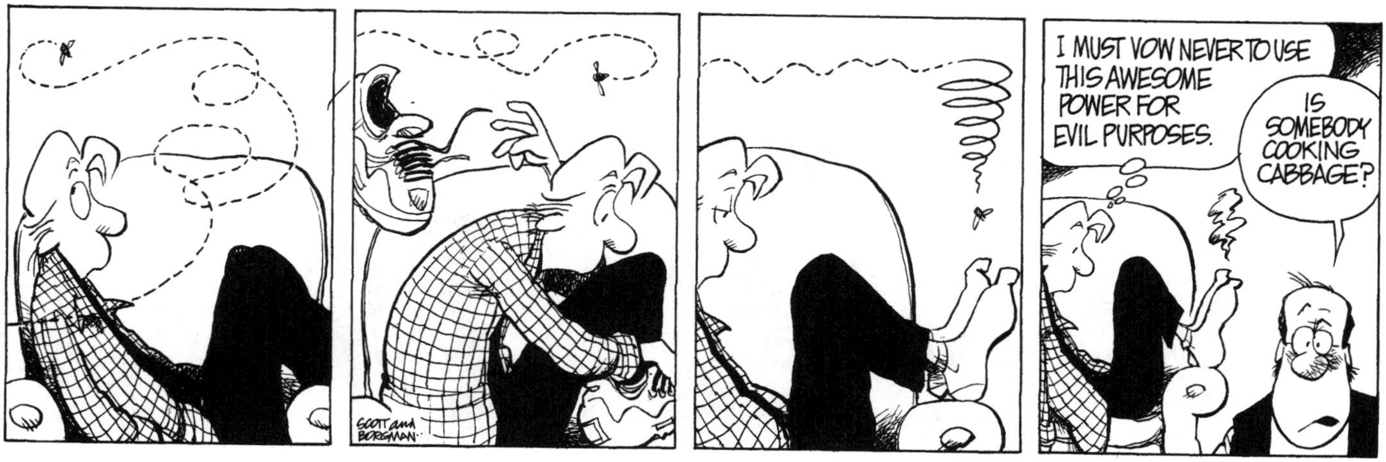
I MUST VOW NEVER TO USE THIS AWESOME POWER FOR EVIL PURPOSES.
IS SOMEBODY COOKING CABBAGE?

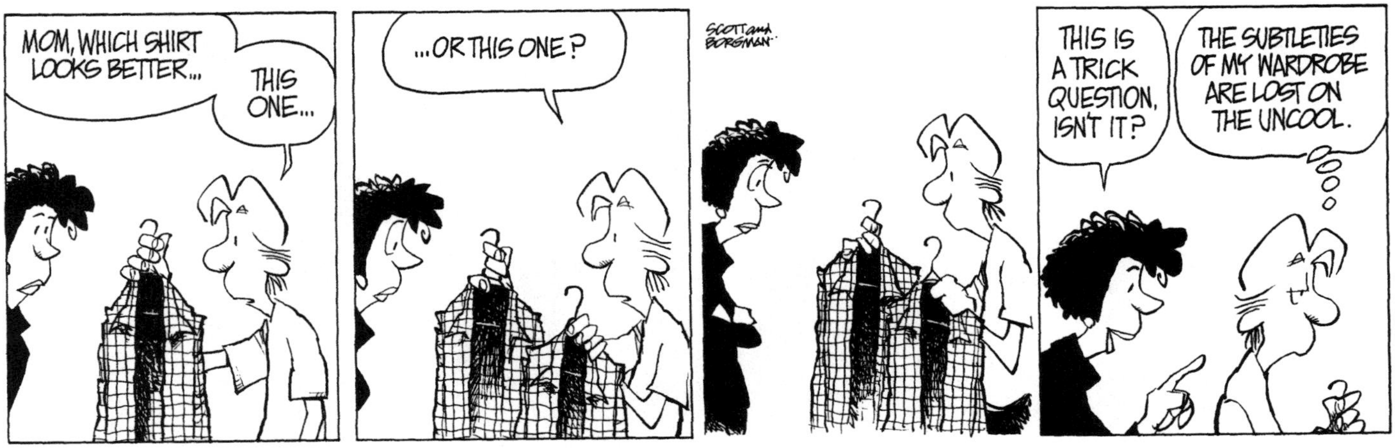
MOM, WHICH SHIRT LOOKS BETTER...
THIS ONE...
...OR THIS ONE?
SCOTT and BORGMAN
THIS IS A TRICK QUESTION, ISN'T IT?
THE SUBTLETIES OF MY WARDROBE ARE LOST ON THE UNCOOL.

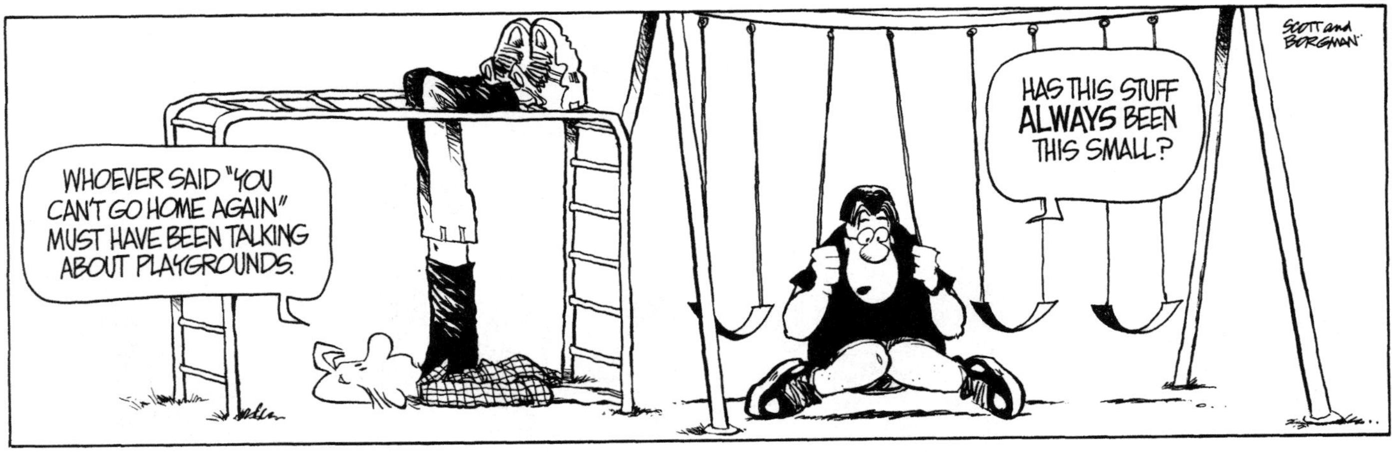
SCOTT and BORGMAN
WHOEVER SAID "YOU CAN'T GO HOME AGAIN" MUST HAVE BEEN TALKING ABOUT PLAYGROUNDS.
HAS THIS STUFF **ALWAYS** BEEN THIS SMALL?

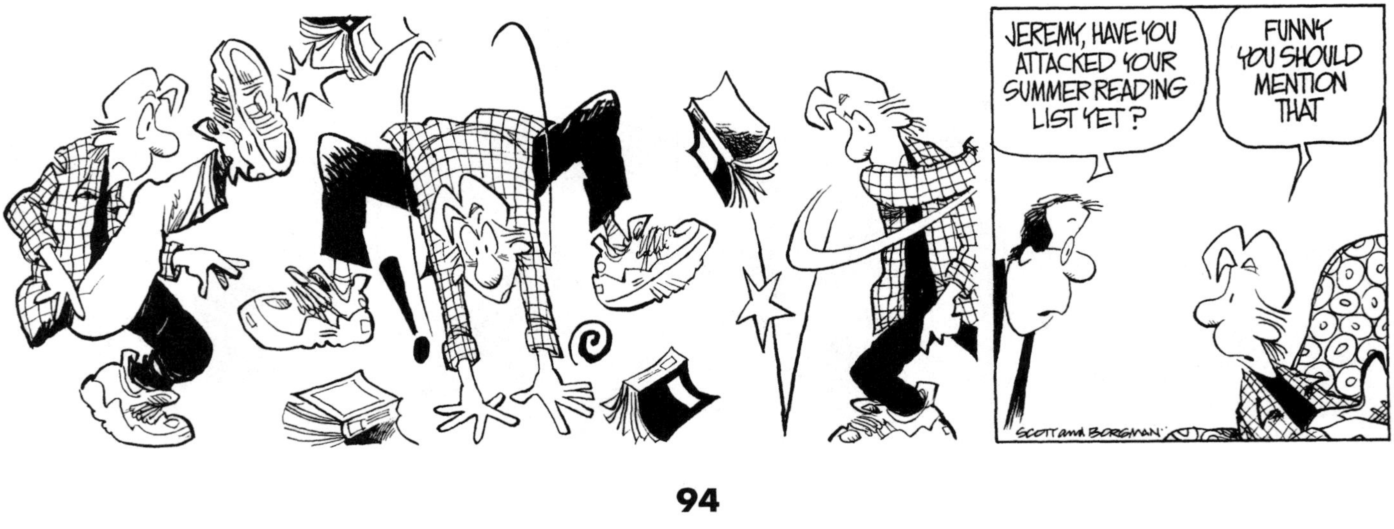
JEREMY, HAVE YOU ATTACKED YOUR SUMMER READING LIST YET?
FUNNY YOU SHOULD MENTION THAT
SCOTT and BORGMAN

Zits
by JERRY SCOTT and JIM BORGMAN

SCOTT and BORGMAN
JEREMY!
TRIP!
SHEESH!
I NEVER SAW ANYBODY GET SO UPSET OVER A COUPLE OF SHOES ON THE FLOOR!

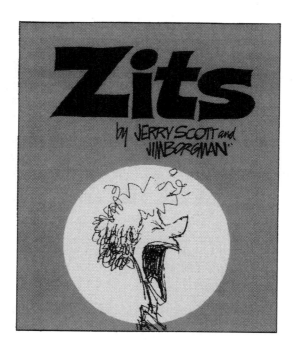

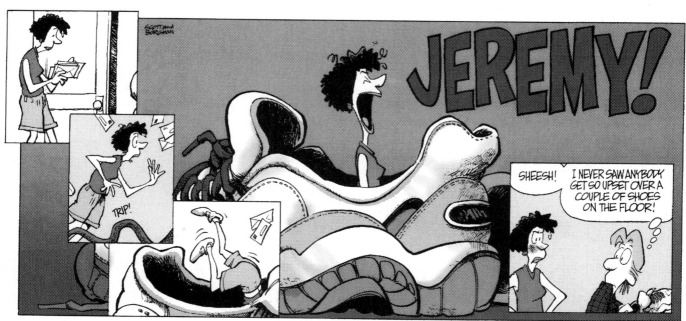

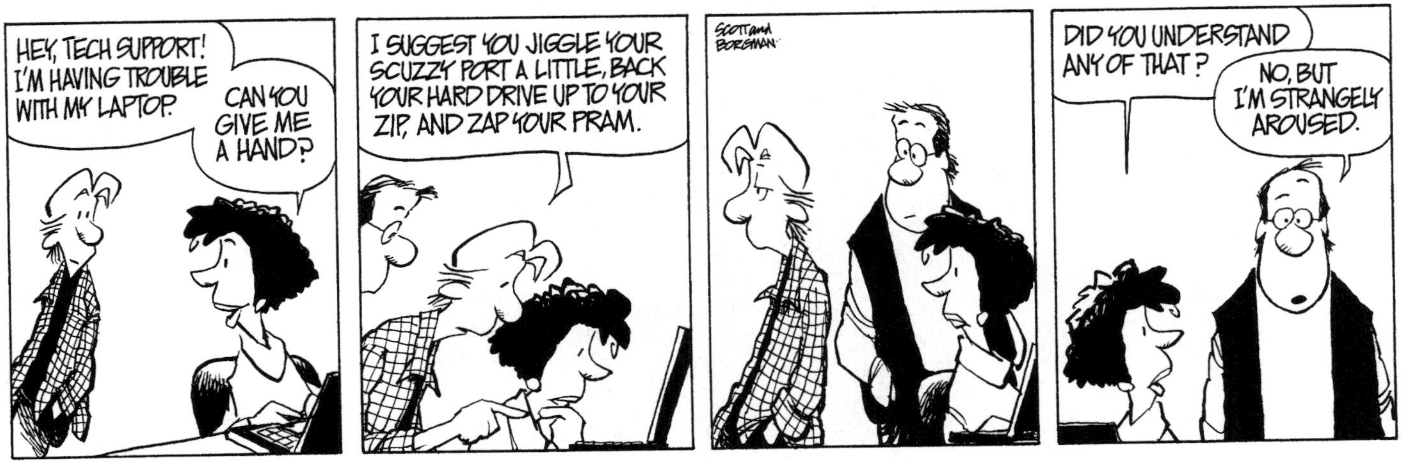
HEY, TECH SUPPORT! I'M HAVING TROUBLE WITH MY LAPTOP.
CAN YOU GIVE ME A HAND?
I SUGGEST YOU JIGGLE YOUR SCUZZY PORT A LITTLE, BACK YOUR HARD DRIVE UP TO YOUR ZIP, AND ZAP YOUR PRAM.
SCOTT and BORGMAN
DID YOU UNDERSTAND ANY OF THAT?
NO, BUT I'M STRANGELY AROUSED.

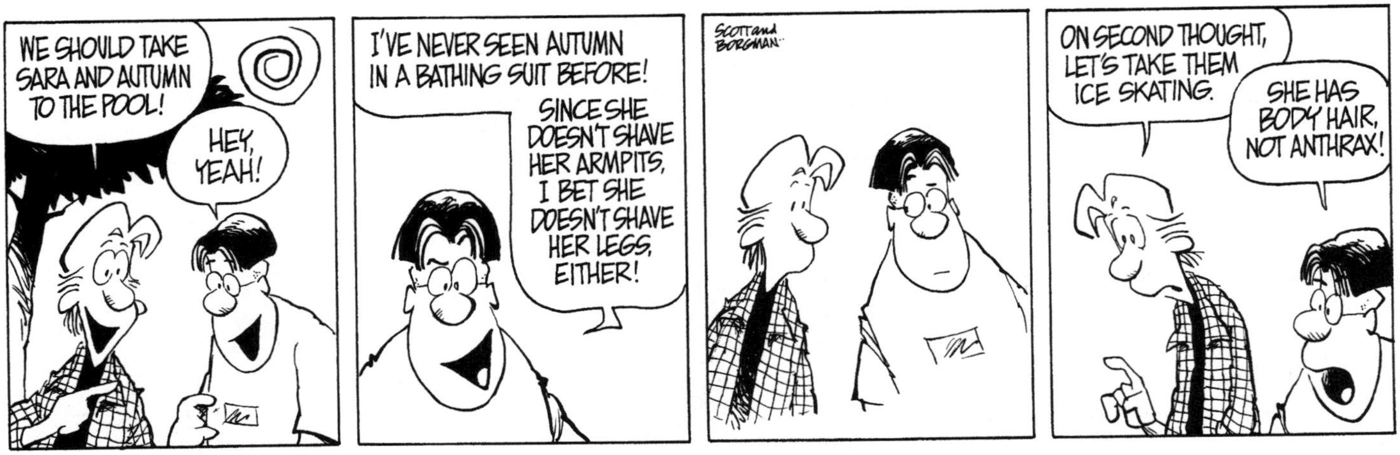
WE SHOULD TAKE SARA AND AUTUMN TO THE POOL!
HEY, YEAH!
I'VE NEVER SEEN AUTUMN IN A BATHING SUIT BEFORE!
SINCE SHE DOESN'T SHAVE HER ARMPITS, I BET SHE DOESN'T SHAVE HER LEGS, EITHER!
SCOTT and BORGMAN
ON SECOND THOUGHT, LET'S TAKE THEM ICE SKATING.
SHE HAS BODY HAIR, NOT ANTHRAX!

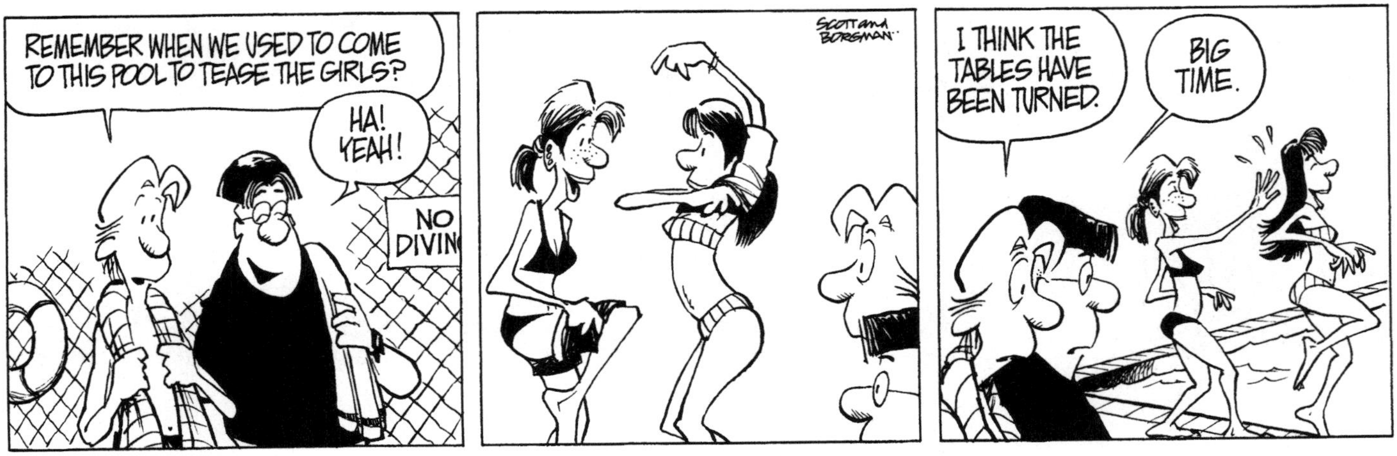
REMEMBER WHEN WE USED TO COME TO THIS POOL TO TEASE THE GIRLS?
HA! YEAH!
NO DIVIN
SCOTT and BORGMAN
I THINK THE TABLES HAVE BEEN TURNED.
BIG TIME.

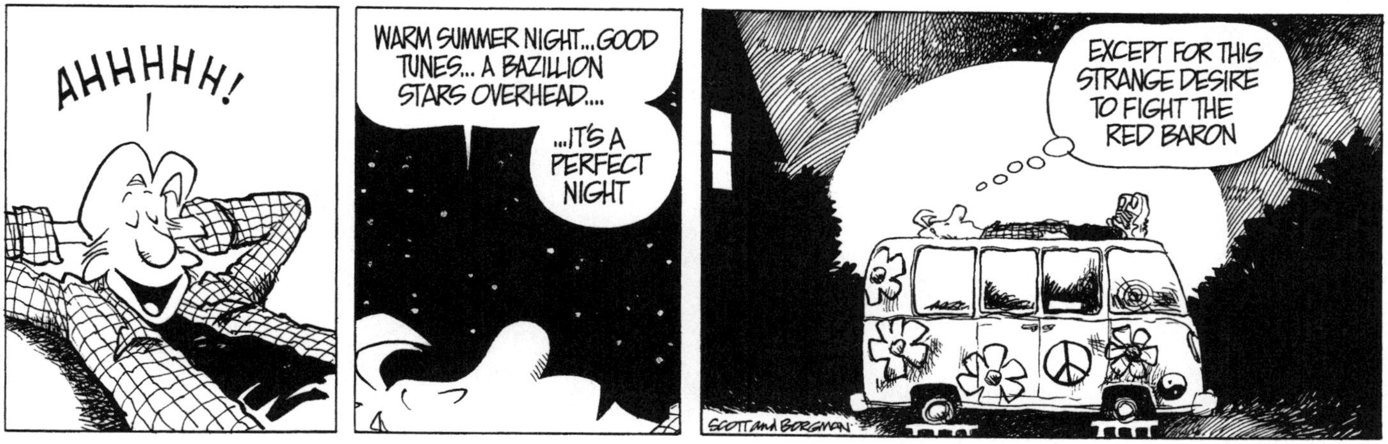
AHHHHH!
WARM SUMMER NIGHT...GOOD TUNES... A BAZILLION STARS OVERHEAD....
...IT'S A PERFECT NIGHT
EXCEPT FOR THIS STRANGE DESIRE TO FIGHT THE RED BARON
SCOTT and BORGMAN

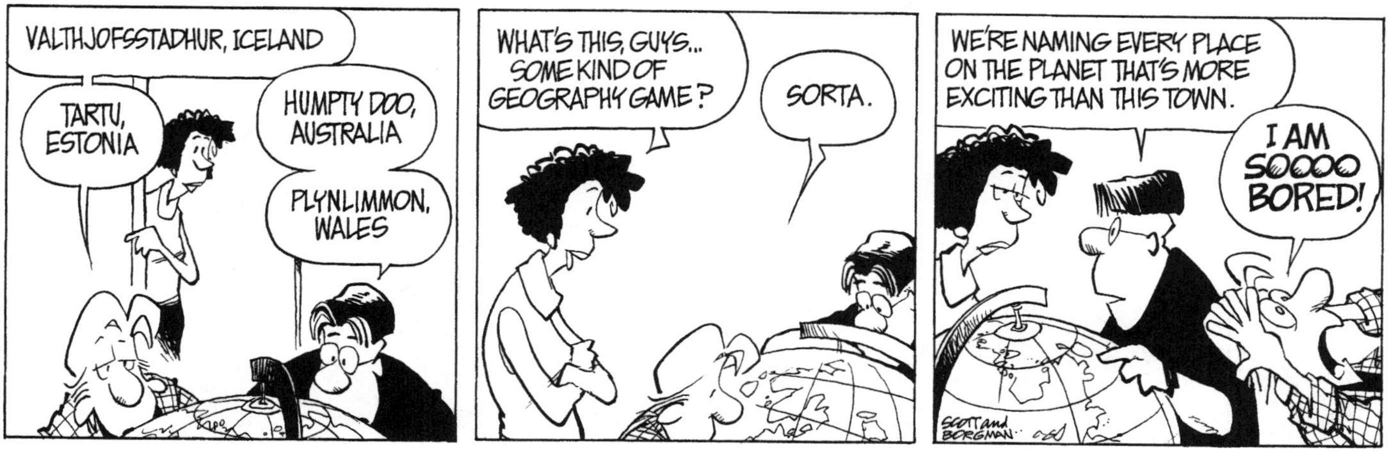
VALTHJOFSSTADHUR, ICELAND
TARTU, ESTONIA
HUMPTY DOO, AUSTRALIA
PLYNLIMMON, WALES
WHAT'S THIS, GUYS... SOME KIND OF GEOGRAPHY GAME?
SORTA.
WE'RE NAMING EVERY PLACE ON THE PLANET THAT'S MORE EXCITING THAN THIS TOWN.
I AM SOOOO BORED!
SCOTT and BORGMAN

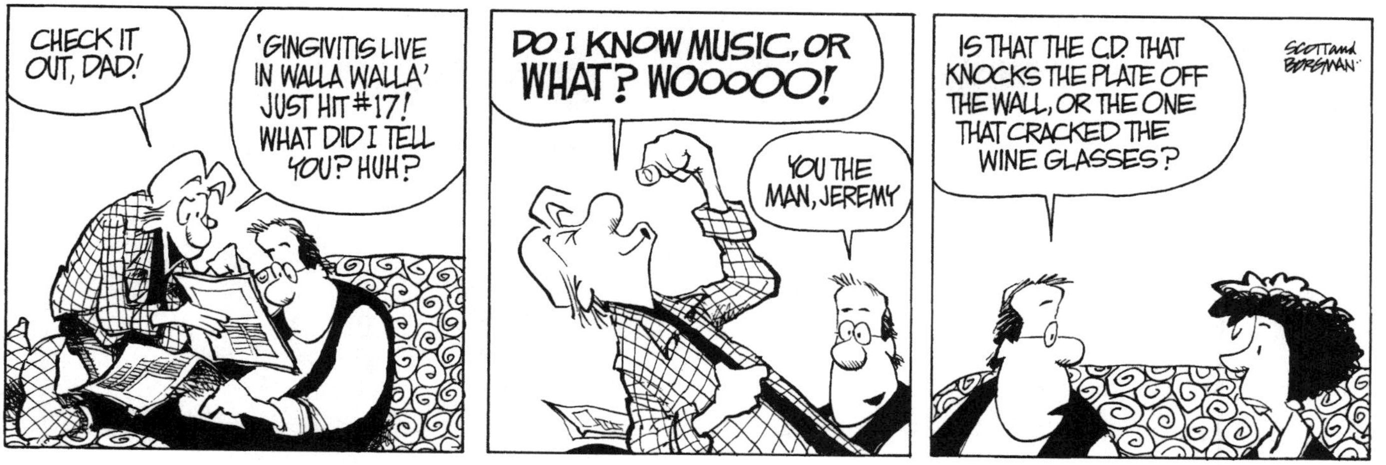
CHECK IT OUT, DAD!
'GINGIVITIS LIVE IN WALLA WALLA' JUST HIT #17! WHAT DID I TELL YOU? HUH?
DO I KNOW MUSIC, OR WHAT? WOOOOO!
YOU THE MAN, JEREMY
IS THAT THE C.D. THAT KNOCKS THE PLATE OFF THE WALL, OR THE ONE THAT CRACKED THE WINE GLASSES?
SCOTT and BORGMAN

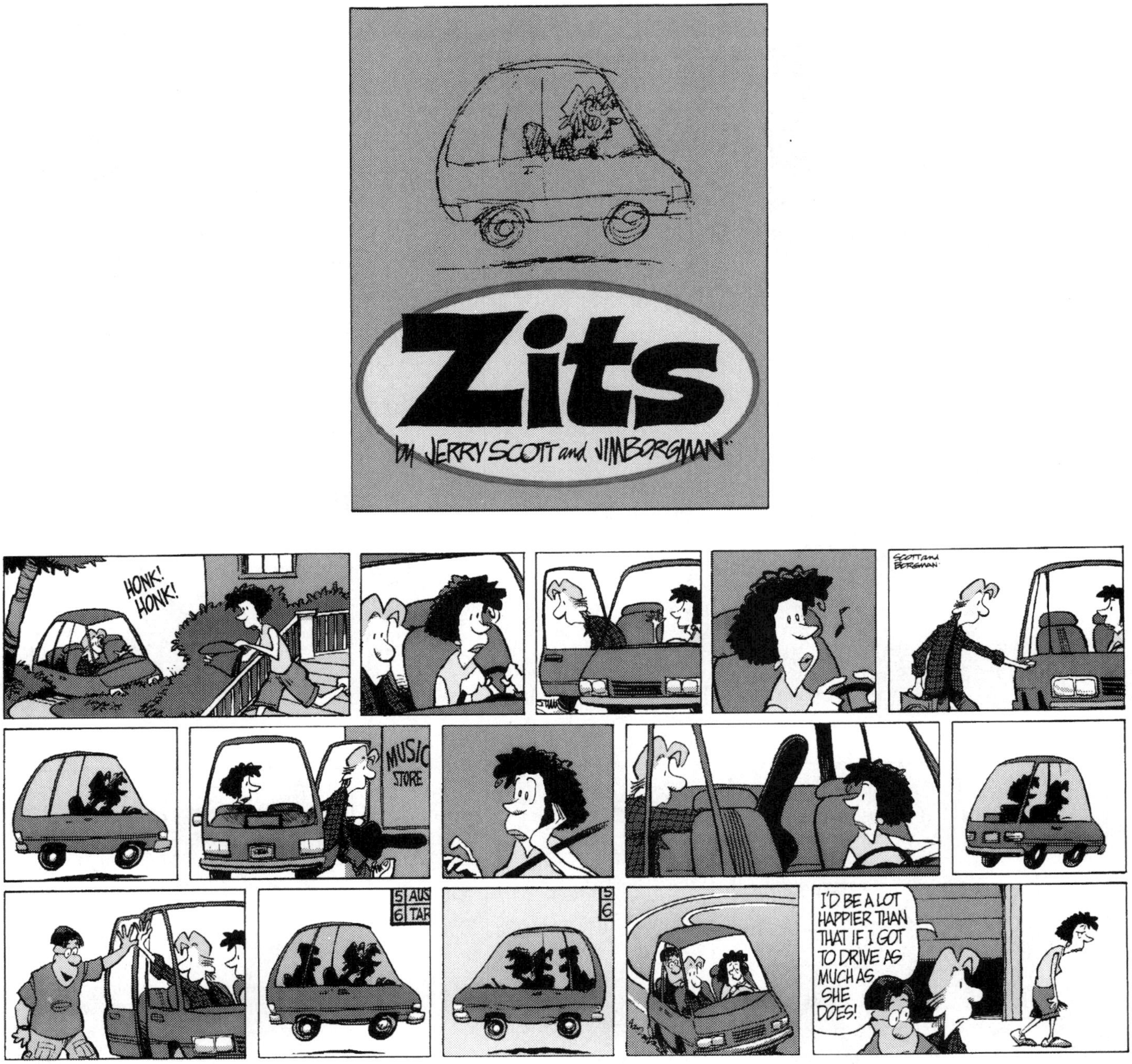
Zits
by JERRY SCOTT and JIM BORGMAN
HONK! HONK!
SCOTT and BORGMAN
MUSIC STORE
I'D BE A LOT HAPPIER THAN THAT IF I GOT TO DRIVE AS MUCH AS SHE DOES!

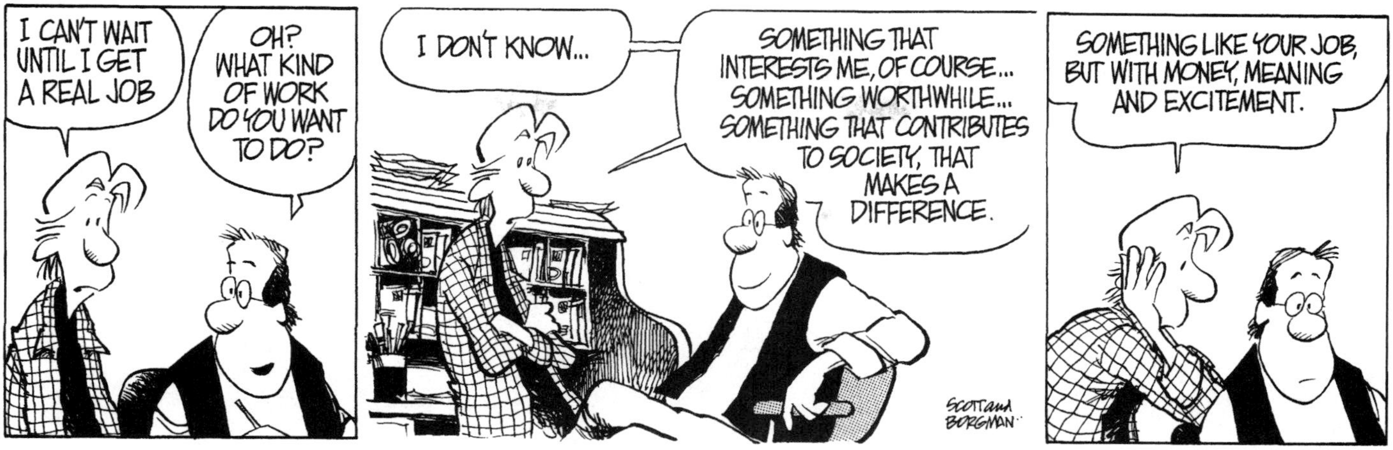
I CAN'T WAIT UNTIL I GET A REAL JOB
OH? WHAT KIND OF WORK DO YOU WANT TO DO?
I DON'T KNOW...
SOMETHING THAT INTERESTS ME, OF COURSE... SOMETHING WORTHWHILE... SOMETHING THAT CONTRIBUTES TO SOCIETY, THAT MAKES A DIFFERENCE.
SCOTT and BORGMAN
SOMETHING LIKE YOUR JOB, BUT WITH MONEY, MEANING AND EXCITEMENT.

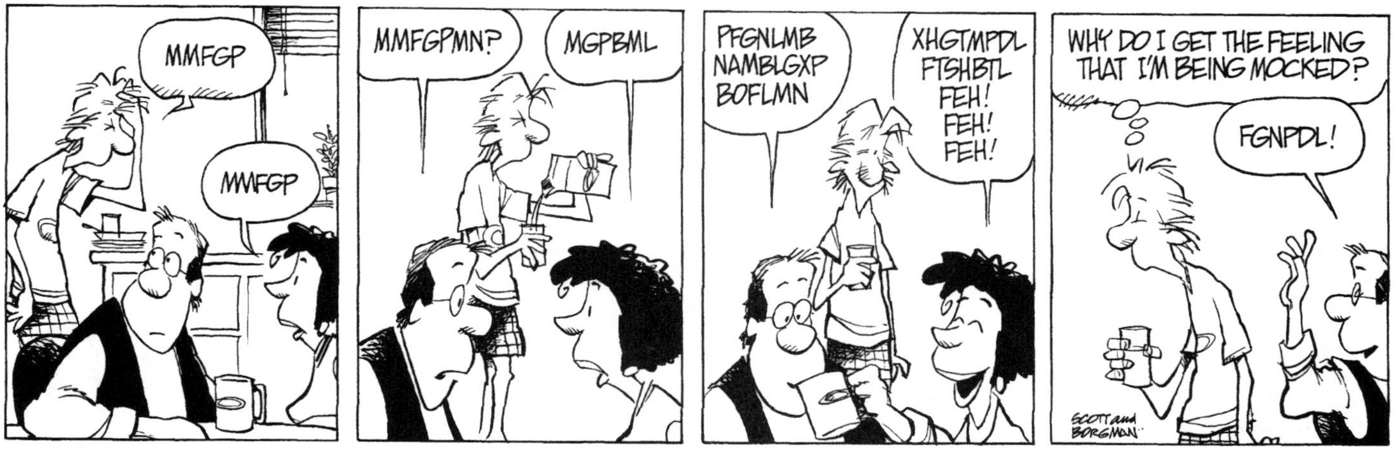
MMFGP
MMFGP
MMFGPMN?
MGPBML
PFGNLMB NAMBLGXP BOFLMN
XHGTMPDL FTSHBTL FEH! FEH! FEH!
WHY DO I GET THE FEELING THAT I'M BEING MOCKED?
FGNPDL!
SCOTT and BORGMAN

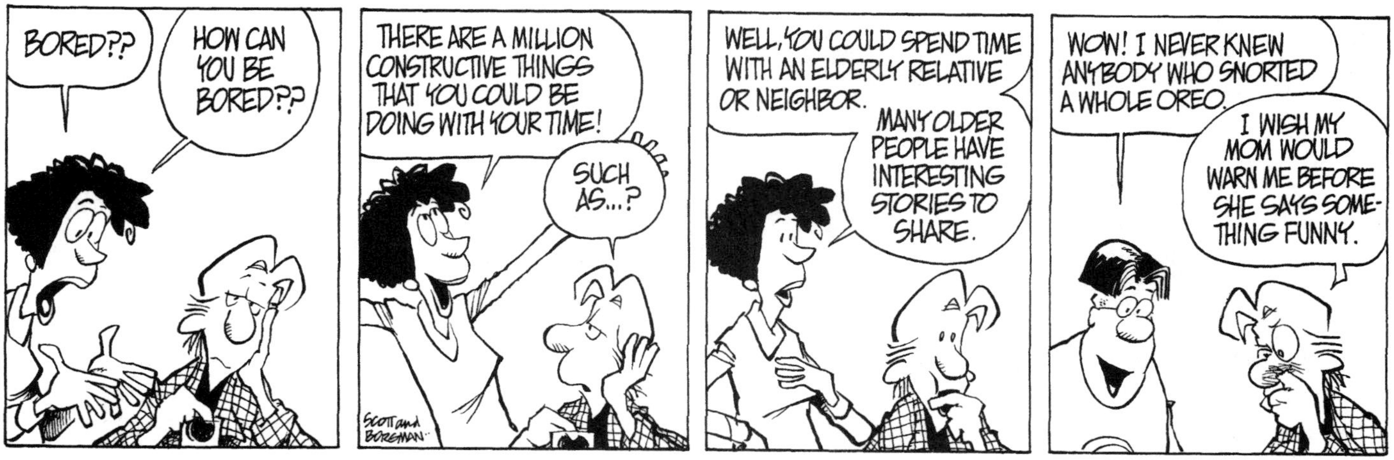
BORED??
HOW CAN YOU BE BORED??
THERE ARE A MILLION CONSTRUCTIVE THINGS THAT YOU COULD BE DOING WITH YOUR TIME!
SUCH AS...?
SCOTT and BORGMAN
WELL, YOU COULD SPEND TIME WITH AN ELDERLY RELATIVE OR NEIGHBOR.
MANY OLDER PEOPLE HAVE INTERESTING STORIES TO SHARE.
WOW! I NEVER KNEW ANYBODY WHO SNORTED A WHOLE OREO.
I WISH MY MOM WOULD WARN ME BEFORE SHE SAYS SOME-THING FUNNY.

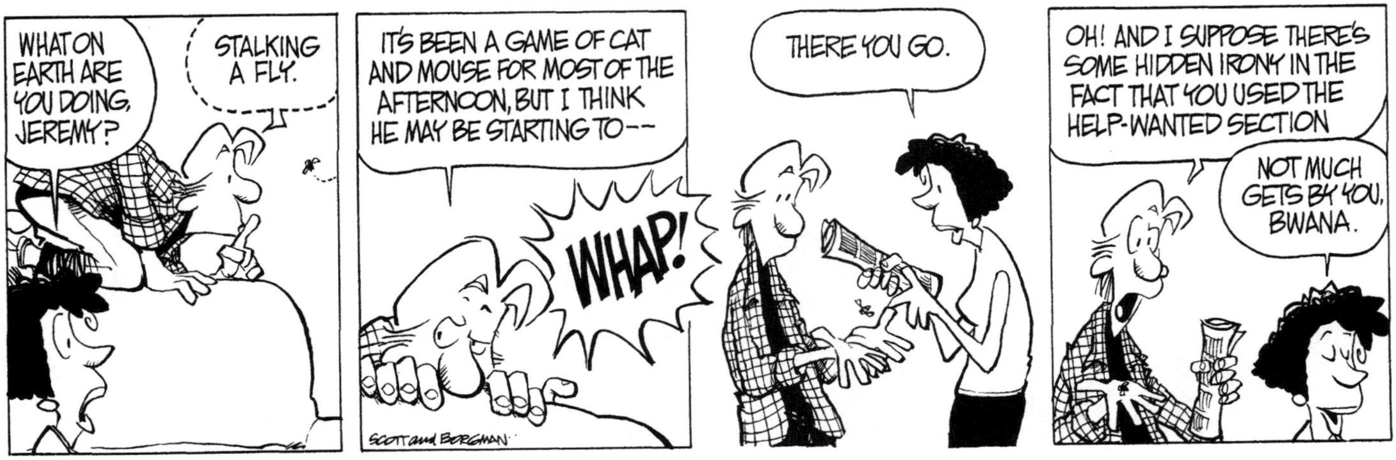
WHAT ON EARTH ARE YOU DOING, JEREMY?
STALKING A FLY.
IT'S BEEN A GAME OF CAT AND MOUSE FOR MOST OF THE AFTERNOON, BUT I THINK HE MAY BE STARTING TO--
WHAP!
SCOTT and BORGMAN
THERE YOU GO.
OH! AND I SUPPOSE THERE'S SOME HIDDEN IRONY IN THE FACT THAT YOU USED THE HELP-WANTED SECTION
NOT MUCH GETS BY YOU, BWANA.

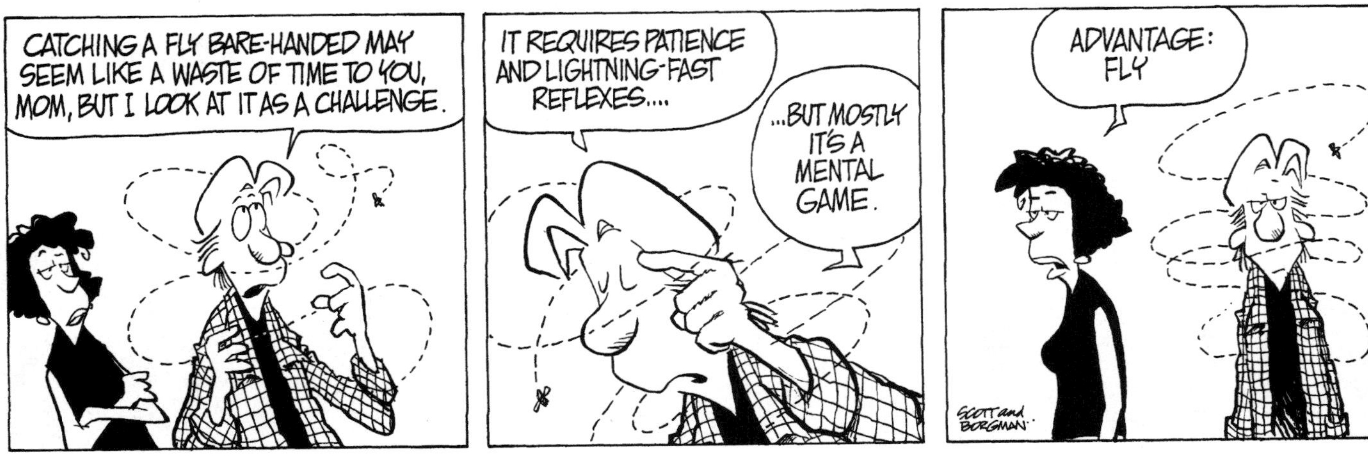
CATCHING A FLY BARE-HANDED MAY SEEM LIKE A WASTE OF TIME TO YOU, MOM, BUT I LOOK AT IT AS A CHALLENGE.
IT REQUIRES PATIENCE AND LIGHTNING-FAST REFLEXES....
...BUT MOSTLY IT'S A MENTAL GAME.
ADVANTAGE: FLY
SCOTT and BORGMAN

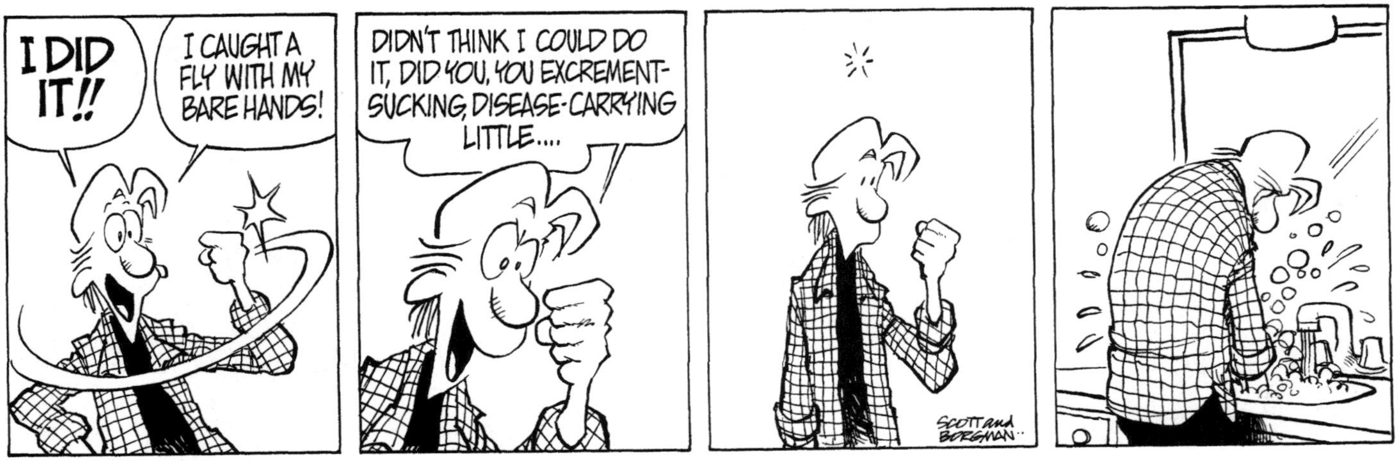
I DID IT!!
I CAUGHT A FLY WITH MY BARE HANDS!
DIDN'T THINK I COULD DO IT, DID YOU, YOU EXCREMENT-SUCKING, DISEASE-CARRYING LITTLE....
SCOTT and BORGMAN

Zits
by JERRY SCOTT and JIM BORGMAN
GRUNT!
OOF!

GRUNT!
OOF!
PUFF!
PANT!
UNGHH!
OKAY, THAT SHOULD DO IT, JEREMY.... TURN ON THE WATER!
SCOTT and BORGMAN
WOOHOOOOOOOOOOOO
YOU MAY BE ABLE TO FIX SPRINKLERS, DAD, BUT I COULD TEACH YOU A THING OR TWO ABOUT STRESS REDUCTION.
I'LL PASS.

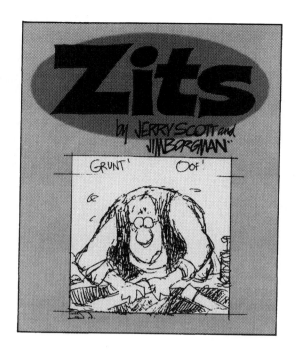

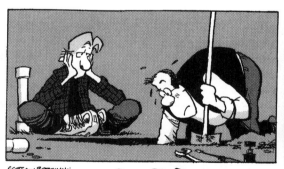

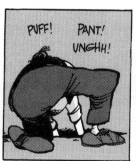

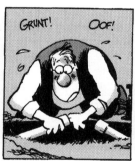

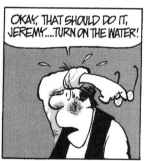

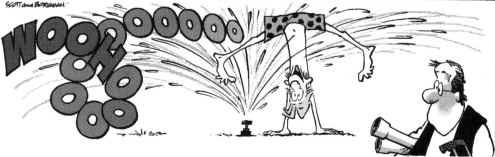

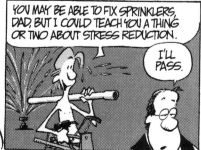

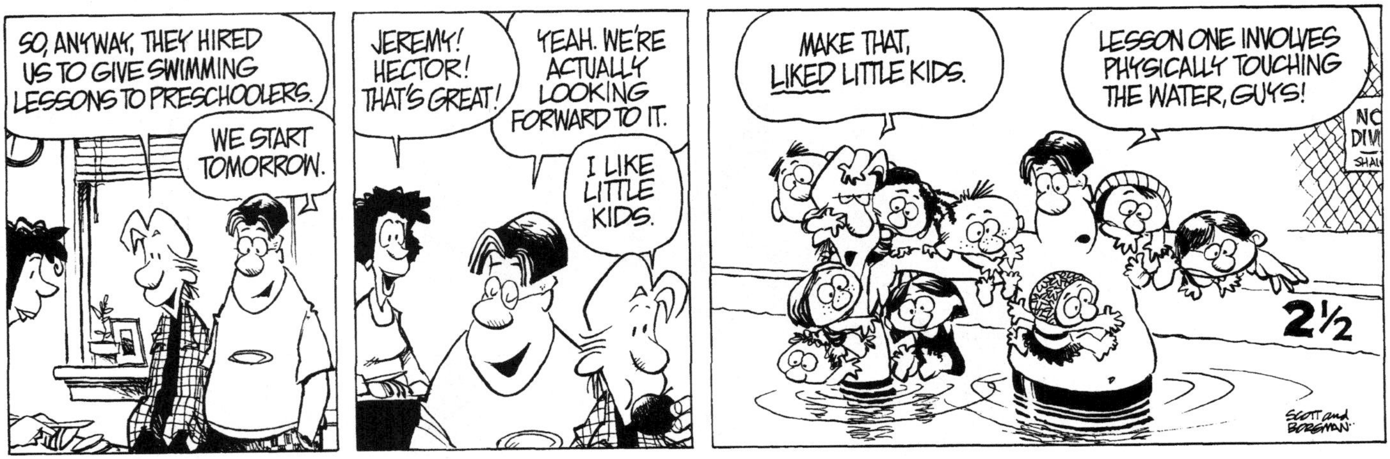
SO, ANYWAY, THEY HIRED US TO GIVE SWIMMING LESSONS TO PRESCHOOLERS.
WE START TOMORROW.
JEREMY! HECTOR! THAT'S GREAT!
YEAH. WE'RE ACTUALLY LOOKING FORWARD TO IT.
I LIKE LITTLE KIDS.
MAKE THAT, LIKED LITTLE KIDS.
LESSON ONE INVOLVES PHYSICALLY TOUCHING THE WATER, GUYS!
2½
SCOTT and BORGMAN

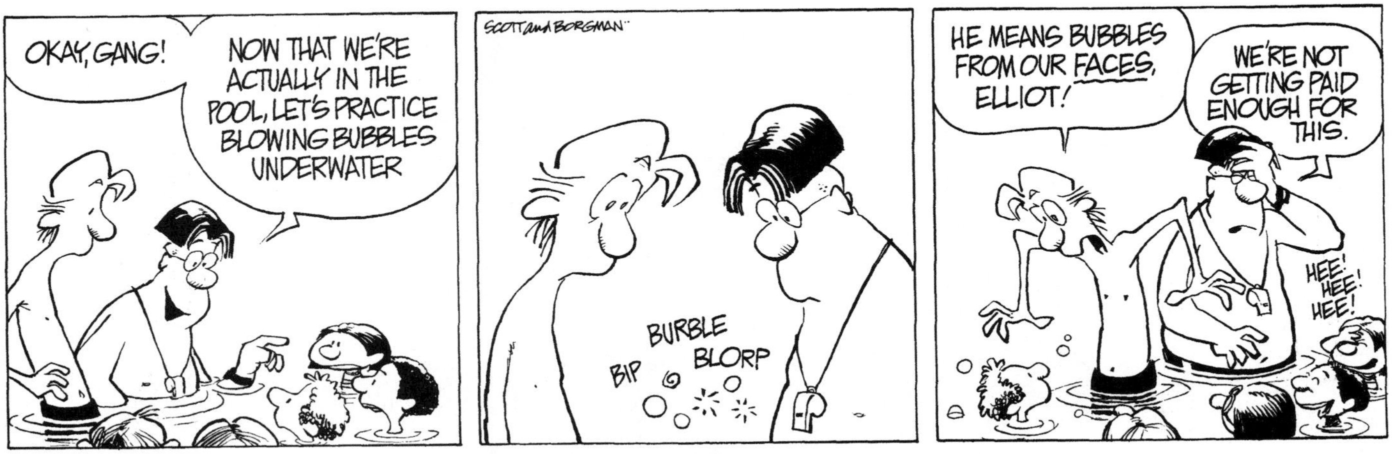
SCOTT and BORGMAN
OKAY, GANG!
NOW THAT WE'RE ACTUALLY IN THE POOL, LET'S PRACTICE BLOWING BUBBLES UNDERWATER
BURBLE
BIP
BLORP
HE MEANS BUBBLES FROM OUR FACES, ELLIOT!
WE'RE NOT GETTING PAID ENOUGH FOR THIS.
HEE! HEE! HEE!

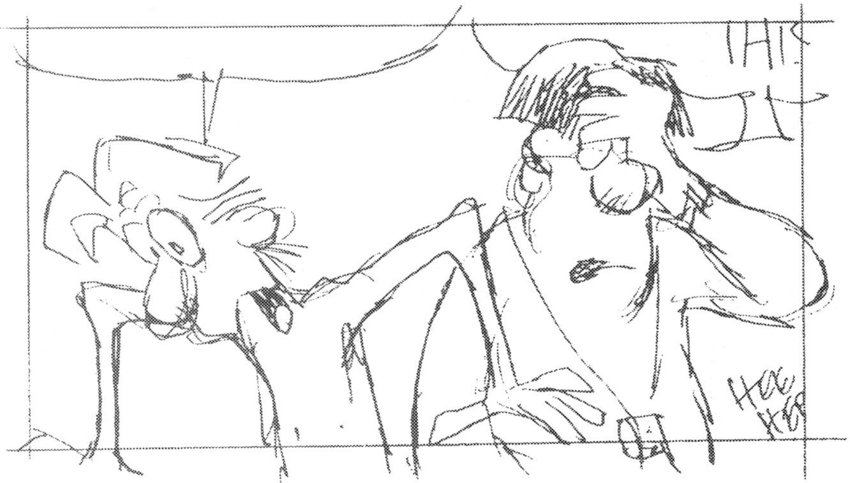

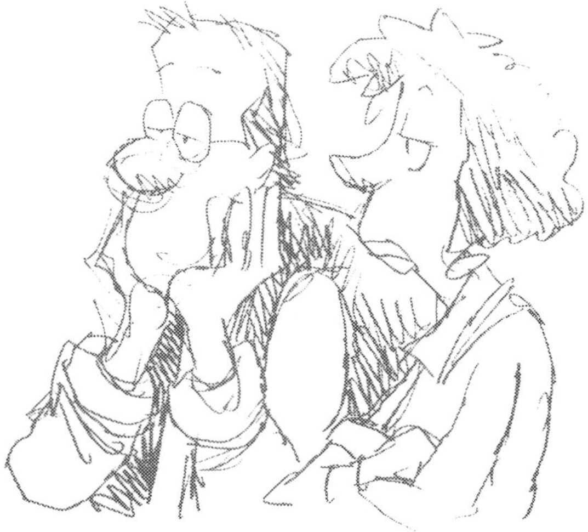

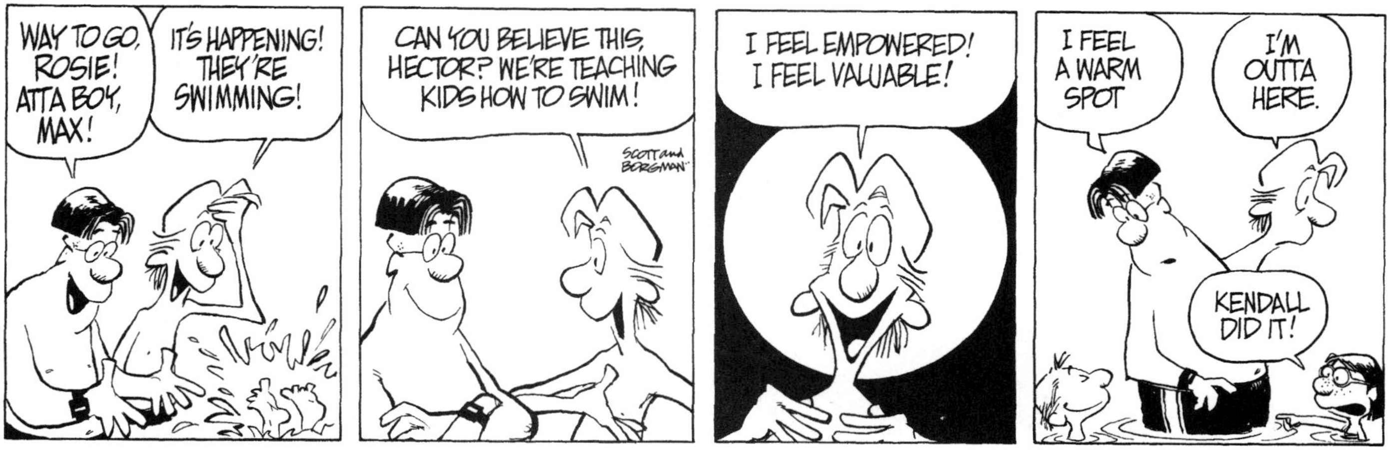
WAY TO GO, ROSIE! ATTA BOY, MAX!
IT'S HAPPENING! THEY'RE SWIMMING!
CAN YOU BELIEVE THIS, HECTOR? WE'RE TEACHING KIDS HOW TO SWIM!
SCOTT and BORGMAN
I FEEL EMPOWERED! I FEEL VALUABLE!
I FEEL A WARM SPOT
I'M OUTTA HERE.
KENDALL DID IT!

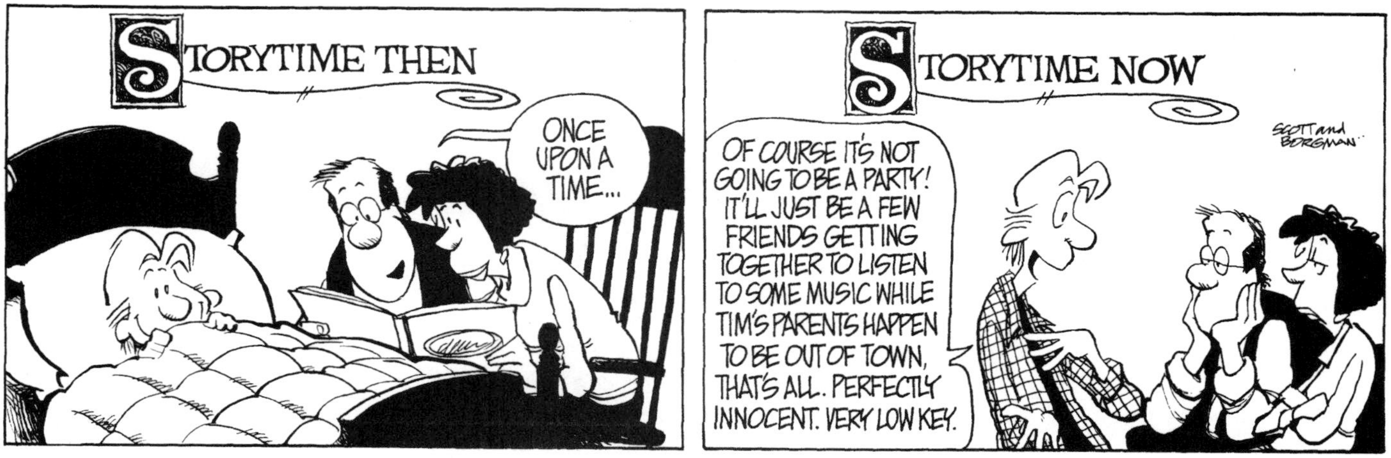
STORYTIME THEN
ONCE UPON A TIME...
STORYTIME NOW
SCOTT and BORGMAN
OF COURSE IT'S NOT GOING TO BE A PARTY! IT'LL JUST BE A FEW FRIENDS GETTING TOGETHER TO LISTEN TO SOME MUSIC WHILE TIM'S PARENTS HAPPEN TO BE OUT OF TOWN, THAT'S ALL. PERFECTLY INNOCENT. VERY LOW KEY.

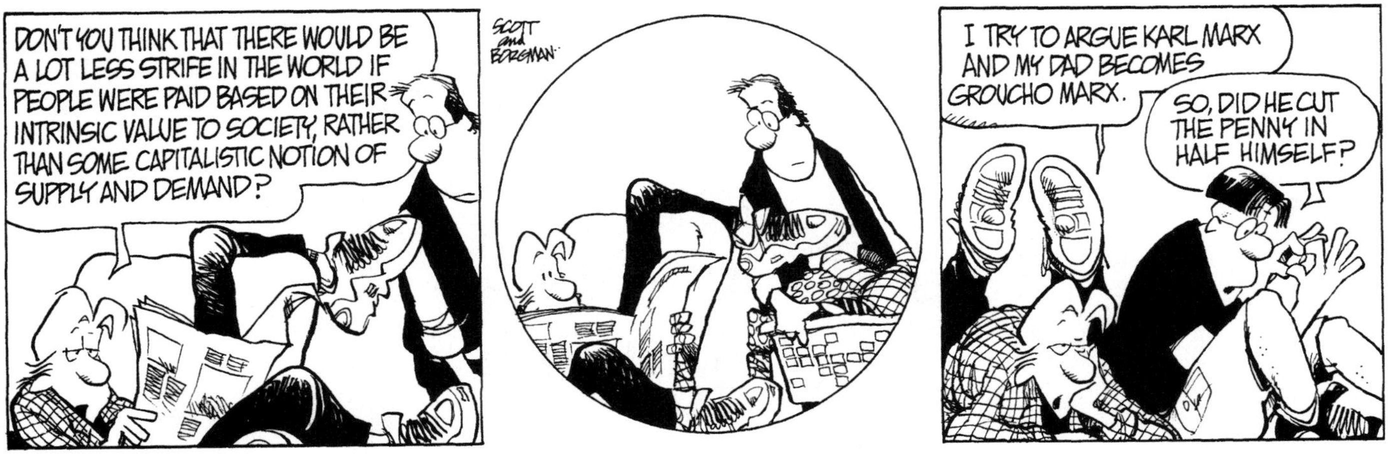
DON'T YOU THINK THAT THERE WOULD BE A LOT LESS STRIFE IN THE WORLD IF PEOPLE WERE PAID BASED ON THEIR INTRINSIC VALUE TO SOCIETY, RATHER THAN SOME CAPITALISTIC NOTION OF SUPPLY AND DEMAND?
SCOTT and BORGMAN
I TRY TO ARGUE KARL MARX AND MY DAD BECOMES GROUCHO MARX.
SO, DID HE CUT THE PENNY IN HALF HIMSELF?

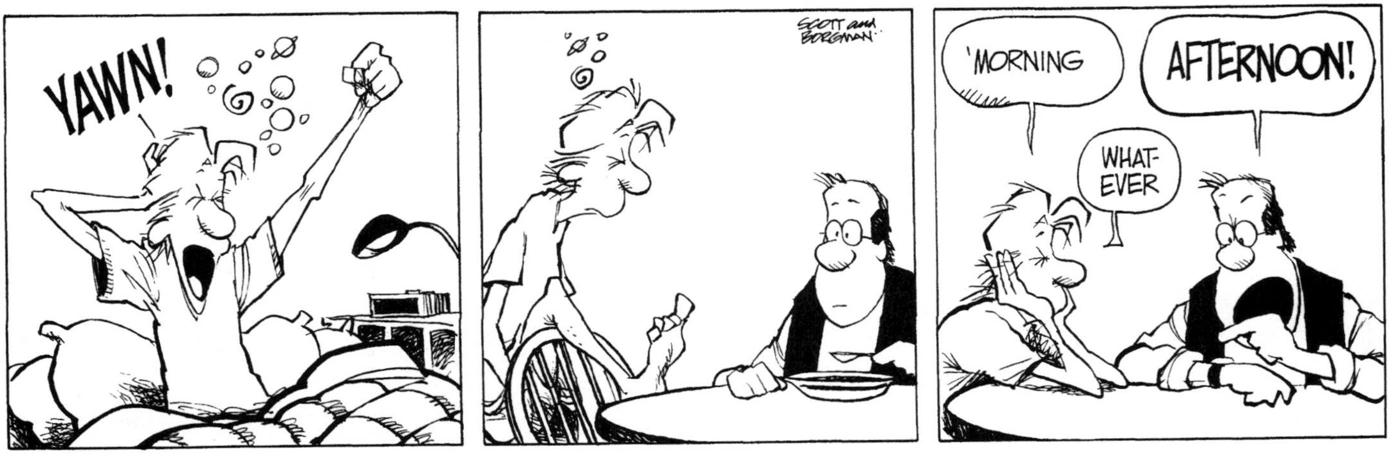
YAWN!
SCOTT and BORGMAN
'MORNING
AFTERNOON!
WHAT-EVER

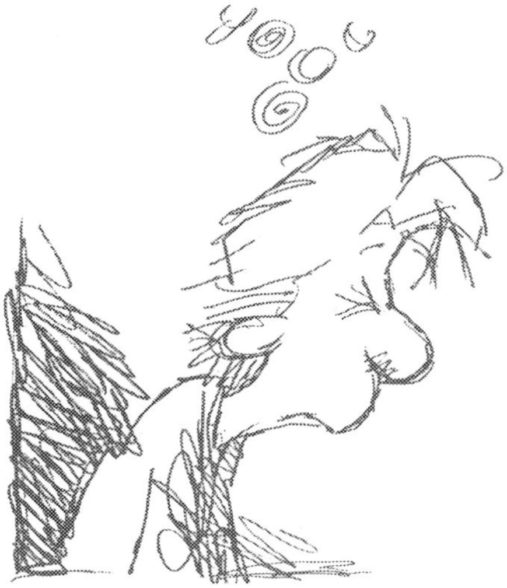

Zits
by JERRY SCOTT and JIM BORGMAN

HECTOR! CHECK IT OUT!

OUR OLD TREE FORT!

I CAN'T BELIEVE THIS THING IS STILL HERE!

IT'S NOT IN BAD SHAPE, EITHER.

MAN, DOES THIS BRING BACK MEMORIES!

BACK THEN WE WERE JUST A COUPLE OF GOOFY-LOOKING KIDS WITH NOTHING BETTER TO DO THAN SIT UP IN A TREE ALL DAY SPYING ON GIRLS.

THANK GOODNESS WE'RE BEYOND THAT STAGE.

SHHH! DO YOU WANT THEM TO HEAR US??

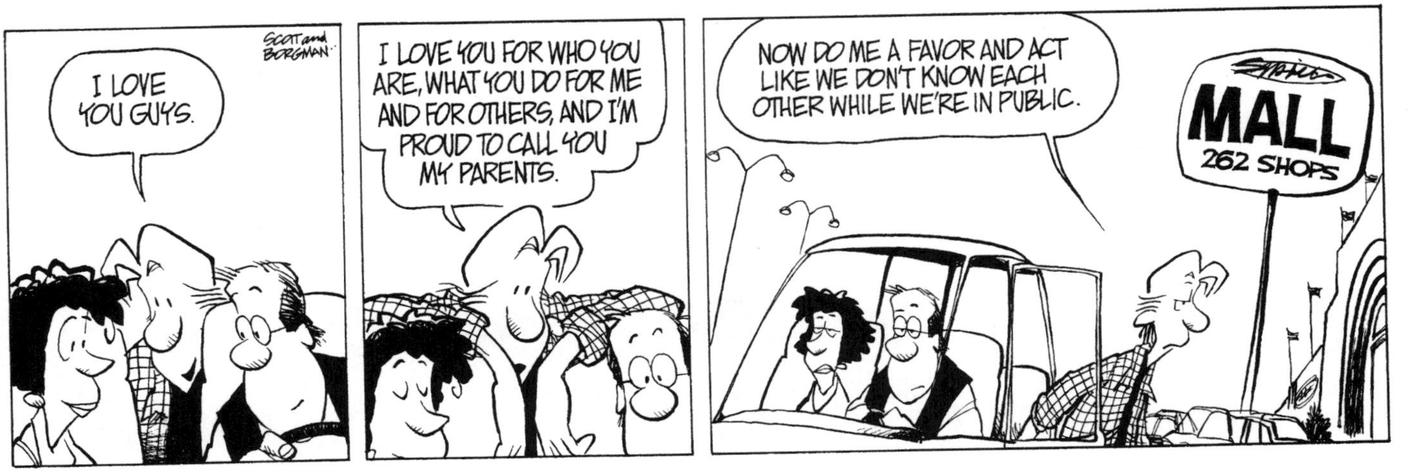
SCOTT and BORGMAN
I LOVE YOU GUYS.
I LOVE YOU FOR WHO YOU ARE, WHAT YOU DO FOR ME AND FOR OTHERS, AND I'M PROUD TO CALL YOU MY PARENTS.
NOW DO ME A FAVOR AND ACT LIKE WE DON'T KNOW EACH OTHER WHILE WE'RE IN PUBLIC.
MALL
262 SHOPS

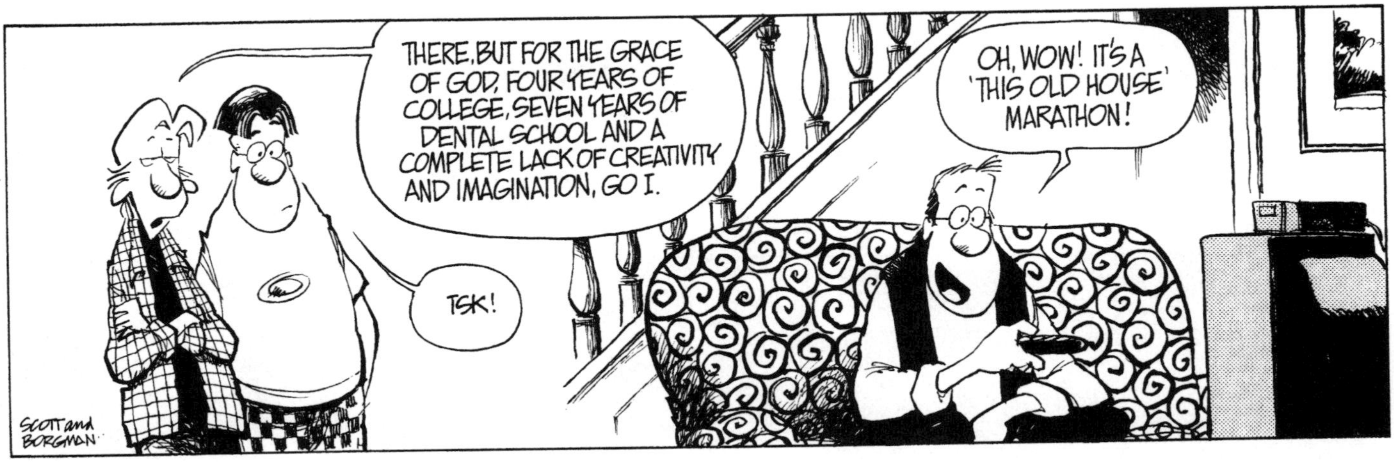
THERE, BUT FOR THE GRACE OF GOD, FOUR YEARS OF COLLEGE, SEVEN YEARS OF DENTAL SCHOOL AND A COMPLETE LACK OF CREATIVITY AND IMAGINATION, GO I.
TSK!
OH, WOW! IT'S A 'THIS OLD HOUSE' MARATHON!
SCOTT and BORGMAN

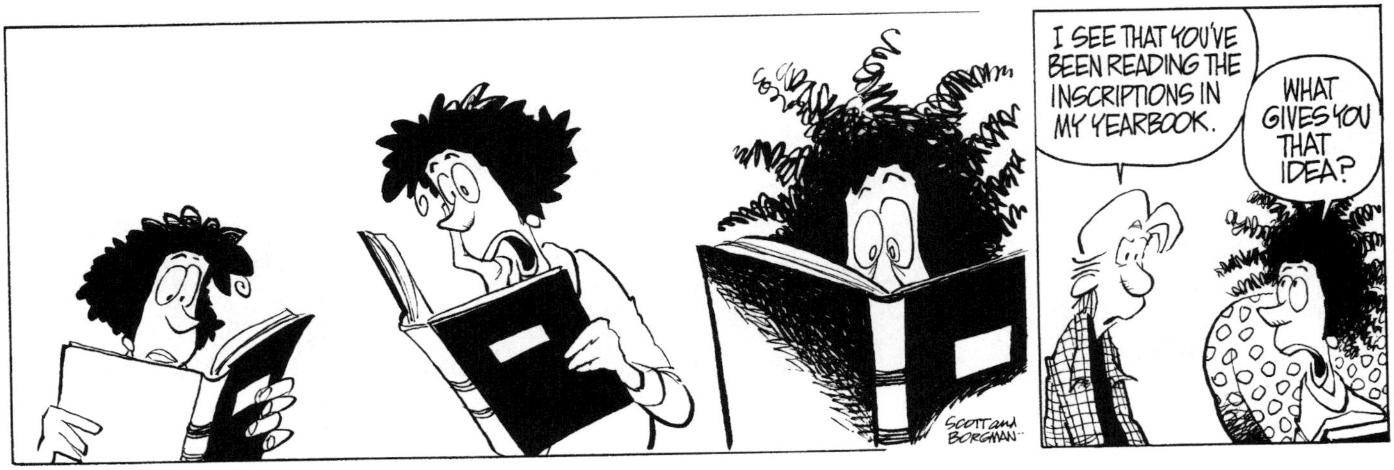
SCOTT and BORGMAN
I SEE THAT YOU'VE BEEN READING THE INSCRIPTIONS IN MY YEARBOOK.
WHAT GIVES YOU THAT IDEA?

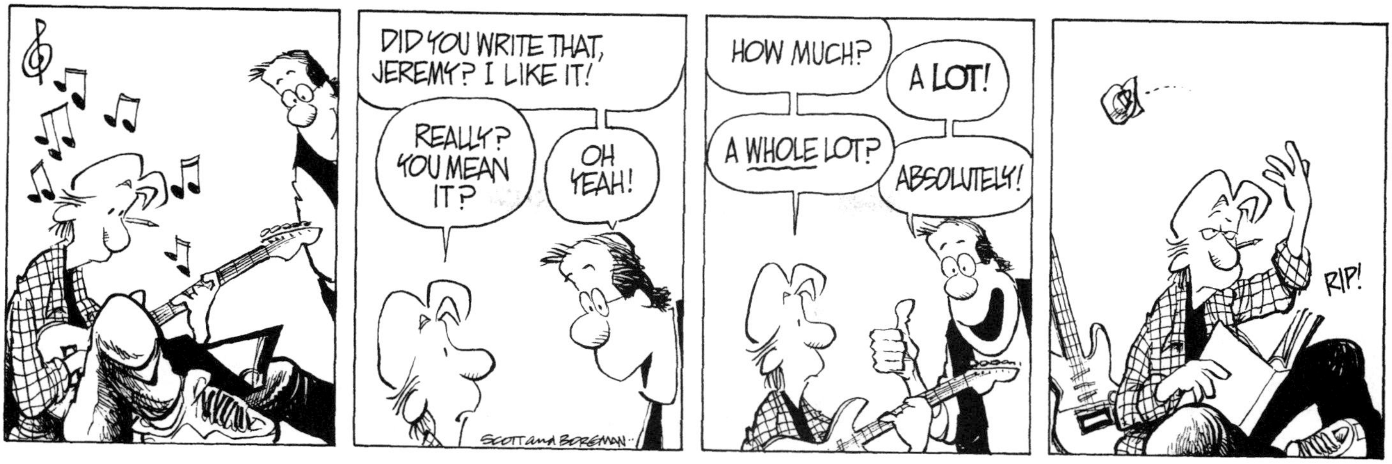
DID YOU WRITE THAT, JEREMY? I LIKE IT!
REALLY? YOU MEAN IT?
OH YEAH!
SCOTT and BORGMAN
HOW MUCH?
A LOT!
A WHOLE LOT?
ABSOLUTELY!
RIP!

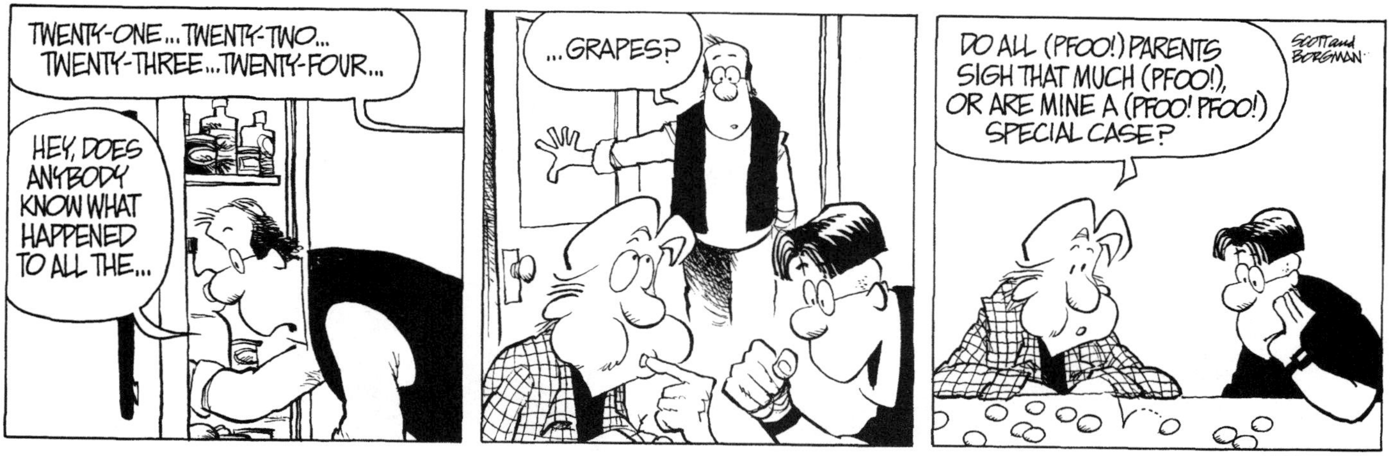
TWENTY-ONE... TWENTY-TWO... TWENTY-THREE... TWENTY-FOUR...
HEY, DOES ANYBODY KNOW WHAT HAPPENED TO ALL THE...
...GRAPES?
DO ALL (PFOO!) PARENTS SIGH THAT MUCH (PFOO!), OR ARE MINE A (PFOO! PFOO!) SPECIAL CASE?
SCOTT and BORGMAN

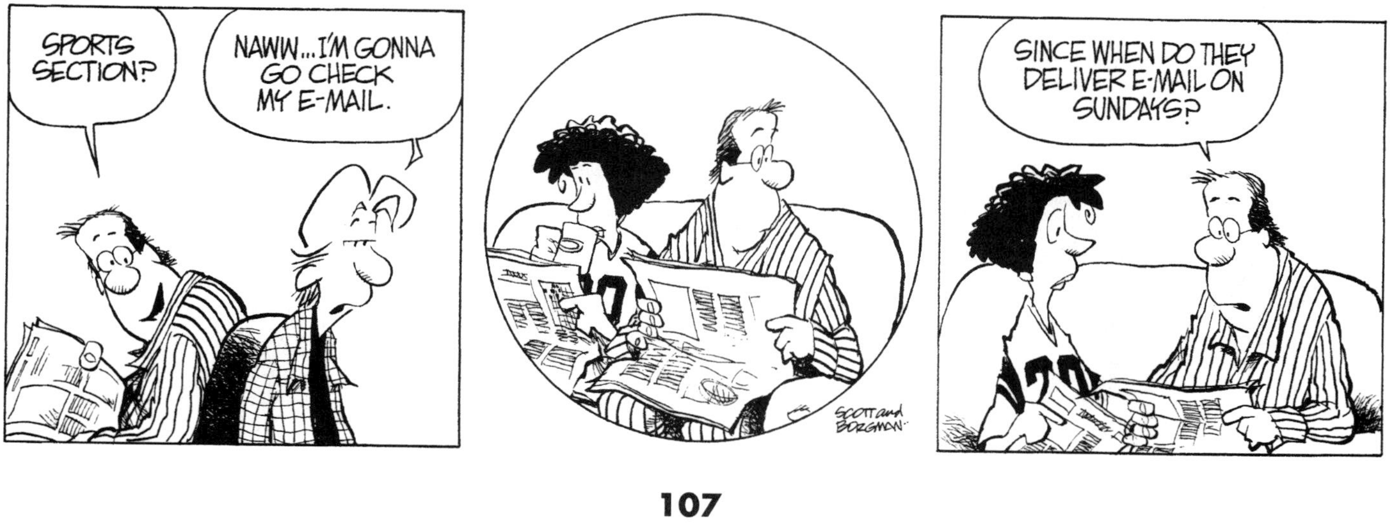
SPORTS SECTION?
NAWW... I'M GONNA GO CHECK MY E-MAIL.
SCOTT and BORGMAN
SINCE WHEN DO THEY DELIVER E-MAIL ON SUNDAYS?

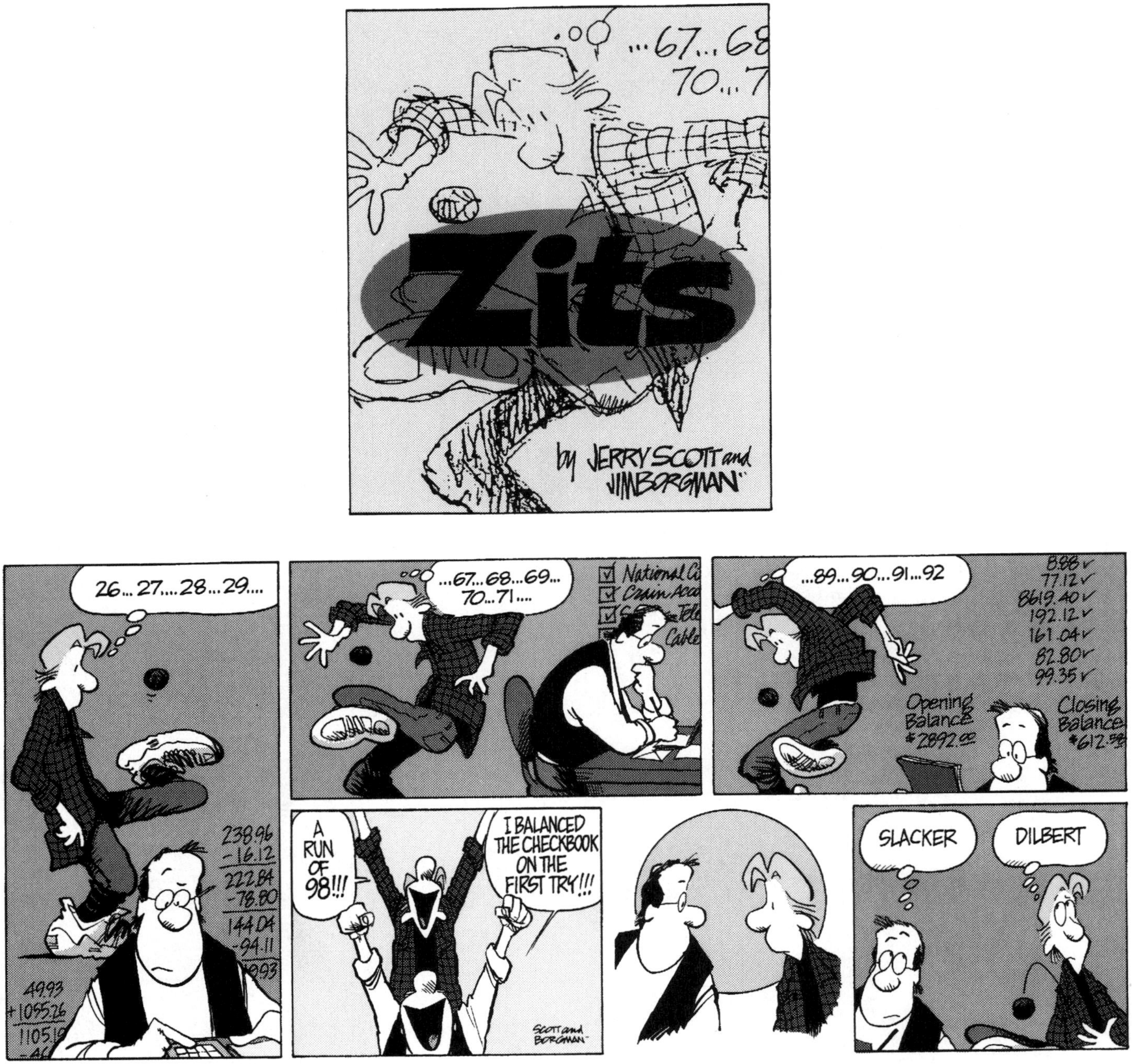

Zits
by JERRY SCOTT and JIM BORGMAN
26... 27.... 28... 29....
238.96
-16.12
222.84
-78.80
144.04
-94.11
49.93
+1055.26
...67...68...69...
70...71....
National
Cable
...89...90...91...92
8.88
77.12
8619.40
192.12
161.04
82.80
99.35
Opening Balance $2892.00
Closing Balance $612.58
A RUN OF 98!!!
I BALANCED THE CHECKBOOK ON THE FIRST TRY!!!
SCOTT and BORGMAN
SLACKER
DILBERT

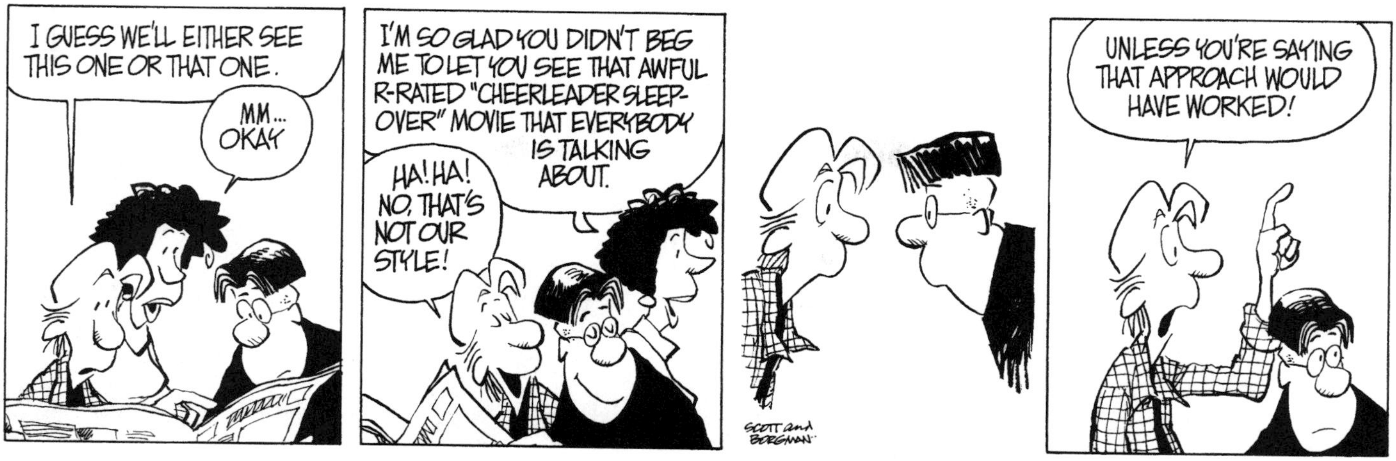
I GUESS WE'LL EITHER SEE THIS ONE OR THAT ONE.
MM... OKAY
I'M SO GLAD YOU DIDN'T BEG ME TO LET YOU SEE THAT AWFUL R-RATED "CHEERLEADER SLEEP-OVER" MOVIE THAT EVERYBODY IS TALKING ABOUT.
HA! HA! NO, THAT'S NOT OUR STYLE!
UNLESS YOU'RE SAYING THAT APPROACH WOULD HAVE WORKED!
SCOTT AND BORGMAN

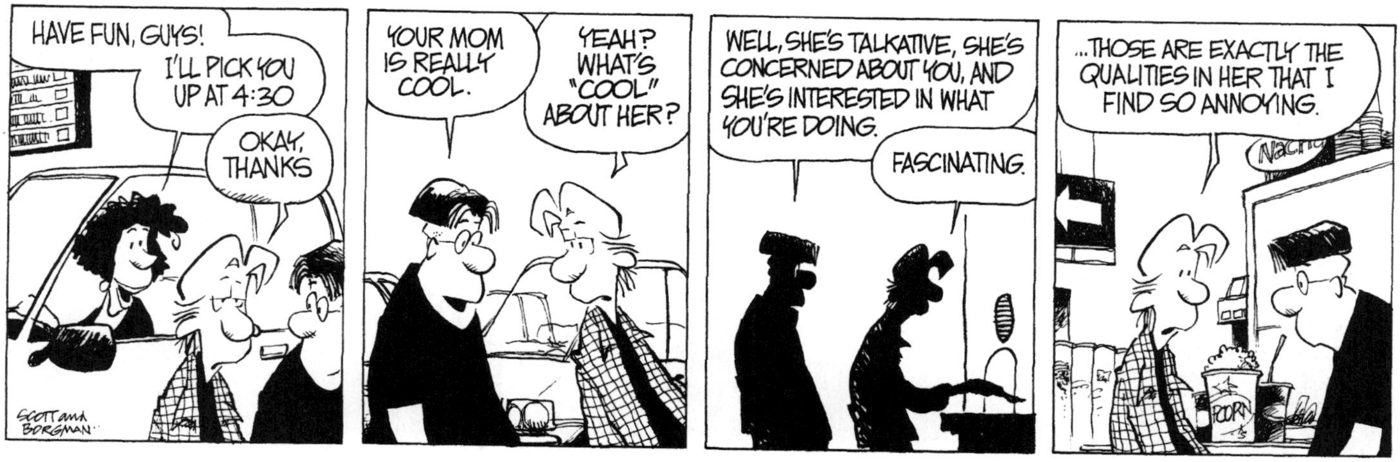
HAVE FUN, GUYS!
I'LL PICK YOU UP AT 4:30
OKAY, THANKS
SCOTT AND BORGMAN
YOUR MOM IS REALLY COOL.
YEAH? WHAT'S "COOL" ABOUT HER?
WELL, SHE'S TALKATIVE, SHE'S CONCERNED ABOUT YOU, AND SHE'S INTERESTED IN WHAT YOU'RE DOING.
FASCINATING.
...THOSE ARE EXACTLY THE QUALITIES IN HER THAT I FIND SO ANNOYING.

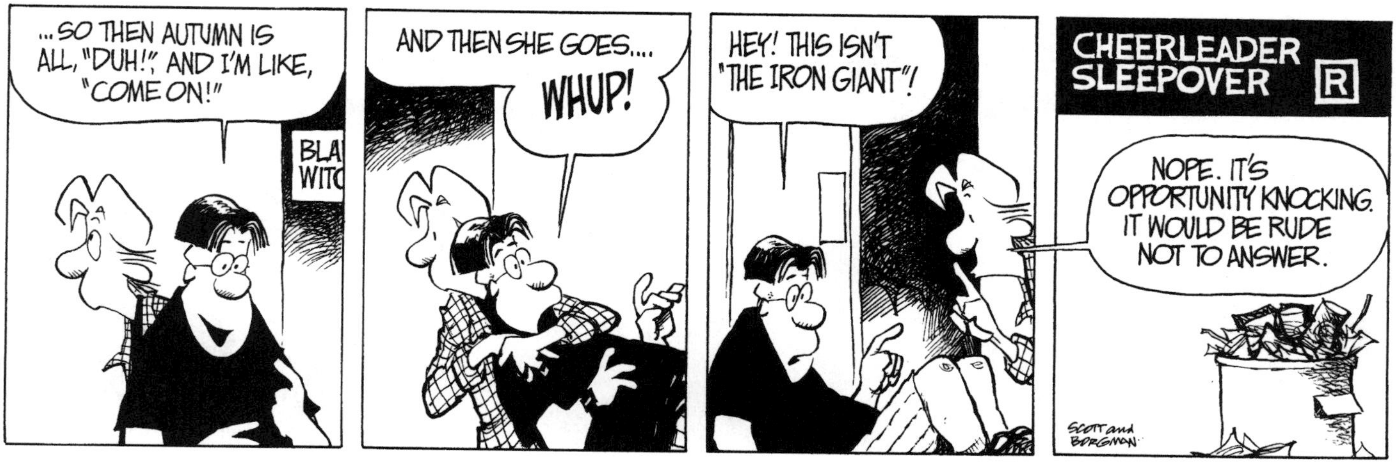
...SO THEN AUTUMN IS ALL, "DUH!", AND I'M LIKE, "COME ON!"
AND THEN SHE GOES....
WHUP!
HEY! THIS ISN'T "THE IRON GIANT"!
CHEERLEADER SLEEPOVER R
NOPE. IT'S OPPORTUNITY KNOCKING. IT WOULD BE RUDE NOT TO ANSWER.
SCOTT AND BORGMAN

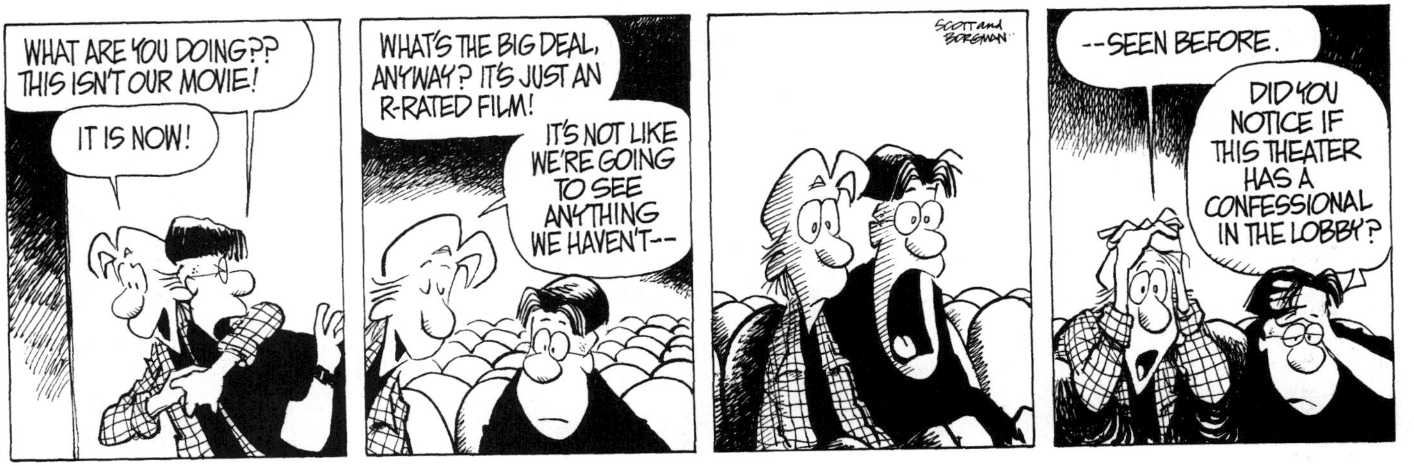
WHAT ARE YOU DOING?? THIS ISN'T OUR MOVIE!
IT IS NOW!
WHAT'S THE BIG DEAL, ANYWAY? IT'S JUST AN R-RATED FILM!
IT'S NOT LIKE WE'RE GOING TO SEE ANYTHING WE HAVEN'T--
SCOTT and BORGMAN
--SEEN BEFORE.
DID YOU NOTICE IF THIS THEATER HAS A CONFESSIONAL IN THE LOBBY?

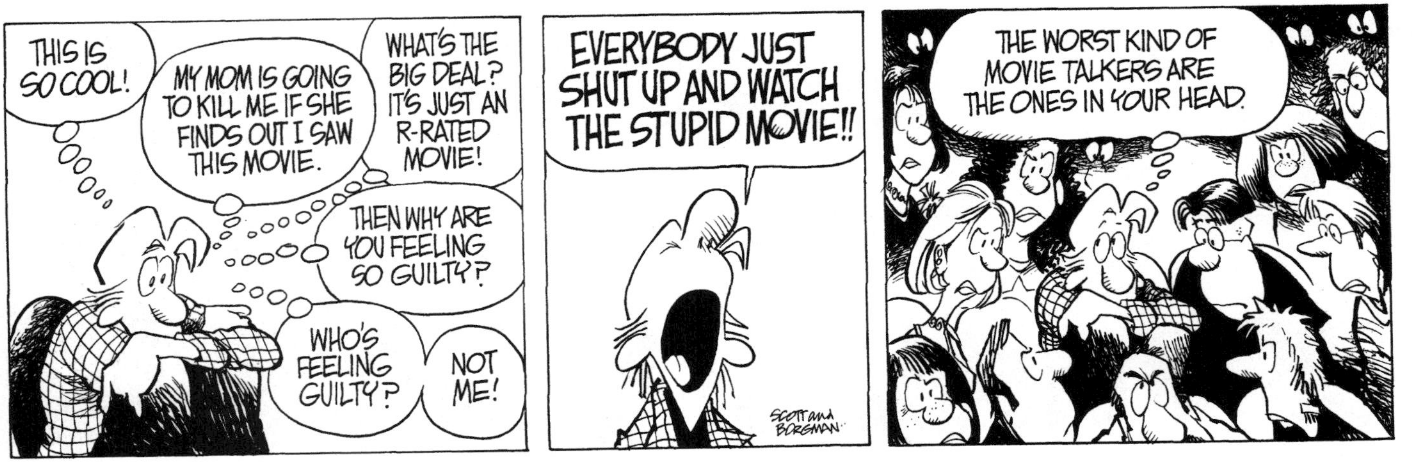
THIS IS SO COOL!
MY MOM IS GOING TO KILL ME IF SHE FINDS OUT I SAW THIS MOVIE.
WHAT'S THE BIG DEAL? IT'S JUST AN R-RATED MOVIE!
THEN WHY ARE YOU FEELING SO GUILTY?
WHO'S FEELING GUILTY?
NOT ME!
EVERYBODY JUST SHUT UP AND WATCH THE STUPID MOVIE!!
SCOTT and BORGMAN
THE WORST KIND OF MOVIE TALKERS ARE THE ONES IN YOUR HEAD.

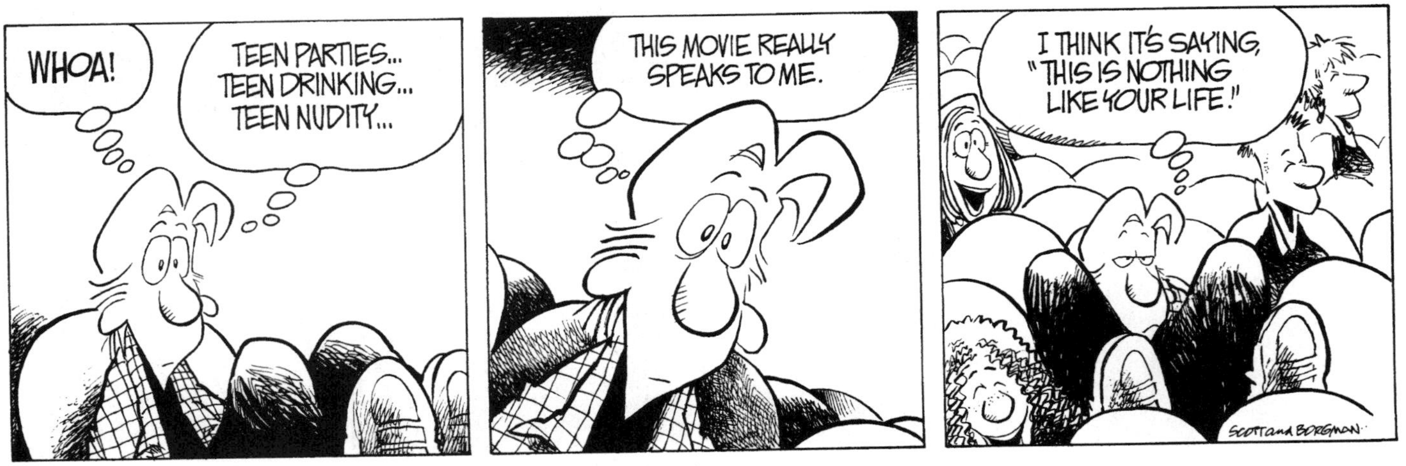
WHOA!
TEEN PARTIES... TEEN DRINKING... TEEN NUDITY...
THIS MOVIE REALLY SPEAKS TO ME.
I THINK IT'S SAYING, "THIS IS NOTHING LIKE YOUR LIFE."
SCOTT and BORGMAN

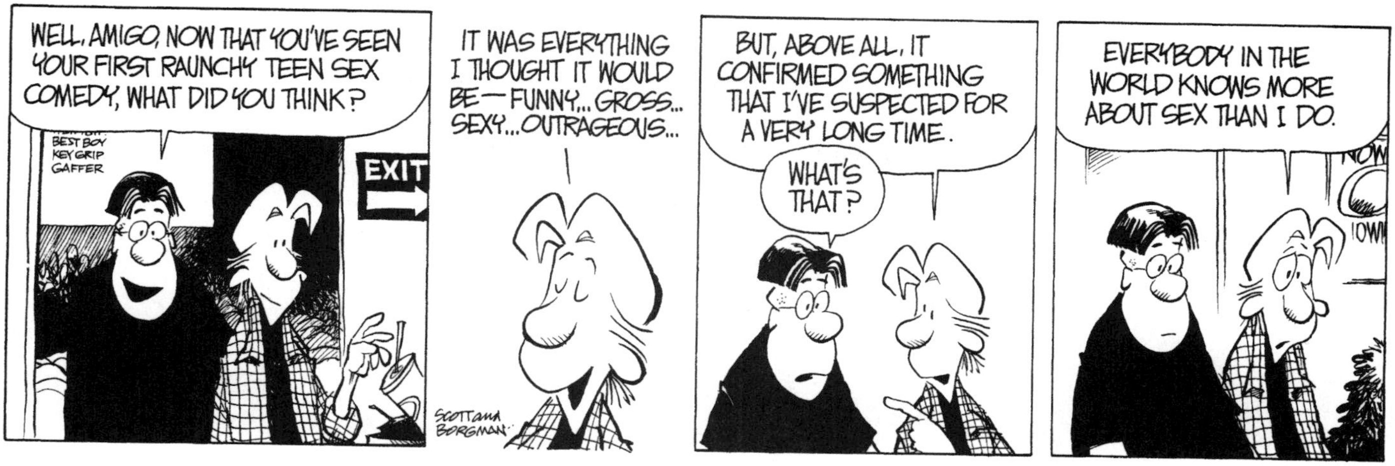
WELL, AMIGO, NOW THAT YOU'VE SEEN YOUR FIRST RAUNCHY TEEN SEX COMEDY, WHAT DID YOU THINK?
BEST BOY
KEY GRIP
GAFFER
EXIT
IT WAS EVERYTHING I THOUGHT IT WOULD BE— FUNNY... GROSS... SEXY... OUTRAGEOUS...
SCOTT and BORGMAN
BUT, ABOVE ALL, IT CONFIRMED SOMETHING THAT I'VE SUSPECTED FOR A VERY LONG TIME.
WHAT'S THAT?
EVERYBODY IN THE WORLD KNOWS MORE ABOUT SEX THAN I DO.

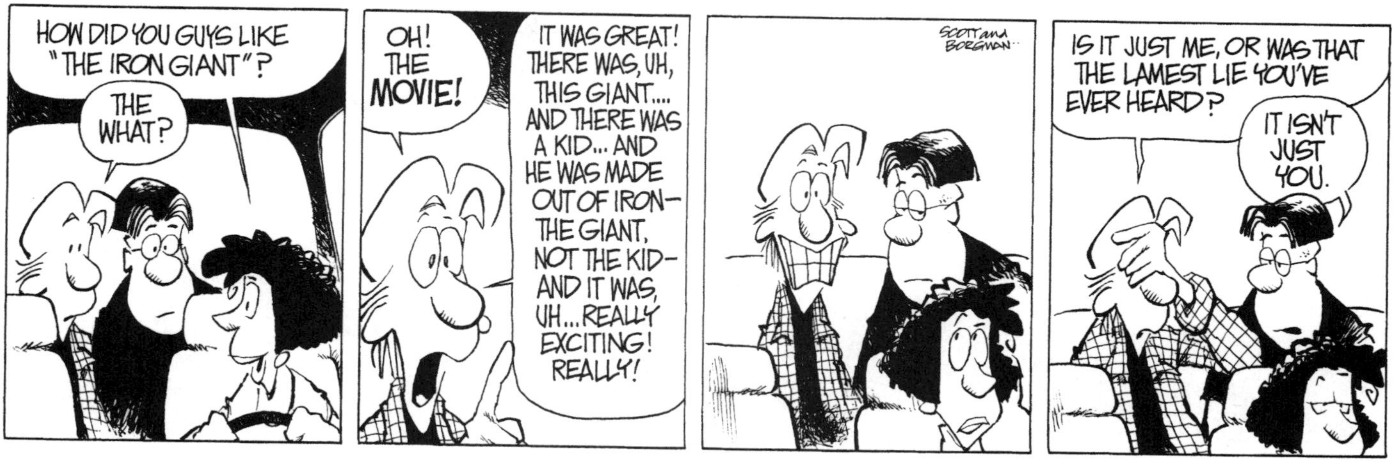
HOW DID YOU GUYS LIKE "THE IRON GIANT"?
THE WHAT?
OH! THE MOVIE!
IT WAS GREAT! THERE WAS, UH, THIS GIANT.... AND THERE WAS A KID... AND HE WAS MADE OUT OF IRON— THE GIANT, NOT THE KID— AND IT WAS, UH... REALLY EXCITING! REALLY!
SCOTT and BORGMAN
IS IT JUST ME, OR WAS THAT THE LAMEST LIE YOU'VE EVER HEARD?
IT ISN'T JUST YOU.

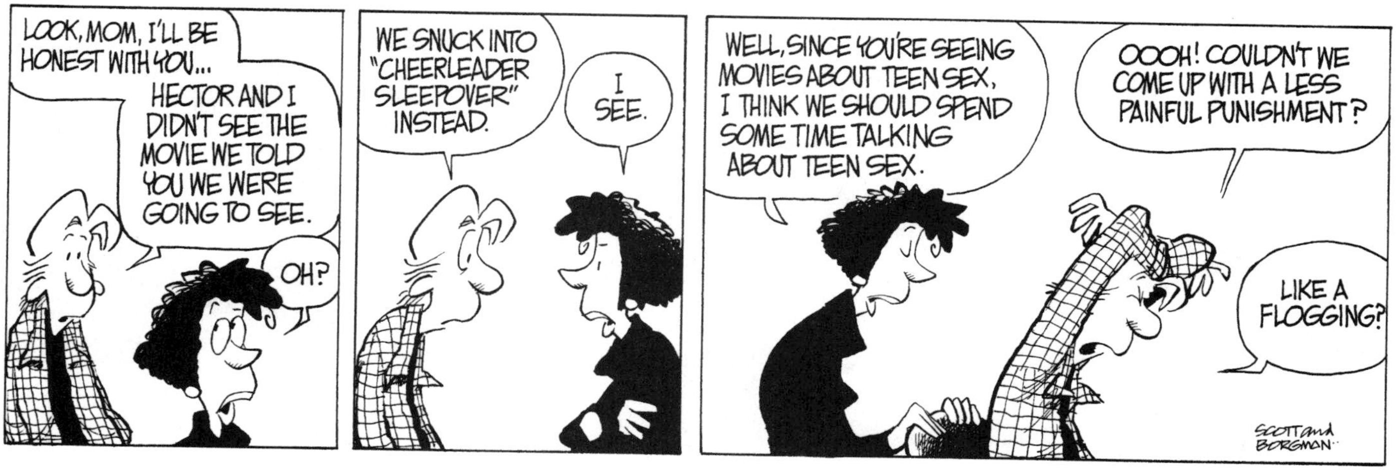
LOOK, MOM, I'LL BE HONEST WITH YOU...
HECTOR AND I DIDN'T SEE THE MOVIE WE TOLD YOU WE WERE GOING TO SEE.
OH?
WE SNUCK INTO "CHEERLEADER SLEEPOVER" INSTEAD.
I SEE.
WELL, SINCE YOU'RE SEEING MOVIES ABOUT TEEN SEX, I THINK WE SHOULD SPEND SOME TIME TALKING ABOUT TEEN SEX.
OOOH! COULDN'T WE COME UP WITH A LESS PAINFUL PUNISHMENT?
LIKE A FLOGGING?
SCOTT and BORGMAN

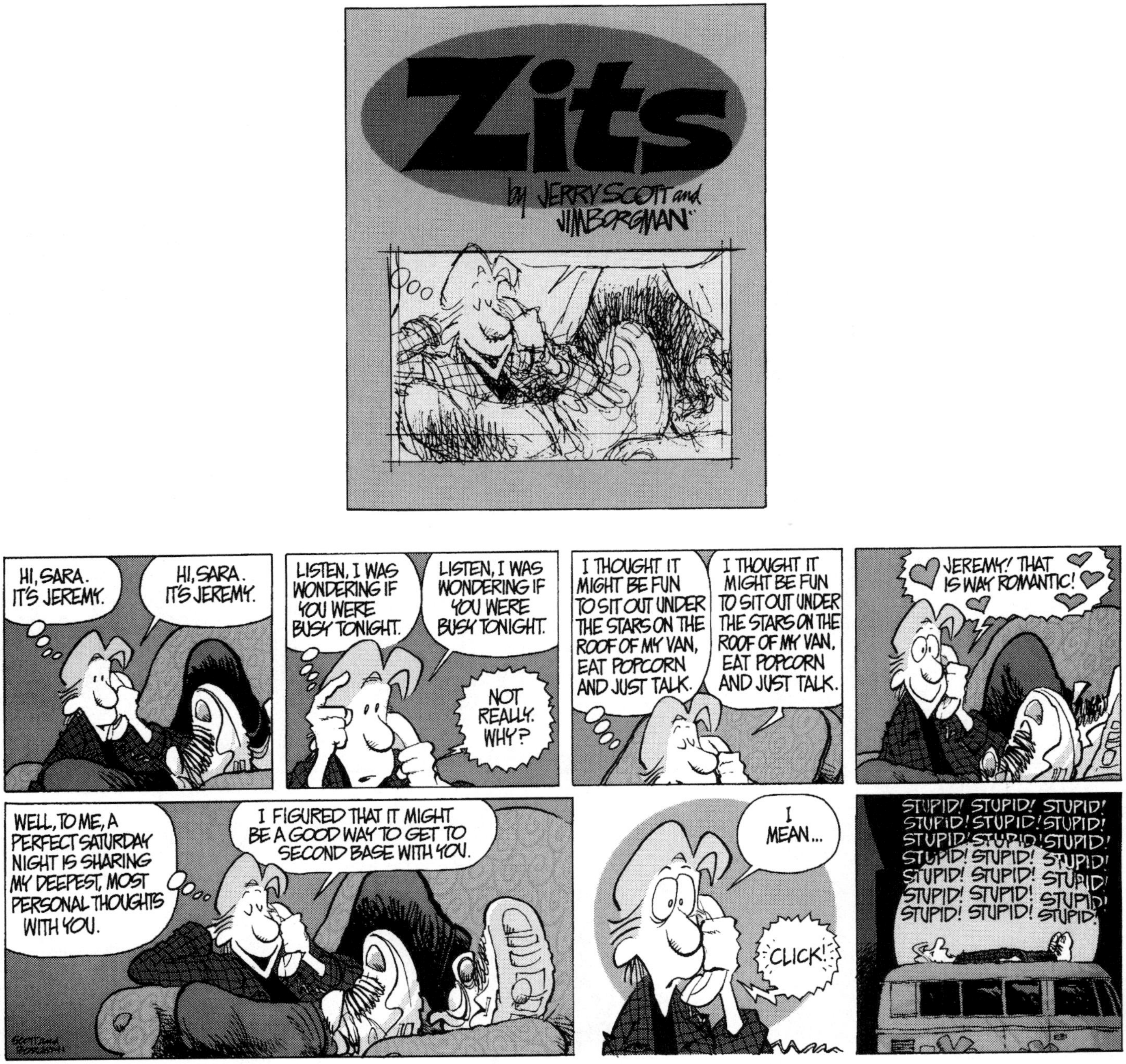
Zits
by JERRY SCOTT and JIM BORGMAN
HI, SARA. IT'S JEREMY.
HI, SARA. IT'S JEREMY.
LISTEN, I WAS WONDERING IF YOU WERE BUSY TONIGHT.
LISTEN, I WAS WONDERING IF YOU WERE BUSY TONIGHT.
NOT REALLY. WHY?
I THOUGHT IT MIGHT BE FUN TO SIT OUT UNDER THE STARS ON THE ROOF OF MY VAN, EAT POPCORN AND JUST TALK.
I THOUGHT IT MIGHT BE FUN TO SIT OUT UNDER THE STARS ON THE ROOF OF MY VAN, EAT POPCORN AND JUST TALK.
JEREMY! THAT IS WAY ROMANTIC!
WELL, TO ME, A PERFECT SATURDAY NIGHT IS SHARING MY DEEPEST, MOST PERSONAL THOUGHTS WITH YOU.
I FIGURED THAT IT MIGHT BE A GOOD WAY TO GET TO SECOND BASE WITH YOU.
I MEAN...
CLICK!
STUPID! STUPID!

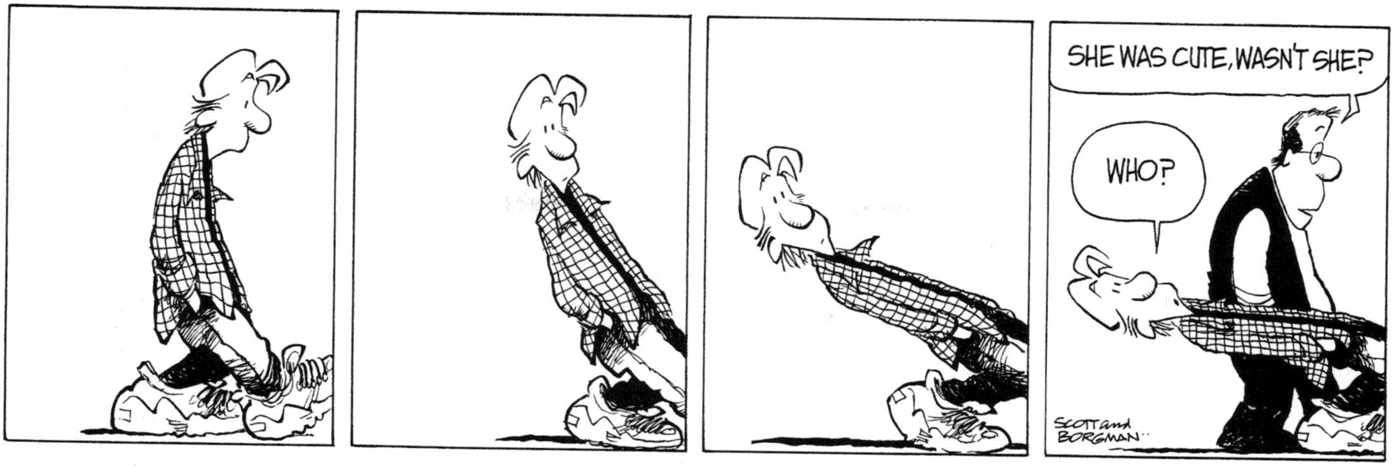
SHE WAS CUTE, WASN'T SHE?
WHO?
SCOTT and BORGMAN

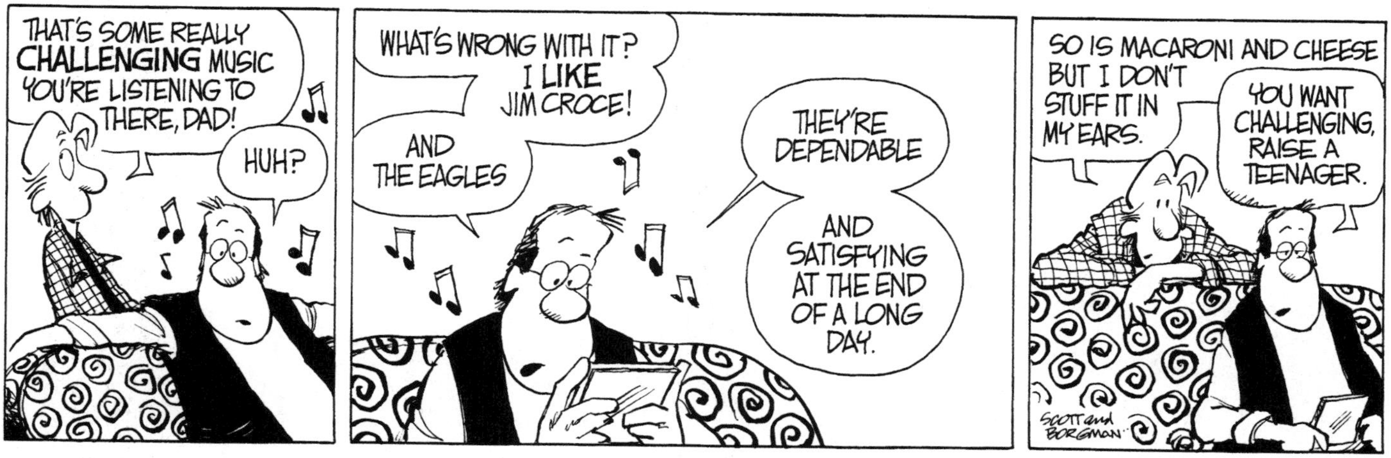
THAT'S SOME REALLY CHALLENGING MUSIC YOU'RE LISTENING TO THERE, DAD!
HUH?
WHAT'S WRONG WITH IT? I LIKE JIM CROCE!
AND THE EAGLES
THEY'RE DEPENDABLE
AND SATISFYING AT THE END OF A LONG DAY.
SO IS MACARONI AND CHEESE BUT I DON'T STUFF IT IN MY EARS.
YOU WANT CHALLENGING, RAISE A TEENAGER.
SCOTT and BORGMAN

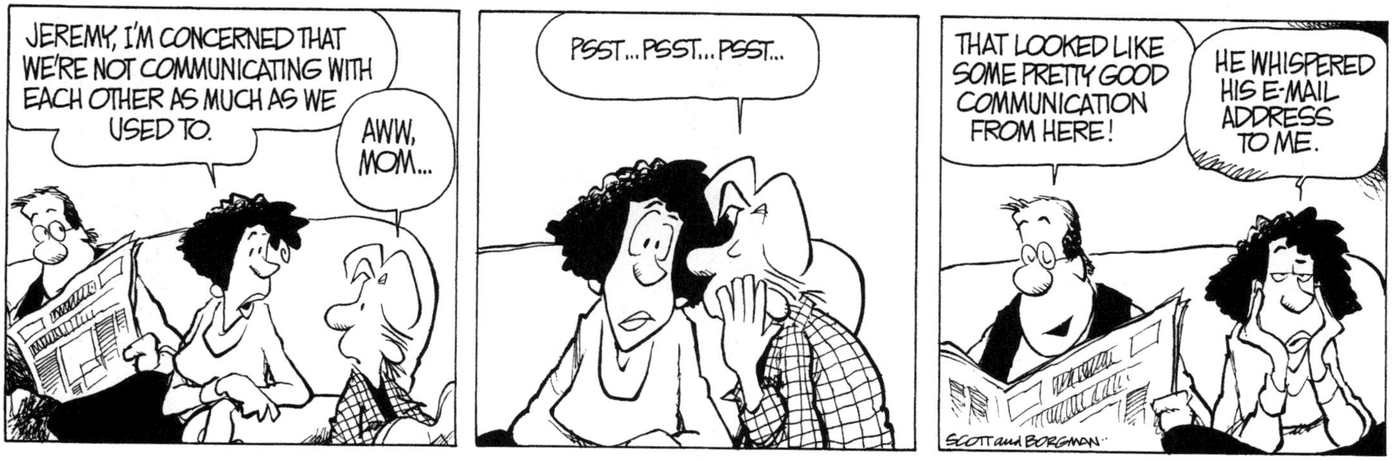
JEREMY, I'M CONCERNED THAT WE'RE NOT COMMUNICATING WITH EACH OTHER AS MUCH AS WE USED TO.
AWW, MOM...
PSST... PSST... PSST...
THAT LOOKED LIKE SOME PRETTY GOOD COMMUNICATION FROM HERE!
HE WHISPERED HIS E-MAIL ADDRESS TO ME.
SCOTT and BORGMAN

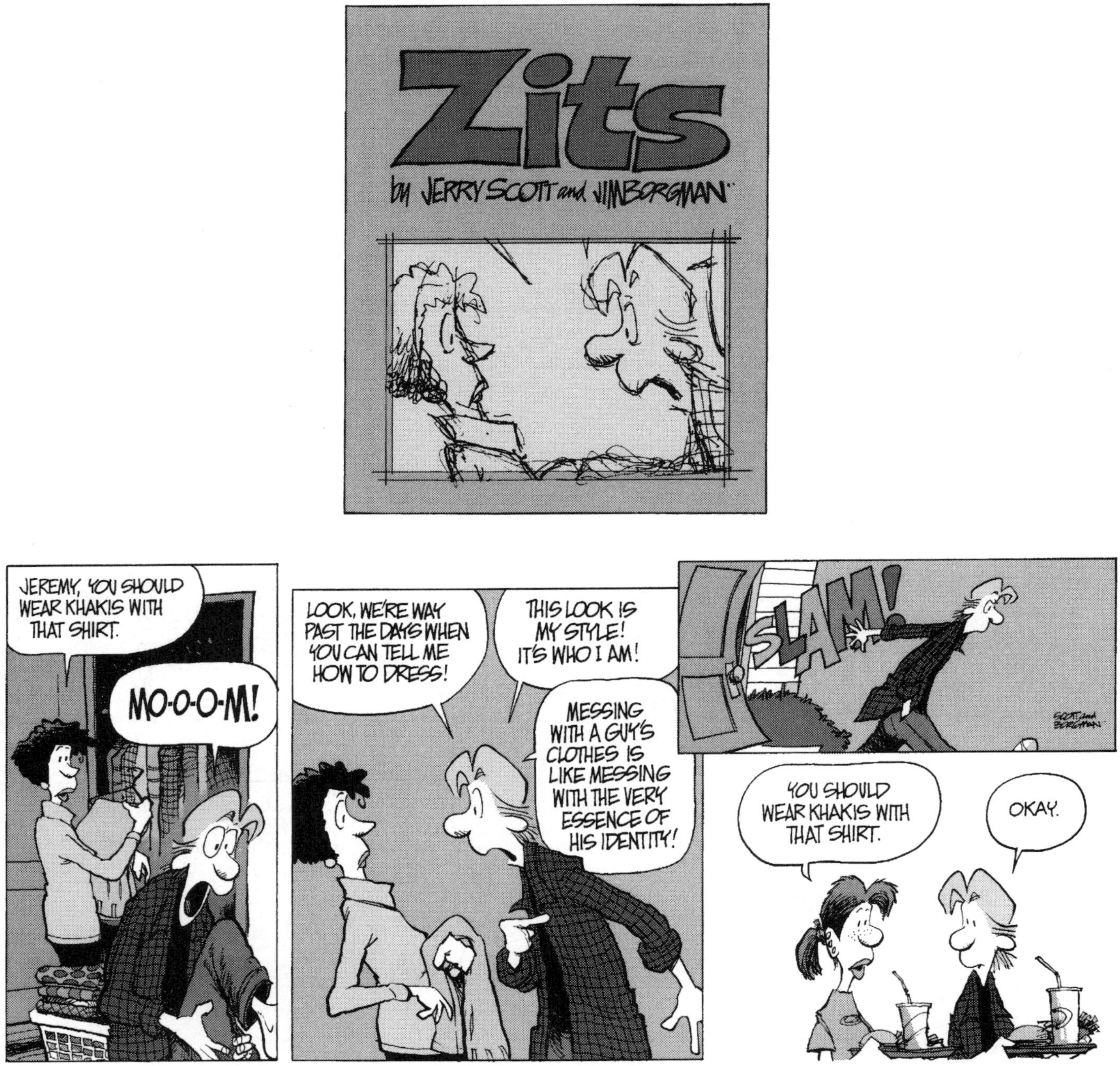
Zits
by JERRY SCOTT and JIM BORGMAN
JEREMY, YOU SHOULD WEAR KHAKIS WITH THAT SHIRT.
MO-O-O-M!
LOOK, WE'RE WAY PAST THE DAYS WHEN YOU CAN TELL ME HOW TO DRESS!
THIS LOOK IS MY STYLE! IT'S WHO I AM!
MESSING WITH A GUY'S CLOTHES IS LIKE MESSING WITH THE VERY ESSENCE OF HIS IDENTITY!
SLAM!
SCOTT and BORGMAN
YOU SHOULD WEAR KHAKIS WITH THAT SHIRT.
OKAY.

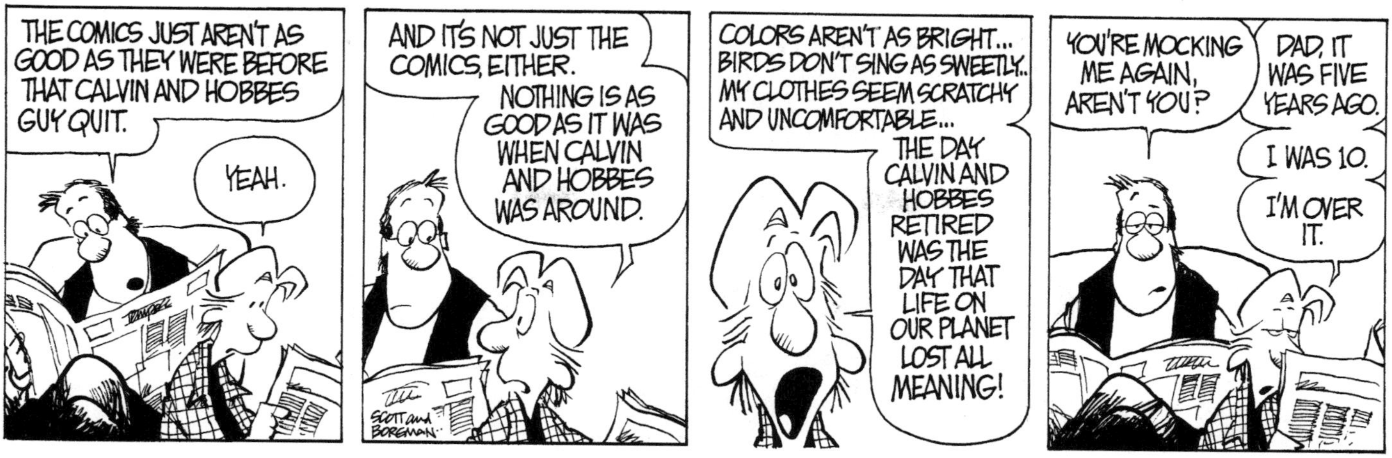
THE COMICS JUST AREN'T AS GOOD AS THEY WERE BEFORE THAT CALVIN AND HOBBES GUY QUIT.
YEAH.
AND IT'S NOT JUST THE COMICS, EITHER.
NOTHING IS AS GOOD AS IT WAS WHEN CALVIN AND HOBBES WAS AROUND.
SCOTT and BORGMAN
COLORS AREN'T AS BRIGHT... BIRDS DON'T SING AS SWEETLY... MY CLOTHES SEEM SCRATCHY AND UNCOMFORTABLE...
THE DAY CALVIN AND HOBBES RETIRED WAS THE DAY THAT LIFE ON OUR PLANET LOST ALL MEANING!
YOU'RE MOCKING ME AGAIN, AREN'T YOU?
DAD, IT WAS FIVE YEARS AGO.
I WAS 10.
I'M OVER IT.

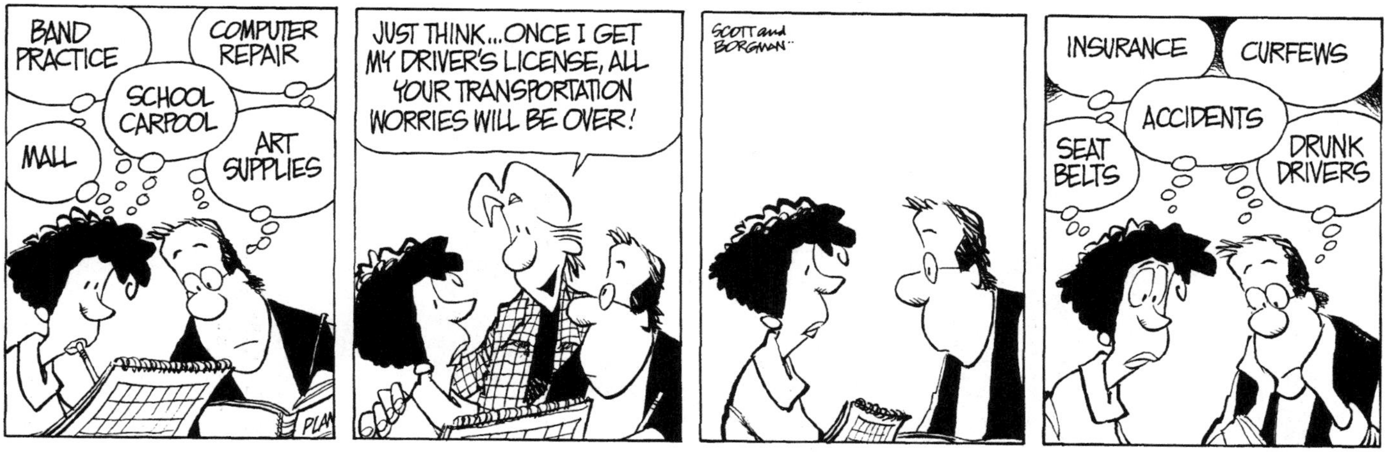
BAND PRACTICE
COMPUTER REPAIR
SCHOOL CARPOOL
MALL
ART SUPPLIES
JUST THINK... ONCE I GET MY DRIVER'S LICENSE, ALL YOUR TRANSPORTATION WORRIES WILL BE OVER!
SCOTT and BORGMAN
INSURANCE
CURFEWS
ACCIDENTS
SEAT BELTS
DRUNK DRIVERS

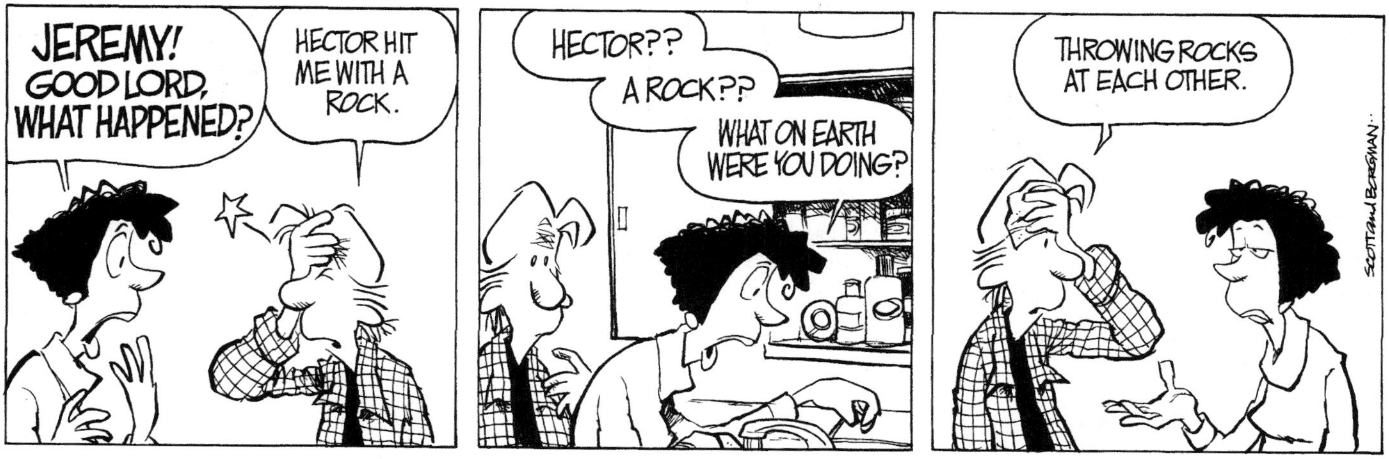
JEREMY! GOOD LORD, WHAT HAPPENED?
HECTOR HIT ME WITH A ROCK.
HECTOR??
A ROCK??
WHAT ON EARTH WERE YOU DOING?
THROWING ROCKS AT EACH OTHER.
SCOTT and BORGMAN

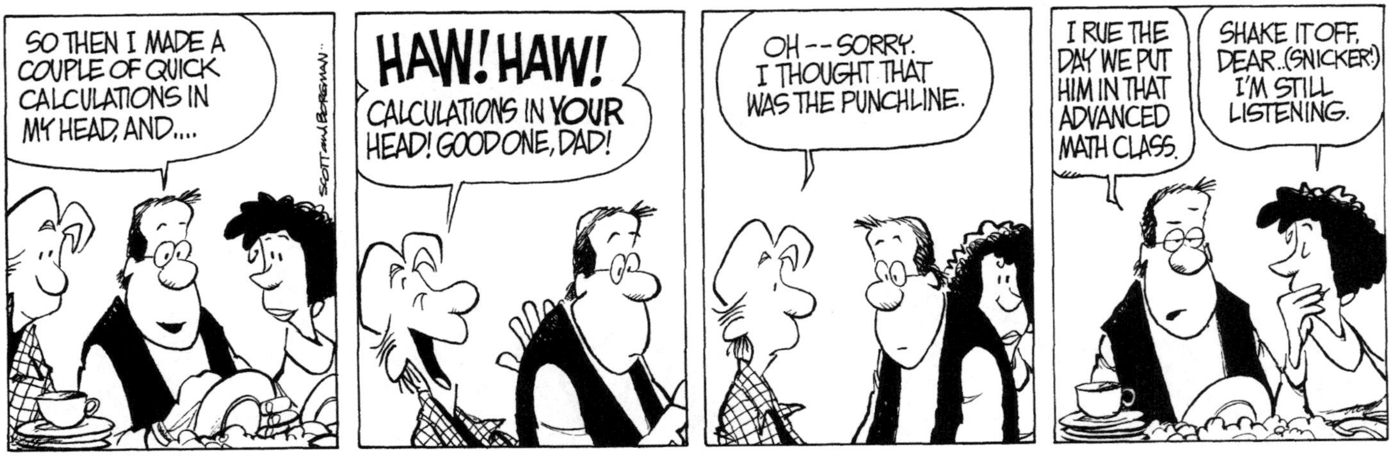
SO THEN I MADE A COUPLE OF QUICK CALCULATIONS IN MY HEAD, AND....
SCOTT and BORGMAN
HAW! HAW!
CALCULATIONS IN YOUR HEAD! GOOD ONE, DAD!
OH -- SORRY. I THOUGHT THAT WAS THE PUNCHLINE.
I RUE THE DAY WE PUT HIM IN THAT ADVANCED MATH CLASS.
SHAKE IT OFF, DEAR..(SNICKER!) I'M STILL LISTENING.

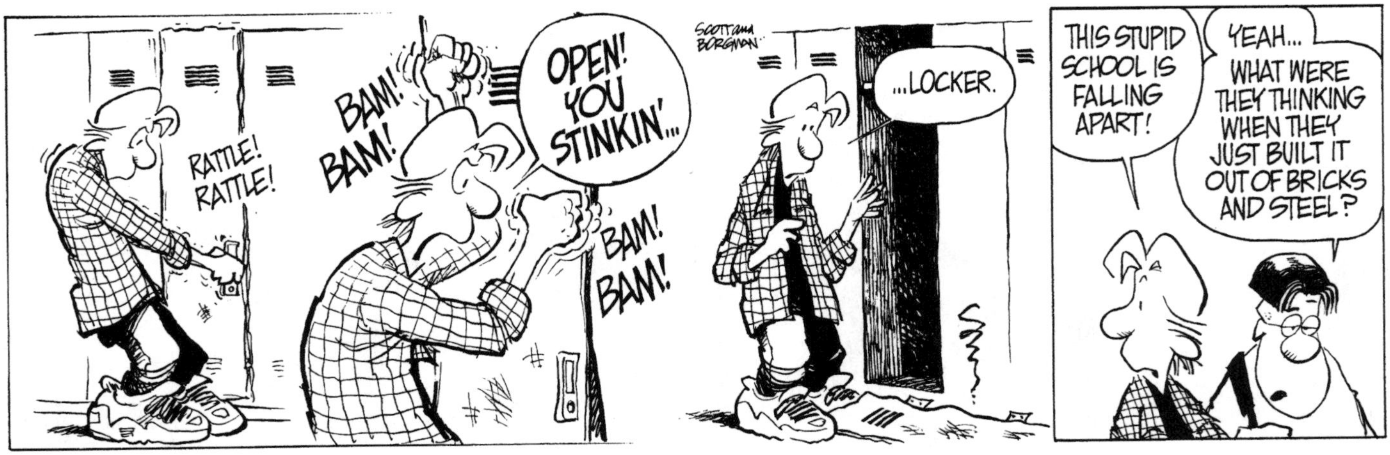
RATTLE! RATTLE!
BAM! BAM!
OPEN! YOU STINKIN'...
BAM! BAM!
SCOTT and BORGMAN
...LOCKER.
THIS STUPID SCHOOL IS FALLING APART!
YEAH... WHAT WERE THEY THINKING WHEN THEY JUST BUILT IT OUT OF BRICKS AND STEEL?

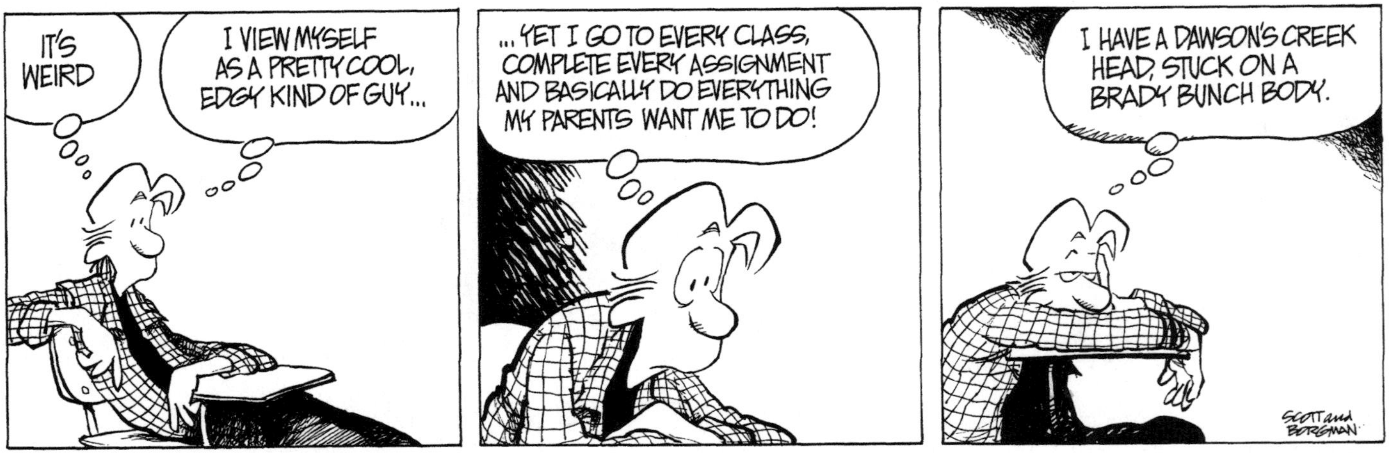
IT'S WEIRD
I VIEW MYSELF AS A PRETTY COOL, EDGY KIND OF GUY...
...YET I GO TO EVERY CLASS, COMPLETE EVERY ASSIGNMENT AND BASICALLY DO EVERYTHING MY PARENTS WANT ME TO DO!
I HAVE A DAWSON'S CREEK HEAD, STUCK ON A BRADY BUNCH BODY.
SCOTT and BORGMAN

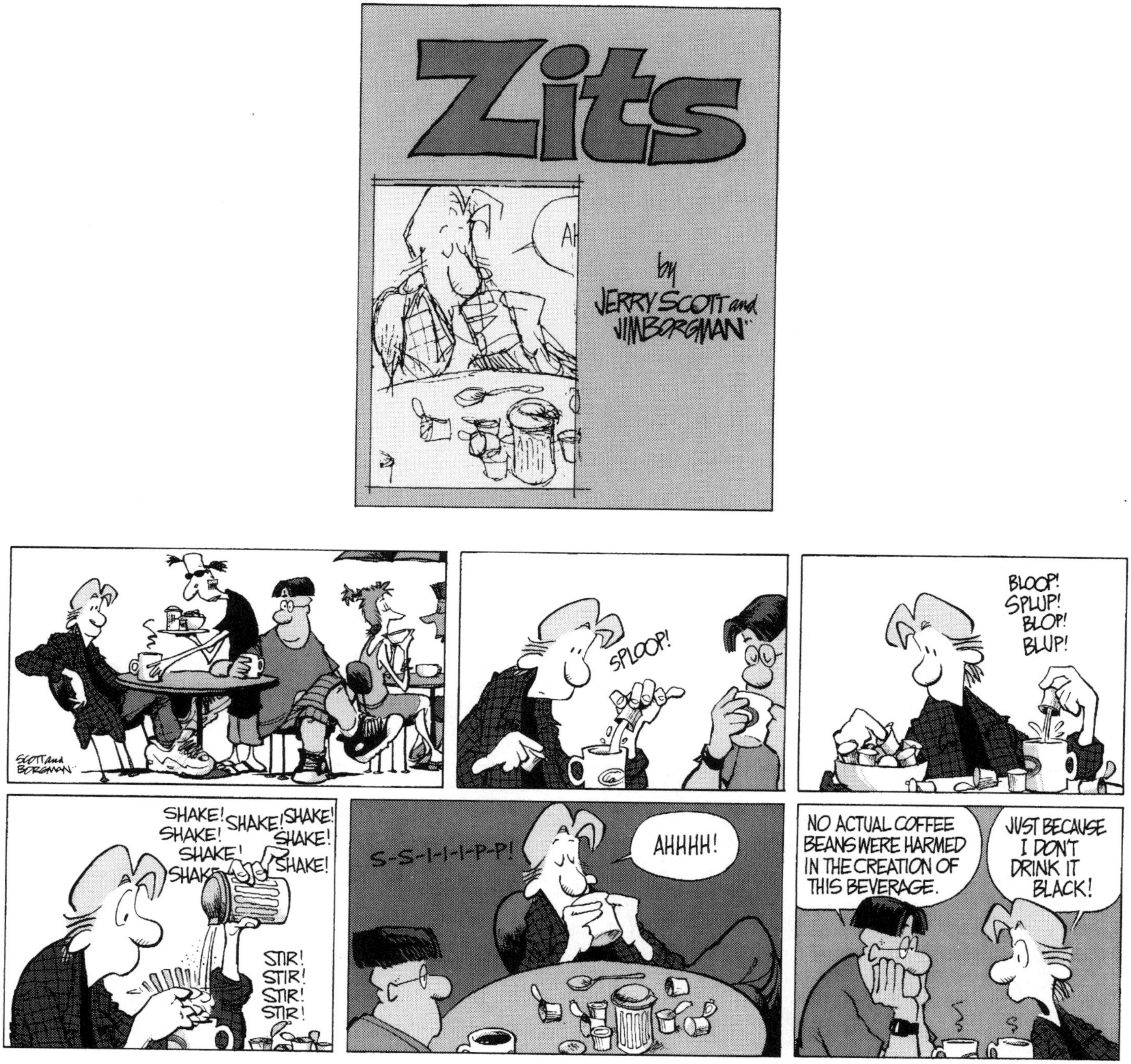
Zits
by JERRY SCOTT and JIM BORGMAN
SCOTT and BORGMAN
SPLOOP!
BLOOP! SPLUP! BLOP! BLUP!
SHAKE! SHAKE! SHAKE! SHAKE! SHAKE! SHAKE! SHAKE! SHAKE!
STIR! STIR! STIR! STIR!
S-S-I-I-I-P-P!
AHHHH!
NO ACTUAL COFFEE BEANS WERE HARMED IN THE CREATION OF THIS BEVERAGE.
JUST BECAUSE I DON'T DRINK IT BLACK!

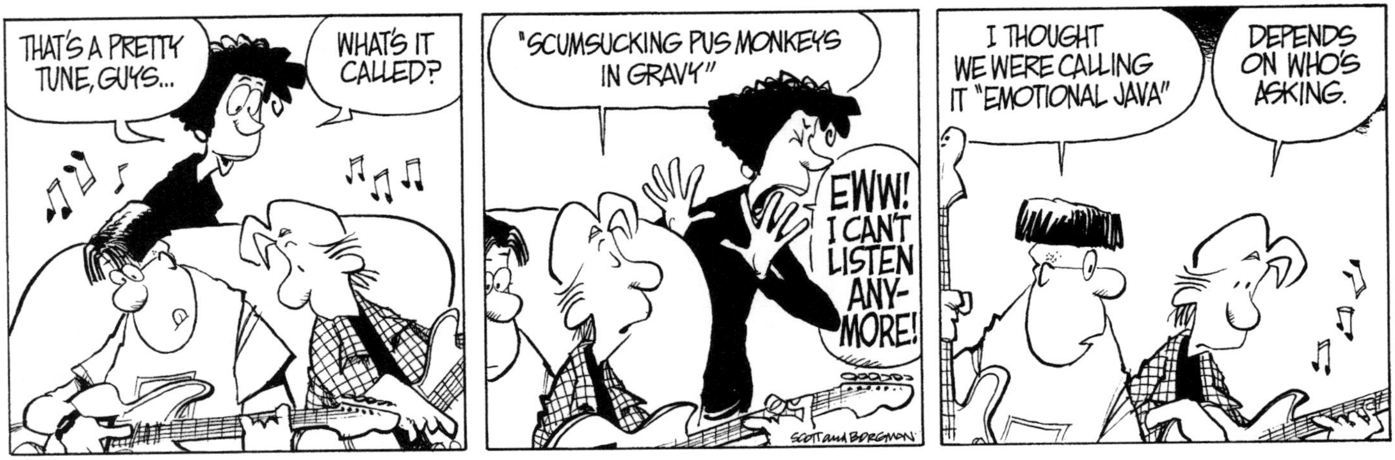
THAT'S A PRETTY TUNE, GUYS...
WHAT'S IT CALLED?
"SCUMSUCKING PUS MONKEYS IN GRAVY"
EWW! I CAN'T LISTEN ANY-MORE!
I THOUGHT WE WERE CALLING IT "EMOTIONAL JAVA"
DEPENDS ON WHO'S ASKING.
SCOTT and BORGMAN

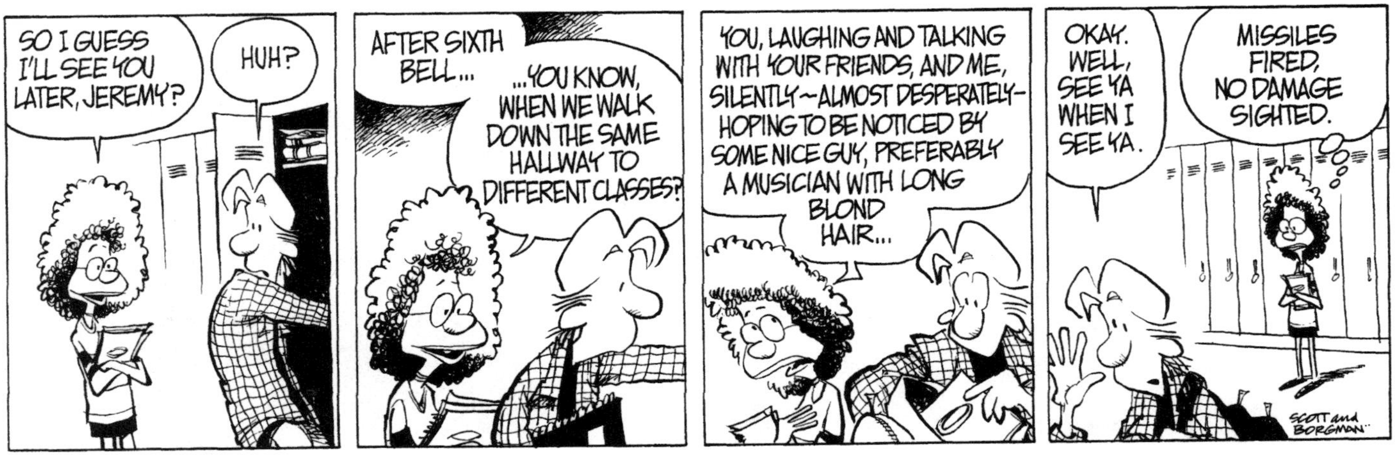
SO I GUESS I'LL SEE YOU LATER, JEREMY?
HUH?
AFTER SIXTH BELL...
...YOU KNOW, WHEN WE WALK DOWN THE SAME HALLWAY TO DIFFERENT CLASSES?
YOU, LAUGHING AND TALKING WITH YOUR FRIENDS, AND ME, SILENTLY—ALMOST DESPERATELY—HOPING TO BE NOTICED BY SOME NICE GUY, PREFERABLY A MUSICIAN WITH LONG BLOND HAIR...
OKAY. WELL, SEE YA WHEN I SEE YA.
MISSILES FIRED, NO DAMAGE SIGHTED.
SCOTT and BORGMAN

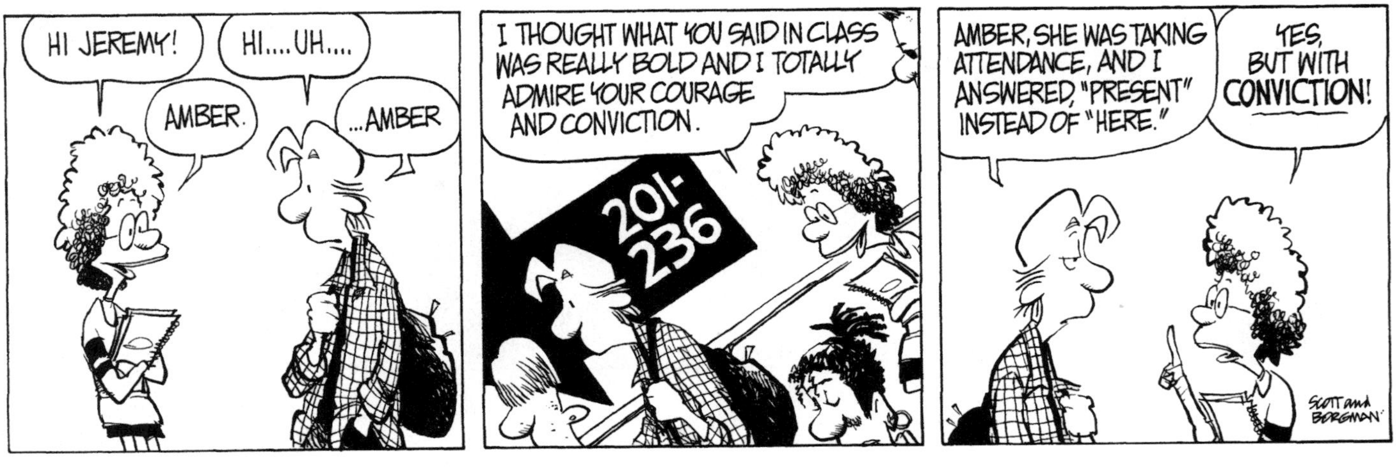
HI JEREMY!
HI.... UH....
AMBER.
...AMBER
I THOUGHT WHAT YOU SAID IN CLASS WAS REALLY BOLD AND I TOTALLY ADMIRE YOUR COURAGE AND CONVICTION.
201-236
AMBER, SHE WAS TAKING ATTENDANCE, AND I ANSWERED, "PRESENT" INSTEAD OF "HERE."
YES, BUT WITH CONVICTION!
SCOTT and BORGMAN

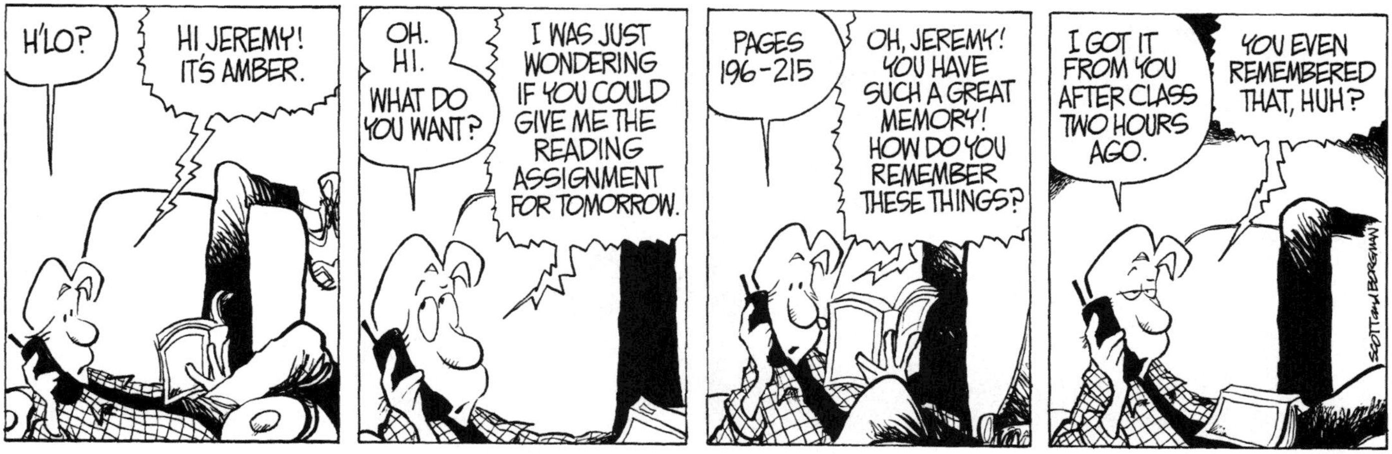
H'LO?
HI JEREMY! IT'S AMBER.
OH. HI.
WHAT DO YOU WANT?
I WAS JUST WONDERING IF YOU COULD GIVE ME THE READING ASSIGNMENT FOR TOMORROW.
PAGES 196-215
OH, JEREMY! YOU HAVE SUCH A GREAT MEMORY! HOW DO YOU REMEMBER THESE THINGS?
I GOT IT FROM YOU AFTER CLASS TWO HOURS AGO.
YOU EVEN REMEMBERED THAT, HUH?
SCOTT and BORGMAN

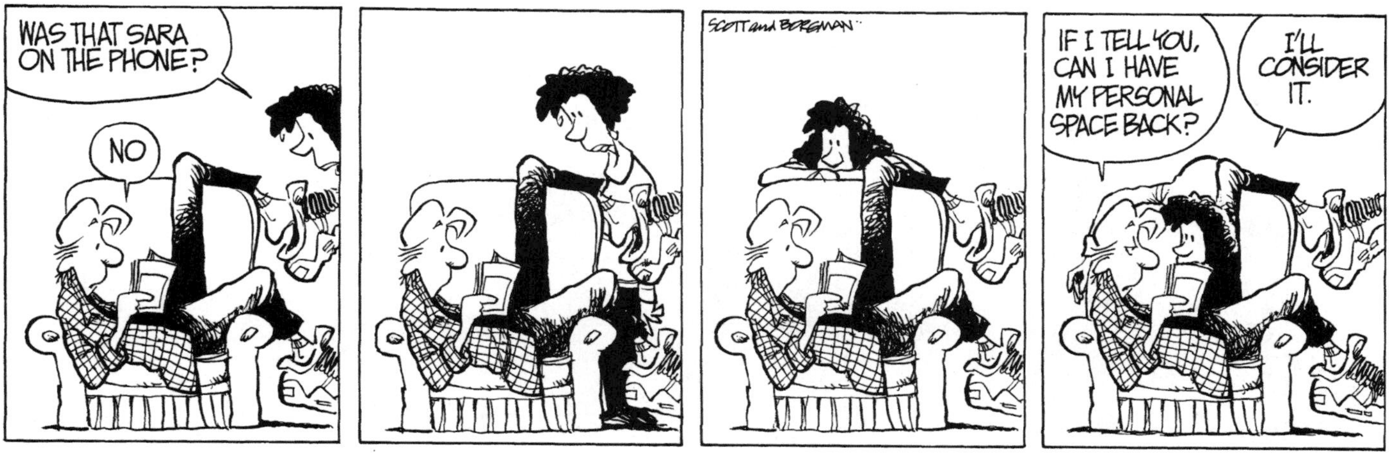
WAS THAT SARA ON THE PHONE?
NO
SCOTT and BORGMAN
IF I TELL YOU, CAN I HAVE MY PERSONAL SPACE BACK?
I'LL CONSIDER IT.

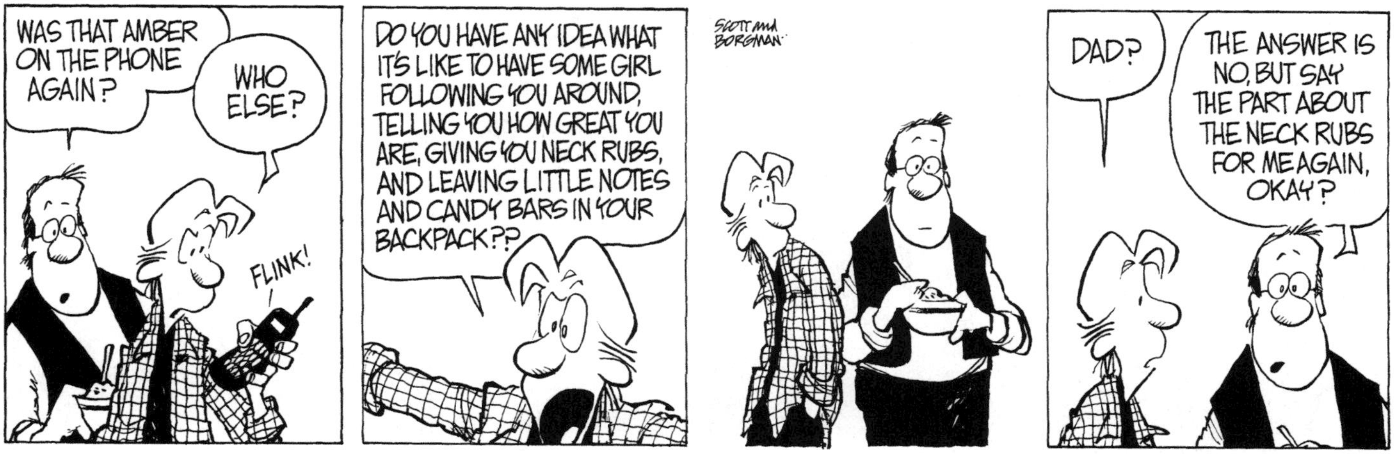
WAS THAT AMBER ON THE PHONE AGAIN?
WHO ELSE?
FLINK!
DO YOU HAVE ANY IDEA WHAT IT'S LIKE TO HAVE SOME GIRL FOLLOWING YOU AROUND, TELLING YOU HOW GREAT YOU ARE, GIVING YOU NECK RUBS, AND LEAVING LITTLE NOTES AND CANDY BARS IN YOUR BACKPACK?!?
SCOTT AND BORGMAN
DAD?
THE ANSWER IS NO, BUT SAY THE PART ABOUT THE NECK RUBS FOR ME AGAIN, OKAY?

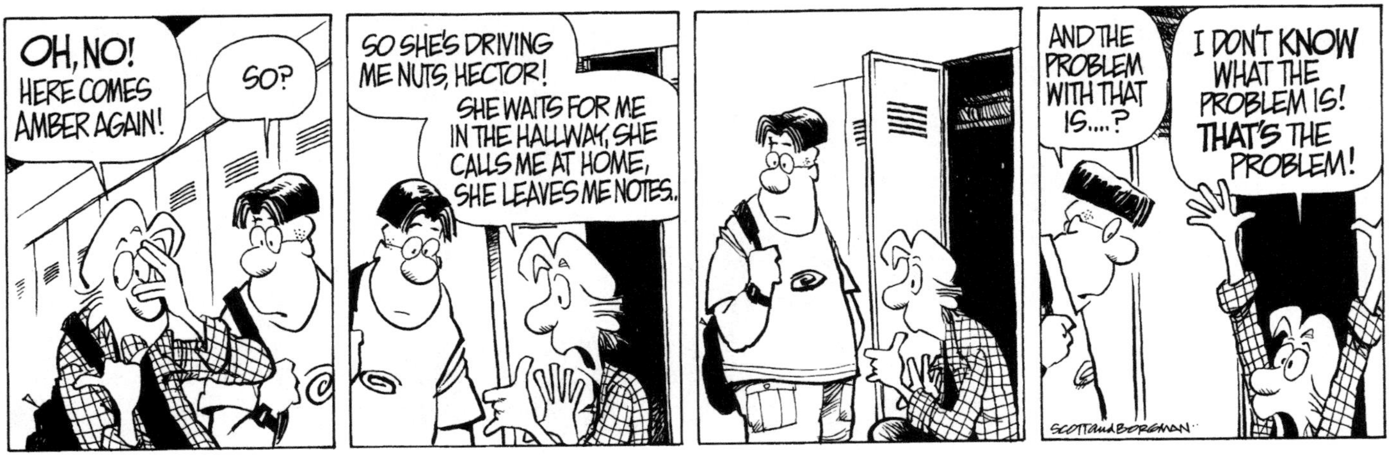
OH, NO! HERE COMES AMBER AGAIN!
SO?
SO SHE'S DRIVING ME NUTS, HECTOR!
SHE WAITS FOR ME IN THE HALLWAY, SHE CALLS ME AT HOME, SHE LEAVES ME NOTES.
AND THE PROBLEM WITH THAT IS....?
I DON'T KNOW WHAT THE PROBLEM IS! THAT'S THE PROBLEM!

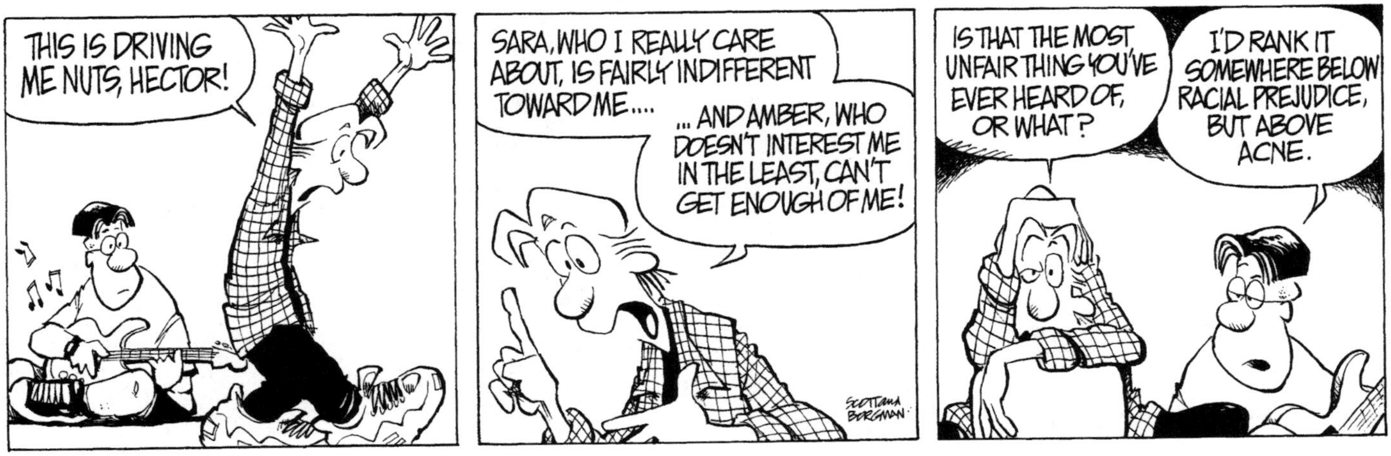
THIS IS DRIVING ME NUTS, HECTOR!
SARA, WHO I REALLY CARE ABOUT, IS FAIRLY INDIFFERENT TOWARD ME....
... AND AMBER, WHO DOESN'T INTEREST ME IN THE LEAST, CAN'T GET ENOUGH OF ME!
IS THAT THE MOST UNFAIR THING YOU'VE EVER HEARD OF, OR WHAT?
I'D RANK IT SOMEWHERE BELOW RACIAL PREJUDICE, BUT ABOVE ACNE.

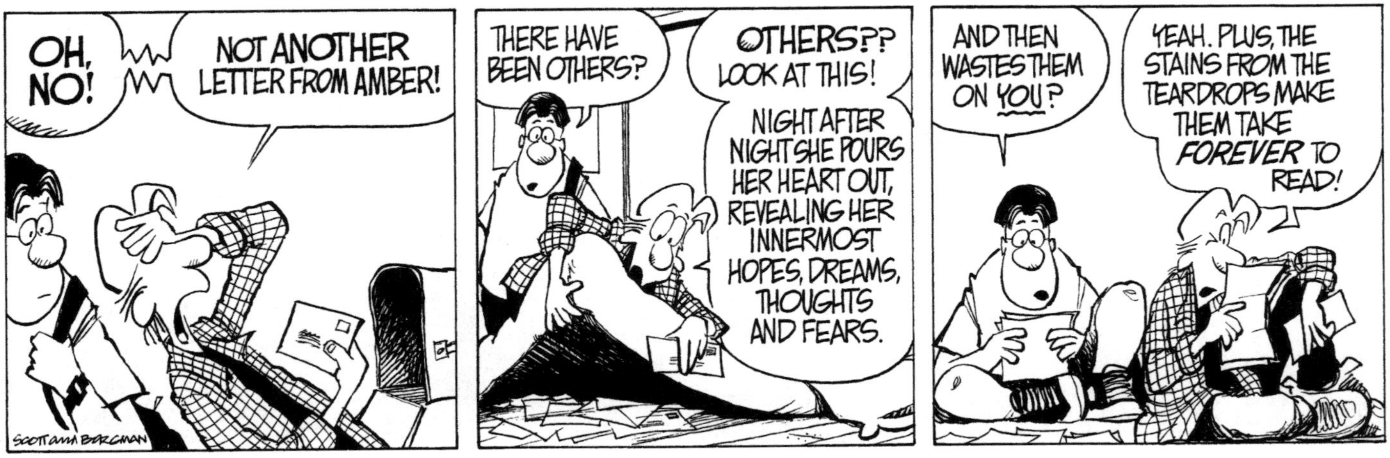
OH, NO!
NOT ANOTHER LETTER FROM AMBER!
THERE HAVE BEEN OTHERS?
OTHERS?? LOOK AT THIS!
NIGHT AFTER NIGHT SHE POURS HER HEART OUT, REVEALING HER INNERMOST HOPES, DREAMS, THOUGHTS AND FEARS.
AND THEN WASTES THEM ON YOU?
YEAH. PLUS, THE STAINS FROM THE TEARDROPS MAKE THEM TAKE FOREVER TO READ!

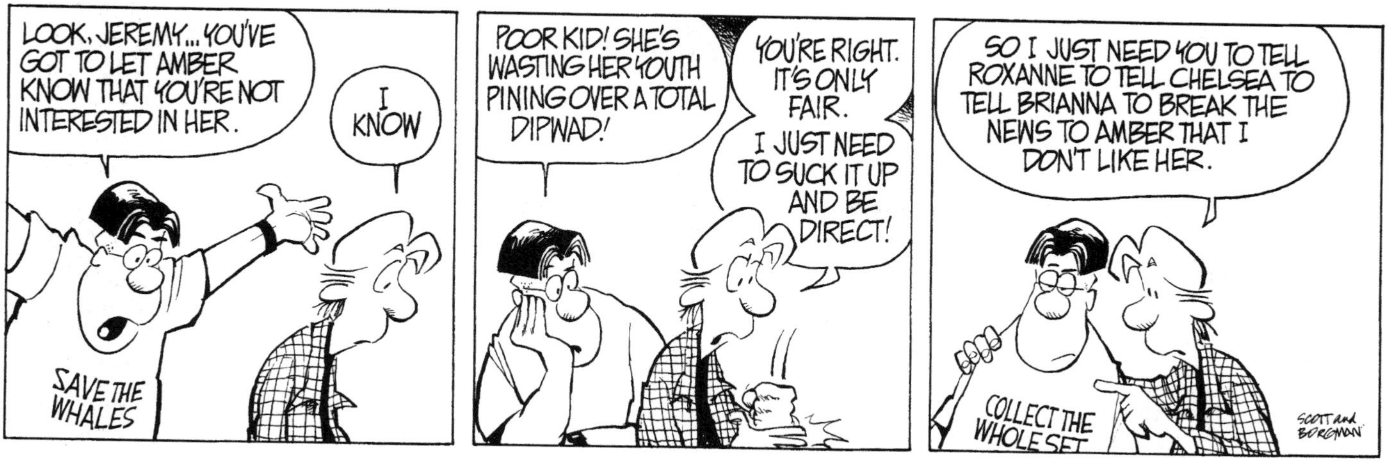
LOOK, JEREMY... YOU'VE GOT TO LET AMBER KNOW THAT YOU'RE NOT INTERESTED IN HER.
I KNOW
SAVE THE WHALES
POOR KID! SHE'S WASTING HER YOUTH PINING OVER A TOTAL DIPWAD!
YOU'RE RIGHT. IT'S ONLY FAIR.
I JUST NEED TO SUCK IT UP AND BE DIRECT!
SO I JUST NEED YOU TO TELL ROXANNE TO TELL CHELSEA TO TELL BRIANNA TO BREAK THE NEWS TO AMBER THAT I DON'T LIKE HER.
COLLECT THE WHOLE SET
SCOTT and BORGMAN

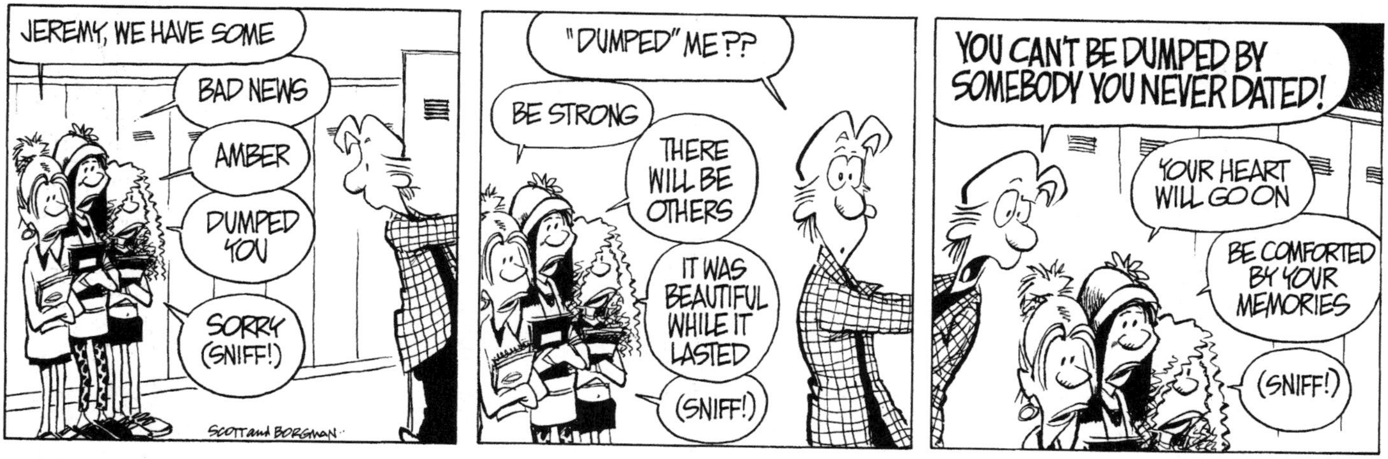
JEREMY, WE HAVE SOME
BAD NEWS
AMBER
DUMPED YOU
SORRY (SNIFF!)
SCOTT and BORGMAN
"DUMPED" ME??
BE STRONG
THERE WILL BE OTHERS
IT WAS BEAUTIFUL WHILE IT LASTED
(SNIFF!)
YOU CAN'T BE DUMPED BY SOMEBODY YOU NEVER DATED!
YOUR HEART WILL GO ON
BE COMFORTED BY YOUR MEMORIES
(SNIFF!)

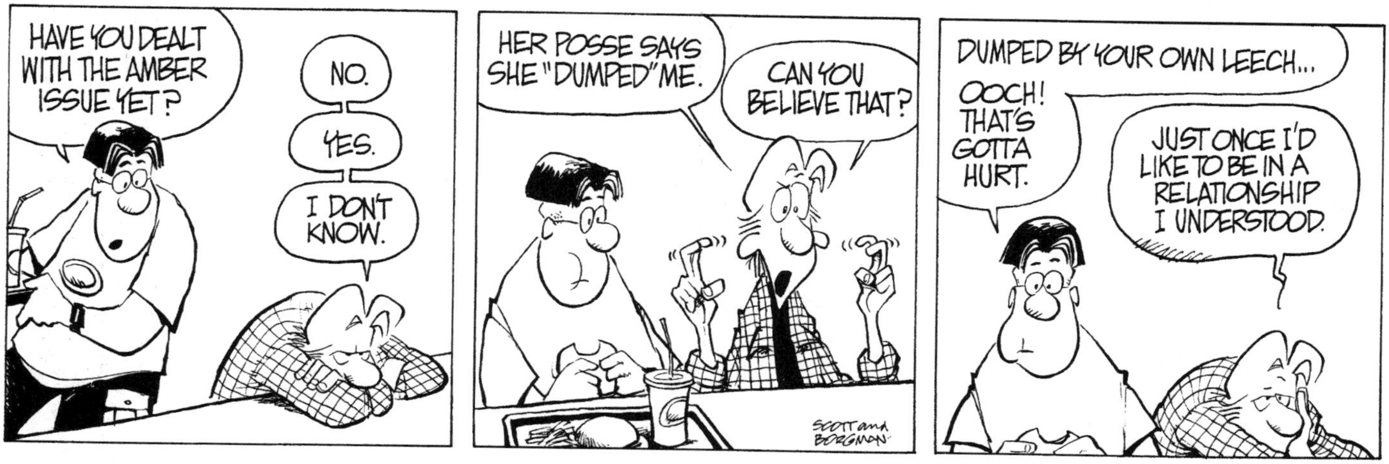
HAVE YOU DEALT WITH THE AMBER ISSUE YET?
NO.
YES.
I DON'T KNOW.
HER POSSE SAYS SHE "DUMPED" ME.
CAN YOU BELIEVE THAT?
SCOTT and BORGMAN
DUMPED BY YOUR OWN LEECH...
OOCH! THAT'S GOTTA HURT.
JUST ONCE I'D LIKE TO BE IN A RELATIONSHIP I UNDERSTOOD.

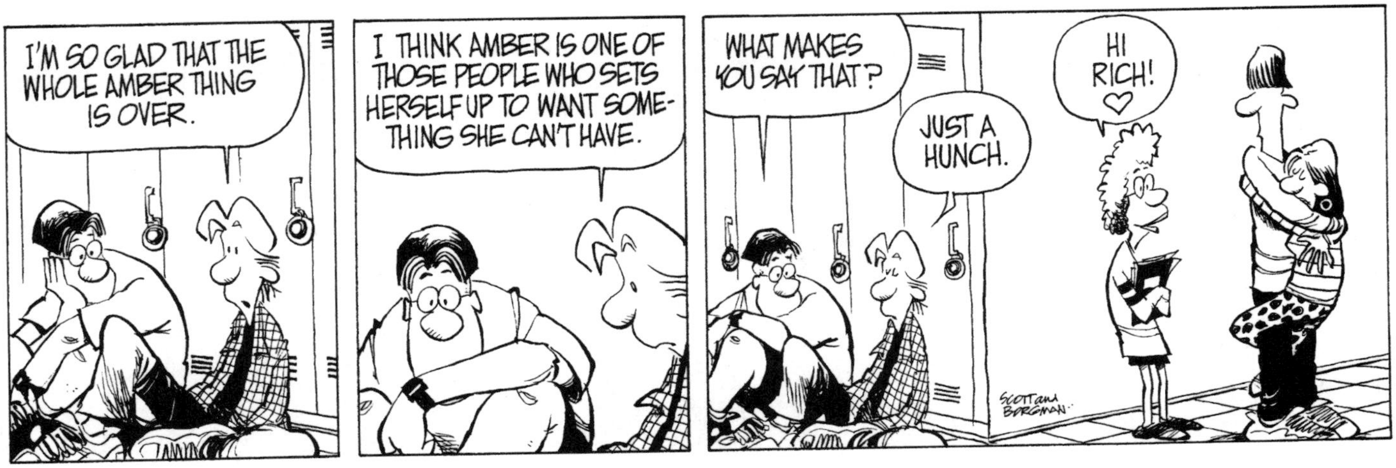
I'M SO GLAD THAT THE WHOLE AMBER THING IS OVER.
I THINK AMBER IS ONE OF THOSE PEOPLE WHO SETS HERSELF UP TO WANT SOMETHING SHE CAN'T HAVE.
WHAT MAKES YOU SAY THAT?
JUST A HUNCH.
HI RICH! ♡
SCOTT and BORGMAN

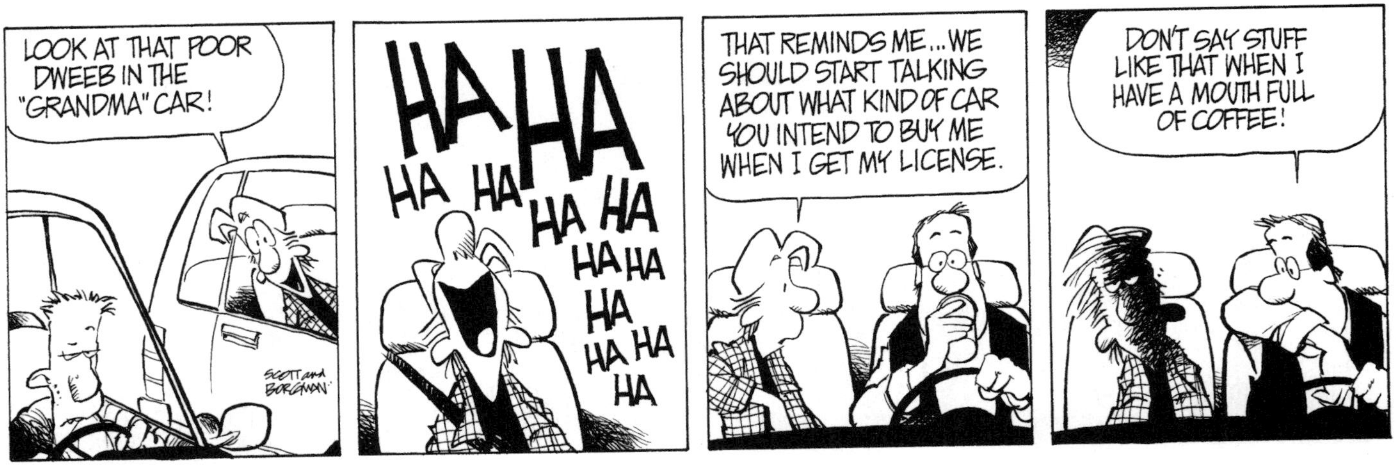
LOOK AT THAT POOR DWEEB IN THE "GRANDMA" CAR!
SCOTT and BORGMAN
HA HA HA HA HA HA HA HA HA HA HA HA HA HA
THAT REMINDS ME... WE SHOULD START TALKING ABOUT WHAT KIND OF CAR YOU INTEND TO BUY ME WHEN I GET MY LICENSE.
DON'T SAY STUFF LIKE THAT WHEN I HAVE A MOUTH FULL OF COFFEE!

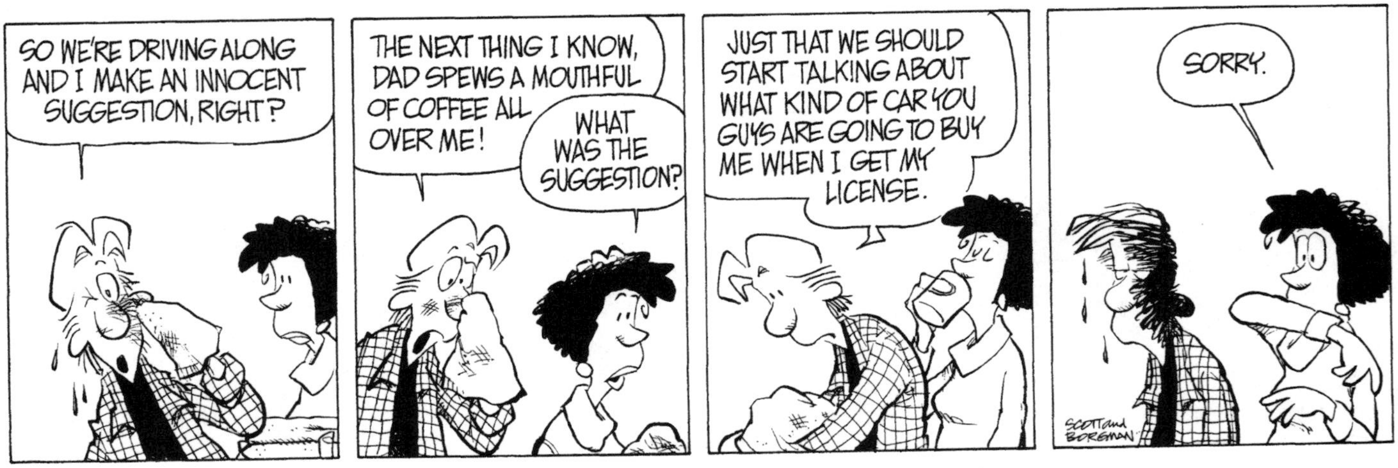
SO WE'RE DRIVING ALONG AND I MAKE AN INNOCENT SUGGESTION, RIGHT?
THE NEXT THING I KNOW, DAD SPEWS A MOUTHFUL OF COFFEE ALL OVER ME!
WHAT WAS THE SUGGESTION?
JUST THAT WE SHOULD START TALKING ABOUT WHAT KIND OF CAR YOU GUYS ARE GOING TO BUY ME WHEN I GET MY LICENSE.
SORRY.
SCOTT and BORGMAN

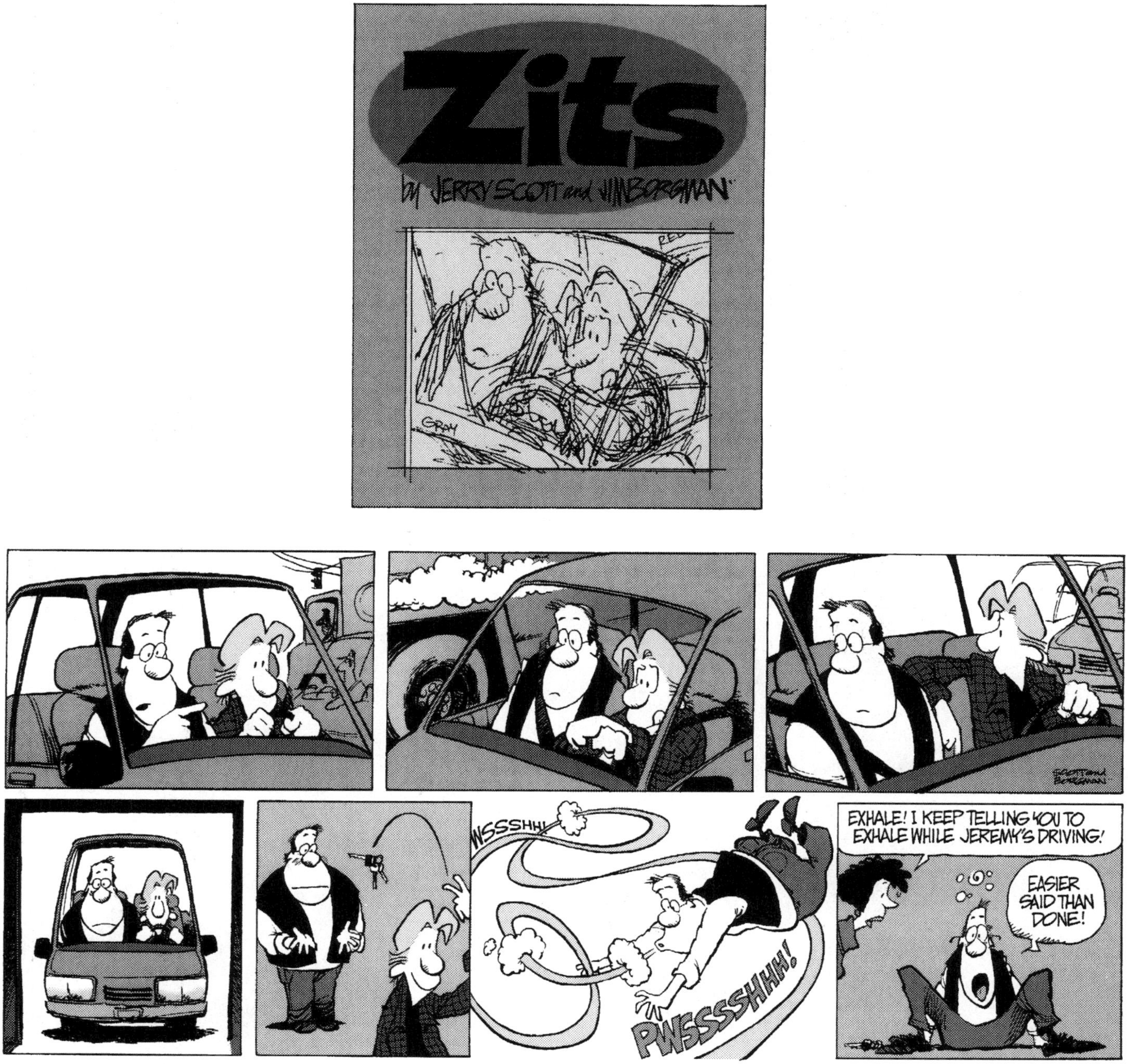
Zits
by JERRY SCOTT and JIM BORGMAN
WSSSHH
PWSSSSSHHH!
EXHALE! I KEEP TELLING YOU TO EXHALE WHILE JEREMY'S DRIVING!
EASIER SAID THAN DONE!

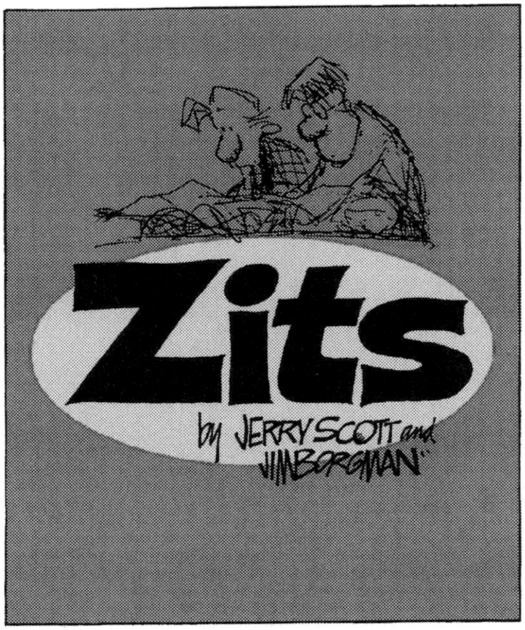
Zits
by JERRY SCOTT and JIM BORGMAN

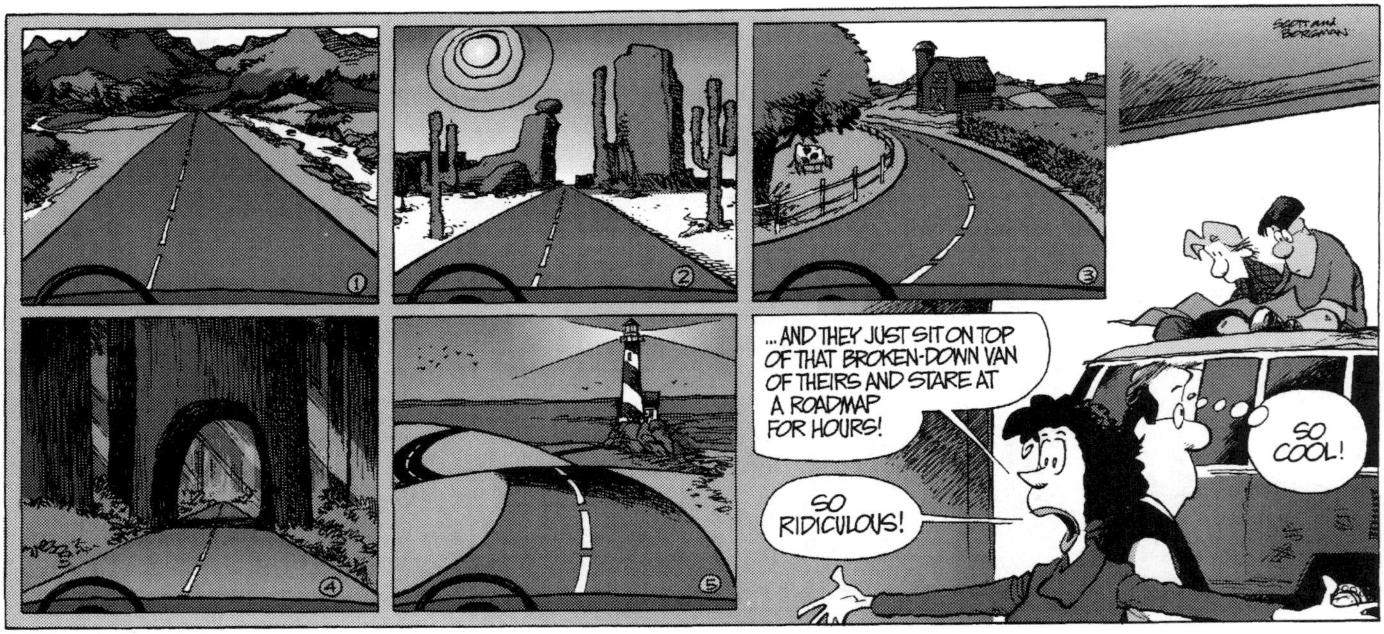
SCOTT AND BORGMAN
...AND THEY JUST SIT ON TOP OF THAT BROKEN-DOWN VAN OF THEIRS AND STARE AT A ROADMAP FOR HOURS!
SO RIDICULOUS!
SO COOL!

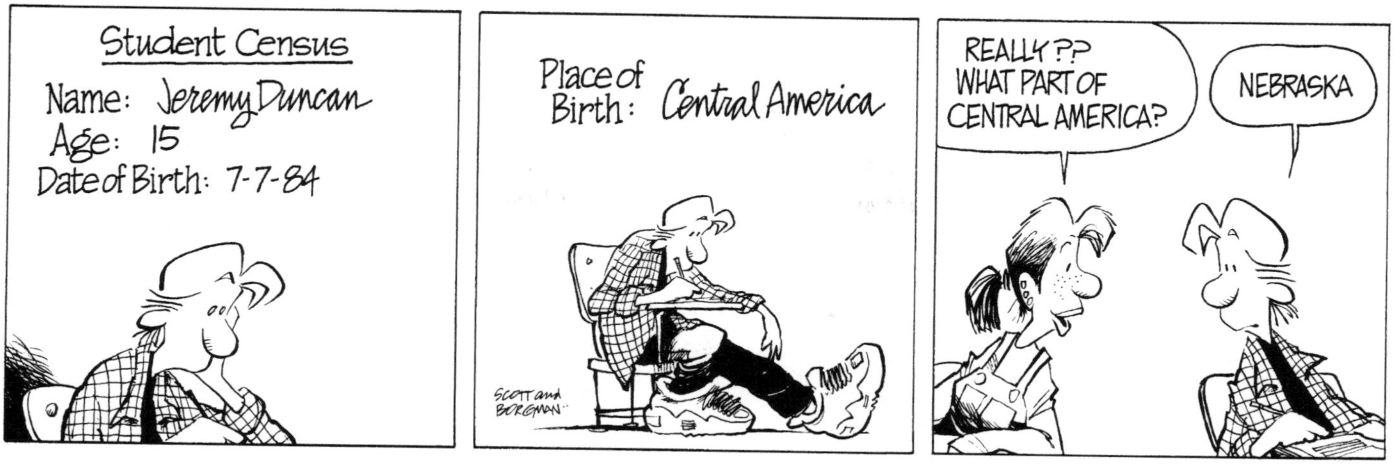
Student Census
Name: Jeremy Duncan
Age: 15
Date of Birth: 7-7-84
Place of Birth: Central America
SCOTT and BORGMAN
REALLY?? WHAT PART OF CENTRAL AMERICA?
NEBRASKA

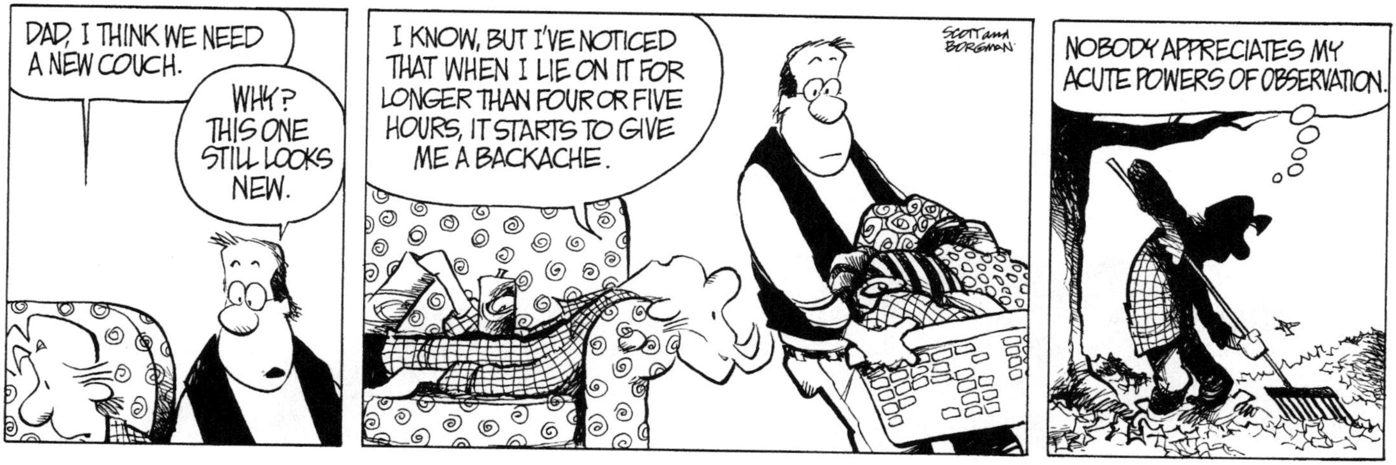
DAD, I THINK WE NEED A NEW COUCH.
WHY? THIS ONE STILL LOOKS NEW.
I KNOW, BUT I'VE NOTICED THAT WHEN I LIE ON IT FOR LONGER THAN FOUR OR FIVE HOURS, IT STARTS TO GIVE ME A BACKACHE.
SCOTT and BORGMAN
NOBODY APPRECIATES MY ACUTE POWERS OF OBSERVATION.

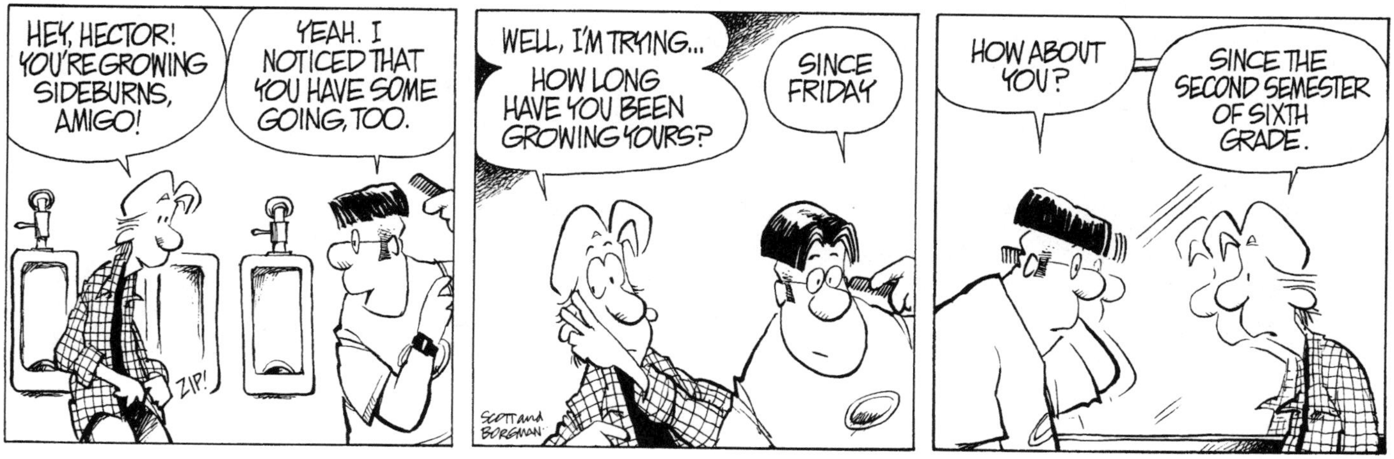
HEY, HECTOR! YOU'RE GROWING SIDEBURNS, AMIGO!
YEAH. I NOTICED THAT YOU HAVE SOME GOING, TOO.
ZIP!
WELL, I'M TRYING... HOW LONG HAVE YOU BEEN GROWING YOURS?
SINCE FRIDAY
SCOTT and BORGMAN
HOW ABOUT YOU?
SINCE THE SECOND SEMESTER OF SIXTH GRADE.

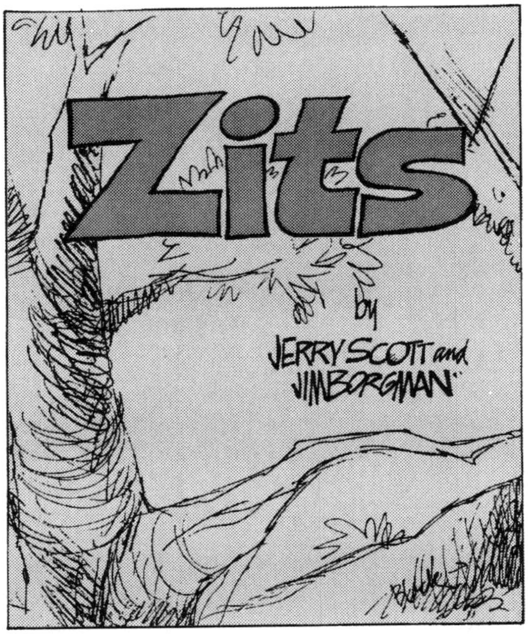
Zits
by
JERRY SCOTT and
JIM BORGMAN

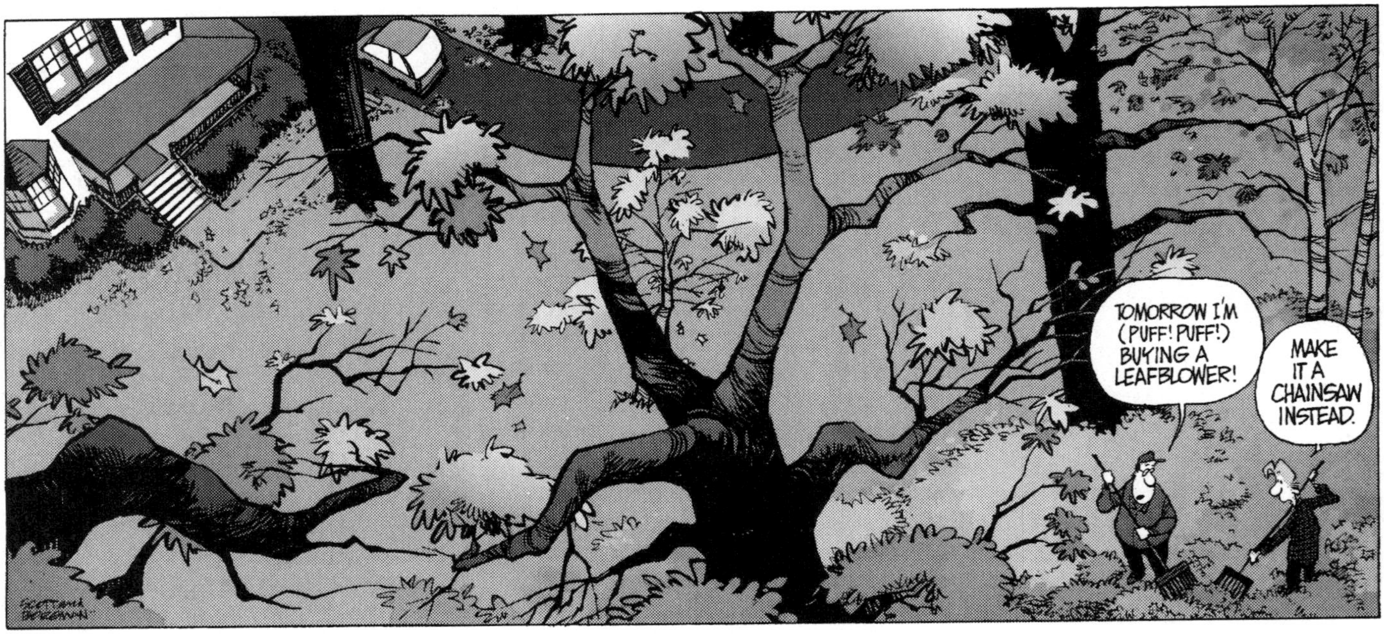
TOMORROW I'M (PUFF! PUFF!) BUYING A LEAFBLOWER!
MAKE IT A CHAINSAW INSTEAD.

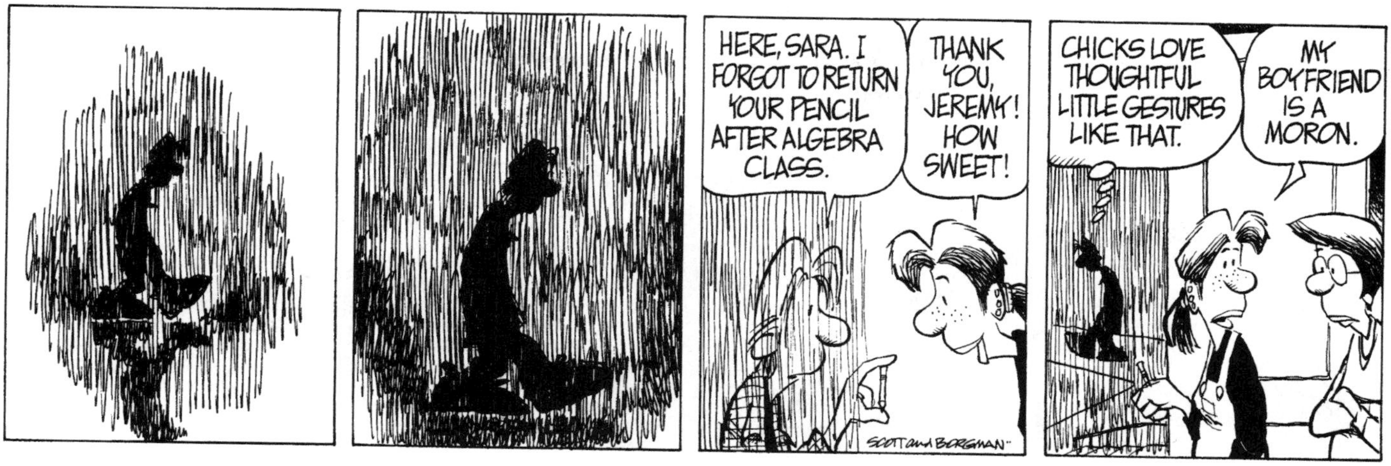
HERE, SARA. I FORGOT TO RETURN YOUR PENCIL AFTER ALGEBRA CLASS.
THANK YOU, JEREMY! HOW SWEET!
SCOTT and BORGMAN
CHICKS LOVE THOUGHTFUL LITTLE GESTURES LIKE THAT.
MY BOYFRIEND IS A MORON.

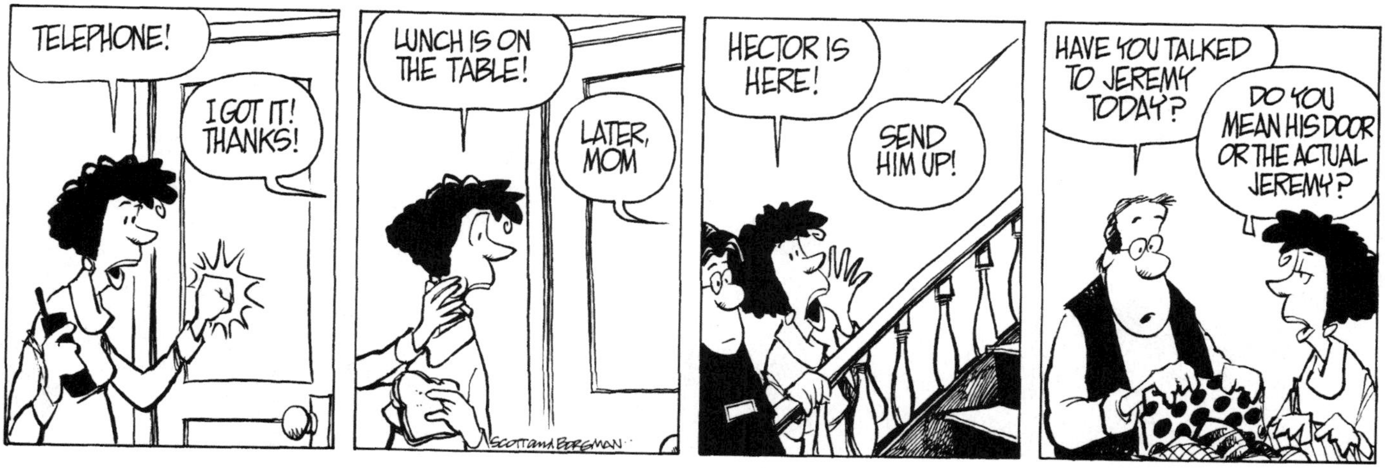
TELEPHONE!
I GOT IT! THANKS!
LUNCH IS ON THE TABLE!
LATER, MOM
SCOTT and BORGMAN
HECTOR IS HERE!
SEND HIM UP!
HAVE YOU TALKED TO JEREMY TODAY?
DO YOU MEAN HIS DOOR OR THE ACTUAL JEREMY?

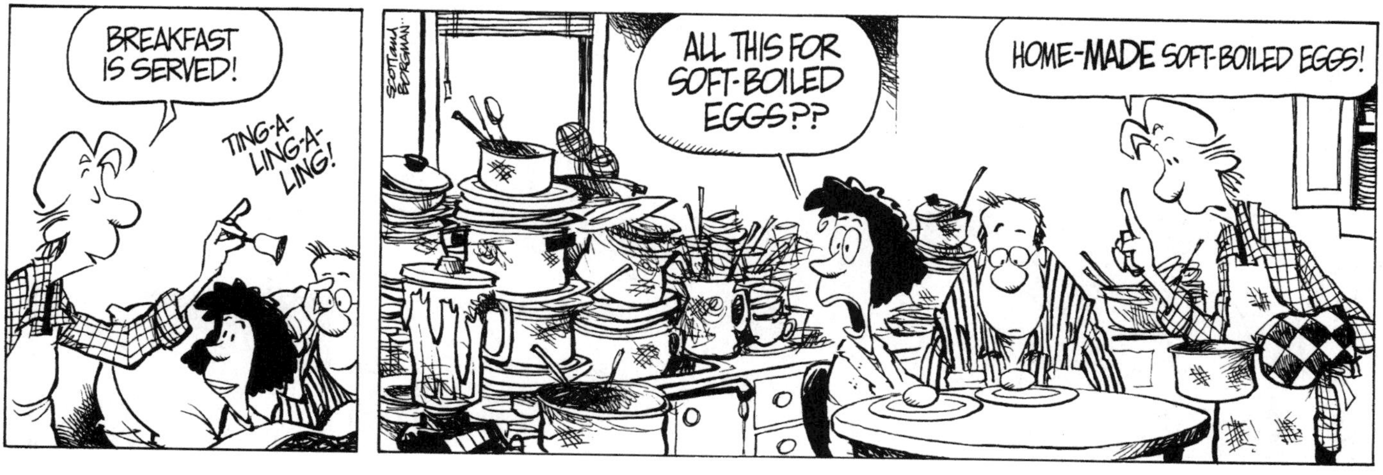
BREAKFAST IS SERVED!
TING-A-LING-A-LING!
SCOTT and BORGMAN
ALL THIS FOR SOFT-BOILED EGGS??
HOME-MADE SOFT-BOILED EGGS!

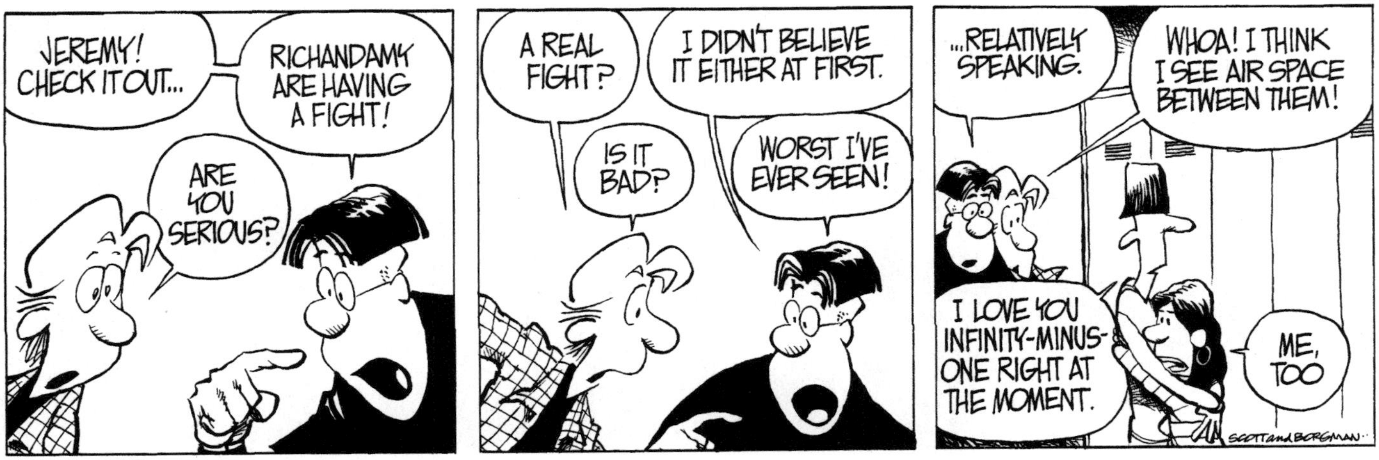
JEREMY! CHECK IT OUT...
RICHANDAMY ARE HAVING A FIGHT!
ARE YOU SERIOUS?
A REAL FIGHT?
I DIDN'T BELIEVE IT EITHER AT FIRST.
IS IT BAD?
WORST I'VE EVER SEEN!
...RELATIVELY SPEAKING.
WHOA! I THINK I SEE AIR SPACE BETWEEN THEM!
I LOVE YOU INFINITY-MINUS-ONE RIGHT AT THE MOMENT.
ME, TOO
SCOTT and BORGMAN

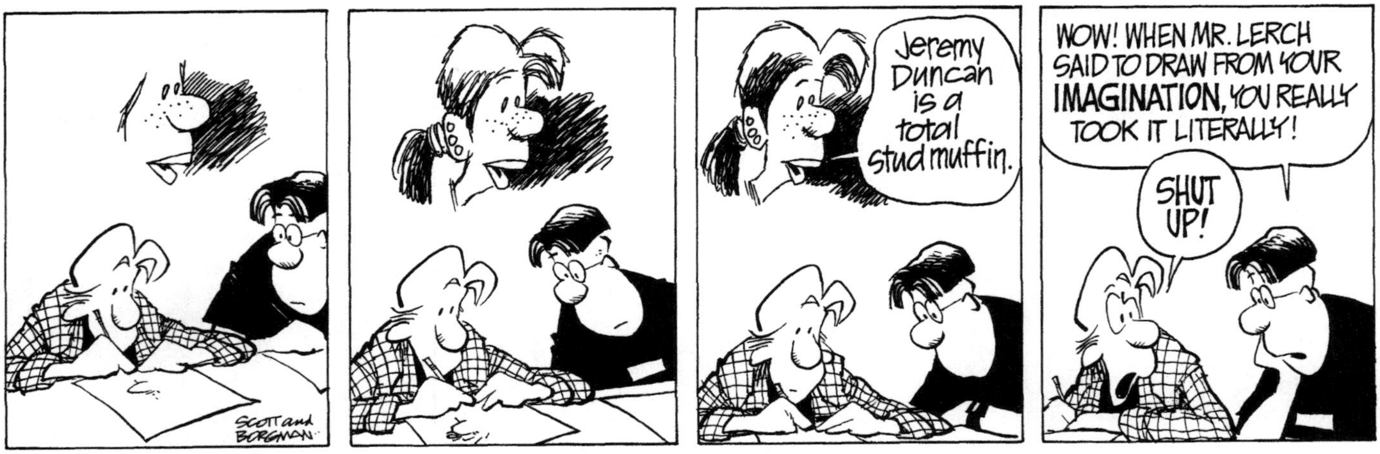
SCOTT and BORGMAN
Jeremy Duncan is a total studmuffin.
WOW! WHEN MR. LERCH SAID TO DRAW FROM YOUR IMAGINATION, YOU REALLY TOOK IT LITERALLY!
SHUT UP!

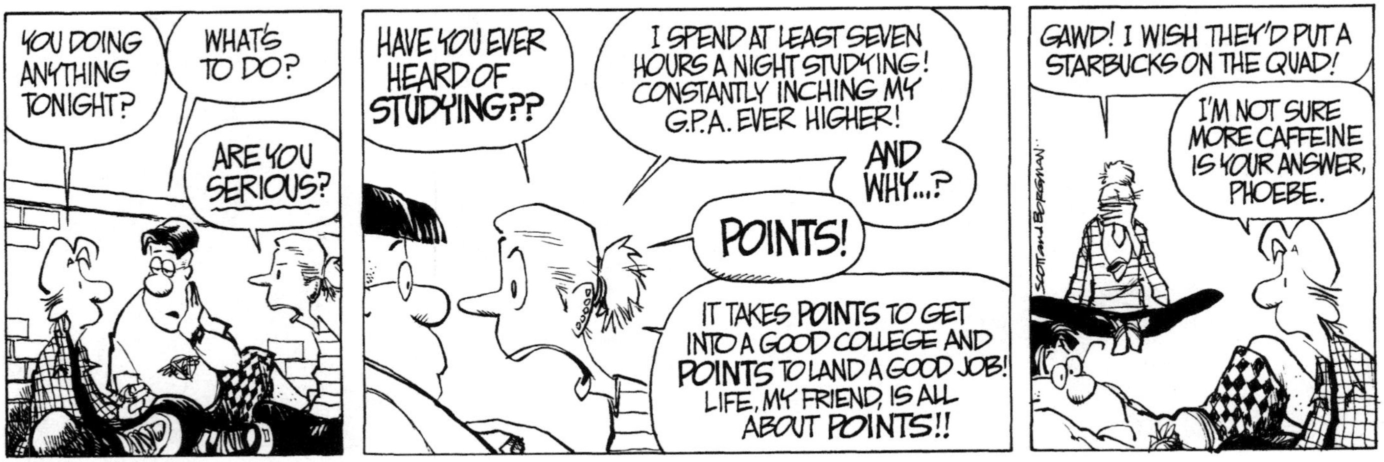
YOU DOING ANYTHING TONIGHT?
WHAT'S TO DO?
ARE YOU SERIOUS?
HAVE YOU EVER HEARD OF STUDYING??
I SPEND AT LEAST SEVEN HOURS A NIGHT STUDYING! CONSTANTLY INCHING MY G.P.A. EVER HIGHER!
AND WHY...?
POINTS!
IT TAKES POINTS TO GET INTO A GOOD COLLEGE AND POINTS TO LAND A GOOD JOB! LIFE, MY FRIEND, IS ALL ABOUT POINTS!!
SCOTT and BORGMAN
GAWD! I WISH THEY'D PUT A STARBUCKS ON THE QUAD!
I'M NOT SURE MORE CAFFEINE IS YOUR ANSWER, PHOEBE.